A progressive education?

Manchester University Press

A PROGRESSIVE EDUCATION?

How childhood changed in mid-twentieth-century English and Welsh schools

LAURA TISDALL

Manchester University Press

Copyright © Laura Tisdall 2020

The right of Laura Tisdall to be identified as the author of this work has been asserted by her in accordance with the Copyright, Designs and Patents Act 1988.

Published by Manchester University Press
Oxford Road, Manchester M13 9PL

British Library Cataloguing-in-Publication Data
A catalogue record for this book is available from the British Library

ISBN 978 1 5261 3289 5 hardback
ISBN 978 1 5261 7456 7 paperback

First published 2020
Paperback published 2023

The publisher has no responsibility for the persistence or accuracy of URLs for any external or third-party internet websites referred to in this book, and does not guarantee that any content on such websites is, or will remain, accurate or appropriate.

Typeset by Sunrise Setting Ltd, Brixham

For my grandma, Shirley Kane neé Innes (1936–2007)
and for my grandad, Jim Kane (1935–)

– secondary modern school pupils made good.

Contents

Acknowledgements	ix
List of abbreviations	xi
Introduction: the rise and fall of progressive education?	1
1 What is a progressive education?	25
2 Stages of development, educational psychology and child-centred education	50
3 'Trendy, airy-fairy methods': teachers' resistance to progressive education	83
4 A half-reformed education? Teaching practice and local change	108
5 Primary school teachers, gender and concepts of childhood	138
6 Secondary school teachers, class and status	176
7 The 'backlash' against progressivism	215
Conclusion: the reinvention of childhood?	245
Bibliography	251
Index	273

Acknowledgements

I would like to acknowledge the consistent encouragement and emotional support of my parents, Alison Kane and Simon Tisdall, throughout all of my education and my historical career so far. My sister, Polly Tisdall, is my creative and intellectual collaborator in so many ways, and the work we have done together has fed into this book. I would also like to thank Sebastian Nye for his patient, thorough and insightful reading of various drafts of this book, and of related articles and conference papers.

I am very grateful to both Lucy Delap and Siân Pooley; both have gone out of their way to offer me advice and guidance on both this and other projects. Mathew Thomson, Peter Mandler and Angela Davis have also helped me in numerous ways, not least by reading earlier chapter drafts of this book. Thanks also to Clare Jackson, for supporting this project from the start. For help with book proposals and chapter outlines, I would like to acknowledge Alana Harris, Laura Kounine, Laura King and Laura Kelly; and for discussions and source suggestions on 'gifted' children, Jenny Crane. Kathryn Hannan at the Institute of Education helped me source an appropriate cover image. Derek Gillard's wonderful website, *Education in England: the history of our schools* (www.educationengland.org.uk/history/index.html) has been an invaluable resource for primary documents and timelines; he deserves the gratitude of all historians and students of English education.

The anonymous reviewers of both my original book proposal and sample chapters, and of the full manuscript, offered invaluable and constructive advice that has made this book much stronger. I would also like to thank the anonymous reviewers and editors of two of my journal articles that have fed into this work: 'Inside the "blackboard jungle": male teachers and male pupils at British secondary modern schools in fact and fiction, 1950–59', *Cultural and Social History*, 12, 4 (2015), and 'Education, parenting and concepts of childhood in England, c. 1945 to c. 1979', *Contemporary British History*, 31, 1 (2017).

Finally, I would like to thank my wonderful elementary and primary school teachers, Ms Mitchell, Ms Natalini and Mr Evans, and my wonderful comprehensive school history teachers, Mr Bartholomew, Mr Daniels, Ms Sayers and Ms Trueman.

The original research for this book was supported by the Arts and Humanities Research Council, grant number AH/ I010645/1, and I completed its final draft while funded by the Leverhulme Trust, grant number ECF-2017-369.

List of abbreviations

ADHD	attention deficit hyperactivity disorder
ATCDE	Association of Teachers in Colleges and Departments of Education
ATO	Area Training Organisation
CACE	Central Advisory Council for Education
CLASP	Consortium of Local Authorities Special Programme
CSE	Certificate of Secondary Education
DES	Department of Education and Science
ESN	educationally subnormal
GCE	General Certificate of Education
HMI	His/Her Majesty's Inspector of Schools/Inspectorate
HORSA	Hutting Operation for the Raising of the School-leaving Age
ILEA	Inner London Education Authority
LCC	London County Council
LEA	local education authority
NAS	National Association of Schoolmasters
NFER	National Foundation for Educational Research
NUT	National Union of Teachers
NUWT	National Union of Women Teachers
Ofsted	Office for Standards in Education
ORACLE	observational and classroom learning evaluation
PGCE	Postgraduate Certificate in Education
ROSLA	Raising of the school-leaving age
Schoolmaster	*The Schoolmaster and Woman Teacher's Chronicle* [the *Teacher* after 1963]

SCI	Senior chief inspector
TES	*Times Educational Supplement*
WEP	Wartime Evacuation Project
WHO	World Health Organisation

Introduction: the rise and fall of progressive education?

'I sometimes think that all the master problems of life will have to be solved in the nursery and the schoolroom; that if we wait for their solution till the child has grown to manhood and hardened into what we call maturity, we shall have waited too long', wrote Edmond Holmes in 1913.[1] Holmes had been a school inspector in England from 1875 to 1911, rising to chief inspector of schools before becoming convinced that a syllabus which 'relieved [the teacher] ... of the necessity for thinking' had wrecked the education of children, and resigning his post.[2] Holmes's ideas, expressed in key works such as *The Tragedy of Education* (1913) and *What Is and What Might Be* (1918), alongside the American writer Homer Lane's *Talks to Parents and Teachers* (1928), which described the philosophy of his Dorset-based Little Commonwealth, were profoundly influential for a wider utopian educational project in inter-war England and Wales.[3] Early progressive pioneers tended not to work within the state system, but set up their own schools. For example, Lane's Little Commonwealth opened in 1913, A. S. Neill's Summerhill in 1921, Bertrand Russell's Beacon Hill in 1927 and Kurt Hahn's Gordonstoun in 1934. For these educationalists, the key concern of the school was to free the child from outside interference. They believed that children were distorted by being exposed to adult norms; if they were allowed to obey their own natural laws of growth, a new generation would be produced that was free of damaging neuroses, a generation unlike any other in the history of the world. As Holmes put it: 'the child's outlook on life, before it has been perverted by education, is fundamentally right, while the adult's is fundamentally wrong'.[4]

These utopian educationalists tended to be heterogeneous in their methods and curriculums. As Neill wrote in 1937, he had 'no interest in how children learn', and he stated later in life that 'there is *nothing* in *any* school subject that is *really* important'.[5] What was important, in Neill's eyes, was that children's development was not controlled by adults. Summerhill famously taught along relatively familiar lines but allowed its students to select which classes they attended. Drawing from psychoanalysis, Neill considered that part of his job was to allow students to explore repressed emotions and work out their neuroses via his 'private lessons'. To facilitate this, he demanded that children and adults relate to each other on equal terms. 'When Billy, aged five, told me to get out of his birthday party because I hadn't been invited, I went at once without hesitation', he wrote, and in the self-governing school meeting, each individual's vote counted equally.[6] Other utopian progressives did not always agree with Neill's approach. Bertrand Russell, despite his utopian views, was relatively conservative in his educational suggestions. In *On Education* he sketched out a familiar curriculum, inspired by the American psychologist and philosopher of education John Dewey, that focused on academic subjects such as geography, history, maths and science, but related these to children's interests; he did not suggest that children would be allowed to choose what they studied.[7] Novel educational methods such as the Dalton Plan, Project Method or Play Way, all of which allowed children to self-direct their education within a certain framework, might form part of utopian educational projects, but did not define them. Instead, this psychoanalytical vision for education centred on organisation and management, with School Councils – where pupils met to have a say in how the school was run – and other forms of self-government set up in almost all progressive schools.

As the 'morbid age' of the 1920s and 1930s dawned in Britain, and as a second war with Germany seemed increasingly likely, a revolutionary generation was even more desperately required.[8] As Russell wrote in his profoundly influential *On Education* (1926), young people who were brought up in a climate of 'fearless freedom' might avoid being 'twisted and stunted and terrified in youth, to be killed afterwards in futile wars'.[9] The influence of these utopian progressives therefore intensified in the 1920s and 1930s. Norman MacMunn, who founded his own school at Tiptree Hall, reflected a wider feeling among

Introduction

educationalists when he stated in a second edition of his book *A Path to Freedom in the School* (1914), renamed *The Child's Path to Freedom*, in 1921, that the experience of the First World War had made it easier to grasp 'new truths' about education.[10] Progressive ideas chimed with wider shifts in attitudes to childhood and youth in inter-war Britain, fuelled not only by the tragic experience of war but by the falling birth rate, the experience of mass unemployment and changing concepts of crime and punishment for juveniles.[11] In their most radical iterations, these concepts of childhood positioned children as the hope for the future, and the British state as corrupted and outdated.

The non-utopian progressive pedagogy that also developed in the inter-war period but became increasingly popular after the Second World War in mainstream schools was diametrically opposed to utopian progressive assertions about childhood, although its exponents saw themselves as part of the wider progressive movement in education. Non-utopian progressive educationalists argued that the child needed to develop healthily, not only physically and mentally but also emotionally and socially, in order to become a fit citizen of the welfare state.[12] Adults played a key role in guiding the child's development, because children's capabilities were so limited in comparison to those of their parents and teachers. A child-centred curriculum, therefore, not self-government, was at the centre of this 'educational revolution'; non-utopian progressive pedagogy advised that if subjects were taught in accordance with children's natural interests, and in line with their capabilities at various stages of development, then pupils would learn most effectively. Finally, it was the developmental psychology of researchers such as Jean Piaget that became central, rather than the psychoanalytical ideas that had shaped early utopian progressive schools. Adult development was seen as a healthy, completed process, rather than as an unhealthy knot of repressed and sublimated desires that must be unpicked. The child was repositioned as a problem that needed to be managed by adult society, rather than as a being that had anything to teach fully mature individuals.

'Underlying all educational questions is the nature of the child himself', stated the influential non-utopian progressive Plowden Report on English primary schools in 1967, summing up the task that its writers believed educationalists had been undertaking since the publication of the Hadow Report on *The Primary School* in 1931. Healthy development could only be ensured through the use of biological, psychological and social-scientific knowledge about children as a group. Because non-utopian progressive educationalists aimed to 'fit the education to the child, rather than the child to the education', finding out what children were like at different stages of development was central to their mission.[13] In contrast, Neill summed up his lack of interest in child development in 1931 when he wrote that 'I have been dealing with children for many years now . . . but I confess that I know comparatively little about child nature.'[14] Historians of education have tended to conflate these two radically different schools of thought because they both used the terms 'progressive' and 'progressivism'. For example, architectural historian Andrew Saint, writing on post-war school building, suggests that non-utopian progressive education is best defined negatively, as it 'denies that the needs of the state, the church or the economy ought to shape the development of a child's expanding consciousness'.[15] However, the schools that he considers would not have subscribed to this utopian commitment to negative freedom; in post-war Britain, the progressive movement had come to centre on whether education was able to fit the child to fulfil the needs of the state, rather than on whether adults could set the rising generation free.

So what *was* a 'progressive' education, if the term encompassed two such divergent forms of pedagogical practice and social analysis? Emily Robinson's work on the language of progressive politics in nineteenth- and twentieth-century Britain offers some vital insights. As a 'forward-looking' term, she argues, '[t]o be progressive is to anticipate the future and, in doing so, it is to bring that future into being'.[16] However, unlike terms such as 'modern', this necessarily entails a relationship with the past, as progressivism aims 'to transcend the past, but also to fulfil it'.[17] Robinson's book does not directly consider childhood and schooling, but it is clear why the term 'progressive' proved so useful for educationalists. As children already symbolised the future, envisaged as 'human becomings' who would eventually emerge into profitable adulthood, the language of progressivism was a natural fit for this social group.[18] In its turn, adolescence could be seen as a stage that emerged only in a modern society, which allowed the extension of cultural education beyond biological puberty.[19] Importantly, Robinson notes that before the late 1960s, the term 'progressive' was not necessarily associated with left-wing politics or the 'liberal elite'. Earlier in the twentieth century, it could be – and was – claimed by those with a wide range of political persuasions.[20] Therefore, any automatic association between, say, 'progressive' and 'permissive' education and parenting must be discarded.

'Progressive', instead, was a term used by those who wanted to associate themselves with 'new schools' and was often employed as a way to emphasise the innovation of 'modern methods', which were contrasted with an old-fashioned 'traditional education'. However, there was little evidence that this 'traditional education' had ever existed as an organised body of thought, or, indeed, that it had eschewed all the strategies that progressive educationalists now claimed as their own. For this reason, despite the fact that these two groups did not use this terminology themselves, I have adopted the terms 'utopian progressive' and 'non-utopian progressive' to distinguish the two major strands of reformist pedagogy that developed in inter-war England and Wales, and to avoid the historiographical confusion that has resulted from the battle between these two visions of the future.

Apart from the word 'progressive' itself, the term most often used by non-utopian progressives to refer to their pedagogical practice was 'child-centred'. To an extent, these terms were used interchangeably; however, insofar as they can be disentangled, I would suggest that 'child-centred' denotes a particular set of pedagogical practices, whereas 'progressive' describes an attitude of mind. Often, the difference between the two did not matter; however, when it did, it illustrated central tensions within the non-utopian movement. To be a progressive meant consistently pursuing innovation; inevitably, then, methods that were deemed child-centred by non-utopian progressives in the 1940s became outdated by the 1970s. This led to claims in the latter decade that progressive change had been more apparent than real – but as schools were being measured against a set of standards that was constantly shifting, it was not surprising that they fell short. Moreover, certain child-centred shibboleths actually stood in sharp contrast to the modernity that the non-utopian progressives believed their movement embodied, because they aimed to preserve childhood as a time of bucolic, timeless innocence.

Both utopian and non-utopian forms of progressivism were important and influential in inter-war England and Wales, although neither was able to do much to put its ideas into practice. But private utopian flagship schools such as Summerhill and Beacon Hill would ultimately exercise little influence on the development of progressivism in primary and secondary modern schools after 1945. Instead, child-centred pedagogy entered mainstream educational practice as a tool for shaping good citizens. This thread emerged after 1918 with the discussion of the needs of a 'mass democracy' and, as Mathew Thomson has argued, continued into the post-war period, when progressive education was seen as necessary to fit children for the needs of a social democracy and welfare state.[21] Key legislative developments paved the way for non-utopian progressivism to become dominant in primary and secondary modern schools. The 1944 Education Act raised the school leaving age from fourteen to fifteen and established the principle of separate secondary education, urging the abolition of all-age elementary schools. Although this principle was not enshrined in the Act itself, it led to their widespread replacement with a bipartite system of grammar schools and secondary moderns.[22] Because of the limited impact of grammar schools on social mobility and the detrimental impact on those who 'failed' the 11-plus entrance exam and had to attend a secondary modern school, sociologists and historians have rightly tended to focus on the conservative aspects of this legislation.[23] However, it also arose from fundamentally child-centred considerations about the different needs of different groups of children, both in terms of age and ability and the need to provide an education that would suit them.[24]

Even more significantly for the implementation of child-centred practice in mainstream schools, central funding for education substantially increased in the post-war period, rising from a 2.6 per cent share of GDP to 4.5 per cent in the 1950s.[25] The Second World War played a key role in this shift; as James Cronin has argued, the 'expansion of the state' was restricted, rather than inevitable, in twentieth-century Britain, and big increases in spending were only possible in the aftermath of the two world wars.[26] Education spending was uneven, with more channelled into secondary education, especially grammar schools, than primaries.[27] But the building of new schools, the provision of extensions such as school halls and school libraries to some existing schools and the increased money for books, apparatus and classroom furniture allowed child-centred ideas to gain far more ground than before.

Given these political and economic gains, a familiar story is often told about the rise and fall of progressive education. It is seen as the

Introduction

triumph of 'permissive' teaching methods in Western Europe and the United States in the 1960s and 1970s, followed by a vehement backlash in the 1980s that reasserted central control over education, alongside the imposition of increasingly rigid targets measured by standardised testing such as SATs in the UK and the No Child Left Behind programme in the US. Permissivism was accused of allowing children to do what they wanted, regardless of how pointless and destructive it was, of failing to instil discipline and appropriate moral standards and of encouraging low academic achievement. Furthermore, it is remembered as having been driven by radical, left-wing teachers and resisted by the institutions of the central state.[28] Some historians of education have modified this simplistic narrative – considering the deep roots of progressive pedagogy in the nineteenth century and the inter-war period, and noting the beginnings of resistance from the 1960s – but not fundamentally challenged it.[29] However, little in this story stands up to scrutiny.

For both right- and left-wing cultural and political commentators, the central feature of this story lies in the association of utopian progressivism with non-utopian progressive or child-centred education, and of both with 'the permissive society'. Sympathisers defend child-centred education by arguing that children need freedom and autonomy to learn; detractors claim that child-centred education led to the decline of educational standards and the rise of disciplinary problems in the classroom. In other words, this story suggests that there was a direct line of inheritance from schools such as Neill's experimental Summerhill in the 1920s and 1930s to the post-war child-centred primary schools praised in the Plowden Report (1967) to 1970s scandals such as the closure of the William Tyndale Junior School by the Inner London Education Authority (ILEA) in 1976. But this is not the case. To understand the differences between utopian progressivism on the one hand and non-utopian child-centred progressivism on the other, we should start by recognising that they rested on different concepts of childhood.

The divisions within the movement that has been called 'progressivism' have been obscured or elided because historians of childhood have not tended to consider the classroom, whereas historians of education have often forgotten about the child.[30] When considering late nineteenth- and early twentieth-century childhood in Western Europe, historians can scarcely avoid paying some attention to the growth of compulsory elementary education, a major factor in what Viviana Zelizer has termed the evolution of 'the priceless' but economically useless child.[31] However, mid- and late-twentieth-century British historians have, on the whole, been more concerned with childhood in the clinic, the court and the family than in the school.[32] Their works share a nebulous chronology which suggests that childhood generally got better from the late nineteenth century onwards as child labour was more tightly regulated, material conditions improved and the child's needs came to the forefront in education and parenting, before a sharp downturn in the 1970s and 1980s as the permissive shift was curtailed.[33]

At the same time, the history of education has been peculiarly and unfairly neglected by historians who do not specialise in it. Peter Mandler has put forward a compelling case for its integration into the wider narrative of modern British history: '[Education] is one of the places where the state enters most regularly and directly into the lives of its citizens. It helps to make us whom we are.'[34] However, historians of education, while also positioning the 1970s as a turning-point, have shown little interest in childhood or youth as a category, focusing on institutional and structural issues in education such as social mobility, gender-differentiated academic achievement and the relationship between the educational system and the central state. Furthermore, as David Cannadine, Nicola Sheldon and Jenny Keating note in their recent monograph on the history of history teaching in twentieth-century Britain, the history of 'taught subjects' – defined as the relationship between the curriculum and actual practice in schools – has been neglected, reflecting earlier arguments about the lack of knowledge of a 'lived curriculum' or the 'social history of the classroom' made by Peter Cunningham and Harold Silver.[35] This suggests, crucially, that child-centred education has still not been analysed in practice, despite recent methodological work that has promised to open up 'the black box of schooling' by considering the range of sources that can be handled by historians of the classroom.[36] Without considering how teachers actually understood, implemented and developed child-centred pedagogy, we cannot assess how it affected classroom practice, or how it reshaped teachers' concepts of childhood.

The top-down nature of the historiography of education partly explains why there has never been a satisfactory history of this kind of pedagogical practice. Child-centred ideas were rewritten by the teachers who employed them and the contexts within which they were actually used. *A Progressive Education?* will suggest that child-centred education was only ever half-implemented in English and Welsh primary and secondary modern schools. Far from being promoted by 'trendy' teachers, these new ideas met significant resistance from within the teaching profession. Even enthusiastic proponents of child-centred practice were restricted by inadequate school buildings, a lack of materials, uncooperative colleagues and large class sizes. Most importantly, as we shall see, the child-centred education that did become mainstream in primary and secondary modern schools after the Second World War was *not* progressive in the utopian sense. However, non-utopian progressive education not only enabled a deliberate rethinking of childhood but was moulded by the context within which it operated. These post-war ideas about childhood were new.

Positioning this shift after the Second World War expands upon current historical work that views the 1950s as a social, cultural and emotional turning-point in British history. Historians such as Claire Langhamer, Thomas Dixon, Carolyn Steedman, Martin Francis, Michal Shapira and Frank Mort, alongside Thomson, have argued that there were fundamental changes in how selfhood was presented and understood after 1945.[37] These new approaches both challenge the chronology of a 'permissive shift', traditionally dated to the 1960s, and question the utility of the concept.[38] As Nick Thomas suggests, quoting Abigail Wills, the 'exact nature of what has been termed the "permissive shift" remains strangely elusive.'[39] These arguments reflect Alan Petigny's assertion that the 'permissive turn' in the United States should be dated to the 1940s, not the 1960s, due to the increasing popularisation of modern psychology.[40]

However, despite Petigny's argument that 'permissive' parenting, primarily inspired by the work of Dr Spock, played a key part in this 'transformation of moral values', the relationship between child-centred practice at home and school and 'a permissive society' – whatever that might mean – is not straightforward.[41] Child-centred education was not inherently permissive, and it did not value the power and agency of young people. A child-centred school could, and usually did, preserve the teacher's traditional authority; altering the curriculum did not change the fact that it was still imposed from above. Conservative critics who decided that child-centred methods had caused a decline in behavioural and academic standards told a story that began with the utopian educationalists of inter-war Britain and ended with the 'exploding school' movement of the 1970s, which aimed to break down barriers between the school and the community; as I have already suggested, this is not a story to which non-utopian progressive education, or, indeed, mainstream educational practice, truly belongs. Child-centred methods did lead to a significant shift in concepts of childhood, but they tended to reduce, rather than to promote, the freedom of the child.

This shift can be understood as follows. While childhood and adolescence were established categories by the beginning of the twentieth century, the gap between these two age stages, on the one hand, and adulthood, on the other, widened after the Second World War. The sequential, maturational development of childhood and youth was compared with the completed 'steady state' of healthy adulthood, and children were re-envisioned as incomplete and incapable, rather than as merely inexperienced. Chronological age became much more significant, as it was claimed that children could only acquire certain capacities, such as logical thought, by getting older, rather than, for example, acquiring more life experience. As child-centred educational methods were increasingly introduced into schools, teachers were encouraged to understand childhood in developmental psychological terms. Teachers sought ways to teach classes more easily and effectively, reshaping what they had been told about children in the context of their own practice. At the same time, they blamed child-centred parenting and teaching for what they perceived to be an entitled, selfish and delinquent generation of children and adolescents, even as the developmental psychology it championed reframed both children and adolescents as egotistic, unable to extend genuine empathy to others.

While this book is rooted in a case study of progressive education in England and Wales, its broader findings are strongly relevant to the histories of both childhood and education in the United States and in Western Europe. The progressive education movement was influential in all these countries, and English pioneers exchanged ideas and practices in the inter-war period with key American and European figures such as John Dewey, Maria Montessori, Charlotte Bühler and Arnold Gesell.[42] After the Second World War, teachers were encouraged to

Introduction

visit schools in other countries and to share child-centred practice.[43] Most notably, the English progressive primary school movement became a key source of inspiration for reformers in the United States in the 1960s and 1970s; in 1974, Ian Lister, head of the department of education at the University of York, called the notably progressive local education authority (LEA) of Leicestershire 'that shrine in England visited by so many US pilgrims'.[44] Vincent Rogers, an American teacher, claimed 'I have not been quite the same' after visiting Brize Norton and two other experimental Oxfordshire primary schools, Tower Hill and Bampton, and he produced an edited collection of essays by English reformers to allow other American teachers to learn from his experience.[45] Similarly, Charles Silberman, who published the well-known American text *Crisis in the Classroom*, in 1970, was hugely impressed by the teaching he saw in London, Leicestershire and the West Riding of Yorkshire: 'Not even the most informal American kindergartens ... have the incredible richness and variety of materials found in the average informal English infant or junior school classroom.'[46]

American historians of education such as William J. Reese and Diane Ravitch have noted the importance of the English example in shaping progressive educational movements in the United States in the 1960s and 1970s.[47] While the LEAs visited by Rogers and Silberman were not representative of educational practice throughout England and Wales – all were known for their radical progressivism – these selective experiences were profoundly influential for what Neville Bennett called the 'droves of Americans' who descended upon English primary schools from the early 1970s onwards.[48] However, the history of non-utopian progressive education and its associated concepts of childhood in England and Wales is important for understanding international experiences not only because English and Welsh pioneers exercised disproportionate influence. While my findings on the implementation of non-utopian progressive education are situated in English and Welsh contexts, they also point to central contradictions within the philosophy and pedagogy of child-centred education as practised throughout Europe, and how it potentially influenced conceptions of childhood outside as well as inside England and Wales.

The argument of this book proceeds across seven chapters. In Chapter 1, I explore how 'utopian progressive' and 'non-utopian progressive', or 'child-centred', educationalists developed two fundamentally opposed sets of ideas about the capabilities, development and potential of children. Having demonstrated that utopian progressivism had relatively little impact on mainstream educationalists and on the significant series of inter-war reports produced by the Board of Education, I define what practices and ideas were signified by a 'child-centred' education before 1945. I suggest that the simultaneous commitment to providing an 'individual' and a 'natural' education for children introduced an inherent tension into this pedagogical programme. However, this tension was largely dormant during the inter-war period itself, as early child-centred experiments such as the Malting House School dealt with small groups of children, and so were able to provide a genuinely individualised education. Citizenship, a key concern for child-centred educationalists, was also conceived of in more individualistic terms in the 1920s and 1930s than after the advent of a collectivistic welfare state in the 1940s.

Chapter 2 considers how teachers themselves engaged with developmental psychology both before and after the Second World War, demonstrating that they claimed to be mystified by key theorists such as Piaget, while unconsciously absorbing the language he used about childhood. By considering the thought of two dominant educational thinkers in Britain before 1945, the psychoanalyst Susan Isaacs and the educational psychologist Cyril Burt, I will show that ideas about maturational developmental stages were resisted in inter-war Britain, and that this ambivalence was evident in teaching manuals and popular journals as well as in the more theoretical work of Burt and Isaacs. The adoption of developmental stages by child-centred educationalists was magnified by the practical reorganisation of schooling around chronological age from the 1930s onwards, emphasising the importance of 'stages of development', which were presumed to be closely linked to a particular age group. This redefined both childhood and adolescence as fundamentally divided from adulthood, because young people were still progressing through a sequence of stages that would allow them to acquire full cognitive and emotional capacities.

Teachers, as we shall see, rarely grasped the full complexities of the psychological theories that they encountered. However, the ways they used psychology and how it influenced their concepts of childhood were not solely reliant on a misunderstood and confused version of the arguments of key theorists. Rather than being an empty atheoretical vessel into which psychological knowledge was poured, the teaching profession had its own model of craft knowledge that both resisted and adapted the novel theories with which it was presented.[49] This argument is developed further in Chapter 3, which focuses on teachers' resistance to the child-centred educational methods that emerged from the findings of developmental psychologists. Teachers often felt they had to pay lip service to child-centred methods even if they were not convinced by them, intensifying the influence of simplistic and limiting concepts of childhood and youth. Even when they self-defined as 'progressive', they were liable to believe that this mindset tended to introduce too many changes too quickly, so teachers could not keep up with changing 'trends' in child-centred practice.

In Chapter 4, I consider the implementation of non-utopian progressivism in English and Welsh primary and secondary modern schools since 1918, contending that it was precisely because child-centred practice was only ever half-implemented in primary and secondary modern schools in England and Wales that it transformed teachers' concepts of childhood so profoundly. Psychological ideas about childhood were shaped by the reactions and needs of the teaching profession, one of their major targets and consumers. For example, teachers who had to manage classes of forty or fifty pupils prodded psychological theorists towards generalisations about childhood; they wanted to be told 'how seven-year-olds learn', rather than being informed that they ought to provide an individualised education for each child. In this chapter, I consider how teacher trainers, inspectors, headteachers and teachers shaped both theory and policy at the local level, using four case studies of LEAs: Oxfordshire, Cambridgeshire, Sheffield and Monmouthshire. I suggest that non-utopian progressive education posed a threat to teachers' notions of expertise, shaping a limited concept of the pupil that nevertheless served a practical purpose in the classroom, especially given large class sizes, poor buildings and scant apparatus. Primary and secondary modern schools – and, later, comprehensives – rather than grammar schools or private schools are focused upon for three key reasons. First, they educated the majority of the population during this period.[50] Second, given this, the relative historical neglect, especially of the secondary modern school, is significant.[51] Third, relatively unencumbered by external examinations, they tended to be the sites for pedagogical experimentation.[52]

A progressive education?

In Chapters 5 and 6, I consider how class and gender shaped not only teachers' responses to child-centred education after the Second World War but their images of the children they taught. I suggest that progressive education was itself gendered feminine, due to its association with infant and primary schools and the 'mothering' role of the teacher.[53] While both male and female teachers felt their traditional craft expertise and subject knowledge to be under threat, men in secondary modern schools were more likely to resist these innovations than their female counterparts in primary schools. Using a case study of the secondary modern school in the 1950s and 1960s, I extend these arguments about male teachers' status anxieties to explore why media depictions of the 'sec. mod.' or 'modern school' were so fraught with violence and conflict during this period. Class is a key variable; the 1944 Education Act had brought a new influx of working-class children within the ambit of state education at the same time as the teaching profession, especially at secondary level, was attracting more middle-class recruits. However, teachers from working-class backgrounds also had a vested interest in maintaining a 'cultural gap' between themselves and their pupils. Although some teachers criticised the negative media portrayals of the 'blackboard jungle', others embraced them. The anxieties engendered by progressive teaching methods, I suggest, increasingly defined the interests of the child and teacher not as a unity but in opposition to each other. Non-utopian progressive education contributed to this shift by emphasising the gulf between the abilities of children and of adults, reconfiguring childhood and youth as *negatively* defined by what young people were unable to do before they reached adulthood. Both children and adolescents were characterised by their essential egotism, their orientation towards practical and concrete experience that directly related to their own lives and their lack of capacity for abstract reasoning.

Finally, in Chapter 7, I consider the 'backlash' against 'child-centred' education in the 1970s and question whether education in England and Wales was ever truly progressive. This does not mean that child-centred ideas ceased to have any impact upon concepts of childhood and adolescence; instead, the child-centred remodelling of youth was increasingly internalised, divorced from its origins. The emergence of ideas such as Anthony Fyson and Colin Ward's 'exploding school' recalled the earlier utopian ideals of progressives such as Neill and

Russell, but, like the experimental schools that were founded in interwar Britain, these variants ultimately failed to have much impact on mainstream education, although they were often taken as representative of a system that had failed.[54] The impact of child-centred education upon marginalised groups – girls, ethnic minority or immigrant pupils, working-class pupils and disabled pupils – is further considered, and it is ultimately argued that, while these groups were the most deeply affected, all children and adolescents were defined by non-utopian progressive educationalists as abnormal, seen as incomplete versions of adults despite reformers' assertions to the contrary.

Age remains an inconstant variable throughout this book. With the exception of the case studies of childhood (seven- to eleven-year-olds) in Chapter 5 and of adolescence (eleven- to fifteen-year-olds) in Chapter 6, I mainly consider the seven- to fifteen-year-old age range as a whole in my discussion of the impact of non-utopian progressive education, deliberately omitting the infant school years, which followed a very different historical trajectory.[55] This decision was made for a number of reasons. First, it mirrors the institutional experience of the majority of children and teachers during this period; all-age elementaries were the norm before 1944 and, despite the provision for separate secondary education in the 1944 Education Act, many children remained in these all-age schools into the 1960s, especially in Wales.[56] Second, it reflects the sources I consulted for these sections: teaching manuals and periodicals rarely highlighted the age group under discussion, unless speaking explicitly about the problems of adolescence or of the primary school child. Due to the envisaging of both childhood and adolescence as segmented into a series of developmental stages, post-war educationalists often found that these life-stages had much more in common with each other than with adulthood, and so tended to deal with them together. In contrast, images of the infant and young child, as Shapira has argued, unlike images of the older child and adolescent, were shaped primarily by psychoanalysis after the Second World War, and so were dominated by an alternative set of concerns.[57] Third, even when schools dealt with separate age groups, there was a consistency in the curriculum between the primary and the secondary modern or comprehensive school, reflecting the largely unspoken assumption that progressive methods were especially appropriate for the less academic child – and that such children would never develop into fully mature beings.

In this book, I consider the development of ideas about childhood in different social contexts: from influential academics such as Jean Piaget attending conferences and collaborating with colleagues, to the teacher struggling to teach a class of fifty-four primary-aged children in an isolated and dilapidated rural Oxfordshire school. Tracing concepts of childhood, even in the more recent past, poses a challenge for historians because children, like women, have often been made invisible in the historical record; as Charlotte Hardman has argued, both are 'muted groups'.[58] While it is not this book's main purpose to attempt the significantly more difficult endeavour of uncovering the voice of the child itself, even adult ideas about children are not easily accessible. This is especially true in the context of classroom practice in schools, which has also been 'hidden from history'. For this reason, this book combines both social and cultural approaches to history, drawing on an exceptionally wide range of sources to trace these discourses where they can be found.

How can we get inside the 'black box' of the classroom and understand how child-centred education worked in practice? English and Welsh education was not tightly controlled from the centre during the period under investigation, although Welsh education was not able to develop independently.[59] As Wooldridge has put it, somewhat negatively, 'English education was a shambles rather than a system', suggesting that the political elite were simply not concerned about mass education as they had no vested interest in its institutions.[60] The nature of the relationship between central government and the schools is summed up in the titles of the handbooks issued infrequently by the Board of Education: they were known as handbooks of *suggestions* to teachers.[61] While the Board produced a steady stream of reports, memorandums, pamphlets and guides, teachers were not bound to obey any of them. It was rare that legislation compelled the local authority to offer any particular service – medical inspections, school meals and the raising of the school leaving age were exceptions – and legislation did not affect the curriculum except in the anomalous case of religious education, which was compulsory in maintained schools.[62] At the local level, schools were likewise loosely accountable to the LEA. The LEA controlled schools' funds, so schools were forced to appeal to the LEA via their boards of governors for repairs, equipment, staff needs and so forth, but the local authority rarely interfered directly in

Introduction

the curriculum. It was nationally employed inspectors who, indirectly, wielded the most influence over teaching methods. Additionally, teacher training colleges affected the views and methods of teachers entering the profession, but central control was, again, minimal after 1926, when the Board of Education relinquished control of examinations at the same time as it relaxed regulations for the school curriculum.[63]

The decentralised nature of the English and Welsh education system has led to the assumption that local differences are crucial to understanding teaching practice in this period.[64] The four local case studies that I draw from throughout this book actually demonstrated a surprising uniformity of practice, despite the fact that two of the LEAs (Oxfordshire and Sheffield) had a 'child-centred' reputation, whereas the other two (Cambridgeshire and Monmouthshire) did not. Using school logbooks, His/Her Majesty's Inspector of Schools' (HMI) reports, school correspondence, punishment books, teaching journals, oral history archives and other records that span the period from the 1920s to the 1970s, this book demonstrates that we can access what was actually happening in the classroom – and that practice was remarkably geographically consistent. To explain why schools were so similar and why teachers' practice was seemingly so co-ordinated we must turn to the role of the national inspectorate, the systems of promotion utilised by local authorities, and the teacher training colleges. It was progressive HMIs and teacher trainers who became crucial in spreading child-centred practice.

School logbooks, mandated by the Board of Education from 1862 and sometimes checked by the local inspector or HMI, are a useful and relatively underutilised source for the history of twentieth-century schooling, although David Nunn, Hester Barron and Andrew Burchell have made use of them recently to consider the responses of schools to the First World War, the inter-war period and post-war period respectively.[65] One reason for their relative neglect is that their coverage is patchy and uneven. Different counties have widely varying numbers of extant logbooks, and the individual histories of the schools in question often determine whether or not they survive; as Siân Pooley has pointed out, logbooks often did not enter archives until the 1970s or 1980s, and so the survival of a logbook for a particular school may depend on whether or not the school survived into the late twentieth century.[66] Headteachers were required to make entries in these logbooks, but their use of them varied widely. Entries range from a cursory dozen records for a year to those of the Cambridgeshire headmaster Derek Skeet who took the time in 1964 to write a mini-essay in the closing pages of his volume about the structure and purpose of the logbook, musing that '[t]he log is a unique form of literature created by many hands. From its dry pages, cryptic as manuscript music, with entries as similar as tesserae, emerges an art form, built out of dedicated living . . . It is the life of a school.'[67]

Moving outside my local authority case studies, I use teachers' journals to gain another angle on teachers' responses to progressive education and how this affected their views on childhood. *Teachers World* [sic] and *The Schoolmaster and Woman Teacher's Chronicle* (*Schoolmaster*), which became the *Teacher* in 1963, form the two major case studies, as they had the widest readership during this period and the greatest appeal to primary and secondary modern school teachers, as opposed to the grammar and private-school readership catered to by the *Times Educational Supplement* (*TES*).[68] Peter Cunningham estimates that 25 per cent of state primary teachers read *Teachers World* in 1969, comparing favourably to the *TES*, at 23 per cent. The *Teacher*, however, the official journal of the National Union of Teachers (NUT), came out top, at 47 per cent.[69] This perhaps represents the composition of the survey, which included only primary school teachers; as Cunningham indicates, *Teachers World* had less appeal to primary teachers than secondary teachers.[70] Both the *Teacher* and the NUT itself were hence more representative of primary school teachers than secondary school teachers in the post-war period.[71] Unfortunately, there are no figures for secondary school teachers' reading practice, although there are anecdotal reports that some read these periodicals.[72] The *Teacher* boasted in 1972 that 120,000 teachers read the paper, a figure that included primary and secondary teachers; given that the total workforce in UK public-sector schools at the time was around 480,000, this represented 25 per cent of all teachers.[73] There are no readership figures for the earlier part of our period; however, many teachers who taught between the wars recalled these periodicals or found them familiar when prompted with a copy during oral history interviews.[74]

The format and content of these journals changed over time. The *Teacher* shifted from a magazine to tabloid newspaper layout post-war, and by 1971 it was being distributed free to all schools. *Teachers World* had been popular in earlier decades because of its practical focus; as Cunningham argues, it was 'closer to the reality of the primary school world' because it focused on printing material for use in lessons, such as its colour poster insert.[75] However, its 'teaching tips' were proving less competitive by the early 1960s, and the *Teacher* recalled that it had cut down on this kind of feature under the editorship of Nicholas Bagnall (1961–65) because *Teachers World* was 'slumping badly'.[76] There was a contraction in the education journal market in the late 1970s; the *Teacher* became a much shorter periodical dominated by job listings rather than news or opinion pieces, while *Teachers World* stopped publishing after 1975.[77] Alongside teaching journals, therefore, I read popular teaching advice guides, focusing on key texts that went through numerous reprints and/or frequently appeared on the book lists of training colleges. Both journals and manuals demonstrate significant shifts after the Second World War in both teaching practice and in conceptions of childhood.

Finally, I use both written self-narratives and transcripts of oral history interviews throughout this book. These represent two very different types of autobiographical account. As Alessandro Portelli puts it, unlike the fixed text of a written self-narrative, '[w]hat is spoken in a typical oral history interview has usually never been told *in that form* before', and, even when it has, it has never been told to that listener.[78] Furthermore, a written self-narrative is usually prompted by the subject's decision to write an autobiographical account, whereas an oral history interview is usually prompted by the interviewer. Much has been written on the 'intersubjectivity' created by the interviewer and interviewee in an oral history interview, and it is crucial to reflect upon the ways in which the interviewee's story is mediated and shaped, especially if you have not conducted the interviews yourself. Nevertheless, as April Gallway has argued, archived oral histories are still a valuable resource, as even the original interviewer's understanding of the contexts that shaped the interview will be partial.[79]

I draw from four oral history archives in this book: first, the archive created by David Cannadine, Nicola Sheldon and Jenny Keating for *The Right Kind of History*; both the original questionnaires sent to respondents and the transcripts of selected interviews are available online.[80] Sheldon and Keating undertook the bulk of the interviewing for this project.

Second, I examine the transcripts and audio recordings available in the Oxfordshire History Archive. In contrast to the Cannadine archive, these interviews were not undertaken by professional and/or academic interviewers, but took place in a range of situations, from a local radio programme called *My Choice*, where the participant chose a range of songs that meant something to them and informally discussed their life and career, to interviews between colleagues who were already known to each other. This inevitably affected the accounts that emerged from the interviews, in contrast to the more structured approach of Sheldon and Keating. The third archive is the hundred or so transcripts produced by the Wartime Evacuation Project (WEP), led by Phil Gardner and Peter Cunningham from 1998 to 2002, which considered how teachers' experiences of evacuation influenced their teaching practice.[81] Finally, I make use of a set of ten oral history interviews that I conducted in Oxford in 2015. Interviewing teachers who had started teaching in the City of Oxford or Oxfordshire in the 1970s, I adopted a 'life history' approach to consider how teachers' attitudes towards their pupils had changed as they themselves grew older, focusing especially on their initial teacher training, early teaching experiences and their engagement with psychological discourses. I supplemented these interviews with fifteen qualitative questionnaires, including some from respondents who completed an initial questionnaire but were not interviewed.[82]

The shift in ideas about childhood and adolescence in England and Wales after 1945 reflected wider understandings about the role of the post-war state. Moreover, it suggested an emotional change in how adults imagined the future. In the supposedly pessimistic inter-war period, British utopian educationalists saw a distorted world that could be made good by the rising generation. The world was fundamentally flawed, but it could also be fundamentally transformed. This optimism was reflected by children's self-narratives, which tended to imagine exciting and glamorous futures.[83] This was an unusual historical moment, although we may perceive some parallels with the recent positive coverage in Britain and the United States of the coming of age in a time of crisis of Generation Z, born in the late 1990s and early 2000s.[84] As Geoffrey Pearson has argued, concern about the declining moral standards of the young had been the steady state of affairs in Britain for three centuries.[85] In contrast, in the supposedly affluent

Introduction

and self-confident 1950s, fears and worries about children and adolescents intensified, and children's writing about imagined futures became more practical, less ambitious and more anxious.[86] If Britain had really 'never had it so good', it stood that British citizens also had more to lose. More was required of adults who formed part of a collectivist, social-solidaristic welfare state; it had to be ensured that the generation that followed them had the moral, social and intellectual capacity to preserve the world they had won.

Notes

1 Holmes, *Tragedy of Education*, pp. 99–100.
2 Holmes, 'Confessions and hopes of an ex-inspector', p. 277.
3 Selleck, *English Primary Education and the Progressives*. Lane was accused of the sexual abuse of adolescent girls in his charge in 1918; see Delap, 'Disclosures of child sexual abuse', pp. 83–5.
4 Holmes, *Tragedy of Education*, p. 5.
5 Neill, *Dreadful School*, p. 35; Purdy, *Neill*, p. 9.
6 Neill, *Summerhill*, pp. 9, 40.
7 Russell, On *Education*, pp. 166–73.
8 Overy, *Morbid Age*.
9 Cited in Selleck, *English Primary Education and the Progressives*, p. 97.
10 MacMunn, *The Child's Path to Freedom*, p. 11.
11 Pearson, *Hooligan*, p. 216; Tisdall, 'Life in Bridgeburn', pp. 358–60.
12 Thomson, *Lost Freedom*; King, 'Future citizens'. Similarly, the Progressive Movement in the United States envisaged education as a key part of the development of a modern society; see Marten (ed.), *Children and Youth*.
13 This quotation has been attributed to John Dewey and Johann Pestalozzi, but I have been unable to trace its precise origin, although the phrasing frequently reoccurs.
14 Neill, 'Introduction' in Mannin, *Common Sense*, p. 13.
15 Saint, *Towards a Social Architecture*, p. 39.
16 Robinson, *Language of Progressive Politics*, p. 4.
17 Ibid.
18 James and Prout, in *Constructing and Reconstructing Childhood*, use the term 'human becomings'.
19 Burchell, 'The Adolescent School Pupil', p. 74.
20 Robinson, *Language of Progressive Politics*, pp. 13–14, 158.
21 Thomson, *Lost Freedom*.
22 Technical schools, the third leg of a 'tripartite' system, were rarely established; see Sanderson, *Missing Stratum*, pp. ix, 147.

23 For example, Thom, 'The 1944 Education Act'. Peter Mandler discusses the 'compromise' nature of the Act and its impact on working-class children in 'Educating the Nation I', pp. 216–35.
24 Tisdall, 'Inside the "blackboard jungle"'; Carter, '"Experimental" secondary modern education'.
25 O'Hara, *Governing Post-war Britain*, p. 7.
26 Cronin, *Politics of State Expansion*, pp. 2–4.
27 DES, *Children and Their Primary Schools*, p. 389.
28 Most recently, every step of this narrative has been rehearsed in Blundell, *Education and Constructions*, pp. 5, 125, 140–56, and in Howlett, *Progressive Education*.
29 For the earlier period, see Lowndes, *Silent Social Revolution*, and Selleck, *English Primary Education and the Progressives*. For the counter-attack on progressive education, see Lowe (ed.), *The Changing Primary School*, Jones, *Beyond* and Lowe, *The Death of Progressive Education*.
30 Blundell, *Education and Constructions* is an exception, but Blundell solely considers educational ideas and institutions, rather than practice in schools.
31 Zelizer, *Pricing the Priceless Child*. On nineteenth-century and early-twentieth-century education, see Rose, *Intellectual Life*; Heathorn, *For Home, Country and Race*; Hurt, *Elementary Schooling*.
32 Rose, *Governing the Soul*; Cox, *Gender, Justice and Welfare*; Shapira, *The War Inside*.
33 Hendrick, *Child Welfare: Historical Dimensions*; Hendrick, *Child Welfare: England 1872–1989*; Hendrick, *Children, Childhood and English Society*; Cunningham, *Children and Childhood in Western Society*; Heywood, *History of Childhood*.
34 Mandler, 'Educating the Nation I', p. 6.
35 Cannadine *et al.*, *The Right Kind of History*, p. 219; Cunningham, *Curriculum Change in the Primary School*, pp. viii, 2; Silver, 'Knowing and not knowing', pp. 104–6.
36 Braster *et al.*, *Black Box*.
37 Langhamer, *The English in Love*; King, *Family Men*; Davis, *Modern Motherhood*; Thomson, *Psychological Subjects*; Todd, *Young Women, Work and Family*; Dixon, *Weeping Britannia*; Steedman, 'State-sponsored autobiography'; Field, *Blood, Sweat and Toil*; Francis, 'Tears, tantrums and bared teeth'; Shapira, *The War Inside*; Mort, 'Social and symbolic'; Waters, 'Dark strangers'.
38 Permissivism in the 1960s is discussed in Marwick, *The Sixties*; Donnelly, *Sixties Britain*, p. 12.
39 Thomas, 'Will the real 1950s please stand up?', p. 228.
40 Petigny, *Permissive Society*.
41 Petigny, *Permissive Society*, pp. 2, 16, 40–1.
42 Hirsch, 'Apostle of freedom'; Rose, *Governing the Soul*; Giardiello, *Pioneers in Early Childhood Education*; Nawrotski, 'Froëbel is dead'.

Introduction

43   D. Jordan, 'The quaint, rude, undisciplined British', *Teacher,* 1 July 1966, p. 17.
44   Lister, *Deschooling*, p. 2.
45   Rogers (ed.), *Teaching in the British Primary School*, p. v.
46   Silberman, *Crisis in the Classroom*, p. 221.
47   Ravitch, *Left Back*.
48   Silberman, *Crisis in the Classroom*, p. 262; Bennett, *Teaching Styles*, p. 8.
49   Middleton and May, *Early Childhood Herstories* makes the similar point that teachers have always used theory.
50   Todd, *The People*.
51   McCulloch and Sobel, 'Towards a history of secondary modern schools', p. 275; Carter, 'Experimental secondary modern education', p. 24.
52   Grosvenor and Lawn, 'Days out of school', p. 382.
53   Indeed, Mathew Thomson suggests that popular psychology was itself 'feminised' in post-war Britain, due to its association with motherhood. Thomson, *Psychological Subjects*, p. 292.
54   Fyson and Ward, 'Streetwork'.
55   Giardiello, *Pioneers in Early Childhood Education*; Davis, *Pre-School*.
56   DES, *Primary Education in Wales*, p. 4.
57   Shapira, *The War Inside*.
58   Hardman, 'Can there be an anthropology of children?', p. 85.
59   Jones, 'Perspectives from the brink of extinction'; Jones, 'Which nation's curriculum?', pp. 6–7.
60   Wooldridge, 'The English state', pp. 232–3.
61   Major re-issuings of this *Handbook* from 1900–67 occurred in 1905, 1909, 1918, 1926, 1937 and 1959.
62   Wooldridge, 'The English state', p. 233.
63   Cunningham and Gardner, 'Teacher trainers and educational change', p. 240; Grace, 'Teachers', p. 207.
64   Cunningham, *Curriculum Change in the Primary School*.
65   Barron, 'Little prisoners of city streets'.
66   Pooley, 'Parenthood and child-rearing', p. 36.
67   Cambridgeshire Archives, St Luke's, Cambridge, Boys: Logbook, Uncatalogued, entry at back of logbook, c. 1964.
68   *Teachers World*'s ungrammatical title has been the subject of much confusion among historians of education. The title changed across time: it was *The Teacher's World* from 1918, *The Teachers' World* from 1922 and *Teachers World* from 1930, when it started producing 'Junior School' and 'Senior School' editions, and it retained this title from 1940, when the two editions became one again. I have referred to the journal as *Teachers World* throughout.
69   Cunningham, *Curriculum Change in the Primary School*, p. 109.
70   Cunningham, *Curriculum Change in the Primary School*, p. 110.
71   Tropp estimates that in 1956 the total membership of the NUT was 240,400, including retired and trainee teachers. 79.7% of primary teachers were

members in 1956 compared with 66.7%, or exactly two thirds, of secondary modern teachers. See Tropp, *The School Teachers*, p. 266.
72 For example: WEP A064, 27/11/01, p. 37; A086, 22/1/01, p. 33.
73 M. Wilkinson, 'The voice of the profession', *Teacher,* 14 January 1972, p. 9; History in Education, 'Analysis of teacher numbers' (2010).
74 For example: WEP A039, 17/8/00, p. 28; D016, 10/5/01, p. 41, A016, 3/10/00, p. 25; A071, 24/1/01, p. 18.
75 Cunningham, *Curriculum Change in the Primary School*, p. 110.
76 *Teacher*, 14 January 1972, p. 19.
77 *Teacher*, 8 January 1971, p. 19.
78 Portelli, *The Battle of Valle Giulia*, p. 4.
79 Gallway, 'Rewards of using archived oral histories'.
80 History in Education Project, www.history.ac.uk/history-in-education/index.html.
81 Cunningham and Gardner, 'Oral history and teachers' professional practice'; Hussey, 'The school air-raid shelter'. This archive is currently only available to researchers for comparative purposes, so I have been unable to quote directly from any WEP transcripts, although I am able to cite individual interviews in footnotes when considering broader trends.
82 I have anonymised all respondents' names and the schools at which they taught in accordance with respondents' wishes.
83 Langhamer and Barron, 'Children, class, and the search for security'.
84 For example, 'How Generation Z will change the world', *Time,* 23 April 2018, http://time.com/5250542/generation-z/.
85 Pearson, *Hooligan*.
86 Highmore, 'Playgrounds and bombsites'; Oxford, Bodleian Libraries: Opie 35, Folder 1, Folios 1–220, essays on 'What I want to be when I leave school' written between 1951 and 1952 by children aged seven to thirteen.

1

What is a progressive education?

'"Give the child freedom," is the insistent cry of the New Education', wrote Homer Lane in *Talks to Parents and Teachers* in 1928. '[B]ut then its exponents usually devise a "system" which, although based upon the soundest of principles, limits that freedom and contradicts the principle . . . I look to the child himself to initiate the methods that govern his development. No matter how much freedom is given by a particular system, at some point the child is disappointing because he does not fit.'[1] Here, Lane was not criticising the 'traditional' education that was depicted as a significant opponent by many contemporary writers, but the group of new educational movements which he might have been expected to welcome. As a utopian progressive, however, Lane was suspicious of the methodologies that had been put forward by a range of non-utopian progressive educators, and argued that the 'freedom' that they were offering the child moved within very limited bounds. Far from espousing permissive philosophies that discarded the old shibboleths of traditional education, Lane suggested that child-centred education tended to create rigid sets of rules of its own.

In inter-war England and Wales, both utopian and non-utopian progressives agreed that education should offer freedom to the child, and that freedom could be defined as the opportunity to develop your natural abilities and fully realise your innate potential. However, they disagreed over the question of who possessed definitive knowledge of the true nature of the child, and hence how freedom should be offered to the pupil. Child-centred educationalists suggested that the educator, guided by the precepts of what was sometimes called the 'new psychology' – an umbrella term that included all the psychological schools that addressed the unconscious – was best positioned to ensure a natural course of development, and hence tended to argue that children should be carefully guided along their path to adulthood.[2] They positioned such claims in relation to a mythical 'traditional' education, which purportedly gave the child no freedom at all. In contrast, utopian progressives thought that the child itself was the sole authority on his or her own nature. The 'leave-the-child-alone' school of thought, in the phrasing of L. B. Pekin, an early historian of the movement, argued that adults must allow the child to be guided by his or her own innate expertise by interfering as little as possible with his or her activities.[3] In other words, while utopian progressives offered the child *freedom from* constraints, non-utopians thought their job was to give the child the *freedom to* develop into a psychologically healthy adult.[4]

What was the 'New Education' about which Lane was so concerned? Progressive pedagogical ideas coalesced in England and Wales in the inter-war period within both departments of education and teacher training colleges, were expressed in a range of education and psychology journals, and became especially influential at the Board of Education. Such endeavours were connected with a disparate range of interested parties through the international New Education Fellowship, founded by Beatrice Ensor in 1921, and its journal, the *New Era*. The Fellowship – which held seven international conferences in Western Europe between 1921 and 1936 – linked developmental psychologists and psychoanalysts such as Susan Isaacs and Jean Piaget to child-centred philosophers such as John Dewey and early years educators such as Maria Montessori.[5] Utopian progressives formed a part of this programme; Neill, for example, was an assistant editor of *New Era* and attended at least one of the Fellowship's conferences. But in Lane's eyes, founders of experimental utopian schools, such as his own Little Commonwealth, were to some degree set apart from the other new educational movements that proliferated in England and Wales in the 1920s and 1930s, because they were the only ones who were genuinely trying to set children free.

Child-centred educationalists rarely defined child-centred educational methods clearly, although historians of education have offered a number of retrospective definitions.[6] John Howlett, who has written the most recent history of the ideas of progressive educational movements, defines non-utopian progressivism as 'a child-centred curriculum, activities directly relevant to the needs and desires of the child, the child as an active learner and a high degree of freedom within the context of the school setting for both teachers and pupils'.[7] Leaving aside the circularity of defining progressivism as child-centred, and the unlikely assertion that child-centred education necessarily gave teachers more freedom, Howlett's definition identifies three key commitments: education should be practical, allowing children to be 'active learners'; enjoyable, or 'relevant to the needs and desires of the child'; and local, because such relevance was seen as embedded in the child's immediate environment. However, this definition arguably leaves out the two most important commitments for non-utopian progressives, buried in the idea of a 'child-centred curriculum': the need for education to be both individual and natural, recognising the differences between children but also mapping the course of development towards adulthood which all children shared.

Child-centred, or non-utopian progressive, education was hence split by three tensions. First, as Lane had identified, the child-centred definition of freedom was often muddled, claiming to give children more choices while actually restricting what they were allowed to explore, practise or learn. If freedom was defined as the freedom to develop one's natural abilities, and if those abilities were defined by adults, it could be theoretically extended without offering any choices at all to the child who was being educated, as the Montessori system, which required children to perform a series of very repetitive exercises in the name of 'sense-training', demonstrated. (Neill wrote in *New Era* in 1921 that it was a 'a dead, apparatus-ridden system'.[8]) 'The Montessori approach presented itself as offering an ideologically progressive freedom, but one that did not degenerate into socially unacceptable disorder', Mathew Thomson has argued, highlighting the difficult balance that child-centred education had to strike between social needs and individual development.[9] Child-centred educationalists also framed this balance in precisely those terms, suggesting that freedom must be limited. As Philip Ballard noted, pupils should 'not be *left* to find out things for themselves, but *led* to find out things for themselves'.[10]

Second, as Valerie Walkerdine and Peter Cunningham have suggested, an inherent contradiction developed within non-utopian progressivism between the idea of an 'individual' and a 'natural' education, stemming from the sense that a child's development must be guided by adults.[11] Child-centred educationalists continually emphasised that children all had their own unique abilities, interests and talents, and that this should be reflected in their education. The stress placed upon the development of individual character both reflected older nineteenth-century discourses about the aim of education, now repurposed for working-class as well as elite pupils, and, from the 1930s, was developed in contrast to the negative image of a homogenised body of Nazi Youth in Hitler's Germany.[12] However, as child-centred pedagogy also argued that education should be suited to the natural course of development experienced by the growing organism, using psychological and psychoanalytical knowledge to define the child's needs at different stages, the idea that each child should progress along his or her own particular life course might, in practice, collapse into the dominant model of normal development.

Third, non-utopian progressivism could not decide whether childhood was best positioned as a preparation for adulthood, or as a life stage that was valuable in its own right and should be nurtured without any reference to either the needs of society or the needs of the child's own adult self. A 1938 report on 'The Extra Year', written by a Joint Committee of Investigation representing the Association of Education Committees and the NUT in anticipation of the raising of the school leaving age from fourteen to fifteen, warned that too much focus on preparation for adult life, even in the adolescent years, could be self-defeating, as it meant that schools were not adequately serving the adolescent's current stage of development. For this reason, the report rejected 'specialised vocational training'.[13] Nevertheless, child-centred language could just as easily be used to defend vocational education as to dismiss it. For example, in 1940, Marjorie Reeves wrote in the New Education Fellowship's journal New Era in an article entitled 'Education after the war' that all post-primary education should be 'technical or vocational' as 'one of the main interests of the adolescent is the real world with real jobs to be done in it'.[14] In other words, should childhood, adolescence and adulthood be seen as three entirely separate stages of life, or should educators recognise an essential continuity of experience between age groups?

Child-centred pedagogy, as indicated by the terms 'New Education' or 'new educational movements', also defined itself against the idea of 'a traditional education'. But this was an imagined enemy. In order to promote child-centred education, non-utopian progressive educationalists created a coherent concept of a 'traditional' education that had never actually existed. Theoretical ideas of what it was to be a 'traditional' teacher rarely matched teachers' actual experiences of teaching in 'non-progressive' ways during the 1920s and 1930s. This straw man allowed child-centred theorists to present themselves as thoroughly 'progressive', moving away from the practices of the past, despite the fact that they rejected the radical ideas of more utopian thinkers.

Utopian and non-utopian progressivism

By the beginning of the Second World War, non-utopian progressivism had come to dominate reformist educational thinking. However, the more radical conception of freedom promoted by utopian progressives was initially influential beyond its own narrow social circle in England and Wales. John Adams, professor of education at the University of London, wrote a series of educational texts in the inter-war period that envisaged a practical programme for its implementation in more mainstream schools. In *The Evolution of Educational Theory* (1912), he postulated that education 'may begin to lead instead of following'.[15] In later, more practically orientated texts, he discussed what that might mean. Writing of the Play Way and the Project Method in *Modern Developments in Educational Practice* (1924), he explained that all the new teaching methods were 'paidocentric', which he defined as 'a complete surrender to the child's point of view', but this was not a development that he viewed as problematic.[16] More broadly still, mainstream teaching journals such as *The Schoolmaster* and *Teachers World* both reported upon, and were influenced by, such utopian views of childhood in the inter-war period, a strand of discourse that had almost completely vanished by 1945.

Teachers World often discussed freedom in education and teaching methods that facilitated self-government.[17] From 1921 onwards, the periodical ran a series of features on the 'school without a timetable', one of which explicitly acknowledged the influence of the radical utopian educator E. F. O'Neill, who had headed Prestolee school at Kearsley Clough in Greater Manchester since 1918, focusing on the education of eight to eleven-year-olds.[18] O'Neill allowed his pupils freedom to move around the classroom and to pursue their own projects, although, in contrast to non-utopian child-centred educationalists, he insisted on starting each day with a period of drill in the 'three Rs'.[19] In 1922, *Teachers World* began to debate the self-governing Dalton Plan, which similarly provided for self-directed education.[20] There was also a growing interest in how experiments with freedom in education in other countries – especially those who were proving to be formidable industrial and geopolitical rivals – might provide a model for Britain. These ranged from a 1923 article on 'Freedom in education: its development in Germany' to a 1925 discussion of 'An American teacher's view' on the Dalton Plan, which was a report of a talk given by a teacher from Philadelphia to the Conference of Educational Associations, to an article in the same year which criticised Canadian educators, arguing 'there is perhaps less variety, experiment, activity of thought than one would like to see' in Canadian classrooms.[21] Similarly, the *Schoolmaster* expressed an interest in the Dalton Plan, free discipline and self-government in the same period.[22] As Diane Ravitch argues, the activity movement in US elementary schools, characterised by unstructured classrooms, was especially influential in Britain in the 1920s and 1930s.[23]

This interest in new teaching methods had developed into an exploration of utopian ideas about childhood by the early 1930s. In 1932, Philip Ballard was quoted positively by *Teachers World* as having said in a speech to the Dalton Association, which promoted the Dalton Plan, that these schemes 'often . . . proved that the child was a better teacher of the child than the adult'.[24] This fitted well with Ballard's earlier talk in 1931, where he had said 'we do not know what the future will be. We do not therefore know how to mould these children's minds; and the best thing we can do is not to interfere with them at all.'[25] The prominent educationalist Professor Ernest Campagnac, who was Chair of Education at Liverpool, wrote in the journal in the same year in one of his series of articles, 'We have to anticipate [children's needs] . . . and . . . efface ourselves and stand aside, while they get from better sources than ourselves what we have seen that they want . . . and what we are content that they should enjoy without thanking us for it.'[26] In December 1932, editor Horace Shipp summed up the year by writing: 'There probably never was a period when the younger generation were so free and established in their rights.' Mentioning Neill and Russell as educational pioneers, he concluded 'Conscious or unconscious evolutionists, we somehow believe that it is the child or the children's far children who will save our muddled world.'[27] The *Schoolmaster* picked up on similar themes in the 1930s. In 1933, one writer quoted a headteacher approvingly: 'Who are we, the older generation who caused the world war with its attendant incalculable misery and folly, to say that the children now in the schools are not as good as we were? Whatever the present generation may do, they can do nothing worse than that.'[28]

The heterogeneous nature of these journals meant that there was certainly no house line on this topic, and articles and letters that stressed discipline and formal subject-divisions also appeared throughout the 1920s and 1930s, although even these complaints tended to be muted.[29] Nevertheless, such contributions demonstrated a continuing interest in more radical educational change among ordinary classroom teachers. This may have been because utopian progressive ideas, despite their radical nature, were actually more palatable for the average teacher than later child-centred interventions. Unlike later child-centred educationalists, utopian progressives did not challenge the teacher's expertise and craft knowledge by suggesting detailed interventions in curriculum and teaching method, but instead, emphasised the importance of the teacher's role in shaping a better future.[30] As James Douglas wrote in *Teachers World* in 1933, echoing utopian assertions: 'The teacher can arrest the atrophy of the mind which threatens the future of every boy and girl . . . the only hope for humanity is the creation of minds which are capable of growth as they grow older.' His article was entitled 'Why teachers should be well paid'.[31]

Despite this support from the teaching press, mainstream opinion in training colleges and departments of education tended not to be sympathetic to utopian assertions in the inter-war period, although they were often interested in non-utopian progressivism. Percy Nunn, Principal of the London Day Training College from 1922 and Director of the Institute of Education until 1936, explicitly criticised such educational ideas in his extremely influential text, *Education: its data and first principles* (1920). He clearly differentiated himself from utopian thinkers when he argued that the idea that children are naturally good is misguided, although they may have 'a biological bias towards the good'.[32] He indicated that self-government would be ill-advised when he commented: 'The boy is always near to the barbarian, and his societies, if left to themselves, naturally develop the characters of a primitive tribe where custom rules with rod of iron, and eccentricity is ruthlessly suppressed.'[33] Interestingly, Nunn paid lip-service to utopianism when he wrote near the end of his text that 'We stand at an hour when the civilisation that bred us is sick – some fear even to death . . . the problems we and those who came before us have created are problems we cannot hope ourselves to solve; they must be solved, if at all, by the generations who will take up our work.'[34] His concluding sentence expressed his faith in the potential of children when he wrote that 'they have in them a creative power which may remould our best into a life far worthier than we have seen or that it has entered into our hearts to conceive'.[35]

The waning influence of utopian thought was demonstrated by the way that Nunn edited this sentence for his third edition, published in 1945; he emphasised that 'they have in them a creative power which, *if wisely encouraged and tolerantly guided*, may so remould our best that, as the dark shadows pass, "the life of the world may move forward into broad, sunny uplands" and become worthier than any we have yet seen' [my italics].[36] This edit – in a new edition that was otherwise very little altered – emphasised both the need for adults to guide children and, by cutting the 'has entered into our hearts to conceive', indicated that adults were able to imagine this new world, and its creation need not be left solely to the young. Utopian ideas might have exercised a brief influence even upon more conservative educationalists, but had now been firmly abandoned.

Even more significantly for the development of educational practice in England and Wales, utopian ideas exercised little influence on the Board of Education, which published three landmark reports in the 1920s and 1930s under the chairmanship of Sir W. H. Hadow; *The Education of the Adolescent* (1926) and *The Primary School* (1931) focused on the education of children under seven, whereas *Infant and Nursery Schools* (1933) considered questions relating to younger children. None of the utopian progressives contributed to the Hadow Reports, and none of them are cited in the texts. As R. J. W. Selleck argues, far from confirming the ideas of utopian progressives, Hadow's recommendations limited their influence on mainstream schools.[37] Yet the 1926 and 1931 Hadow Reports, in particular, have been frequently identified as the first coherent progressive programme. If this is the case, it was a progressivism that had already excluded half the movement.

Three tensions within child-centred education

Despite the theoretical dominance of non-utopian progressivism by 1939, child-centred ideas were rarely practised in mainstream schools. This allowed non-utopian progressives to either leave the three central tensions within child-centred practice unresolved, or to resolve them in ways that would become less suitable once child-centred practice became mainstream. Most obviously, when teachers were not yet being asked to put these ideas into practice with large groups of children, the individuality of the child could be foregrounded. There was no need to make assumptions about the interests, needs and abilities of children as a group when a single child was the subject under consideration. Similarly, more freedom could be afforded to these theoretical children than to their real-life counterparts, especially when nobody had to worry about the practical barriers to child-centred classroom teaching. Finally, childhood and adolescence were more usually positioned as a preparation for adult life than as valuable periods in their own right during the inter-war period, due to dominant discourses of active citizenship and vocational training.[38] Nevertheless, this produced no inherent conflict with child-centred ideas, because British inter-war educational psychologists tended to perceive a seamless continuity of growth from child to adult, rather than picturing development as a series of sharply demarcated stages. This would not be the case after 1945.

Both the 1926 and 1931 Hadow Reports emphasised the importance of an individualised education, although this assertion was more explicit in the 1931 Report. The 'Terms of Reference' for the 1926 report stated clearly that one of the three key aims of their consideration of secondary school education was 'the desirability of providing a reasonable variety of curriculum [sic], so far as is practicable, for children of varying tastes and abilities'.[39] The aim of 'forming and strengthening the character, both individual and national' harked back to a late-nineteenth-century discourse about the importance of individual difference which had been established by John Stuart Mill's *On Liberty* (1859).[40] The Report perceived the potential conflict between this vital trait and the needs of society, and argued that this contradiction must be carefully balanced in schools: 'If . . . the education of older pupils be kept too general in the supposed interests of individual development, the pupil is apt to find himself ill-equipped on leaving school to cope with the demands of modern life. If, on the other hand, undue stress be laid in the school course on the needs of later life . . . the individual man or woman may be sacrificed to the workman or citizen.'[41] The 1931 Report, which was less concerned with school leavers due to its focus on primary-aged children, was more explicit about the significance of individuality for the teacher, stating in its conclusion that 'He [the teacher] has to teach children, and to do this successfully he must know something of children in general, and he must know – and this is a perpetual obligation – as much as he can of the particular children he is teaching.'[42] Over-dependence on class teaching was criticised because 'it cannot always be adjusted as closely as teaching should be to the varying needs of children' who need 'to proceed at their own pace'.[43] This acknowledged that, despite the hindrance of having to teach large classes, the teacher's attention must always be directed to the individual child.

The stress placed upon individuality perhaps indicated the influence of Nunn, who was a key witness and sat on the drafting sub-committees for both the 1926 and 1931 reports; he had written in *Education* that 'individuality is the ideal of Life', but spent little time considering how this could actually be achieved in the classroom.[44] The other most popular and widely read advice guide in this period was training college lecturers A. G. Hughes and E. G. Hughes's *Learning and Teaching* (1937), which offered a more straightforward and user-friendly text than Nunn. Like *Education*, this text went through multiple reprints in the inter-war years and into the post-war period, and regularly appeared on training college booklists.[45] It also went through a series of revised editions; in the case of Hughes and Hughes, these alterations indicate how their commitment to individuality was reduced, if not effaced, by the late 1940s. On the first page of *Learning and Teaching*, Hughes and Hughes asserted that the teacher is teaching a class of thirty individuals, not a single unit, and argued that children 'make a definite stand . . . as individual persons' as early as five months old.[46]

Interestingly, this strong emphasis on individuality in the 1937 and 1947 editions was tempered in the third revised edition, published in 1959, where an extra paragraph was inserted between the two opening paragraphs on individuality, stating: 'Moreover, as we shall see, the group in which children live, work and play . . . has an important influence on the development of its individual members. The study of groups and of individuals in groups . . . is necessary for a full understanding of the arts of learning and teaching.'[47] This added emphasis on group needs was evident throughout the minimal revisions to the original text; the closing paragraph to the first chapter had reiterated the point that children are all individuals, but an added sentence in the 1959 edition changed the emphasis of the final lines: 'one of the important lessons that everyone has to learn is the art of living, working and playing with others'.[48] These alterations reflect the shift away from the focus on the individual child in post-war educational psychology, and the increased interest in the 'natural' needs of the group; justified in this context by the assertion that however 'individual' the child, he or she still had to learn to conform to social norms. However, these edits to Hughes and Hughes were only published well after the Second World War.

Theoretical ideas about individuality were translated into practical recommendations on teaching methods by both *Teachers World* and the *Schoolmaster* even before the end of the First World War, anticipating rather than simply reflecting the assertions of the two Hadow Reports and popular teaching guides. In April 1918, *Teachers World* positively reviewed J. H. Simpson's *An Adventure in Education*, which recommended 'self-expression, self-determination and personal responsibility' as the key values of the school, drawing on the models of two experimental US educators, Homer Lane's 'Little Commonwealth' (founded in Dorset in 1912 after Lane's work in the US) and William Reuben George's 'George Junior Republic' (founded in New York in 1895 as a self-governing institution for delinquent boys).[49] By the 1920s, the journal was consistently emphasising the importance of individual work, even if the teacher did not adopt novel methods such as the Dalton Plan and had to consider the practicalities of managing a large class.[50] An article on 'The final year in an elementary school', published in 1921, suggested that pupils should keep diaries of their own individual work and assist each other, using the teacher as a guide. The writer recognised that the class would inevitably get smaller as pupils reached the age of fourteen and left for work, making the teaching situation more manageable.[51]

The Hadow Reports also emphasised the idea of a 'natural' education, although this was subordinate to their consideration of children's individuality. The committees collected evidence from a wide range of organisations and individuals that had a stake in education, from teachers and academics to political and union representatives such as the Women's Cooperative Guild and an Education Commission appointed by the Bradford Independent Labour Party, to build up a picture of children's interests at different stages of development.[52] In the case of the 1931 Report, this revealed both the preoccupation with developing an education that would appeal to children and the assumption that their interests were practical and constructive. Stating that, 'a child never works so well as when he is enthusiastically interested', the Report went on to say that 'the interest in making things' is 'one of the most characteristic features of the whole period'.[53] Linking a practical education to a local one, it stated that 'Towards the age of nine, healthy children take more and more to outdoor life. They are still restless and active, but owing to their increasing strength and independence they demand a wider range of movement. At this age the child seeks to explore his immediate environment further afield, and enjoys expeditions to places of interest.'[54] This linked the assertions of early experimental European educationalists such as Johann Pestalozzi and Friedrich Froëbel about the importance of the child exploring nature with newer biological findings on the physical development of the child.[55]

The idea that a natural education would be an innately enjoyable one also permeated the report. The final assertion on this matter, in the conclusion, was to prove to be the most famous line of the 1931 Report: 'We are of opinion that the curriculum of the primary school is to be thought of in terms of activity and experience, rather than of knowledge to be acquired and facts to be stored.'[56] The findings of the Report were further communicated in the *Handbook of Suggestions for Teachers* (1937) which reflected a similar approach when it stated 'The choices of activities and experience should be such as to lead the child to a realisation of the fundamental interests of life in so far as they lie within the compass of childhood.'[57] Hadow suggested that education would be enjoyable for children so long as it centred around their 'natural interests', a phrase that was to be continually repeated throughout this period.[58] The 1931 Report argued that primary-aged children's interests were essentially practical and constructive, hence the focus on what would come to be known as 'learning through doing', rather than on the presumably passive absorption of facts.

Despite their desire to value the life of the child and the particular talents and interests of childhood, child-centred educationalists often argued that their pedagogical programme also best prepared children for living an adult life in a modern society. The idea that schools now had to fit children for 'citizenship', and that the earlier elementary schools had not recognised this greater purpose for education, was central to inter-war child-centred pedagogy. As the 1931 Report put it, '[t]he schools whose first intention was to teach children how to read have thus been compelled to broaden their aims until it might now be said that they have to teach children how to live.'[59] Laura King has argued that the experience of the First World War, and the subsequent Representation of the People Acts of 1918 and 1928, positioned all children as future voters, and hence as 'future citizens'.[60] This theme reoccurred in teaching journals throughout the 1930s; *Teachers World* noted in 1932 that in a speech to the City of London Vacation Course to teachers, the new president of the Board of Education, Lord Urwin, had said that 'the primary concern of those present was to fit the children of to-day to be the citizens of to-morrow', whereas in 1939, as the raising of the school-leaving age became a concrete prospect, the National Association of Schoolmasters (NAS), an all-male teaching union, stated that it was especially important that in 'this extra year', 'the children should be instructed in their rights and responsibilities as citizens'.[61] Child-centred practice was seen as especially suitable for instruction in citizenship; the *TES* noted in 1939, for example, that teaching local geography would encourage a sense of citizenship.[62]

However, the non-utopian progressive claim that this aim was confined to their novel pedagogical recommendations does not stand up to scrutiny. As Nathan Roberts has argued, concerns about the teaching of 'citizenship' to working-class children were evident from the beginnings of compulsory elementary education in the 1870s, although these concerns were often rephrased in the language of 'character'.[63] In the revised Elementary Code published by the Board of Education in 1904, it was stated that the elementary school should aim to 'form and strengthen the character and to develop the intelligence of the children entrusted to it'.[64] Schools should produce useful members of the community by helping children to 'reach their full development as individuals'.[65] Martin Lawn and Ian Grosvenor emphasise the breadth of appeal of such messages by the 1920s and 1930s; for example, the

Association of Education for Citizenship was set up in 1934, and published *Education for Citizenship in Secondary Schools* in 1935.[66] Therefore, while non-utopian progressive educationalists such as Harold Dent, editor of the *TES* from 1940, claimed that their commitment to 'active learning' was the best way to ensure education for citizenship, they were not the only actors to use such language, nor were these ideas especially novel in inter-war England and Wales.[67] Furthermore, this kind of discourse highlighted all three of the tensions within child-centred education by returning to the idea that education should fit a child to live as a productive member of society, and implicitly, that his or her maturation should hence follow a certain path that should be predefined by parents and teachers. After the Second World War, non-utopian progressives would have to find a different way to address these tensions.

Rejecting a 'traditional' education

By claiming to provide greater 'freedom' for the child, by paying attention to the individuality of each pupil, and by aiming to produce active citizens for a mass democracy, child-centred education relied upon the existence of 'traditional' pedagogy to define and defend its territory. Non-utopian progressive writers in the inter-war period tended to characterise traditional elementary school pedagogy in opposition to their own recommendations for the schooling of working-class children. They stated that 'old-fashioned' schools were centred on a set curriculum, divided into a range of tightly defined subjects; that they provided a set body of facts that must be learnt, regardless of the child's own interests; that they offered little opportunity for the child to be active or practical; and that, in terms of teaching method, they relied heavily on 'drill', the memorisation of long strings of information.[68] In terms of discipline, they operated a rigid set of rules, inhibiting any spontaneous activity.[69] Most importantly, however, 'traditional' educators, it was argued, showed no interest in how children learnt or what they enjoyed learning. They had no conception of the broader purpose of education, and saw schools as a shortcut to instilling appropriate work-discipline for manual labourers.[70] However, while some of these child-centred assertions about 'traditional' practice were reasonably accurate, others were far off the mark. Furthermore, they identified their enemy as a coherent body of 'traditionalists' that, in reality, unlike the conservative 'other school reformers' that Adam Laats has considered in the inter-war United States, did not exist as an organised and purposeful movement in this period.[71]

Both utopian and non-utopian progressives told 'origin stories' about their conversion to the new pedagogy after witnessing the miseries of the old, often before the First World War. These testimonies most frequently came from school inspectors, who, as a professional body, were to become key champions of child-centred education. Edmond Holmes, remembering his time as a school inspector in the 1890s, condemned the infamous 'payment by results' system. Payment by results, or, in official terms, the Revised Code, which was introduced in 1862, linked the teacher's pay directly to the number of students who advanced into the next 'standard' when examined by an inspector. The system, as Holmes pointed out, relied on the passive absorption of facts: 'The natural result of this [perpetual examination] is that the pupils, instead of learning to rely on themselves and to use their own powers and resources, become more and more helpless and resourceless, and gradually cease to take any interest in their work for its own sake.'[72] Philip Ballard, who also worked as an inspector for the London County Council (LCC) before 1914, wrote that 'Under the old regime of school discipline, a regime by no means over, the teacher-made laws are so numerous that the margin of free activity left to the child is inordinately small . . . The word most frequently on the teacher's lips is "Don't". . . He would like to say "Don't breathe" if there was any chance of his being obeyed.'[73] F. H. Spencer, who taught from 1886 and became an HMI in Liverpool from 1912, remembered 'the magnificent mechanical discipline of the times', which he contrasted with 'the normal atmosphere of the boys' elementary schools to-day' which was 'happy and . . . pleasant'.[74] While these late-nineteenth and early-twentieth-century schools were not invented or even necessarily atypical, many of the worst abuses recorded by these writers had been theoretically or actually abandoned by 1918; payment by results, for example, was abolished in 1898. While this did not mean there was a dramatic shift of practice in schools themselves, it throws into question the child-centred assertion that 'traditionalists' were wedded to their ways.

Non-utopian educationalists were also reluctant to present themselves as iconoclastic innovators. Histories of child-centred education usually trace the beginnings of the movement back to John Locke, Jean-Jacques Rousseau, Johann Pestalozzi and Friedrich Froëbel, setting inter-war developments within a long and distinguished intellectual tradition.[75] These thinkers were also frequently cited by child-centred educationalists writing after the Second World War.[76] Nevertheless, it is questionable how far the inter-war progressive movement in England and Wales was deeply influenced by these predecessors. Neill was open about the fact that he had never read Rousseau, and his biographer, Bryn Purdy, thought that he had also never read Froëbel, Pestalozzi or Dewey.[77] Non-utopian progressives might name-check Rousseau or Locke, but their writings indicated little engagement with the actual texts. None of these figures were cited in any meaningful way in either the 1926 or 1931 Hadow Reports. While Froëbelian kindergartens developed significant influence in England and Wales from the early twentieth century onwards – the Hadow Report on *Infant and Nursery Schools* (1933) mentioned Froëbel fifty-four times – there is little evidence that these ideas influenced the education of children over seven.[78]

Nikolas Rose has suggested that Rousseau's famous novel about a boy's upbringing, *Emile* (1763), became a 'myth of origins' for child-centred educationalists.[79] However, a more useful concept might be the term coined by Suzanne Schmidt in her discussion of the 'midlife crisis' in the post-war United States: the 'invented precursor'. Inventing a precursor, Schmidt argues, allows ideas that might otherwise seem too novel to be bolstered by scientific – or in this case, philosophical – authority.[80] Citing figures such as Rousseau allowed non-utopian progressives to present their work as having a long history, even though more recent writers such as Dewey were more obviously influential. Again, we can see how non-utopian progressivism maintained an uneasy relationship with the past, wanting to present itself as essentially modern, yet unwilling to move too far from established orthodoxy.

It can also be questioned how far child-centred programmes lived up to their own expectations. The idea of a curriculum centred on 'activity and experience' rather than 'facts to be stored' appeared in the section of the 1931 Hadow Report that dealt with 'The curriculum of the primary school', in which it characterised the 'older' approach as narrowly focused on the acquisition of skills such as reading, writing and ciphering.[81] Child-centred educationalists frequently said that education should not be centred around a body of facts that were organised into a set of school subjects. As Hadow noted, 'the general tendency has been to take for granted the existence of certain traditional "subjects" and to present them to the pupils as lessons to be mastered... [we must] depart from the traditional way of teaching by subjects.'[82]

But child-centred theorists, unlike some of the utopian progressives, rarely suggested dispensing with a curriculum. Indeed, much early child-centred writing developed elaborate new curriculums, such as John Dewey's *The School and Society* (1899). These new plans of study challenged traditional subject-divisions, but did not dispense with content.[83] Journals such as *Teachers World* picked up on these sets of examples to produce their own suggested programmes of study, for example the four-year syllabuses for 'Real life arithmetic', 'A practical course for backward boys' and 'The home as a project' published in 1931.[84] Throughout 1932 the journal ran an inquiry into 'irreducible minima' for all school subjects that emphasised 'the child's point of view' but, in practice, largely consisted of boiling down which facts children should learn, rather than abandoning a list of facts altogether. As one writer commented, the new approach was not characterised by a removal of facts but by a reconceptualisation of the purpose that facts served: 'Are we to teach [the curriculum] for the sake of its content so that children will know "geography" or are we to take the data of geography and use it as a necessary element in the training of the future citizen?'[85] The 1931 Hadow Report itself retained the traditional organisation of school subjects in its discussion of the curriculum, as most 'reformed' schools would after the war.[86] As this demonstrates, splitting 'traditional' and 'progressive' writers into clearly defined and separate camps was often impossible in practice.

Finally, both 'traditional' and 'progressive' teachers and writers suggested in inter-war England and Wales that it was their curriculum alone that satisfied children's natural interests and abilities, indicating how small the gap was between their basic commitments, despite their differences over teaching method. Teachers who emphasised the importance of routine, drill and discipline might note that these practices were in line with knowledge about child development, especially at the primary school stage. Frank Watts, an educational and vocational psychologist who was to contribute to *Teachers World* for several decades, asked readers 'Are you a successful teacher?' in 1921. Despite his psychological expertise on the workings of children's minds, Watts recommended that systematic drill was crucial for habit formation.[87] As a writer for the *TES* commented in 1936, 'Regular drill in penmanship, spelling, arithmetic and diction, with memory exercises in geography and history, is in no way out of keeping with the natural process of learning in children between seven and 12 years of age.'[88] In Nunn's edited collection on the *Education of Backward Children* (1937), F. J. Schonell, an Australian educationalist who worked in Britain and wrote for both *Teachers World* and the *Schoolmaster* in the 1930s on 'backwardness', argued that while self-expression and activity can be helpful in the primary school, 'junior school children like repetition and are even ready to endure drudgery to acquire skills'.[89]

As this suggested, the children's own enjoyment of rote work was a rhetorical strategy that was often deployed, directly linking 'traditional' teaching to a curriculum that pleased its pupils. Furthermore, it was argued, drawing on older psychological knowledge, that it was ideally suited to their stage of development because they possessed a naturally 'retentive' memory.[90] Both *Teachers World* and the *Schoolmaster* published articles that echoed these views throughout the inter-war period, justifying the use of traditional methods by assertions about children's nature. In 1932, *Teachers World* argued that 'even the very young like doing sums', and, in a direct riposte to the more concrete mathematics favoured by child-centred educationalists, the writer stated 'but . . . they "hate doing sums about John"'.[91] Similarly, in the *Schoolmaster* in 1935, Thomas Holland challenged the integrated curriculum of child-centred educationalists by arguing that it was wrong to suggest that 'children hate school subjects'. 'Some do, but many do not.'[92]

Despite such assertions, educationalists did not tend to interview children directly about what interested them, relying instead on observation and inference. When they did conduct such research, it was often distorted by the conclusions they wanted to reach. E. B. Warr's *The New Era in the Junior School* (1937), reviewed positively in the *Schoolmaster*, asked seven to twelve-year-olds what they liked doing in school, distributing a questionnaire to eleven schools and receiving 1,042 replies.[93] While the results were equivocal, Warr's analysis was not. She stated confidently that practical subjects were more popular among the respondents than literary ones, which fits comfortably into the stereotype of the primary child.[94] However, the subjects that respondents chose also suited a 'traditional' interpretation of children's preferences, with 30 per cent of the respondents picking 'drill and games' as their favourite subject, and 13 per cent arithmetic.[95]

Similarly, primary-aged children's essays on 'My ideal school', cited by Agatha Bowley in her *Everyday Problems of the School Child* (1948), did not suggest that they disliked either traditional subjects or subject-divisions; one eight-year-old wrote 'I would send my boy to a school that had fighting and Arithmetic and Spelling and English', while another commented that 'I would have Reading, Writing and Arithmetic. History and Geography'.[96] The idea of primary school children as, in Bowley's words, essentially 'active', focused on 'making and doing', was confounded by the ten-year-old respondent who wanted 'a library where you can sit down and read a book'.[97] Methodologically speaking, this data still did not reveal what children 'really' wanted or liked; children's answers were bound to be constrained by what they believed the questioner wanted to hear, by their own experiences of school to date, and by what they had been told by adults was important in school. However, these considerations hold equally true for any assertions that suggested children 'really' wanted practical child-centred activities.

Jonathan Rose has used oral testimony from working-class men and women who were children during the inter-war period to explore this contemporary thesis that children enjoyed rote learning. Jane Mitchell, born in 1934, recalled that 'I enjoyed the mental drill and exercise I was put through, even the memorising from our geography book of the principal rivers and promontories of the British Isles, going round the coasts clockwise . . . Arithmetic I enjoyed as an agreeable game.' A son of a Cornish fisherman, born a generation earlier, in 1911, said that 'To some modern theorists the chanting of [mathematical] tables is shocking, but we enjoyed it – and learned the tables.'[98] As the reference to 'modern theorists' suggests, such testimonies should be treated with caution, as they were composed in response to the perceived changes in education since the interviewees' childhood.[99] However, the existence of such contemporary and remembered preferences indicates that the assertion that children enjoyed such memorisation is by no means implausible. In any case, as we have seen, 'traditional' educationalists frequently put forward this line of argument, indicating that they wanted to find out what interested children, even if their assumptions were incorrect. Therefore, it became increasingly difficult to separate 'traditional' and 'child-centred' pedagogical commitments, even if the solutions they offered were different.

Child-centred educationalists further suggested that, having sought the views of 'ordinary classroom teachers', they were now better informed about the nature of the child. However, as the witness statements submitted to the 1931 Hadow consultation indicated, teachers often cited their experiential knowledge of children to oppose, rather than to support, child-centred assertions. Some teachers did concur with the image of the essentially practical, active and exploratory image of this age group; the evidence provided by the National Union of Women Teachers (NUWT), for example, emphasised the 'curiosity, constructiveness, acquisition and self-assertion' of junior school children.[100] L. S. R. Jones, the headmaster of Brize Norton, an exceptionally progressive school in Oxfordshire, similarly suggested that practical work was essential for seven to eleven-year-olds, arguing that handicraft and speech 'were the two great media of expression of the child-mind'.[101] Nevertheless, it is unlikely that Jones's views were representative of the majority of schools in 1929, when this evidence was gathered. A number of respondents continued to emphasise an older image of elementary education that focused on routine, drill, handwork and the inculcation of the three Rs. For example, the National Federation of Class Teachers, a union for certificated teachers formed in 1890, outlined a clear curriculum and argued that children needed to master four fundamental rules in maths, that 'definite drill in spelling was necessary during the Junior stage', and that accurate writing must be achieved before thinking about composition.[102] Similarly, the headteacher of a Roman Catholic school in Durham argued that 'So much stress is now laid upon the "self-activity" of children that school methods are now dominated by the presumed necessity for providing scope for its exercise. Routine methods are looked at askance.'[103]

In the published version of the Report, the Committee did not cite such evidence but, instead, suggested that its vision for education was supported by 'the evidence of practical teachers'. It argued that observation of primary children in the classroom supported the psychological claim that 'junior children are little workmen'. [104] This section of the report implied that teachers' craft knowledge confirmed the scientific findings of progressivism. However, alongside the dissenting views outlined above, the idea of a 'little workman' did not come from 'the evidence of practical [junior] teachers' at all but from Mr W. E. Urwick, an inspector of secondary schools, who stated 'children were little workmen on the lookout for jobs to do'.[105] Again, it was school inspectors, rather than teachers, who were making the most explicitly child-centred assertions. Appealing to teachers as natural experts was not likely to get child-centred pedagogy very far. Furthermore, it is clear that some of the key commitments of child-centred educationalists – to provide a curriculum that interested children, to position school as a preparation for life in a modern society, and to consider how teaching methods reflected known facts about child psychology – were shared by their 'traditionalist' enemies.

Child-centred education between the wars was, on the whole, as 'traditional' as it was 'progressive'. Indeed, it could be argued that child-centred educationalists created an invented opponent in the form of 'traditional' education in England and Wales, suggesting that it was much more coherent, intransigent and persistent than it actually was in order to present themselves as moving towards a better future. The novelty of child-centred pedagogy did not lie in suggesting that education should suit the nature of the child, but on a set of particular claims about what children were really like. While theorists often argued that children could gain the freedom of an individualised education while still being educated in citizenship along the lines of their natural psychological development, these 'middle way' arguments were not tested in practice in the inter-war period. Indeed, such assertions would become increasingly difficult to sustain as child-centred theory started to filter into the overcrowded and under-resourced classrooms of the post-war state.

Notes

1 Lane, *Talks to Parents and Teachers*, pp. 110–11.
2 Adams, *Modern Developments in Educational Practice*, p. 253.
3 Pekin, *Progressive Schools*, p. 47.
4 Berlin, 'Two concepts of liberty'.
5 Howlett, *Progressive Education*, p. 143; Brehony, 'A new education for a new era', p. 733.

A progressive education?

6 Wooldridge, *Measuring the Mind*, p. 24. Histories of education are usually not focused upon progressive practice. Lowe, *Education in the Post-War Years*, and Jones, *Education in Britain* discuss progressivism, but do not clearly define it.
7 Howlett, *Progressive Education*, p. 272.
8 Stewart, *Progressives and Radicals*, p. 220.
9 Thomson, *Psychological Subjects*, p. 122.
10 Ballard, *The Changing School*, p. 71.
11 Cunningham, *Curriculum Change in the Primary School*, p. viii, gestures towards this inherent tension. Valerie Walkerdine has mounted a radical critique of progressive education along similar lines. See Walkerdine, 'Child-centred pedagogy', p. 155, and Walkerdine, 'It's only natural', p. 86.
12 Roberts, 'Character in the mind'. On concerns about German child-rearing and education in the 1930s and 1940s, see Beekman, *The Mechanical Baby*, p. 173 and Selleck, *English Primary Education and the Progressives*, pp. 87–8.
13 *The Extra Year*, pp. 7–10.
14 M. Reeves, 'Education after the war,' *New Era*, June 1940, pp. 137–9.
15 Cited in Findlay, *The Children of England*, p. 186.
16 Adams, *Modern Developments in Educational Practice*, p. 14.
17 For example, Letters page, *Teachers World*, 25 April 1934, p. 159; A. Gruber, 'The New Art', *Teachers World*, 1 May 1935, p. 177; Report from the NUT's Margate conference, *Teachers World*, 20 April 1938, p. 2.
18 'Another "school without a time-table"', *Teachers World*, 19 January 1921, p. 703.
19 Holmes, *The Idiot Teacher*, p. 124.
20 *Teachers World*, 4 January 1922, p. 608; 11 January 1922, p. 667.
21 *Teachers World*, 31 January 1923, 'Freedom in education: its development in Germany', p. 872; 7 January 1925, 'An American teacher's view', p. 695; Mrs H. A. L. Fisher [Lettice Ilbert], 'Education in Canada', 14 January 1925, p. 769. While cited by *Teachers World* solely as the wife of H. A.L. Fisher, President of the Board of Education until 1922 and remembered for the 1918 Education Act, Ilbert was an economist and historian in her own right, and founded the National Council for the Unmarried Mother and her Child in 1918.
22 For example, *Schoolmaster*, 4 June 1931, p. 1054; A. E. Henshall, 'The claims of education upon the nation', *Schoolmaster*, 1 April 1932, p. 597; A. Bechervaise, 'Self-management and free discipline', *Schoolmaster*, 2 February 1933, p. 166.
23 Ravitch, *Left Back*, p. 395.
24 '500 speeches on education', *Teachers World*, 13 January 1932, p. 510.
25 Cited in Selleck, *English Primary Education and the Progressives*, p. 118.
26 E. Campagnac, 'The teaching of literature', *Teachers World*, 29 June 1932, p. 490.
27 *Teachers World*, 21 December 1932, p. 423.
28 F. Evans, 'Are our schools better than they were?' *Schoolmaster*, 6 July 1933, p. 28.

29 For example, in the *Schoolmaster*, 4 February 1937, p. 232, three letters complained about 'stunts and fads' in teaching, but a further two letters protested that 'the attitude of mind revealed in these letters is one which is alien to the majority of the profession'. In *Teachers World*, a letter on 'Individual Work' on 17 February 1932, p. 706, complained about 'queer ideas of discipline' but conceded 'on the ideal [individualisation] we all agree'.
30 This was reflected in contributions to these journals. For example, 'The teacher as citizen' *Teachers World*, 31 July 1935, p. 659; 'A message from the Lord Mayor of London', *Teachers World*, 4 December 1935, p. 433; 'The changing responsibility of the teacher', *Teachers World*, 10 August 1938, p. 29; George H. Green, 'Just out of college', *Schoolmaster*, 11 July 11 1935, p. 50; *TES*, 6 March 1937, p. 77.
31 J. Douglas, 'Why teachers should be well paid', *Teachers World*, 22 February 1933, p. 733.
32 Nunn, *Education*, 1st edn, p. 99.
33 *Ibid.*, p. 195.
34 *Ibid.*, p. 219.
35 *Ibid.*, p. 220.
36 Nunn, *Education*, 3rd edn, p. 276.
37 Selleck, *English Primary Education and the Progressives*, p. 32.
38 Barron, 'Little prisoners of city streets', p. 173.
39 Board of Education, *Education of the Adolescent*, p. iv.
40 Board of Education, *Education of the Adolescent*, p. xxiii; Roberts, 'Character in the mind'; Mill, *On Liberty*, pp. 56–74.
41 Board of Education, *Education of the Adolescent*, p. 101.
42 Board of Education, *The Primary School*, p. 150.
43 Board of Education, *The Primary School*, p. 152.
44 Wooldridge, *Measuring the Mind*, p. 2, discusses Nunn's introduction of psychology to teacher training.
45 London County Council Archives, Camden Emergency Training College: General Files, LCC/EO/TRA/2/7, Sample letter to student, 5 February 1948; London County Council Archives, Wandsworth Training College: General Files, LCC/EO/TRA/2/28, Booklist, 1946. Also see Frisby, 'The History of Educational Psychology', p. 116. Hughes and Hughes, *Learning and Teaching*, 1st edn; Hughes and Hughes, *Learning and Teaching*, 2nd edn.
46 Hughes and Hughes, *Learning and Teaching*, 2nd edn, p. 2.
47 Hughes and Hughes, *Learning and Teaching*, 3rd edn, p. 2.
48 Hughes and Hughes, *Learning and Teaching*, 3rd edn, p. 7.
49 *Teachers World*, 'Self-government in school', 10 April 1918, p. 27.
50 For example: 'J. St. C.H'., 'Liberty or license', *Teachers World*, 14 January 1920, p. 563; 'The fetish of method', *Teachers World*, 4 January 1922, p. 623; John Adams, 'The knell of class teaching', *Teachers World*, 11 January 1922, p. 665.

51 'The final year at an elementary school: individual work, private study and sectional teaching', *Teachers World*, 5 January 1921, p. 606.
52 National Archives, ED 10/148.
53 Board of Education, *The Primary School*, p. 49.
54 Board of Education, *The Primary School*, p. 50.
55 Pestalozzi, *How Gertrude Teaches Her Children*, pp. 25, 28; Fletcher and Welton, *Froëbel's Chief Writings*, p. 50.
56 Board of Education, *The Primary School*, p. 139.
57 Scotland and Wood, *The Book of Interests*, p. 4.
58 Board of Education, *The Primary School*, p. 156.
59 Board of Education, *The Primary School*, p. 93.
60 King, 'Future citizens'.
61 *Teachers World*, 10 August 1932, p. 676; *Teachers World*, 18 January 1939, p. 19.
62 *Times Educational Supplement*, 4 March 1939, p. 80.
63 Roberts, 'Character in the mind'.
64 Cited in Roberts, 'Character in the mind', p. 180.
65 Cited in Cunningham, 'Primary education', p. 14.
66 Grosvenor and Lawn, 'Days out of school', p. 379.
67 Grosvenor and Lawn, 'Days out of school', p. 380.
68 For example, see H. R. Hamley, 'Introductory survey', in Nunn (ed.), *The Education of Backward Children*, p. 10; Shelton, *Thoughts of a Schoolmaster*, p. 142; Hughes and Hughes, *Learning and Teaching*, 1st edn, pp. 261–6; *The Extra Year*, p. 53; Spencer, *Inspector*, p. 146. The idea of learning to 'reason' or to 'love knowledge' rather than learn facts was hardly novel in inter-war Britain; it had been expressed by Locke, *Some Thoughts Concerning Education*, p.28 in 1689 and by Owen, 'A new view of society', p. 134.
69 For example, see Daniel, *Activity in the Primary School*, p. 96; Hamilton, *The Teacher on the Threshold*, pp. 170–2.
70 Ballard, *The Changing School*; Warr, *New Era in the Junior School*; Isaacs, *The Children We Teach*.
71 Laats, *The Other School Reformers*.
72 Holmes, 'The confessions and hopes of an ex-inspector of schools', p. 278.
73 Ballard, *The Changing School*, p. 67.
74 Spencer, *Inspector*, pp. 146, 195.
75 Giardiello, *Pioneers in Early Childhood Education*, pp. 27, 40, 43; Thomas, *Education*, p. 21; Blundell, *Education and Constructions*, pp. 36–49, 126.
76 Atkinson, *Junior School Community*, p. 34; Rogers (ed.), *Teaching in the British Primary School*, p. 36.
77 Howlett, *Progressive Education*, p. 276; Purdy, *A. S. Neill*, p. 10.
78 Nawrotski, 'Froëbel is dead'.
79 Rose, *Governing the Soul*, p. 179.
80 Schmidt, 'Feminist origins of the midlife crisis', p. 511.
81 Board of Education, *The Primary School*, pp. 91–3.

82 Board of Education, *The Primary School*, pp. xxii, 104.
83 Dewey, *School and Society*, pp. 32–8.
84 'Real life arithmetic', *Teachers World*, 7 January 1931, p. 558; Fred Hughes, 'A practical course for backward boys', *Teachers World*, 21 January 1931, p. 636; Ada L. Nixon, 'The home as a project', *Teachers World*, 4 February 1931, p. 716.
85 Dr A. D'arcy Chapman, 'Another view on the "irreducible minimum" in geography', *Teachers World*, 13 April 1932, p. 68.
86 Swinnerton, 'The 1931 Report of the Consultative Committee on the Primary School', p. 84.
87 F. Watts, 'Are you a successful teacher?', *Teachers World*, 12 January 1921, p. 636.
88 *Times Educational Supplement*, 5 December 1936, p. 437.
89 Schonell, 'Causes of backwardness', in Nunn (ed.) *The Education of Backward Children*, p. 42.
90 For example, in Bloor, *The Process of Learning*, p. 119.
91 *Teachers World*, 3 February 1932, p. 649.
92 *Schoolmaster*, 7 March 1935, p. 380.
93 Warr, *New Era in the Junior School*, pp. 58, 67; *Schoolmaster*, 5 August 1937, p. 224.
94 Warr, *New Era in the Junior School*, p. 59.
95 *Ibid.*, p. 58.
96 Bowley, *Everyday Problems of the School Child*, p. 130.
97 Bowley, *Everyday Problems of the School Child*, pp. 67, 130.
98 Rose, *The Intellectual Life*, pp. 165–6.
99 Jacob Middleton makes this point in relation to Rose's interviewees' views on corporal punishment in 'Corporal punishment', pp. 256–8.
100 Miss A. A. Kenyon, President of the NUWT, E. E. Crosby, Chairman of the NUWT Education Committee, C. Neal, Former President of the NUWT, and E. E. Froud, Secretary of the NUWT, 'Summary of evidence given on behalf of the NUWT, 25/1/29', National Archives, ED 10/148, p. 3.
101 Mr L. S. R Jones, headteacher of Brize Norton Council School, Oxfordshire, 23 May 1929, National Archives, ED 10/148.
102 Mr R. Morley, President of the National Federation of Class Teachers, and Mr L. A. Grudgings, Vice-President, 'Summary of evidence given on behalf of the National Federation of Class Teachers, 25th/1/1929 [sic],' National Archives, ED 10/148, p. 3.
103 T. Caden, Head Teacher of the Towneley Memorial Intermediate Roman Catholic School, Stanley, Co. Durham, memorandum, National Archives, ED 10/148, p. 1.
104 Board of Education, *The Primary School*, pp. 50–1.
105 Mr W. E. Urwick, Inspector of Secondary Schools, 23 May 1929, National Archives, ED 10/148.

2

Stages of development, educational psychology and child-centred education

Non-utopian progressive educationalists in inter-war and post-war England and Wales argued that education needed to be designed to suit the nature of the child. In order to maintain this assertion, they sought scientific validation for their claims about children's nature. By making the relatively novel findings of developmental psychologists central to their project, they could claim to have discovered the necessary data to justify child-centred methods. The elaboration of earlier schemes of 'normal' development had built on discredited recapitulation theory, which postulated that the development of the child recapitulated the development of the race. In other words, as humans had evolved from fish to mammals to monkeys, or from 'savage races' to civilised Europeans, so the child had moved from an atavistic embryo to a fully fledged adult.[1] Most importantly, however, the idea of chronological and discontinuous 'stages of development' allowed educationalists to make generalised assertions about the 'natural' interests and abilities of a large group of children – provided they were all the same age. This allowed post-war educationalists to start to address one of the central tensions within their philosophy: how a teacher could design his or her teaching to suit the nature of a large number of children at the same time.

The practical utility of developmental psychology helps to explain why it became so significant for the child-centred programme – rather than, for example, paediatric biology or psychoanalysis – but this was not the only reason for its centrality. Most obviously, Harry Hendrick has contended that inter-war and post-war Britain witnessed a shift of focus 'from bodies to minds'. Although medical inspections and free school meals spread rapidly in this period, child-centred educationalists, especially after the Second World War, were more interested in self-expression and exploration than the conscious cultivation of physically healthy citizens. Even the school meal became a symbol of social development and community cohesion rather than a central plank of good nutrition. As James Vernon argues in his history of hunger and the hungry in Britain and its colonies, while nutritional considerations had initially driven the school meals programme and its institutional expression in the 1944 Education Act, which made it compulsory for all schools to provide meals for children deemed to need them, the environment in which the meals were eaten also became a central concern as it 'was considered critical to the aim of turning out civil and sociable citizens'. In collaboration with the Ministry of Works, the Board of Education designed and built a new range of canteen equipment and designs for prefab canteens, and also produced catalogues of appropriate dining tables, cutlery and crockery.[2]

There was also a relative lack of knowledge about the particular needs of children's bodies. As late as the 1940s there was still little reliable data on the physical development of the child. As David Armstrong has shown, it was wartime surveys that helped to fill this gap, such as the 1943 nutritional survey of schoolchildren in Oxfordshire, London and Birmingham. The 1949 growth survey finally initiated a longitudinal assessment of children's growth, from which growth curves and percentile charts could be derived.[3] Paediatrics, the specialist medical discipline that dealt with childhood illnesses, did not really establish itself until the Second World War. Although the first separate text on childhood, *The Diseases of Children*, was published in 1885 and the British Paediatric Association was founded in 1928, it was not until the 1940s that paediatrics fully emerged, or asserted that the child could not be treated by simply extrapolating back from the adult.[4] Child psychology and psychoanalysis had made these two moves much earlier. Therefore, even once 'biomedical models' of childhood mental illness were available, they were much less influential in Britain than in the US, especially with the increasing dominance of sociological analyses of childhood deprivation from the 1960s onwards, which did not necessarily challenge psychological explanations but often worked in tandem with them.[5]

While psychoanalysis was to prove hugely significant for the care of infants and younger children in post-war Britain, it became much less important in the education of children over seven.[6] While it had been central to the pedagogical thought of utopian progressives such as A. S. Neill, this strand of thinking had already become marginalised by 1939. John Stewart's history of the child guidance movement traces this shift from the individualistic mental hygiene movement of the inter-war period to the 'social problem' approach that developed post-war. He suggests that child guidance clinics, which focused on providing individual psychoanalysis for children, were more significant in the inter-war period than other historians have allowed, with more than sixty clinics active by 1939, and that, as Nikolas Rose has argued, they formed the hub of a movement for mental hygiene.[7] However, Stewart argues, the movement 'seemed outmoded' by the late 1950s as child maladjustment was repositioned as essentially social and embedded within the family, and concern for the 'whole child' took over from the child guidance model with its defined roles for the educational psychologist and the psychiatrist.[8] The provision of psychoanalytic guidance for certain 'maladjusted' children was replaced by regular school visits of the educational psychologist, who focused on maturational progression throughout developmental stages and whose primary tool was intelligence testing.

The early findings of developmental psychology were, to some extent, resisted in inter-war England and Wales due to the opposition of the two leading educational psychologists of the time: Susan Isaacs, herself influenced by Kleinian psychoanalysis, and Cyril Burt. However, as developmental psychologists such as Jean Piaget refined and developed their own practice, their ideas found a much warmer welcome after the Second World War, where they were taken up as the intellectual orthodoxy of teacher training colleges, advice manuals, and the child-centred national inspectorate and Department of Education. Psychoanalysis did not suit the purposes of the emerging child-centred programme, which was now firmly focused – despite theoretical claims to the contrary – on the needs of the group rather than the individual, on limited, prescribed freedom in the classroom, and on the preparation of children to fulfil their purpose in an idealised post-war state. Instead, teachers were encouraged to work with Piaget's 'stages of development' through their education at teacher training colleges, which were becoming normalised as the major route into a teaching career, through teaching advice guides and teaching journals, and through the reorganisation of schools themselves, most notably through the establishment of separate secondary education for all children in the 1944 Education Act, which was justified with reference to the specific needs of the adolescent stage of development. Teaching guides and journals did not make much explicit mention of Piaget before the 1960s. Nevertheless, they normalised psychological language by referring to developmental stages, which were increasingly envisaged as age-linked and discontinuous after the Second World War.

The promotion of developmental psychological ideas about children altered teachers' concepts of childhood, even as teachers themselves engaged reluctantly with the formal study of developmental psychology. This new model of children's physical, intellectual, emotional and social growth encouraged teachers to see childhood and adolescence as entirely separate from adulthood, rather than part of a smooth and continuous maturation, which fit with the post-war child-centred tendency to frame school as a separate and protected stage of life rather than as a preparation for adulthood. It also tended to portray children and adolescents as capable of much less than had previously been believed by emphasising their lack of abstract reasoning and their emotional immaturity, two categories that could be traced directly back to early Piagetian texts. Teachers tended to generalise about the capabilities of an age group rather than treating children as individuals, despite the fact that individuality was supposed to be central to a child-centred education. This was promoted at an institutional level, as teachers were encouraged to train for the specific needs of certain age groups and, despite experiments with 'vertical' or 'family' grouping, where children of different ages worked together in a group throughout the school year, children were increasingly grouped by chronological age, a practice that was not universal before the Second World War.

The theory of developmental stages: reception and revision

The idea of dividing the child's growth into a series of maturational stages was a key theme of most of Jean Piaget's early work in the 1920s, which included *The Language and Thought of the Child* (1923, trans. 1926) and *The Child's Conception of the World* (1926, trans. 1929).

Piaget, a Swiss developmental psychologist who had begun his scientific career as a zoologist, did not pioneer this type of schema, but his meticulous experiments and his initial focus on the development of logical thinking allowed each stage to be defined by much clearer criteria than previous psychologists such as G. Stanley Hall had utilised.[9] As his work developed across several decades, he identified sequential stages in various aspects of child development, ranging from logical to mathematical, linguistic to social. Piaget's work also influenced Arnold Gesell's studies of the 'normal child' in the 1920s and 1930s in the USA. Although Gesell rarely referenced Piaget directly, his loosely conceived trilogy, *Infant and Child in the Culture of Today* (1943), *The Child from Five to Ten* (1946) and *Youth: The Years From Ten to Sixteen* (1956), which reported findings from his observations in the Yale Clinic, utilised the same assumptions and adopted Piagetian terminology when assigning names to the various stages.[10]

The significant claims relevant to concepts of childhood made by Piaget's early work were twofold. First, it suggested that children's individual development was, to some extent, subsumed by their maturational development through a pre-set sequence of stages, although children might accelerate through these steps or lag behind. These stages were portrayed as essentially discontinuous; a child's capabilities at one level were distinctly different in type from his or her capabilities at the next level. Second, it emphasised the gulf between the intellectual and social abilities of adults and children, suggesting there was something fundamentally different about how children approached the world that could not be simply put down to their limited experience of it.

In inter-war England and Wales, while stages of development, alongside older recapitulationist thought, were beginning to enter educational discourse, especially from the late 1920s onwards, their impact was minimised and modified by reference to the uniform growth of intelligence, the individuality of the child and the very few essential differences between children and adults. This was in large part due to the critical influence of Susan Isaacs and Cyril Burt. Isaacs had originally trained as an infant school teacher, studied general psychology at Cambridge for a year, and become a qualified psychoanalyst, where she came into contact with the thought of Melanie Klein. She ran her own small school at Malting House between 1924 and 1927, where she made the set of observations of children that formed the basis for two significant books, *Intellectual Growth in Young Children* (1930) and *Social Development in Young Children* (1933). Two more popular texts were aimed at parents and teachers respectively: *The Nursery Years* (1929) and *The Children We Teach* (1932). Isaacs established and ran the Department of Child Development at the Institute of Education from 1933 to 1943, and also ran the Cambridge Evacuation Survey during the Second World War. Burt, meanwhile, became best known for his work on mental testing and juvenile delinquency, publishing *The Young Delinquent* in 1938 and popularising Charles Spearman's ideas about 'g', or general intelligence, in Britain. He was appointed as the first educational psychologist at the LCC in 1913, where he promoted statistics, assessment and a focus on individual difference throughout the inter-war years.

Both of Piaget's central claims about childhood were criticised by Burt and Isaacs. Isaacs' methodology, and the way in which she wrote up her findings, foregrounded individual differences between children. Both *Intellectual Growth of Young Children* and *Social Development in Young Children* included lengthy lists of the actions and interactions of individual children, emphasising the messiness of the raw data from which Isaacs drew her conclusions. Typical records for a single child – for example, 'Harold' – might range from examples of 'feelings of inferiority or superiority or general anxiety', such as 'When Mrs I. [Isaacs] and the children sang "Dickory Dickory Dock", Harold called that a "silly tune" and said there were "too many Dickories" in it', to 'friendliness and co-operation', for example, 'Dan cried at lunchtime because he had not been given a brown plate, and when Harold, who had a brown plate, had finished his pudding, he took his spoon off and passed it to Dan – "You can have my brown plate."'.[11] In Isaacs' more popular texts, such as *The Children We Teach* (1932), she emphasised the value of individualised treatment in school. The basis for her assertion of the value of psychological expertise to the teacher was not that the psychologist had had different training or more experience with the maladjusted, but that the psychologist had had the opportunity to get to know individual children better than the teacher.[12]

Burt's approach, perhaps even more so than Isaacs', was centred on the psychology of individual difference.[13] He was concerned with both the differences between children and the psychological difference between the child and the adult. Like Isaacs, his approach in *The Young Delinquent* lay in his synthesis of a large number of individual case studies, which he analysed in great detail, using them as the basis for his wider conclusions about the causes of delinquency. However, he carefully presented this mass of information to the reader, indicating that his conclusions were measured and limited. While suggesting that 'character is less complex' and 'motives simpler' in these young offenders than in adults, he did not attempt to smooth them into a homogeneous mass.[14] Burt's appendix in the 1931 Hadow Report on *The Primary School* concerning the mental development of the seven to eleven-year-old also indicated his interest in individuality, although he was tasked by the Consultative Committee with giving a general picture of the development of this age group. He emphasised how the variability in intellectual growth resulted in a huge range across a class of, for example, ten-year-olds, and how intellectual development was the central factor in the full range of the child's abilities, as 'one such fundamental function underlies all concrete intellectual activities'.[15] Despite his focus on the common interests and characteristics shared by this age group, he assumed that children would be increasingly different from each other as they aged, an assumption that the Report itself adopted.

Burt also challenged the idea that children's development was essentially staged and discontinuous. This arose from his foregrounding of the concept of 'general intelligence', or 'g', which he adapted from the English psychologist Charles Spearman, and its uniform continuous development. Later in his career, Burt was to oppose the 1943 Norwood Report for being 'in conflict with the known facts of child psychology', as he wrote in the *British Journal of Educational Psychology* in the same year.[16] Despite his support for intelligence testing, he disliked the 'tripartite' system for introducing a sharp break in teaching after the age of eleven, and attempting to train certain faculties. Given his focus on the uniform development of 'g', a single factor which 'appears to enter into everything which the child attempts to think, or say, or do', he could not endorse such an educational arrangement, arguing that the idea that the child undergoes waves of growth separated by pauses had already been discredited.[17] In the third edition of his influential *The Young Delinquent* (1938) he pursued a similar line of thought: 'To name a particular birthday as fixing the instant when every person ceases to be young and becomes an adult, is to the psychologist as arbitrary as it is unjust.'[18]

Finally, both Isaacs and Burt resisted the idea that either the mental or social capabilities of children were essentially different from those of adults. Burt's opposition to the idea of developmental stages predated Piaget. In a 1919 article in the *Journal of Experimental Pedagogy*, he argued that all the mental mechanisms necessary for reasoning were present by the age of seven, and this increase in reasoning power did not proceed in a series of clear stages; the only reasons it did increase after seven were because the capacity of the child's memory and attention span grew and the child experienced a greater variety of subject-matter.[19] He was to maintain this assertion throughout the 1920s and 1930s, and it dominated the Board of Education's Hadow Reports. For example, the chapter on 'development' in the 1931 report essentially summarised Burt, and it explicitly dismissed both 'stratification theory' – another term for developmental stages – and recapitulation.[20] Burt's appendix to the 1931 report also reasserted his belief that children were capable of logical argument from the age of seven, footnoting *Intellectual Growth* with the comment that it was 'full of suggestive observations and inferences, made by a most cautious and well-informed observer'.[21] In return, it was clear that Isaacs' idea of fixed intelligence was indebted to Burt.[22]

Isaacs engaged with Piaget's assertions more directly. In all her work, she claimed that the process of thinking in children was not substantially different from that of adults, although their minds were not as developed, and that mental growth was gradual. She argued in her *Intellectual Growth in Young Children* (1930) that 'the difference between . . . the child and the adult, is thus *not* that the former do not reason', and challenged Piaget for using the idea of maturation uncritically, stating that

> If we stress maturation in mental growth too strongly, and treat it too readily as a literal organic fact (of the same order as the facts of embryology), we are likely both to over-emphasise the difference between children and ourselves, and to under-estimate the part played by experience in their development. The behaviour of my group of little children would seem to suggest both that *the general modes of their thought* are not fundamentally different from our own . . . and that the experiences which a particular environment offers them do enter powerfully into their concrete ways of repose.[23]

She linked increased adolescent ability in solving abstract problems not to biological development but to adolescents' greater interest in such questions, which encouraged them to work harder in solving them.[24] Isaacs made similar claims about the social development of children, challenging Piaget's *The Moral Judgment of the Child* (1932). In *Social Development in Young Children*, she argued that sociability has its beginnings in very early childhood, and 'no-one needs to have it proved that little children can be friendly and mutually helpful', contradicting Piaget's assertion that sociability begins at seven or eight years.[25]

In the 1950s, Piaget became, if anything, even more tightly wedded to the concept of maturational stages, which perhaps stemmed from his focus on cognition, and unlike the inter-war period, no significant intellectual challenges were levelled at his studies. Indeed, Nathan Isaacs, Susan Isaacs' widower (she had died of breast cancer in 1948) became a major populariser of Piaget's work in Britain after he was satisfied that Piaget's revised methodology answered his and his wife's earlier criticisms.[26] During this period, Piaget wrote a number of texts in collaboration with his research assistant Bärbel Inhelder, who had originally been his student and who had run a centre dealing with the psychology of schoolchildren during the Second World War.[27] Unlike Piaget, Inhelder, at least in the early 1950s, was more willing to countenance the suggestion that cognitive stages were not fixed and unalterable, which was reflected in their co-authored text *The Growth of Logical Thinking from Childhood to Adolescence*, published in 1955 and translated into English in 1957. This study suggested that the progression of stages of development might be related to social context, which implied that this sequence was not absolutely fixed.[28] However, discussions at a conference on the psychosocial development of the child, run by the World Health Organisation (WHO) in 1953, indicated that this was Inhelder's view, rather than Piaget's.[29] Furthermore, this text was relatively neglected by English and Welsh educationalists in comparison with Piaget's earlier work.

Teacher training, pedagogical advice and educational psychology, 1918 to 1979

Between 1918 and 1979, teacher training colleges became the predominant route for entry to teaching in a primary or secondary modern school.[30] By 1962, there were 109 training colleges in England and Wales, rising from 86 in 1910 and 83 in 1944 after a significant increase on expenditure on teacher training in the post-war period; 17 of these were former emergency training colleges, the remainder of the 54 that had been opened during the war.[31] Links between training colleges and the education departments of universities began to emerge from the 1930s as joint examination boards were established, but these meant little until Area Training Organisations (ATOs) emerged in 1946, recommended by the McNair Report of 1944.[32] Each of the universities in England and Wales had its own ATO, co-ordinating the work of training colleges and Institutes of Education. This brought training college practice into closer contact with academic research, and encouraged 'refresher courses' [in-service training].[33] This trend was confirmed by the James Report of 1972, which proposed a new set of teaching qualifications that would be administered by colleges of education and universities. The report recognised that new teachers often found it difficult to absorb and utilise theoretical content, so advised its limitation in teacher training courses while promoting its inclusion in an expanded programme of in-service training.[34] However, teachers' own recollections indicate that the amount of practical training available remained very variable throughout the 1970s, with certain progressive providers, such as Sussex, pioneering a more practical course, while many others remained theoretical.[35]

As this indicates, training colleges retained extensive freedom throughout most of the period under consideration. M. V. C. Jeffreys, the director of the Institute of Education from 1947, stated in 1961 that 'a college can do anything that it can get the appropriate board or committee of the Institute [of Education] to approve', as the Ministry of Education had withdrawn central control over the approval of syllabuses and the assessment of practical teaching.[36] Whether they were voluntary or maintained, colleges varied hugely in size, philosophy and staffing – from specialist Froëbel colleges to established progressive hubs such as Goldsmiths and Homerton. The Postgraduate Certificate in Education (PGCE) remained an alternative route to becoming a qualified teacher, but only a small number of prospective teachers trained in this way. Only 17 per cent of those who qualified in 1967 had taken a postgraduate course, and the majority of these went on to teach in secondary schools.[37] University graduates could enter teaching without taking a further qualifying course until 1973, and their numbers increased over the course of the 1970s. By 1980, 53.8 per cent of secondary school teachers and 16.5 per cent of primary school teachers employed in the public sector were graduates, a rise from 35.7 per cent and 4.2 per cent respectively in 1965–66.[38] However, postgraduate and graduate teachers tended to be concentrated in grammar schools rather than primaries, secondary moderns and comprehensives until at least the early 1970s, highlighted by the relatively low take-up of the B.Ed, which was aimed at prospective primary school teachers.[39]

Teachers rarely encountered developmental psychology during their training in the inter-war period. While 'psychology' featured on the inter-war syllabus, it was often outdated and did not deal specifically with more recent work on children. William McDougall, a well-known 'new psychologist' whose *An Introduction to Social Psychology*, first published in 1908, was in its twenty-second edition by 1931, dominated throughout the inter-war period, as Mathew Thomson has argued, despite increasing criticism from academics of his popularised approach to instinct.[40] Psychoanalysis only rarely featured in exams, and psychology was also sometimes collapsed 'under the umbrella' of philosophy of education, which continued to dominate inter-war training courses.[41] It was only thoroughly taught at progressive colleges such as Homerton and Goldsmiths, and even then, only from the 1930s onwards, as J. H. Frisby has shown.[42] At Darlington Training College in Durham in 1937, the inspectors thought that the treatment of psychology was both 'too academic' and 'unsystematic'. This was because 'One approach is through individual Child Study which in many respects is without a clear objective... The other approach is through the formal study of general psychology. These two approaches do not bring the students to the common ground where theory and practice should normally unite.'[43] This suggested that the students were expected to extrapolate from 'general psychology' using their experience of observing individual children. Darlington's syllabus did not exploit the resources available from inter-war writers such as Isaacs and Burt.

The amount of time spent on educational psychology in teacher training courses increased after 1945, but this did not necessarily indicate that developmental psychology had become central to syllabuses. In 1962, an enquiry by the Association of Teachers in Colleges and

Departments of Education (ATCDE) and the British Psychological Society indicated that 10-15 per cent of the total course in the 109 training colleges was devoted to educational psychology.[44] Philosophy of education, the other major component of theoretical work in training colleges, was in decline by the 1960s. Jeffreys commented that students found the subject difficult and irrelevant, and blamed staffing, stating that 'for every ten competent psychologists among professors and lecturers in Education, there is not more than one with any philosophical training.'[45] However, the ATCDE enquiry found that the content of psychology curriculums still lagged behind the most recent research. Having surveyed a thousand examination papers from 1959, the enquiry concluded that few questions were set on Piaget; on the other hand, McDougall still appeared occasionally. Of the time spent on educational psychology during the course, a quarter was spent on child development, a quarter on learning, and more than a third on attainments, abilities and psychometrics, indicating the continuing dominance of older ideas of intelligence testing compared with newer work on maturational growth. Nevertheless, new priorities were being established. The colleges surveyed by ATCDE claimed that developmental psychology was the most important part of educational psychology, and that this should be focused on the age group that students were training to teach. They ranked intellect and educational attainment fourth in their list of priorities, after the psychology of learning and social adjustment.[46] This indicates that while the colleges were responding to the post-war psychological climate, it was not yet clearly reflected in their syllabuses.

Staffing problems in teacher training colleges and the persistence of formal teaching methods also affected teachers' responses to training courses. Psychology was infrequently taught by trained specialists until the 1950s. The limited number of honours degrees offered in psychology meant that the lecturers' qualifications were often non-existent, piecemeal or unsuitable.[47] In the inter-war period, finding qualified staff was a particular problem, as the records of training colleges demonstrate. For example, at Sheffield City Training College from 1935–36, the inspector thought that the lecturer in education for men had 'studied psychology to good purpose' but was not 'a professed psychologist', while the lecturer in education for women did not have a sufficient 'intellectual grasp of psychology . . . to allow her to handle this subject effectively.'[48] This lack of qualified staff was unsurprising, given that psychology was still establishing itself as an academic discipline in Britain during the 1930s. As Nikolas Rose notes, there were only six university chairs in psychology by 1939, and thirty lecturing staff.[49]

Nevertheless, this issue was not confined to inter-war Britain. Citing the ATCDE enquiry, Frisby noted that even by 1962, more than a third of lecturers in educational psychology were not formally qualified; fifteen of the seventy-two colleges surveyed had no psychological specialist, and twenty-six were unable to answer the question. Furthermore, Frisby suggested, some of the qualifications held by the two-thirds of qualified lecturers may not have been adequate. For example, many diploma courses were biased towards the descriptive study of behaviour, rather than a true engagement with psychology as a science.[50] In addition to staffing problems, training colleges often used formal methodology to teach child-centred methods, failing to practise what they preached, and hence not engaging their students. Selleck argued that, in the inter-war period, 'crowded rooms of would-be teachers often listened to lectures bemoaning the inefficiency of lessons to large classes, and students solemnly copied out notes from lectures which extolled "activity" methods.'[51] Isaacs herself noted the poor balance between theory and practice, writing in an examiners' report on a college psychology course: 'I do wish we could give up teaching these dreary old theories of play. It seems to me pathetic that students spend so much time on discussing Schiller, Groos, etc. instead of . . . going direct to children at play and seeing for themselves what play does for children's development.'[52]

It was only after the Second World War that teaching methods became more active in the majority of colleges. While the ATCDE enquiry found that the lecture still dominated in 1962, it now stood in a 4:3:2 ratio to discussion groups and seminars.[53] Ian Dawson, who trained in 1973, recalled, 'I did PGCE and suddenly there was this wonderful man called Bob Unwin who wanted to make history interesting in the classroom. He'd got seventy-five ways of starting a lesson so that the children were enlivened and became drawn in.'[54] However, teachers who trained in the 1960s and 1970s still intermittently remembered formal and uninspiring teaching. Patricia Dawson, who trained in secondary teaching at the Institute of Education in the 1960s, remembered that 'it was all lectures all the time ... I remember a Friday morning, we had three consecutive hours of lectures ... people were bored to tears; they were leaving and walking out.'[55] Lynn, who completed a PGCE in primary school teaching at Westminster College in 1972–73, remembered a theoretical curriculum dominated by lecturers who had been 'teaching the same class for a very long time'.[56]

These methodological problems highlighted a broader issue; training college lecturers lacked teaching experience, especially within the kind of schools for which they were preparing their students. Lecturers tended to be middle-class graduates, and while many did possess some teaching experience, their teaching careers tended to be brief simply by virtue of the fact that they had become teacher trainers.[57] In addition, they were more likely to have taught in independent, private or grammar schools than primary or secondary moderns. T. H. B. Hollins noted in 1971 that around 80 per cent of training college lecturers had taught at secondary rather than primary level.[58] Plowden recognised that the need for 'well qualified specialists' in 'main subjects' at the training college made this weighting towards former secondary-level teachers almost inevitable, and noted that '[s]pecialists in psychology and sociology may, like other specialists, know too little of the primary schools'.[59] This meant that lecturers' experience was not necessarily closely related to the needs of the majority of trainees.

Training college set texts tended to be more up-to-date than both training college courses and the people who staffed them. Standard interwar set texts concurred with contemporary wisdom by emphasising the individuality of the child, minimising the significance of developmental stages, and underlining the continuity between childhood and adulthood, as in the earlier editions of Percy Nunn's *Education: its data and first principles* (1920) and A. H. Hughes and E. H. Hughes's *Learning and Teaching* (1937). References to maturational stages of development became more frequent and more specific from the late 1940s onwards in both new set texts and revised editions of familiar authorities. Hughes and Hughes responded to the shift in emphasis by more tightly linking chronological and developmental age in their later editions, although without retracting their argument that there was no fundamental difference between childhood and adulthood. In their 1947 edition, it was already emphasised that there would be mental differences between classes of differing ages; by 1959, this statement was amended to suggest that the teacher must also be aware of any children below the average age of the class, as this slight age difference might affect their achievements.[60]

Changing attitudes to developmental psychology were also reflected in teaching journals, which may have been more widely read than training college set texts by primary school teachers. In the inter-war period, teaching journals tended to engage only with developmental stages insofar as they were making broad generalisations about children of a specific age, and even these references were limited. In line with Isaacs and Burt, *Teachers World* and the *Schoolmaster* often rejected the utility of stage-concepts entirely, asserting that there were no sharp divisions between childhood and adulthood.[61] *Teachers World*'s references to stages were clustered around the publication of the 1931 Hadow Report and the revised *Handbook of Suggestions* in 1937.[62] The more progressive *Schoolmaster* went even further than *Teachers World* in the 1930s and 1940s in emphasising the malleability of stages and the abilities of even very young children, in line with the arguments of Isaacs and Burt. While it welcomed the 1931 Report, it also argued that the Board of Education had misinterpreted its instructions on the age of transfer to secondary education – in particular, a footnote that stated that the age of eleven 'is not intended to be used in a precise chronological sense'. The journal went on to argue that classification by age within the school should also not be seen as a necessary corollary of Hadow.[63] In contrast, stages of development appeared with relative regularity in both the *Schoolmaster* and *Teachers World* after 1945.[64]

Primary school teachers also turned to informal authorities such as M. V. Daniel's *Activity in the Primary School* (1947), which had been reprinted at least seven times by 1966, and provided more specific information on teaching this age group than training college set texts.[65] Daniel was the principal of Hereford Training College as well as an inspector of schools for Manchester LEA. In her text, the importance of individual treatment was still noted, but the emphasis was on the 'outstanding characteristics' of the seven-to-eleven age group, and, anticipating the 1959 edition of Hughes and Hughes, Daniel argued that the child must be able to both express individuality and conform to the requirements of the group.[66] It was noted, in line with the inter-war emphasis on continuous growth, that '[d]evelopment is gradual', but a normative image of the child was presented, asserting that, when designing teaching methods, 'the general characteristics of children of primary school age must remain the most important consideration', perhaps reflecting the practical point that individual teaching in large classes would be a struggle for most teachers.[67] Therefore, set texts, journals, and popular teaching guides such as Daniel's tended to be more in step with broader post-war developments, even if syllabuses were not.

Stages of development assumed even greater significance in the reports of the Ministry of Education (the Department of Education and Science from 1964).[68] The *Handbooks* issued to teachers – which many of the WEP interviewees recognised or spontaneously mentioned – continued to toe the 1931 line by emphasising individuality and giving only a broad account of stages of development that made little reference to Piaget.[69] For example, *Primary Education* (1959) focused on the enormous variation in individual development and gave only a brief account of the common characteristics of children in this age group – although, in contrast to the 1931 Report, it did split the group into seven to nine-year-olds and nine to eleven-year-olds, indicating a closer, more precise attention to differences in age and their relationship to children's abilities and interests.[70] Its stance on the difference between children and adults was less cautious. The difference between children and adults, it suggested, lay in attitude rather than experience: 'though girls and boys want to be like adults, they can be like them only within limits. They do not yet look far ahead; it is the present or easily foreseeable future that is all-important to them.'[71] This, on balance, cleaved more closely to the idea of an absolute separation than the continuum postulated by Isaacs, because the handbook also argued that children were incapable of fully understanding time 'until nearly the end of the primary period', which implied that their present-orientated stance was maturational and inescapable rather than experience-linked and optional.[72]

The Plowden Report (1967), which sold 70,000 copies in its first year of publication and was also widely discussed in the US, took this shift a step further by explicitly engaging with Piaget and asserting a fully maturational account of children's growth and development.[73] While still careful to recognise individual difference, Plowden emphasised sequential developmental stages, concluding its section on the role of the teacher with the assertion that 'our study of children's development has emphasised the importance of maturation to learning'.[74]

Unlike many advice guides, Plowden recognised that Piagetian stages could not be tied tightly to chronological ages.[75] However, the writers of the report also took an interest in the biology of child development, a body of thought that suggested that growth was pre-planned and, while not unrelated to experience, mediated by physical realities. As well as briefly exploring the ethological literature on 'critical periods', the report took a strong stand on recent research into the development of the brain, asserting that it was

> probable that the higher intellectual abilities also appear only as maturation of certain structures occurs ... Piaget and Inhelder have described the emergence of mental structures in a manner strongly reminiscent of developing brain or body structures; the mental stages follow in a sequence, for example, which may be advanced or delayed, but not altered. There seems good reason to suppose that Piaget's successive stages depend on progressive maturation or at least progressive organisation of the cerebral cortex.[76]

This suggested that, while brain development may vary between individuals, experience alone was not sufficient to account for the difference between children and adults; the difference was, at least to some extent, neurologically determined. Plowden, therefore, was committed to both maturational stages of development and the separation between childhood and adulthood.

While more nuanced interpretations of Piaget's developmental stages that decoupled them from chronological age and took sociological factors into account were emerging in educational research by the 1970s, these were not usually reflected in popular teaching guides for either primary or secondary school teachers. Robinson noted in an MSc thesis of 1971 produced at the University of London's Institute of Education that five recent texts were commonly recommended on college reading lists.[77] Three of these cleaved to older orthodoxies. Both Molly Brearley's *Fundamentals in the First School* (1969) and Leonard Marsh's *Alongside the Child in the Primary School* (1970) rehearsed misleading material on maturational developmental stages.[78] Lorna Ridgway and Irene Lawton's *Family Grouping in the Primary School* (1968) emphasised chronological age by using character sketches of each age group, as Gesell had done: 'The 6-year-old is going through an unsettled period ... The 7-year-olds can manage long periods of purposeful self-direction'.[79] Even when popular texts published in this period explicitly recognised the complexity of Piaget's formulations, usually in their introductions, the ideas were simplified in later chapters to offer practical advice to teachers.[80] For example, Ruth Beard's *An Outline of Piaget's Developmental Psychology for Students and Teachers* (1969), which was reprinted again that year, annually for four more years and was still in print in 1986, explained in its first chapter, in line with Piaget's original work, that age-stages were developmental, not chronological, but then simplified this statement in the main body of the book. For example, Beard wrote 'Until about nine years, most children continue to find some difficulties in understanding relationships between classes.'[81] This kind of language was likely to be confusing to teachers, especially if they had skipped the theoretical preamble to get straight to the bits of their set text that were about the practical teaching situation in the classroom.

Teachers' engagement with educational psychology and stages of development, 1918 to 1979

Recalling his teacher training at Thornlea in Exeter from 1975 to 1976, Michael, an Oxfordshire teacher, wrote 'Worst was the 1st term . . . "learning"! about child Psychology, Piaget and history of education'.[82] Throughout this period, teachers in England and Wales tended to recall predominantly negative responses to the psychology component of their training courses in retrospective self-narrative accounts, although post-war teachers were more likely to remember specific information about course content than their inter-war counterparts. The WEP interviews indicate that teachers who trained in the inter-war period were not likely to remember studying the subject at all, while teachers who trained post-war were more aware of psychology even if they did not see it as relevant, given the greater number of respondents who mentioned it spontaneously in their interviews. Post-war teachers were also more likely than inter-war respondents to have found psychology important in their teaching, or at least to have believed that the subject had some value. Conversely, they were more likely than inter-war respondents to deny outright that it was important, suggesting that they had thought about it, or come into contact with it frequently enough to have formed a strong opinion. Notably, contemporary surveys of teachers tended to reflect less negative responses to educational psychology than both inter-war and post-war teachers' remembered accounts of their careers, indicating that teachers' reactions changed over time.

Earlier work on teachers' engagement with developmental psychology has tended to assume that as Piaget was 'unknown' among teachers before the 1960s, his ideas were unknown to them as well. This is unlikely to have been the case.[83] It is certainly clear that direct engagement with Piaget was uncommon among teachers until his name emerged abruptly in teaching journals in the 1960s.[84] The WEP interviews, which routinely asked respondents if they had heard of Piaget, showed that most of the WEP teachers had either not heard of Piaget at all, or had only heard of him after they had been teaching for some time; several tied his influence explicitly to the 1960s or 1970s. When asked to summarise what Piaget's work had said, few respondents were able to say anything accurate. The handful of better-informed respondents tended to have trained in the 1960s or 1970s, or had encountered him by taking a special interest in child psychology that the majority of teachers would not have pursued, such as attending a special vacation course or even taking a year's diploma in child development.[85] This was also evident in the History in Education and Oxfordshire interviews. For example, Brian, who trained between 1975 and 1979, asserted that 'everybody remembers Piaget', but, having taken a B.Ed in History and Psychology, he was an atypical respondent. Michael recalled that 'Pierjetay [his pronunciation of Piaget] . . . meant very little to me'.[86] However, although teachers may not have come across Piaget's actual name before the 1960s, it is evident that, when they did, this material built on a series of assumptions that had been instilled both by earlier post-war pieces and training college set texts and teaching guides. Teachers did not need to know who Piaget was to have been deeply affected by popularised versions of his assumptions about the way that children thought and how they developed.

Teachers who had trained in the 1950s and 1960s regularly used psychological language, even if they found it difficult in retrospective interviews to recall the names of theorists such as Piaget. In the Oxfordshire interviews, virtually all respondents recalled learning about 'stages of development' in their initial teacher training. Most strikingly, even teachers of this generation who denied the importance of psychology, or who did not mention it, used ideas about children and teaching that were drawn from psychological assumptions about child education, a language that was largely lacking in the inter-war teachers' interviews.[87] These references became increasingly specific among teachers who had trained in the 1970s. Ann, who trained at the University of York from 1973–74, remembered 'The idea of building learning in ways that match the age and stage of learners . . . I do think there was an effort to place us in the shoes of the learner at their different ages and stage in order to match our teaching to pupils/students.'[88] As this indicates, teachers' response to developmental psychology, and the extent to which it influenced their teaching practice, was mediated by the cohort with which they trained. Interestingly, the age of the trainee was much less significant. Even the few WEP teachers who started their training later in life tended to adopt the stance of the group that they trained with, even though most of their cohort was significantly younger, suggesting that it was not age as such that divided teachers, but their experience of training college.[89] This was also evident among the cohort of emergency trained teachers, who tended to be older on average than the usual recruits. A number of teachers recalled that one of the most useful things about training college had been sharing ideas with their fellow students, indicating how certain assumptions about teaching may have developed within particular cohorts.[90]

Teachers' responses to developmental psychology was also conditioned by the amount of teaching experience they had already had. Teachers who were looking back over the course of their careers from the vantage point of retirement tended to dismiss the relevance of psychology, at least when they were considering the early years of their teaching career. These remembered impressions are corroborated by some contemporary evidence. Howard Peach left training college in 1954, and claimed in an article in the *Teacher* nine years later that it had not been a useful experience, as it had given no practical advice on discipline: 'I never remember taking down notes on what to do with, for instance, non-stop talkers, the pupil who refuses to submit to a caning, the buffoon, the unruly, the lout.'[91] In 1966, the progressive educationalist Sybil Marshall, author of *An Experiment in Education*, published that year, commented in the same journal, 'I have met many teachers in training who have expressed to me the same bewilderment about the content and purpose of the education course offered to them at their colleges of education; as one of them said, "The course was nearly over before I caught on to what it was all about."'[92] The

1972 James Report concurred, arguing that trainee teachers predominantly found psychology difficult, confusing and/or irrelevant to the practical business of teaching:

> Many courses place too much emphasis on educational theory at the expense of adequate preparation for students' responsibilities in their first professional assignments. The knowledge that in-service opportunities are scanty leads to a similar overloading of initial programmes... Such frustrations can be detected only too readily whenever teaching practice is discussed.[93]

However, teachers' responses to developmental psychology were not uniformly negative across all career stages. In the course of this period, two groups of teachers were more likely to respond positively to psychological knowledge: teachers who had very little practical teaching experience, and teachers in their mid-career, who had built up a great deal of experience. A. Lloyd-Evans's 1935–36 survey of a group of female teachers who were about to leave college indicated that the majority of the 135 respondents thought psychology was important.[94] These findings were partly replicated by the 560 recruits surveyed by the NUT's National Young Teacher Advisory Committee between 1964 and 1967, 45 per cent of whom had found educational psychology useful – not a majority, but a very significant minority, especially when compared with the 31 per cent who had found sociology useful and the 15 per cent who had found philosophy of education useful.[95] Once teachers had gained some teaching experience, though, this age differentiation became less significant. Patricia Ashton et al.'s 1975 survey on 'progressive' and 'traditionalist' approaches to primary teaching – where 'progressive' teachers were those who agreed with the statement that teachers had to create a favourable psychological and physical environment – indicated that there was no significant age differentiation between those who agreed and those who didn't, once teachers were practising in schools.[96]

Teachers encountered psychology not only in their initial teacher training but also in the 'refresher courses' that experienced exponential growth in the 1950s and 1960s, becoming codified as in-service training in the 1970s. This led to a number of teachers suggesting in retrospective interviews that they had found educational psychology important in their teaching careers, but only after they had built up a significant amount of practical experience in the classroom, and perhaps after they had re-encountered these ideas in a different setting.

Carol, who trained between 1966 and 1970, recalled 'I think I didn't benefit from my initial training as much as I could have done had I been more mature.' She found refresher courses much more useful, and also pointed to the importance of a career break, after which she had gone 'back into primary school where I'm much more excited about the development of children's minds and how they learn through play, I got really excited about it a bit later in the day.'[97] Brian felt that his training in psychology became 'subconsciously' useful later in his teaching career, although he seemed to be referring to his B.Ed from Oxford, which he completed in 1979, rather than his initial disappointing teacher training at Westminster.[98] The James Report recognised the greater effectiveness of in-service training in engaging teachers with theoretical ideas, arguing that 'all teachers ought to have opportunities to extend and deepen their knowledge of teaching methods and of educational theory'.[99]

Even teachers who did not engage directly with educational or developmental psychology itself experienced the shift towards tighter age- and stage-classifications in the practical reorganisation of schooling from the 1950s onwards. The most significant landmark was the 1944 Education Act, which established the principle of 'separate secondary education for all', enshrining a formal divide between junior and senior schools. This act has become associated with the tripartite system of grammar, secondary modern and technical schools that developed in the immediate post-war years, but this system, promoted by the 1943 Norwood Report on *Curriculum and Examinations in Secondary Schools*, was not in fact formally mandated by the 1944 legislation. In popular memory, the 1944 Act was part of a conservative programme that relied on intelligence testing to separate academic and non-academic children; in reality, the Norwood Report, as Adrian Wooldridge has argued, was sceptical about educational psychology and IQ tests.[100] As we have seen, Cyril Burt condemned the report for separating children into three distinct 'types' rather than adopting his ideas about the uniform distribution of intelligence; in other words, he did not believe children possessed different 'kinds' of intelligence but were either good at everything or at nothing. Instead of viewing the 1944 Act as a wholly conservative piece of legislation, therefore, we should also see the tripartite system as a natural corollary of the emerging non-utopian progressive movement. If one had to suit pedagogy to the needs of the child, it made sense to divide children into different groups according to their 'age, ability and aptitude' so that schools could cater for them accordingly.

Inter-war schools were not necessarily organised by chronological age. Classes in the 1920s tended to be separated into 'standards', which reflected a child's progress through set schemes of work rather than his or her age, a relic of the 1862 Revised Code. The LCC reported in 1924 that children of thirteen could be found everywhere between Standard 1 and Standard 6, and promotion by ability rather than age only ceased when the Elementary Regulations were abolished in 1926.[101] Even as schools started to adopt chronological age-grouping, this may initially have had less to do with psychological justifications and more to do with a deliberate rejection of the form of organisation that had been associated with payment by results. The reorganisation of schools into infant, primary and secondary departments, with each associated with a distinct stage of development, was first suggested by the Hadow Report of 1931. This basic organisational change emphasised the importance of a child's age and developmental stage, and put the onus on the teachers to use appropriate methods in the smaller age ranges they now had to deal with. It highlighted both a basic discontinuity between different age groups and the belief in a set of abilities that were specific to a group of children that shared a chronological age.

These assumptions were not necessarily shared by practising teachers in the inter-war period, who were accustomed to teaching under a different system. In the early 1920s, *Teachers World* suggested that teachers should be moved between primary and secondary schools as the need arose, and that this was desirable: 'Let us get rid of the notion that there are inevitable and wide gaps between one type of work and another.'[102] This was tied into a broader professional commitment to ensure mutual respect between different 'types' of teacher in the context of disputes over pay, after the cuts in government expenditure made by the 'Geddes axe' after the First World War and the negotiation over the Burnham salary scales that had been introduced in 1919 and made compulsory in 1925.[103] Later, the journal explicitly questioned both the 1926 and 1931 Hadow Reports' definition of adolescence as a chronological age-stage. In 'Is There A Break at 11?' (1929), Philip Ballard argued that, because of the individuality of children, '*There is no universal change or psychical crisis at eleven years of age.*' The problem

Stages of development

with universal transfer at eleven, he stated, while it might be necessary for administrative purposes, was that 'some education authorities expect children to reach the same stage of development at eleven years of age', which he considered to be ludicrous.[104]

Once the 'break at eleven' was made compulsory by the 1944 Act, it took some time to implement in practice, but was virtually complete by the 1960s. The Plowden Report noted that while 59 per cent of English schools were all-age in 1933 and 35 per cent in 1949, this dropped to 12 per cent in 1955 and only 1 per cent in 1965.[105] Data from individual counties, such as Cambridgeshire, largely bears out this national pattern. The head of St Albans' Roman Catholic mixed all-age school bemoaned the fact in 1960 that 'This is possibly (and we all hope so) the last year in the career of this the only remaining "all-age" school in the city of Cambridge,' hoping that the new secondary school would be completed by 1961.[106] St Albans had lagged behind other schools in Cambridge, which had virtually all been reorganised in the 1930s, but was more in step with rural Cambridgeshire, where all-age schools persisted for longer. In rural areas, schools might have been technically 'reorganised' into separate departments but continued to be housed in the same building, distorting Plowden's figures to some extent. In Wales, with its large rural authorities, reorganisation proceeded more slowly, with 3.1 per cent of Welsh children still in all-age schools in 1965.[107]

Despite the slow progress of formal reorganisation, especially in rural areas, teachers and inspectors after the Second World War became more concerned with avoiding large age-ranges, maintaining a junior-senior divide, and ensuring that teachers had been trained for, or had had experience of teaching, the age group that they worked with although, in practice, teachers frequently taught a range of age groups. Due to the nature of logbook evidence, which dealt with practical issues relating to the school rather than educational philosophies, explicit references to stages of development were not made by headteachers, but these shifts can be witnessed in inspectors' reports. For example, in 1948, the inspector thought that the headmistress of Horspath in Oxfordshire, which had been reorganised as a junior school in 1946, was 'finding it extremely difficult to adapt her outlook and methods to the changed conditions' as she had always taught the senior class before.[108] Other Oxfordshire schools faced the same problem. At Goring, in 1949, in a small two-teacher rural junior school, the inspector commented that: 'Both teachers have been accustomed to dealing with older children and have no doubt found it difficult ... to adjust their methods and outlook to the needs of younger pupils.'[109] The same complaint occurred after the reorganisation of Garsington in 1947.[110] Interestingly, HMIs never commented that junior teachers struggled with teaching senior classes. This may have been because reorganised senior schools tended to employ new staff, or because the 1931 Hadow Report had focused attention on the needs of junior-age children.[111]

Teachers also became increasingly aware across this period of the importance of age-appropriate education. Teachers who taught in an earlier period tended to be less concerned with age divisions, or might actually prefer teaching in all-age schools, like W. D. Campbell, who was a headmaster in Berkshire in the 1930s and 1940s after starting to teach in 1929. When interviewed on the BBC Oxford radio programme *My Choice* in 1984, he remembered 'I had in the end children from the age of five to fifteen, boys and girls.' When the interviewer asked him, 'Which age group do you prefer?' he failed to understand why the question was relevant:

> That was the happiest time of my teaching experience, which I had them right through from beginning to when they left ... We never had any trouble, it was a marvellous time. And those I had till they were fifteen have never forgotten me. When wretched alterations came they took them and sent them away at eleven, to secondary moderns ... grammar school type if they'd passed the 11+, they forgot all about me.[112]

Connie Norman, who started teaching in the late 1930s in Croydon, took a different view in her *My Choice* interview; she remembers making a deliberate decision to switch to teaching infants in 1943, when she moved to Oxford. She thought that it was a 'very different sort of teaching, but I believe it's something that would be good for all teachers to do ... I think you should try the little ones, and get to know the real essence of teaching'.[113] This suggested that teaching younger children was a different kind of thing altogether than teaching juniors or seniors, and also implied that the kind of all-age school that Campbell remembered fondly would not be viable.

Teachers who trained even later, in the 1950s and 1960s, tended to train for a single age group and stick to it, as David Cannadine's interview transcripts and the WEP interviews indicate.[114] This had been less common among teachers who trained before the war unless they planned to teach infants.[115] For example, Patricia Dawson, who started teaching in the 1960s, only ever taught at secondary schools, as did Evelyn Hinde, who started teaching in 1957 and remembered clearly making that choice during her training at Stockwell. When asked, 'So what age group were they aiming at training you for?', she answered 'Oh I went for secondary. Now that was unusual. There had been ... nearly all teacher training colleges trained for infant or junior.'[116] Similarly, Roberta Wood, who trained during the 1960s, only ever taught in junior schools, and recalled 'I've never taught anything older than 9'.[117] My Oxfordshire respondents made similar assertions: 'I've taught right across the school but I must say my preferred age group is KS2 [seven to eleven-year-olds]... teaching Reception and ... Y1 [four to six-year-olds] is a completely different mindset'; 'Although I was secondary trained ... the middle school [nine to thirteen-year-olds]... I loved that age range'; 'The older the better ... 13–19 ... I take my hat off to primary school teachers.'[118] The key shift was not that all teachers had stopped switching age groups, but that teaching one age group was increasingly envisaged as the ideal, feeding into norms about children's homogenous and monolithic development.[119]

By the late 1960s, 'family grouping' or 'vertical classification' was increasingly floated as a credible alternative to age-grouping in the primary school, and this was often linked with the integrated day. The Plowden Report (1967) on *Children and Their Primary Schools* in England was cautious and implicitly critical of extending family grouping to the junior school, although it recognised that the practice had some advantages in infant schools.[120] In contrast, its Welsh equivalent, the Gittins Report (1967) more enthusiastically recommended that schools should experiment with family grouping, although this was probably due to the fact that 23.7 per cent of Welsh children were already organised in mixed-age classes in 1964 because of the large number of rural schools in Wales.[121] The promotion of family grouping might seem to suggest that it was being increasingly recognised that chronological and developmental age did not necessarily align, and that children should hence not be grouped strictly by chronological age. This was certainly an argument put forward by some of its advocates. Edith Moorhouse, senior adviser for primary education in Oxfordshire, who led a team of advisory teachers to promote non-utopian progressive education in the county from 1946, thought there was no purpose in organising children into age groups, complaining that 'in many schools age is still sacrosanct and intellectual, emotional and social differences are ignored'.[122]

However, most arguments made in support of family grouping said nothing about developmental age. George Baines, head of the flagship Oxfordshire progressive school, Eynsham County Primary, saw vertical classification as the 'normal' pattern, bringing school closer to the home environment.[123] Plowden thought that children in vertical groups were able to learn from each other and 'gained from a longer association with one teacher'.[124] Therefore, although a few exceptionally progressive educators were emphatically reasserting the original philosophy of individuality that had motivated child-centred pedagogy, it was not obvious that this belief was especially widespread. Teachers also resisted the adoption of family grouping, and even when it was enforced upon a particular school by a headteacher or the inspectorate, they might accept the new form of organisation only grudgingly.

Mel Summers was the headteacher of West Oxford School until his retirement in 1981. The school had started off as a junior and secondary school housed in the same building – an all-age school in all but name – and then acquired an infant department after the closure of another local school, St Thomas's. Mel felt that he had to adopt what he called 'school family grouping' even though he was 'personally not too happy' about it. When the interviewer asked 'So you were largely sort of directed in this way by the administration?' Mel answered 'That's right.' He encountered practical problems with the reorganisation: 'It wasn't very easy in our school, because of the way the school was built . . . later schools, they had the open plan right from the word go but we couldn't do an open plan very well unless you had quite small classes, which did come about . . . so we were able to put them in groups.' Unlike purpose-built flagship schools such as Brize Norton, most Oxfordshire schools were housed in older buildings. Mel disagreed that family grouping improved his pupils' educational experience: 'you had children of five, six, seven all in one group, and usually it was the older ones doing most of the work.'[125]

As Mel's experience suggested, 'family' or 'vertical' grouping could often simply provide sociological and psychological justification for the persistence of all-age education in small rural schools in the 1970s, a practice that had been seen as undesirable since the Second World War but which was difficult to eradicate, especially given the child-centred idealisation of this kind of school.[126] The Plowden Report alluded to this when it stated 'It is of some interest that many of the heads of junior schools . . . in the National Foundation for Educational Research (NFER) streaming survey complained of the difficulties of a wide age range in a large class . . . They share, that is to say, the conditions of a school which voluntarily widens the age range in its classes.' Plowden went on to note that it was becoming 'relatively common' to move in the opposite direction by making age ranges in particular classes as small as six months.[127] The 1978 HMI survey indicated that while 49 per cent of classes for nine-year-olds and 42 per cent of classes for eleven-year-olds spanned more than a year's age range, 24 per cent and 23 per cent of these, respectively, were in schools that were too small to have precise year-groups, so this was not a choice but a necessity, as was the case in Wales.[128] Therefore, the use of 'family grouping' could be solely an attempt to seem more 'up-to-date' when forced to teach large groups. The ideal for most teachers and local educational authorities, even in the 1970s, remained a school divided into year-groups by the pupils' chronological age.

As developmental psychology became more established in Britain after the Second World War, its assumptions about childhood were increasingly dominant in teaching guides and journals, if not always in training colleges before the 1960s and 1970s. Both inter-war and post-war teachers often struggled to understand and engage with formal educational psychology, due to its heavy theoretical content, poor teaching and staffing, and its seeming irrelevance to the practical teaching situation, although new teachers might be excited by the possibilities it offered, and others sometimes changed their minds after significant classroom experience. However, psychological concepts still shaped teachers' concepts of childhood. The basic assumptions about child development that were suggested by a simplified version of Piagetian stages filtered into teaching practice through the dominance of child-centred education, which frequently cited developmental psychological claims to support its assertions about the capabilities and incapabilities of children. They also came through the practical reorganisation of schools, centring chronological age as a key characteristic of classes and presenting development as maturational and discontinuous, and by the adoption of psychological language by teachers themselves. Most teachers' resistance to educational psychology was consistent and often vehement. However, especially when such resistance was expressed by practising teachers, this may have had less to do with the content of training college and refresher course syllabuses, and more to do with the threat that developmental psychology posed to their own ideals of professional expertise. Far from being at the vanguard of progressive reform, a significant number of teachers resisted progressive innovations because they felt they posed a challenge to their own authority, knowledge and professional identity.

Notes

1. Wooldridge, *Measuring the Mind*, p. 45.
2. Vernon, *Hunger*, pp. 169, 171–2.
3. Armstrong, *Political Anatomy of the Body*, p. 56.
4. Armstrong, *Political Anatomy of the Body*, pp. 13, 27, 55, 60–1.
5. Smith, 'Hyperactive around the world?', p. 775. On sociological and psychological explanations working in tandem, see Hayward, 'The invention of the psychosocial'.
6. Shapira, *The War Inside*.
7. Stewart, *Child Guidance in Britain*, pp. 5, 7, 171.
8. Stewart, *Child Guidance in Britain*, pp. 164, 167, 171.
9. Hall, *Adolescence*.
10. Riley, *War in the Nursery*, p. 36.
11. Isaacs, *Social Development in Young Children*, pp. 67, 99. Presumably Harold had been used to singing '*Hickory* Dickory Dock'.
12. Isaacs, *The Children We Teach*, p. 12.
13. Wooldridge, *Measuring the Mind*, p. 73.
14. Burt, *The Young Delinquent* (3rd edn), p. 19.
15. Board of Education, *The Primary School*, p. 258.
16. Burt, 'The education of the young adolescent', p. 140. Wooldridge, *Measuring the Mind*, p. 243.
17. Wooldridge, *Measuring the Mind*, p. 237.
18. Burt, *The Young Delinquent* (3rd edn), p. 18.
19. Burt, 'The development of reasoning', pp. 123-4, 126-7.
20. Wooldridge, *Measuring the Mind*, p. 228.
21. Board of Education, *The Primary School*, p. 268.
22. Wooldridge, *Measuring the Mind*, p. 121.
23. Isaacs, *Intellectual Growth in Young Children*, pp. 57, 84. Wooldridge, *Measuring the Mind*, p. 122.

24 Isaacs, *Intellectual Growth in Young Children*, pp. 70-1.
25 Isaacs, *Social Development in Young Children*, pp. 11, 24.
26 Smith, *To Understand and to Help*, p. 173; Giardiello, *Pioneers in Early Childhood Education*, p. 114.
27 Tanner and Inhelder (eds), *Discussions on Child Development*, p. 30.
28 This recalled Margaret Mead's anthropological work on adolescence; for example, in *Coming of Age in Samoa*.
29 Tanner and Inhelder (eds), *Discussions on Child Development*, pp. 85, 90, 93.
30 The course was two years long until 1960, when it was extended to three years.
31 Tanner and Inhelder (eds), *Discussions on Child Development*, p. 162; Edwards, *Women in Teacher Training Colleges*, p. 13; Lowe, *Education in the Post-War Years*, p. 28.
32 Jeffreys, *Revolution in Teacher-Training*, pp. 10-11.
33 Jeffreys, *Revolution in Teacher-Training*, p. 13.
34 DES, *Teacher Education and Training*, pp. 7, 20.
35 History in Education, David Burrell interviewed by Nicola Sheldon (2009), pp. 26, 33-4.
36 Jeffreys, *Revolution in Teacher-Training*, p. 13. Dent, *The Training of Teachers*, p. 118.
37 History in Education, 'Analysis of teacher numbers' (2010).
38 *Ibid*.; DES, 'B.Ed degree course'.
39 History in Education, J. Keating, 'Teacher training – up to the 1960s' (2010).
40 Frisby, 'The History of Educational Psychology Teaching', p. 100; Thomson, *Psychological Subjects*, p. 57; McDougall, *An Introduction to Social Psychology*, 22nd edn.
41 Thomson, *Psychological Subjects*, p. 59; Frisby, 'Educational Psychology', pp. 105, 109.
42 National Archives, ED 115/2, Homerton Training College, 1932-33, 9-11; ED 115/48, London, Goldsmiths' College Training Department, 27 November 1937, pp. 23-4.
43 National Archives, ED 115/11, Darlington Training College, Durham, 30 October 1937, 4, 7. Also National Archives, ED 115/7, Truro Training College, Cornwall, 1937, 3-4.
44 Frisby, 'Educational Psychology', pp. 160-2.
45 Jeffreys, *Revolution in Teacher-Training*, p. 46.
46 Frisby, 'The History of Educational Psychology Teaching', pp. 160-2.
47 Frisby, 'The History of Educational Psychology Teaching', p. 50.
48 National Archives, ED 155/89, Sheffield City Training College 1935-36, 6. Also ED 155/81, York Training College, 1931-32, 5 and ED 155/47, Gipsy Hill Training College, London, 1930-31, 5.
49 Rose, *The Psychological Complex*, p. 4.
50 Frisby, 'The History of Educational Psychology Teaching', pp. 160, 167, 176.

51 Cited in Partington, *Teacher Education in England and Wales*, p. 38.
52 Drummond, 'Susan Isaacs' in Hilton and Hirsch (eds), *Practical Visionaries*, p. 229.
53 Frisby, 'The History of Educational Psychology Teaching', p. 162.
54 History in Education, Ian Dawson interviewed by Nicola Sheldon (2009), p. 2.
55 History in Education, Patricia Dawson interviewed by Nicola Sheldon (2010), p. 4.
56 Oxfordshire Pilot, Ox.006, interview.
57 Edwards, *Women in Teacher Training Colleges*, p. 92.
58 Hollins, 'Desirable changes', in Hilliard (ed.), *Teaching the Teachers*, p. 90.
59 DES, *Children and Their Primary Schools*, p. 345.
60 Hughes and Hughes, *Learning and Teaching*, 2nd edn, p. 4; Hughes and Hughes, *Learning and Teaching*, 3rd edn, p. 5.
61 *Teachers World*, 6 March 1935, p. 835.
62 See *Teachers World*, 14 April 1937, pp. 1, 21 for a review of the *Handbook* that gives a typically vague account of stages of development linked to the broadly defined periods of infancy, late childhood and adolescence.
63 *Schoolmaster*, 1 April 1932, p. 601.
64 For example: J. J. B. Dempster, 'Stages in the development of the child', *Schoolmaster*, 6 February 1947, p. 135; 'Primary school workshop', *Schoolmaster*, 1 October 1954, p. 431; 'Psychologist', 'Are there any late developers?', *Teachers World*, 31 July 1957, p. 17, S. S. Segal, 'Applied basic skills', *Teachers World*, 5 January 1962, p. 4.
65 Cunningham, *Curriculum Change in the Primary School*, p. 16.
66 Daniel, *Activity in the Primary School*, pp. 39–41, 57.
67 *Ibid.*, pp. 31, 50.
68 Cunningham, *Curriculum Change in the Primary School*, p. 13.
69 WEP A015, 19/5/00, p. 40; A022, 31/3/00, p. 41; A030, 27/3/00, p. 39; A031, 17/4/00, p. 45; A036, 18/10/00, p. 27; A042, 1/5/00, p. 40. It is not usually clear which edition of the *Handbook* the teachers read.
70 Ministry of Education, *Primary Education*, pp. 25, 58.
71 *Ibid.*, p. 57.
72 *Ibid.*, p. 23.
73 Gillard, *Education in England*.
74 DES, *Children and Their Primary Schools*, p. 311.
75 *Ibid.*, pp. 10-18.
76 *Ibid.*, pp. 11-12. This reflected Piaget's own views on the matter.
77 Robinson, 'Ideology in Teacher Education', p. 77, cited in Cunningham, *Curriculum Change in the Primary School*, p. 78.
78 Brearley, *Fundamentals in the First School*, pp. 159, 166; Marsh, *Alongside the Child*, pp. 12–15.
79 Ridgway and Lawton, *Family Grouping in the Primary School*, 2nd edn, p. 53.

80 This was evident in the two other texts cited by Robinson: Rogers (ed.), *Teaching in the British Primary School*; and Brown and Precious, *The Integrated Day in the Primary School*.
81 Beard, *An Outline of Piaget's Developmental Psychology*, pp. 16, 78.
82 Oxfordshire Pilot, Ox.002, questionnaire, p. 1.
83 Cunningham, *Curriculum Change in the Primary School*, p. 79.
84 L. G. Marsh, 'Number apparatus', *Schoolmaster*, 1 July 1960, p. 32, made brief reference to Piaget; John H. Flavell, 'The developmental psychology of Jean Piaget', *Teacher*, 6 September 1963, p. 4; J. Darbyshire, 'Piaget and the teacher', *Teachers World*, 16 September 1966, p. 13.
85 For instance, WEP A015, 19/5/00, p. 39; A029, 1/11/00, p. 27; A031, 17/4/00, p. 34; A038, 12/6/00, p. 45.
86 Oxfordshire Pilot, Ox. 002, interview.
87 WEP A040, 18/7/00, p. 19; C006, 18/6/01, pp. 16–17; C008, 31/7/01, p. 36; C012, 9/8/01, p. 10; C016, 22/8/01, pp. 15–16; C018, 5/9/01, p. 13.
88 Oxfordshire Pilot, Ox.009, questionnaire, p. 2.
89 For example: WEP G006, 28/3/00.
90 Oxfordshire Pilot, Ox.002, questionnaire, p. 1.
91 G. H. W. Peach, 'Where the training colleges fall down', *Teacher*, 7 June 1963, p. 9.
92 *The Teacher*, 4 February 1966, p. 6.
93 DES, *Teacher Education and Training*, p. 20.
94 Cited in Frisby, 'The History of Educational Psychology Teaching', pp. 124–30.
95 Hilliard, 'Theory and practice', p. 38.
96 Ashton et al., *The Aims of Primary Education*, p. 50.
97 Oxfordshire Pilot, Ox.003, interview.
98 Oxfordshire Pilot, Ox.001, interview.
99 DES, *Teacher Education*, p. 7.
100 Thom, 'The 1944 Education Act'; Wooldridge, *Measuring the Mind*, p. 236.
101 DES, *Primary Education in Wales*, p. 52.
102 'The week's causerie', *Teachers World*, 17 January 1923, p. 782.
103 Robinson, 'Experiment'. Also see *Teachers World*, 16 January 1924, p. 786.
104 P. Ballard, 'Is there a "break at 11"?', *Teachers World*, 16 January 1929, p. 829.
105 DES, *Children and Their Primary Schools*, p. 98.
106 Cambridgeshire Archives, Uncatalogued: St Albans School Logbooks, 8 September 1960.
107 DES, *Primary Education in Wales*, p. 4.
108 National Archives, ED 156/54, HMI Report, Horspath Church of England School, 29 January 1948.
109 National Archives, ED 156/54, HMI Report, Goring Church of England School, 7 July 1949.
110 Oxfordshire Archives, S112/1/A1/3, Garsington Church of England School Logbook, 9 December 1947, HMI Report.

111 One in five teachers in the secondary modern schools in 1955 were emergency trained, indicating that they had trained during or after the war. See Taylor, *The Secondary Modern School*, p. 203.
112 Oxfordshire Archives, OXOHA:LT 222 – W. D. Campbell – '*My Choice*', BBC Oxford, interviewed by Penny Faust (1984).
113 Oxfordshire Archives, OXOHA:LT 276 – No.79 Connie Norman, '*My Choice*', BBC Radio Oxford, undated.
114 For example, see WEP D020, 6/6/01, p. 25; G005, 10/4/00, p. 30; G019, 26/11/01, p. 21, C026, 4/12/01, p. 14.
115 For example, see WEP A006, 31/7/98, pp. 1, 15; A016, 18/9/98 and 25/9/98, pp. 10, 18; A030, 27/3/00, p. 7; A033, 25/5/00, p. 13, on training as an infants' teacher; and WEP A084, 25/1/01, p. 21; A088, 15/1/01, p. 16; C010, 7/8/01, p. 8, on teaching a range of ages.
116 History in Education, Patricia Dawson interviewed by Nicola Sheldon (2010); Evelyn Hinde interviewed by Nicola Sheldon (2010), pp. 1, 3. The focus on infant-junior teachers in the 1950s resulted from a national shortage after the wartime baby boom.
117 History in Education, Roberta Wood interviewed by Nicola Sheldon (2010), p. 18.
118 Oxfordshire Pilot, Ox.006, interview; Ox.002, interview; Ox.005, interview.
119 For example, WEP C010, 7/8/01, p. 8.
120 DES, *Children and Their Primary Schools*, pp. 284–7.
121 *Teachers World*, 26 January 1968, p. 7. DES, *Primary Education in Wales*, p. 73.
122 Moorhouse, 'Philosophy', in Rogers (ed.), *Teaching in the British Primary School*, p. 4.
123 Baines, 'Social', in Rogers (ed.), *Teaching in the British Primary School*, p. 201.
124 DES, *Children and Their Primary Schools*, p. 284. Molly Brearley makes the same argument in *Fundamentals in the First School*, p. 143.
125 Oxfordshire Archives, OXOHA:OT 257 – Mel Summers interviewed by Malcolm Graham (1997). Duncan Webster discusses cultural fears of 'Americanisation' in Britain and the ultimate unreality of such fears in *Looka Yonder!*.
126 Galton *et al.*, *Inside the Primary Classroom*, p. 55; Cunningham, *Curriculum Change in the Primary School*, p. 18.
127 DES, *Children and Their Primary Schools*, pp. 285–6.
128 DES, *Primary Education*, p. 21.

3

'Trendy, airy-fairy methods': teachers' resistance to progressive education

In both inter-war and post-war England and Wales, teachers' professional organisations, teaching journals and teacher training colleges were all deeply concerned that teaching should be recognised as a 'profession'.[1] This concern often lay behind shifts in training and pedagogy, for example the moves to normalise a two-year and then a three-year training college course as the central route into teaching, and the emphasis on the acquisition of a body of theoretical knowledge which was increasingly focused on educational and developmental psychology.[2] However, teachers themselves, equally determined to assert their professional status, did not always come up with the same solutions. Instead, they perceived teaching as a learnt craft or skill, rather than a formal discipline that could be taught at college. Craft knowledge could only be acquired through actual experience in the classroom.[3] The declining status of the teacher – which teachers who started teaching in the 1920s perceived as acutely as teachers who started in the 1970s – was not, in teachers' eyes, because of poor training and professional standards, but because of social and cultural change that had led to disrespect from both parents and pupils.

Therefore, teachers' resistance to both educational psychology and child-centred pedagogy should be interpreted not as blind opposition to new ideas, but as a logical response given the way they conceived of professional authority. New methods were untried and untested, and were often advocated by people who had little or no experience of class teaching themselves. When teachers were enjoined to practise child-centred methods, they were often implemented only partially and incoherently. Teachers articulated their reasons for resistance in both contemporary correspondence to teaching journals and retrospective oral history interviews. However, their inability to fully control educational change affected both their teaching practice and their concepts of childhood. Post-war generations of teachers, predominantly qualifying through teacher training colleges rather than through the practical 'student-teacher year' that had been available in the inter-war period, still bought into older definitions of expertise but had less access to this kind of professional authority at the beginning of their teaching careers. Young teachers were stigmatised as 'unprofessional' for adopting 'trendy' methods because they lacked a proper understanding of the children in their care. Meanwhile, older teachers built their expertise on a life-cycle model, claiming that only trial and error had brought them to where they were now.

Recognising the importance of classroom practice for pedagogical change, historians of education Peter Cunningham and Philip Gardner, along with Stephen Hussey, who carried out the bulk of the WEP interviews, have suggested that the Second World War was a significant turning point for non-utopian progressive education.[4] Their argument focuses on the experience of teachers evacuated with their classes, who had to teach under very different conditions and, they claimed, used this relative freedom to experiment with more child-centred teaching methods and also to engage with the surrounding environment. Lacking textbooks, classroom space and apparatus, the argument runs, these teachers had to improvise and discovered the value of practical, local and natural teaching for themselves. Maurice Galton, Brian Simon and Paul Croll similarly consider the impact of evacuation, suggesting that '[a] kind of backlog of progressive ideas and practices built up almost since 1911' was 'reinforced by war-time evacuation experiences, when teachers were driven back onto their own resources and began to act both more autonomously and more flexibly than before'.[5]

Galton *et al.* ultimately argue that the partial abolition of the 11-plus was more significant than evacuation experiences, as primary schools that did not have to prepare pupils for the examination were freer to participate in progressivism. This, they suggest, was the reason why Leicestershire, the West Riding of Yorkshire and Oxfordshire, along with Bristol and London, were especially progressive from the mid-1950s onwards, as they were local education authorities where 'the 11-plus was early abolished or profoundly modified'.[6] Galton *et al.*'s argument is less convincing, however, when it is recalled that these counties possessed substantive progressive traditions well before the mid-1950s. It seems more likely that the more progressive LEAs would have abolished the 11-plus, rather than the other way around.[7] As Martin Francis points out, rural Conservative-controlled local authorities such as Southend and Anglesey were often forced to adopt comprehensive schools early due to the difficulty of providing separate schools for such a scattered population, but this did not lead to progressive policies being adopted in these LEAs.[8] Furthermore, other exceptionally progressive counties, such as Hertfordshire, do not fit this pattern. The 11-plus persisted in Hertfordshire at least until 1956, but it was one of the earliest counties to develop progressive practice and school design under the influence of John Newsom, who was chief education officer for the county from 1940.[9] Galton et al.'s suggestion that progressive education and the 11-plus stood in opposition to each other neglects to consider both the significant influence of non-utopian progressivism on secondary modern schools and that, in many ways, the 11-plus was in harmony with progressive ideals as it aimed to provide different types of education for different types of children.[10]

While the experience of evacuated teachers may have contributed to the widespread adoption of progressivism after the war, this was also not a key turning point for grass-roots practice. Although concurring with Galton et al. that the 1950s were when progressive practice really took off, I highlight the importance of a different set of factors. As we shall see over the course of the next two chapters, the influence of the individual teacher – as opposed to *teachers* as a whole – on teaching methods was limited. Furthermore, the numbers of evacuated teachers in 1939 were not necessarily representative of the profession as a whole, and many of these would not have experienced evacuation long-term.[11] A new cohort of teachers who would not have been evacuated – so-called emergency trained teachers, who entered via a one-year training course – also formed a significant proportion of the profession from the 1940s, and disproportionately altered its attitudes, both because of the new ideas they brought and because of the responses of traditionally trained teachers to them.[12] Teachers certainly did contribute to shaping educational experience in this period, but it was not their enthusiastic adoption of progressive methods that really mattered. As Adrian Wooldridge has argued, progressive teachers had to gain power in schools and local authorities to be truly influential, and 'their influence on educational practice, like their influence on educational policy, probably increased in the 1940s and 1950s, as the recruits of the 1930s moved up the occupational ladder.'[13] Hence, it was a generational shift, rather than the experience of war, that was central to the widespread adoption of child-centred methods, and this was not a shift in which all teachers enthusiastically participated.

'You're in a profession': teachers, practical experience and professional identity

Teachers' claims to professional expertise throughout both the inter-war and post-war periods were based not on the mastery of a body of theoretical knowledge, but on practical experience in the classroom. Compared with classic 'professions' such as medicine and the law, the professional status of teaching remained contested throughout this period, despite strenuous efforts on the part of organisations such as the NUT to establish it on an equal footing. Eric Hoyle and Peter John have explored why teaching does not fit the established professional model. They assert that, in the traditional understanding of a 'profession', knowledge gained through experience is 'important but insufficient' and a profession needs to draw on a body of systematic knowledge, acquired through a lengthy period of higher education. A profession will also set its own code of ethics, possess autonomy in shaping appropriate practice and possess a strong influence in shaping public policy. The rewards of professional practice are a high salary and social status. Hoyle and John dispute the usefulness of this definition, stating that, under it, teaching remains a 'semi-profession', due to its limited reliance on 'special knowledge' and lack of independence and high remuneration.[14] Keith, a thirty-eight-year-old teacher interviewed in the early 1980s, who 'came straight from industry' into teaching, summed up the confused professional claims of teaching from another angle by comparing it to a 'trade':

> My first reaction when kids messed about in class was to give them a smack round the head. And I was soon told that was unprofessional conduct ... but ... what is professional conduct then? ... I don't think I've ever seen a job specification ... What does the profession entail? What are the criteria? What are the norms of behaviour ... until they tell me the rules of the trade, as it were, I don't know what's considered professional or unprofessional.[15]

Teaching, hence, lacked both a body of specialised scientific knowledge and a clear practical rulebook to define its own professional standards.

However, teachers frequently argued that these omissions were inherent in the nature of the job. First, they suggested, you could only become a good teacher by trying things out, and second, teachers' practice was expected to differ, as the majority of the profession did not assume that there was a single set of correct methods that could be disseminated. In this context, teachers' resistance to both developmental psychology and child-centred education was not simply stubborn, old-fashioned behaviour, but a rational response given what they felt it meant to be a teacher. Recognising that practice, not theory, was key to teaching, they were naturally suspicious of methods they had not used successfully before. Indeed, older teachers might suggest that pedagogical innovation was cyclical, and fashions in teaching method would inevitably change, so should not be taken too seriously.

Diana Laffin, who started teaching history in the early 1980s at a comprehensive school, was interviewed in 2009 for the History in Education Project with a group of teachers of varying ages. Throughout the group interview, Diana defended her scepticism about novel teaching methods by reference to her age and experience, often suggesting that these 'trends' had already been tried before. For example, when discussing 'humanities and theme-based teaching', which aimed to eliminate subject divisions by emphasising the connections between the humanities subjects, she stated 'I do feel we've come full circle because I know that humanities and theme-based teaching I think is an in-thing now. So when you're my age you've sort of seen it all really . . . I am a lot older than you two and I have to say, I think there is some continuity in good teaching.'[16] My Oxfordshire respondents, who all started teaching in the 1970s, slightly earlier than Diana, reflected similar views; a male secondary teacher wrote that 'Nothing really phased me as I had seen it all before.'[17] WEP respondents who had started teaching two or more decades earlier often presented the same views, despite the fact that their teaching careers spanned a completely different period.[18]

In this context, the intrusion of formalised child-centred methods was inevitably perceived as a threat to existing ideals of expertise. Therefore, teachers' complaints about educational psychology might be viewed in another light. While many teachers undoubtedly struggled with this academic subject, others might have felt enjoined to decry it as 'useless', even when they found useful things in it, because it was perceived as undermining their own experiential knowledge of children. This kind of reaction could be found among teachers who trained in both the inter-war and post-war period. Ronald Gould, who was to become General Secretary of the NUT from 1947 to 1970, trained at Westminster College from 1922 to 1924. He recalled attending his first lecture on 'The psychology of the unconscious', given by the well-known psychologist and textbook writer J. C. Ross, in his memoir *Chalk Up the Memory* (1976). 'As I . . . had never heard of psychology, could not even spell it correctly, and laboured under the delusion that "unconscious" meant being knocked silly, I did not find this easy to follow.'[19] Gould went on to do well in psychology and the theory of education, but comments later in his memoir that life was 'simpler' for teachers in the 1920s as 'psychologists, sociologists, psycho-metricians and curriculum experts hardly existed'. In some ways, he argued, this was a better situation than in the 1970s, as teachers were not enjoined to use methods they did not feel confident applying.[20] Given his success in psychology examinations, this suggests that his memory of his initial confusion may have been deliberately selected for this memoir to prove a point about the role of psychology in education. More broadly, it is sometimes difficult to disentangle whether teachers who recall not being able to understand psychology in this period were truly baffled, or whether they resisted the idea of a body of expertise external to that of the craft of teaching.

In this context, we can consider the career of one of my Oxfordshire interviewees, Jan, who trained to teach secondary school pupils from 1975–79, undertaking an initial year of training before completing a three-year B.Ed at Westminster. Jan's B.Ed essays indicate a thorough grasp of contemporary work on child psychology, sociology and pedagogy, with subjects ranging from 'Discuss the view that the phenomenon of adolescence may be entirely explained in terms of a ghetto of age' to 'What can be said about either learning theories or theories of motivation advocated by child-centred educationalists?'. Far from struggling with psychology, Jan effectively deconstructed ideas about child-centred education in her latter essay, arguing that it contained a number of inherent contradictions; most notably, it preserved the formal authority of the teacher, as some form of adult criteria always has to be imposed to decide what is taught in schools. 'To claim that to teach the "interests" of the child is good is somewhat deceitful in that what is really being taught is something presupposed by someone else to be the correct thing to teach,' she wrote.[21] Jan received an A grade for this piece of work. Nevertheless, she stated in her interview that she no longer remembered anything about stages of development, and that she was unconvinced by sociology: 'the outcome was determined by the question that you asked. I felt you had a huge power in sociology over... producing the answers you want.'[22] Jan was perfectly capable of understanding psychological and sociological theories of education; she simply didn't agree with them or find them useful in her teaching.

The threat posed by child-centred educational theory was magnified by the decline of alternative routes into teaching that had been based on practical experience in the classroom, and the increasing dominance of a training college education that centred philosophy, psychology and sociology, especially for those teachers who were not university graduates. Peter Cunningham and Philip Gardner have shown that the Board of Education and the NUT were increasingly determined to phase unqualified teachers out of the profession from the 1930s onwards. Pupil-teaching had been abolished in 1907, but the inter-war student-teacher scheme was intended as a chance to gain a year's practical experience before commencing a training college course. However, a number of these recruits went on to gain posts as uncertificated teachers without going through training college, which heightened official concern. Local authorities began to drop student-teacher schemes after a Board of Education Departmental Committee report from 1925 discouraged the practice, and Cunningham and Gardner suggest that by 1939 in most LEAs, and certainly by the late 1940s, the student-teacher year was extinct.[23] This is borne out by case-study evidence. For example, in Oxfordshire, a 1927 Board of Education circular informed headteachers that they were no longer to apply to the Board to recognise the employment of student-teachers or pupil-teachers, although a later letter of the same year indicated that rural pupil-teachers were exempt. The system of rural pupil-teaching was finally discontinued in 1932.[24] So while some teachers who started teaching in the 1930s, and many of the teachers *already* teaching in that decade, may have experienced a student-teacher year, it would not have been an experience shared by those who started teaching from the 1940s onwards except in a handful of localities.

Cunningham and Gardner's conclusions on the closure of this scheme suggest that it ended a period in teacher training which had 'continued to acknowledge among its principles the centrality of the classroom ... [and] a positive role for the practicing teacher'.[25] As this summation implies, the reduction of classroom experience in teacher training meant a reduction in the emphasis placed on the practical expertise of the teacher and a corresponding increase in the significance of theoretical educational psychology. This indicates that there was more at stake for teachers than a conflict between theory and practice. By linking their professional identity to theoretical knowledge, teachers could make stronger claims to be regarded as a profession than if they centred this identity around a skill-based understanding of their pupils gained through work.[26] As Cunningham and Gardner further state, the decline of classroom practice in teacher training also meant the decline 'of a traditional sympathy between schools provided for the working class and teachers who came from the working class'.[27] Jennifer Ozga and Martin Lawn also engage with this question by adopting a 'labour process' approach to their analysis of teaching. Through analysing teaching as work, they are able to explore the relationships between teachers and the state, their employers and their unions, suggesting that professionalisation was a top-down model that sat uncomfortably with the grass-roots origins of teaching.[28] Teaching was becoming a more middle-class profession not solely because of the changing social origins of its recruits, but because it was striving to adopt a middle-class professional ethos.

Older and more experienced teachers might also feel under attack from younger recruits who used their more recent knowledge of educational innovation, garnered from training college courses, to assert authority. In educational discourse in both the inter-war and post-war periods, it was an established cliché that a new teacher would try to introduce innovations in their first school, but that they either should not or would not be able to do this. This assumption linked to the professional ideal by asserting that new teachers needed to fit into an existing school community and accept the guidance and support of longer-serving teachers. As progressive innovation became increasingly linked to youth in the post-war period – perhaps as part of a wider shift in the 1950s and 1960s that identified the young with positive social change – the emphasis shifted from 'should not' to 'could not', but the barrier was evidently still there.[29] An example of the older attitude is provided by a *Teachers World* article from 1939; a Director of Education advised the young teacher to remember that 'the school he will enter will probably have evolved a technique after many years' experience by a staff who are as sensible and as well-qualified as himself' and so he should not adopt 'a superior attitude'. Any scheme he wanted to introduce would probably be rejected by the head.[30] W. W. Sawyer, a maths teacher, put the other side of the case in the *Schoolmaster* in 1946, stating that

> a young teacher with modern ideas of education should take the greatest care in choosing a headmaster or headmistress. It is impossible to teach well without the co-operation of the head ... The keen young teacher who has to work in an old-fashioned school usually becomes embittered and worn out, and ends by believing that children's natures make real education in schools an impossibility.[31]

In reality, young teachers found that they possessed limited space for innovation, at least before the 1950s and 1960s. Kathleen Chapman, who started teaching in the 1920s in Oxfordshire, was asked during her oral history interview in 1974, 'Did you ever try to develop ideas which the school didn't approve of?' Kathleen answered, 'Well I don't think so, not at that time, no. Probably when you after you'd been away to College you came out with ideas you see, but I don't ever remember, you wouldn't be experienced enough or confident enough to do it.'[32] WEP respondents also frequently recalled that, even when their teaching practice had changed during evacuation, they were unable to implement these changes after the war because of the dominant influence of the headteacher: a key factor that limited the impact of wartime experience in promoting educational change.[33]

Young teachers were often associated with a particular visual image by WEP respondents. They were pictured as badly dressed upstarts using 'trendy' methods.[34] This image was reflected in contemporary texts. In 1953, 'Onlooker' attacked the poor dress of younger teachers in *Teachers World*: 'a number had been wearing polo-necked sweaters under their jackets ... a teacher should wear a collar and tie.'[35] Edward Colton also criticised 'The Young Teacher' in 1954, reminding him 'You're in a profession'. He gave the example of a teacher who 'goes to school looking like a tramp' in 'corduroys, a neckerchief instead of a tie, thick crepe-soled shoes and red-and-white socks. His shirt was a loudish check'.[36] 'Onlooker's comment that teachers were dressing like 'tractor driver[s]' indicates that one perceived problem with this mode of dress was that it was undermining the distinction between the profession and manual workers. Several WEP respondents also refer explicitly to the idea that the casual clothes and manners of younger teachers eroded important status distinctions.[37] Catherine Horwood's study of inter-war fashion indicates that typical dress for a male teacher, as a low-paid professional, might have been a cheap suit with a clean collar, shirt and handkerchief, so these outfits contrasted strongly with older expectations of dress.[38]

The identification of youth and progressivism indicates that age was a factor in teachers' assessments. Patricia J. Sikes has argued that a life-cycle approach is particularly relevant when assessing teachers' professional identities, because their position in the life-cycle not only affected their relationships to their colleagues, but to the children they taught. Emlyn, a thirty-three-year-old teacher, stated in the early 1980s that 'They [the pupils] stay young, they stay young and they stay young, and you get older and older . . . That's what I dislike about teaching.' Teachers near the end of their careers felt that they were seen as 'past it' by both pupils and younger colleagues, and resented the fact that their experience was not valued.[39] Interestingly, however, Ashton et al.'s survey indicated that younger teachers were no more likely to be progressive than older ones, so this image may have been based on stereotypes of youth rather than actual experience.[40]

Older teachers defended themselves by emphasising the importance of practical experience in retrospective accounts, demonstrating that they were not simply reacting against new ideas, but asserting a positive ideal of learnt expertise. This was evident in my Oxfordshire oral histories. One female secondary teacher reflected:

> As I have got older and more confident, I have been able to relax more with my classes – I can get them quiet and settled very quickly when I need to. At the start, I was not used to being creative in my discipline methods, when to call for help, and the age gap between me and my oldest students was just four years – so I felt I needed to maintain a firm control. Though actually I have a firmer control now because the students know and understand my expectations.[41]

Women, unlike men, often linked these gains not only to teaching experience but to the experience of parenthood. In contrast, male interviewees usually agreed that becoming a father had been an influence on their teaching career when directly questioned about it, but did not bring up the topic themselves.[42] Alongside gendered norms, this may have been because female teachers often took a 'career break' after having children and returned to the profession later in life, so wanted to quantify what their time out had given them, especially when they encountered pedagogical norms that had dramatically altered once they were back in the classroom.

The 'marriage bar' that operated in most LEAs during the inter-war period prevented the vast majority of female teachers from combining the roles of teacher and mother, forcing them to leave the profession upon marriage.[43] Alison Oram notes that by 1926 about three-quarters of LEAs operated some form of marriage bar, and by 1939 about 80 to 90 per cent had a bar in place.[44] However, in the post-war period, with marriage bars lifted, the phenomenon of 'married women returners' became a recognised phenomenon by the 1960s, with authorities concerned to attract trained women back into teaching.[45] The Ministry of Education's *Education in 1961* report indicated that half of female teachers had left the profession five years after beginning their careers, contributing to a continuing shortage of teachers.[46] Plowden estimated that half of *all* teachers in maintained schools were married women, compared with 10 per cent of *female* teachers in the 1930s at the height of the marriage bars.[47] This linked to a wider trend of married women working in the 1950s and 1960s, but also indicated that teaching was seen as a particularly appropriate profession for a married woman and, given the high birth rate, that female teachers were likely to experience parenthood.[48]

In both the WEP and Oxfordshire pilot interviews, female respondents frequently asserted that having their own children made them relate to their pupils in a different way. Patricia Sikes's study of 'the life-cycle of the teacher' in the early 1980s made similar observations. Sikes noted that female teachers thought they returned more as 'mums' to the children after having a career break: 'The "advantage" mentioned by all mid-career women with children was that of greater understanding and sympathy.' Ann, forty-three, thought that 'Having your own children must change the way you see children . . . you get an understanding of children but you don't really know where you got it from.' The Oxfordshire pilot interviewees who had their own children all emphasised how important the experience of mothering had been for their teaching practice. Debbie thought that 'After having my own child, I became different – better, I think.'[49] Carol, who had her first child in 1977 after she had already been teaching for seven years, stated in her questionnaire that one of 'the biggest influences' on her teaching had been 'my own children! I learnt so much more about child development'.[50]

Even when female teachers had had no children of their own, they would emphasise the importance of getting to know children in different environments. Ruth, my only childless female Oxfordshire interviewee, when asked 'over the course of your career have you found that, as you've got older yourself, has the relationship with the children changed?' turned immediately to discourses about parenting:

> I'm not a mother myself but I've got friends with – whose young children I've looked after and they've grown up with me and I've grown sort of grown older with them – I think that how I deal with children is different . . . Just as a parent gets more confident with the second child than they were with the first child, I think with teaching you get more confident in how to deal with young people.[51]

Taking a career break to become a full-time mother could also alter female teachers' relationship with the theoretical discourses of child-centred education, especially if they also encountered child-centred parenting advice guides such as Benjamin Spock's *Baby and Child Care* (first British edition, 1955) and Penelope Leach's *Baby and Child* (1977).[52] Most obviously, spending time outside the workplace meant that shifts in teaching practice struck women with greater force upon their return. Some WEP respondents went further than this, commenting that they were more favourably disposed to non-utopian progressive pedagogy after becoming mothers. This was reflected by Carol, who felt that 'it's taken me until bringing up my own children' to become really 'excited' about psychological theories of child development, '. . . maybe because I've got practical experience of it'. She told a story about watching her grandson pouring water between different-sized containers – a classic example used by Piaget to illustrate children's shifts in understanding about the conservation of matter – and commented that 'it's really fascinating to think ah, at some point he'll think about this differently'.[53] Another kind of response, however, which tallies with other teachers' narratives of their careers, was to comment on how rapidly things had changed, usually for the worse. Philip Gardner records the testimony of a female teacher, Marian, born in 1905, who returned to teaching in 1952 after a career break. She recalled:

> I thought, "I'll never cope", because by that time, of course, there was a, sort of, different attitude between the children. They just didn't sit still and be told what to do. They'd got minds of their own and very often their minds were very different from what we expected them to be . . . Now, children are inclined to question, which I think is a good thing, but it's the way it's done that makes teaching difficult I think, these days.[54]

However, Marian had started teaching almost two decades earlier than Carol, Ruth and Debbie, and her inter-war training would have been markedly different from theirs, which may help to explain her less enthusiastic response to child-centred practice, alongside the familiar sense among older teachers that their pupils' behaviour and attitudes were getting worse.

Traditional or progressive? Teachers' responses to pedagogical innovations

In June 1967, G. L. Haynes, a primary school teacher who had been teaching for the past thirty years and hence had trained in the inter-war period, wrote to the *Teacher*. While she got good results and had a good relationship with her class, she explained, she felt that 'modern methods' were seen as 'the only aspects of education worthy of discussion and notice', and despite pressure from HMIs, she was resistant to adopting them.[55] Haynes's letter sparked off an outpouring of correspondence that lasted more than three months. A letter from training college student Christine Philips in July ignited the debate. Philips argued that Haynes had given an inaccurate depiction of modern education, and had ignored the need to 'educate the whole child'.[56] Philips' intervention embodied the concerns of many inter-war trained teachers, as Philips had yet had no experience of teaching, and was basing her claims on psychological theory.

A fortnight later, Haynes responded to the disturbance her letter had created. 'So far,' she wrote, 'apart from private discussions among teachers themselves, very little really knowledgeable criticism [of modern methods] is ever voiced in the Press. I have had many letters from teachers all over the country supporting my views.' She was aware of Philips' arguments, she wrote, but felt that she should never have to use methods she did not believe in, and Philips needed at least five or six years of teaching experience before she expressed a view.[57] It was an anonymous letter, in September 1967, that gave the final word on the debate, and, in doing so, not only effectively summed up the exchanges but a wider stance of resistance to child-centred education: 'One shudders to think how many people with the enthusiastic lack of experience of Miss Philips coupled with most excellent paper qualifications may be dictating primary policy from exalted levels', he/she wrote, giving the examples of HMIs, advisers and training colleges. 'I wonder how many primary teachers feel that things are not as they should be, that they are being inundated with new ideas, methods, subjects.'[58] Haynes herself asserted that her reason for writing had been 'so that the country may know what is really going on behind the scenes in education'.[59]

It is evident that older teachers felt especially threatened by the implied criticisms of their methods. Unlike Christine Philips, G. L. Haynes had already been teaching for thirty years, and now, she felt, she was being told that her life's work had been wasted. But what were the 'modern methods' that Haynes resisted and Philips defended? Non-utopian progressive education was never unified around a single set of desirable child-centred practices, but certain broad trends can be identified, especially from the 1950s onwards. These shifts will be considered in greater detail in the next three chapters, but in summary, child-centred educationalists tended to recommend changes in class organisation, a reorientation towards more practical, active and participatory forms of teaching, including the use of novel apparatus, and the integration of subjects rather than the maintenance of formal subject-divisions, especially in the humanities. 'Best practice' for class organisation, especially in primary schools, underwent substantial shifts during the period under consideration. During the inter-war period, child-centred pedagogy promoted individual project-work through schemes such as the Dalton Plan and Project Method. By the 1950s, group work was more popular and, by the 1970s, more elaborate schemes such as the integrated day and family grouping were gaining ground. Similarly, 'practical' teaching could range from relatively passive methods, such as providing children with a 'nature table' in the classroom to which they could add their own finds, to much more participatory strategies that encouraged children to discover facts for themselves. These might utilise familiar forms of technology such as library books, or unfamiliar innovations such as Cuisenaire rods – coloured rods which could be used to teach basic mathematical operations such as addition and subtraction, fractions and sequences. Finally, child-centred educationalists recommended the breakdown of subject-divisions in a range of ways, from integrated 'projects' to humanities topics based around the local community, and 'team teaching' where a range of teachers taught a single class. These methods theoretically expressed the central child-centred commitments to individual, natural, practical, local and enjoyable education, although these commitments, as the next three chapters will explore in greater depth, were not always borne out in practice.

The sequence of correspondence between Haynes and Philips encapsulated teachers' concerns about 'modern methods' in the 1950s and 1960s. A number of discursive strategies were used to attack 'child-centred' or 'progressive' education. One cultural script, used by a number of the WEP respondents, was the idea that children themselves did not enjoy child-centred methods. This argument was particularly appealing because it turned the arguments of child-centred educationalists against them, and so was positioned as the final word on the matter. In texts or interviews, teachers often ended a lengthy critique of child-centred methods with this point, and frequently expanded it into a story of an actual encounter with a child or adolescent.[60] In the second volume of the *Black Papers* (1968) a teacher, June Wedgewood Benn, argued that 'children like peace and quiet' and that child-centred educationalists need to pay more attention to 'the differing responses of individual children. Some do not *like* painting, some hate noise . . .'[61] Even teachers who had trained near the end of this period, and who tended to be more broadly supportive of child-centred methods, often pointed out that they could cause pupils to disengage. Brian, who taught history in secondary schools, criticised the rise of unified 'humanities' curriculums in the 1970s, saying that they were 'killing history' by repeating the same topics across all the subjects, so his pupils became bored. He recalled the class's comments at the start of one of his lessons: 'Don't tell us sir . . . today we must be doing the history of electricity.'[62]

Drawing on accumulated knowledge, teachers also tended to argue, in both the inter-war and post-war periods, that they knew and understood 'normal' children much better than the psychologist or psychiatrist. First, teachers had contact with far greater numbers of children than the other professions. George Green, a lecturer in education at the University College of Wales, wrote to the *Schoolmaster* in 1935, 'No psychologist in his laboratory, no physician in his consulting-room, no child specialist in his clinic, has a tithe of the opportunities of the teacher for learning about children.'[63] Second, it was contended that teachers understood 'normal' as well as 'abnormal' children, giving them a more balanced perspective on their pupils – although this argument was often asserted through stigmatising children with mental health issues or learning disabilities. *Teachers World* put this case in 1954: 'The value of his [the psychologist's] theoretical knowledge is vastly outweighed by the schoolmaster's daily contacts with children – ordinary children, not merely with the freaks.'[64] Third, teachers, unlike any other professionals, had the opportunity for longitudinal observation of their subjects, day after day. In 1959, the periodical commented on the tendency within child guidance services 'for the psychologist or psychiatrist to set up as a tin god – knowing better after a half-hour interview than the teacher, who has known the child for years'.[65]

Another common criticism of progressivism was expressed in the frequently used term 'airy-fairy', suggesting that progressive methods lacked a clear philosophy or expressed aims. The consistency with which the term 'airy fairy' appears in both contemporary complaints and retrospective accounts indicates that teachers were drawing on a broader discourse about young teachers and falling standards that was prevalent in the 1950s and 1960s, as well as in the late twentieth and early twenty-first centuries, when the WEP and Cannadine respondents were interviewed. Patricia Dawson, who trained in the 1960s and was interviewed by Nicola Sheldon for *The Right Kind of History*, remembered how the focus of history teaching switched in the 1970s from telling the story of history to focus on source analysis, which she felt had 'gone too far' because 'they had no framework; it was just too nebulous . . . it was just so airy fairy'.[66] The term, also used by a number of WEP respondents in retrospective interviews, was also linked in contemporary accounts to teachers who were seen to be idealising children or failing to prepare them for the 'real world'.[67] Howard Peach, whom we have already encountered complaining about his training college experience in 1956, wrote to *Teachers World* in 1960 to make a similar complaint about refresher courses, which he felt contained 'too much of the airy-fairy stuff they used to trot out at training college . . . the inevitable concession to psychology'.[68]

Teachers often returned to the idea that public respect for the teaching profession was decreasing due to changing attitudes from pupils, parents and the wider community, and blamed progressive or child-centred innovations for this trend. However, this idea was repeated in both retrospective narratives and contemporary sources throughout this period, whether the teacher had predominantly worked in the 1920s and 1930s or the 1960s and 1970s, and was linked to the recurring worries about younger generations that Geoffrey Pearson has identified.[69] This was a common narrative through all the WEP interviews.[70] Ethel Mace started teaching in Kidlington primary school in 1929. When interviewed in 1997, she recalled that it had been easy to deal with evacuees during the war because 'they weren't tough like they are nowadays', reiterating that discipline was easy in those days because there was respect.[71] Pupils were not the only group who were seen to have lost respect for the teaching profession. Connie Norman, who started teaching in the 1930s in Croydon, was 'quite certain that we had much more respect in those days, particularly from the parents of the children which we taught'.[72]

It was not only inter-war teachers who identified this narrative. My Oxfordshire respondents, who started teaching in the 1970s, almost all put forward the same view. John recalled that 'when I came into teaching there was a lot of respect. Parents appreciated what you did. Now they come in and they're just challenging all the time.'[73] Similarly, children's behaviour was seen to have deteriorated, as in the inter-war narratives. Lynn thought that 'Teachers have to handle much more poor behaviour' nowadays.[74] These repeated scripts suggest that it was not the wider sociocultural climate that was solely at fault, but the perceived lack of respect afforded to older teachers – especially as the younger respondents experienced a 'golden age' of teaching precisely when the older respondents felt everything was going downhill.

However, teachers' expressed resistance to 'progressive' or 'child-centred education' – what Haynes termed 'modern methods' – was not as simple as it seemed. The idea of 'progressive' teaching was often tagged to different sets of pedagogical assumptions, indicating that these teachers were not resisting child-centred education because they identified as 'traditional' rather than 'progressive', but because progressivism, for them, meant something different. Regardless of their own particular practice, teachers tended to present themselves as standing at a 'golden mean' between 'traditional' and 'modern' methods.[75] Haynes, for example, stated that she was aware of the 'social and cultural' aspects of education, indicating her awareness of the greater significance of sociology and the environment in modern pedagogical discourse, but also supported a quiet and orderly classroom.[76]

Despite continuing resistance throughout this period, some earlier child-centred methods became commonplace, although teachers continued to criticise newer innovations. Howard Peach wrote a number of articles for the *Teacher* where he engaged with the subject more carefully, perhaps aware of the more progressive stance of the latter journal. In a 1967 article, Peach focused on mathematics in 'The noise of passing bandwagons', an obvious reference to the emptiness of 'trends'; the idea of 'jumping on a bandwagon' was another commonly used script for criticism of child-centred methods, employed by a number of oral history respondents.[77] Gordon Pemberton wrote in *Teachers World* in 1973 that while teachers should aim for integrated learning, 'the integration of learning is not a bandwaggon [sic] to be jumped on'.[78] Pemberton was far from a traditionalist; he had published articles on modern mathematics in *Teachers World* since the late 1960s, emphasising the use of Cuisenaire rods for concrete work, and had been criticised by J. C. Gagg in 1971 for being 'as hooked on your little rods as some people used to be on their mechanical tables. Is there *nothing* to maths but bits of wood?'[79] Gagg had been seen as a progressive himself in the 1940s and 1950s, advocating free activity in the classroom and proposing an 'Anti-Sum League' in 1950, but now, as he pointed out, he had been repositioned as a reactionary as fashions had changed.[80]

In this context, therefore, progressivism can be seen more as an attitude of mind than a commitment to particular methods or even a certain set of aims for education. You were 'progressive' if you felt that education needed further reform, and became anti-progressive if you thought reform had already gone too far, regardless of how child-centred your methods were. Peach, for example, argued that continual experimentation in maths teaching was confusing, accuracy had been 'debased', and that children needed a 'consistent scheme and basic skills'. However, he added, 'I'm all in favour of mathematical play, experimental, creativity and practical problems' and 'against drill methods unrelated to children's experience or needs'.[81] Given these statements, little divided Peach from a child-centred teacher. His arguments were directed either at a straw man – few schools in England and Wales used a 'Summerhill' framework – or at misapplied child-centred methods, rather than the methods themselves. Interestingly, Philips defended herself against Haynes by insisting that even she was not blindly progressive, using similar phrasing to Peach. She wrote in one of her responses that she believed in modern methods *not* because she wanted to 'jump on the bandwagon' as, at the beginning of her training, 'most of us were fairly sceptical of all this business about freedom and an integrated day', but she had changed her mind after visiting 'experts' teaching at progressive schools. Hence, she related her own convictions back to practical experience, even if the experience in this case was not her own.

Teachers often felt they had to pay 'lip service' to child-centred methods, regardless of their personal beliefs, especially if they did not themselves hold a position of responsibility in the school.[82] Eric Houlder, who trained to teach in 1959, remembered teaching history at North Featherstone County Secondary School in the early 1960s: 'The head was an ex-history teacher . . . he was so enthusiastic, he went on all the courses. He sent me on courses. I enjoyed courses, actually, but he went on them all and he became a bit too enthusiastic on team teaching . . . The team was himself, me, and a student.' Eric 'enjoyed' team teaching, despite his initial reluctance, but thought it was impractical: 'of course the marking was, when you have a whole year group to mark . . . but at least the student could help with that'.[83] Lynn, who trained to teach primary between 1972 and 1973, wrote in her questionnaire that

> in my second school [in Kidlington], the integrated day was fashionable – the day's tasks were outlined in the morning and children were meant to work their way through what was expected over the course of the day at a time of their own choosing. Consequently, some never did much Maths or writing at all! What else could you expect from seven-year-olds? It was another name for chaos.[84]

'Chaos' was a term that was frequently repeated in the 1970s in relation to the integrated day. Gordon Pemberton argued that if teachers were forced into adopting it, this could cause 'chaos', whereas Brenda

Thompson argued in a review of Alice Yardley's *Structure in Early Learning*, which advocated the practice, 'I am afraid teachers who take Miss Yardley's advice too literally and without planning are inviting chaos.'[85] Lynn returned to this theme in her oral history interview, indicating its significance in her own narrative of her career, and adding that she had found this method 'exhausting and draining... It was a really awful, awful way to teach'.[86] Both Eric and Lynn's accounts, therefore, emphasised that they felt they were not only uncomfortable with the methods they were forced to use but that these methods required much more time and energy from the teacher, which was ultimately unsustainable.

'Lip service' could become even more crucial if a teacher was angling for promotion, given the significant influence teachers believed was wielded by the progressive inspectorate. Geoffrey Hearnshaw, who became an HMI in 1967, recalled that 'One disturbing feature was that some teachers obviously felt that HMI were in possession of exclusive inside knowledge.'[87] The Plowden Report noted that some LEAs kept 'promotion lists', which noted 'the records and assessments of their own teachers', and these lists contributed to the teachers' sense that they needed to be seen to conform to modern trends.[88] In some authorities, to get on to 'the promotion list' and to be considered for a headship, a teacher had to satisfy a panel of inspectors, and HMIs could recommend teachers to directors of education and education committees for promotion. Plowden commented that promotion lists do not 'result in the best applicants applying for posts or encourage the interchange of ideas and good practice between different parts of the country', recognising the danger that they posed.

Even where promotion lists were not used, teachers believed that it was important to be seen to support modern methods.[89] *Teachers World* commented in 1966 that a few teachers will pick out the winning 'trends', and 'they will finish at the top of the salary tree', indicating that criticisms of 'trendy' methods tied into the familiar fear of losing out on promotion.[90] Howard Peach's letter to *Teachers World* in 1960, where he deplored 'airy-fairy' methods, also revealed that he experienced this pressure: 'Like many another promotion aspirant, I occasionally attend refresher courses. (Not to do so would mean leaving blank a whole section on that application form for the coveted post!) But what a waste of time they so often turn out to be!'[91]

As we have seen, Peach's attitude to child-centred methods was equivocal; he did not entirely resist innovation, but felt that progressive education could be haphazard and sloppy. Whatever his private views, however, his strategy worked; he finished his career as a headmaster in Yorkshire.[92]

By the late 1960s, ordinary teachers were engaging more closely with professional discourse, creating a shared sense that the 'true professional', drawing as he or she did from practical experience rather than ideological commitments, was not a reactionary traditionalist, or a radical progressive. 'Lip service' meant that some teachers made sure to fulfil the most visible child-centred orthodoxies, while not really understanding why these new methods existed. At its most simplistic, it could mean making physical changes in the classroom while not altering one's own pedagogical style in the slightest, such as moving around the furniture so children were grouped around tables, but continuing to set individual work.[93] Less obviously, teachers might use certain methods but be sceptical about their value, especially if they were enjoined to do so by a more senior colleague. 'Lip service', however, could also mean absorbing certain shibboleths about what children were like, or what they could understand, that had become completely disconnected from their original roots in developmental psychology. Teachers might resist outside expertise, but their relative lack of power in the educational hierarchy meant they had no choice but to adopt some of it, and practical experience of handling a classroom meant that shortcuts that foregrounded children as a group rather than as individuals were much more likely to be taken. The realities of dealing with large classes, inadequate buildings and a lack of basic facilities forestalled genuinely progressive reform throughout the inter-war period and until well after the Second World War.

Notes

1 Gardner, 'Teachers' in Aldrich (ed.), *A Century of Education*.
2 *Teachers World*, 5 January 1962, p. 1, noted that a new three-year training course had been introduced.
3 Scott, *Seeing Like a State*, p. 320. Teachers' claims for professional status also took place in the context of a society where increasing emphasis was placed upon the professional ideal. See Perkin, *The Rise of Professional Society*, pp. xii–xiii.

4 Gardner and Cunningham, 'Oral history and teachers' professional practice'; Gardner, Cunningham and Hussey, 'Wartime experiences and the teachers' role', pp. 6–8; Hussey, 'The school air-raid shelter'.
5 Galton *et al.*, *Inside the Primary Classroom*, p. 39.
6 *Ibid.* Also see Dent, *Education in Transition*, p. 155 and Blackie, *Inside the Primary School*, p. 10.
7 Cunningham, *Curriculum Change in the Primary School*, pp. 49–58, 183, discusses Oxfordshire and the West Riding of Yorkshire, and notes that Hertfordshire was another exceptionally progressive county.
8 Francis, 'A socialist policy for education?', p. 325.
9 Hertfordshire was a case study in Floud *et al.*, *Social Class and Educational Opportunity*, p. 33.
10 On progressive practice in secondary moderns, see Taylor, *The Secondary Modern School*, Dent, *Secondary Modern Schools*, Newsom, *The Education of Girls*, p. 92 and Blishen, 'The task of the secondary modern school,' pp. 303–5.
11 Titmuss, *Problems of Social Policy*, shows that the numbers of evacuated teachers and helpers dropped rapidly from January 1940, with the majority returning by September 1942. There are no figures for the numbers of evacuated teachers alone.
12 Emergency trained teachers formed a sixth of teachers in maintained schools by 1951; Dent, *The Training of Teachers*, p. 127.
13 Wooldridge, *Measuring the Mind*, p. 249.
14 Hoyle and John, *Professional Knowledge and Professional Practice*, pp. 4–7.
15 Sikes, 'The life-cycle of the teacher', p. 37.
16 History in Education, 'Teachers' discussion', interview by Nicola Sheldon (2009), p. 3.
17 Oxfordshire Pilot, Ox.011, questionnaire, p. 4.
18 WEP A003, pp. 9–16; A018, p. 12; A031, p. 35.
19 Gould, *Chalk Up the Memory*, p. 25.
20 *Ibid.*, p. 47.
21 Oxfordshire Pilot, Ox. 012, 'Jan', 'What can be said about either learning theories or theories of motivation advocated by child-centred educationalists?', photocopy of unpub. B.Ed Philosophy essay in author's possession, c.1975–76, p. 4.
22 Oxfordshire Pilot, Ox.012, interview.
23 Cunningham and Gardner, *Becoming Teachers*, pp. x, 40, 229.
24 National Archives, ED 67/36, Oxfordshire Education Committee Circular: letter from Board of Education, 17 January 1927; letter from Board of Education, 21 April 1927; letter from Board of Education, 6 July 1932.
25 Cunningham and Gardner, *Becoming Teachers*, p. 71.
26 James Scott's definitions of *techne* and *metis*-based occupations suggest that this shift is inevitable in a modern state, where 'traditional knowledge' is incorrectly positioned in opposition to progress. Scott, *Seeing Like a State*.

27 Cunningham and Gardner, *Becoming Teachers*, p. 71.
28 Ozga and Lawn, *Teachers, Professionalism and Class*.
29 Marwick, *The Sixties*.
30 'A Director of Education', 'To the teacher in his first post', *Teachers World*, 30 August 1939, p. 15.
31 Sawyer, 'Towards education', *Schoolmaster*, 6 June 1946, p. 515.
32 Oxfordshire Archives, OXOHA:OT 7, Kathleen Chapman interviewed by Gaby Porter (1974).
33 For example: WEP A001, 1/5/98, p. 11; A033, 25/5/00, p. 22.
34 WEP A003, 27/7/98, pp. 9–12; A001, 1/5/98, pp. 11–12; A010, 12/10/98, p. 11.
35 'Onlooker', *Teachers World*, 2 December 1953, p. 2.
36 E. Colton, 'The young teacher: You're in a profession', *Teachers World*, 20 October 1954, p. 5.
37 'Onlooker', *Teachers World*, 2 December 1953, p. 2. Also WEP A019, 8/10/98, p. 9; A022, 31/3/00, p. 28; A002, 1/6/98, p. 19.
38 Horwood, *Keeping Up Appearances*, p. 41.
39 Sikes, 'The life-cycle of the teacher', pp. 27, 55. While these teachers hailed from a slightly later cohort than our chronological focus, their comments about the life-cycle seem to be universal.
40 Ashton *et al.*, *The Aims of Primary Education*, p. 50.
41 Oxfordshire Pilot, Ox.007, questionnaire, p. 4.
42 For example: Oxfordshire Pilot, Ox.001, Ox.002, Ox.005.
43 Wilson, 'Fighting the "damnable" triumph of feminism', pp. 669–70.
44 Oram, 'To cook dinners with love in them', p. 98. Edwards, *Women in Teacher Training Colleges*, p. 11. Also see Copelman, *London's Woman Teachers*.
45 Dent, *Century of Growth*, p. 133.
46 Lowe, *Education in the Post-War Years*, p. 104.
47 DES, *Children and Their Primary Schools*, p. 313; Oram, 'To cook dinners with love in them', p. 98.
48 On married women workers, see Lewis, *Women in Britain since 1945*, p. 2; Brooke, 'Gender and working class identity in Britain', pp. 775–7. On working mothers, see Wilson, 'A new look at the affluent worker', pp. 206–29. On teaching as a particularly appropriate career for women, see Thane, 'Girton graduates', p. 354.
49 Oxfordshire Pilot, Ox.008, questionnaire, p. 2.
50 Oxfordshire Pilot, Ox.003, questionnaire, p. 2.
51 Oxfordshire Pilot, Ox.007, interview.
52 This is explored further in Tisdall, 'Education, parenting and concepts of childhood'.
53 Oxfordshire Pilot, Ox.003, interview.
54 Gardner, 'Classroom teachers and educational change', pp. 40–1.
55 *Teacher*, 23 June 1967, p. 4.
56 *Teacher*, 14 July 1967, p. 4.

57 *Teacher*, 18 August 1967, p. 4.
58 *Teacher*, 15 September 1967, p. 4.
59 *Teacher*, 18 August 1967, p. 4.
60 For example: WEP D007, 3/5/00, p. 8; A003, 27/7/98, p. 11.
61 Cox and Dyson (eds), *Black Paper 2*, p. 94.
62 Oxfordshire Pilot, Ox.001, interview.
63 G. H. Green, 'Just out of college', *Schoolmaster*, 11 July 1935, p. 50.
64 Editorial, 'Keep psychology in its place,' *Teachers World*, 5 May 1954, p. 1.
65 *Teachers World*, 1 April 1959, p. 3.
66 Patricia Dawson, www.history.ac.uk/history-in-education/browse/interviews/interview-patricia-dawson-12-april-2010, pp. 13–16.
67 WEP C009 2/8/01, pp. 19, 30; C012, 9/8/01, pp. 7–8. See also J. C. Gagg, 'Talking Point', *Teachers World*, 10 January 1969, p. 13, who argued that banning corporal punishment was 'airy-fairy'.
68 Letters page, *Teachers World*, 1 April 1960, p. 21.
69 Pearson, *Hooligan*.
70 WEP A002 1/6/98, p. 20; A003, 27/7/98, p. 14; C003, 8/10/98, p. 5.
71 Oxfordshire Archives, OXOHA:OT 363, Ethel Mace and Nita Webber interview (1997).
72 Oxfordshire Archives, OXOHA:LT 276 – No.79 Connie Norman, '*My Choice*', BBC Radio Oxford, undated.
73 Oxfordshire Pilot, Ox.005, interview.
74 Oxfordshire Pilot, Ox.006, interview.
75 For example: J. Russell, *Teachers World*, 1 January 1971, p. 7; 'Strange alliance – deschoolers and traditionalists', *Teachers World*, 17 January 1975, p. 3.
76 *Teacher*, 18 August 1967, p. 4.
77 Oxfordshire Pilot, Ox.008, interview; History in Education, Eric Houlder interviewed by Nicola Sheldon (2010), p. 10.
78 G. Pemberton, 'Integrated learning', *Teachers World*, 5 January 1973, p. 15.
79 G. Pemberton, 'The practical approach to mathematics', *Teachers World*, 12 May 1967, p. 7; G. Pemberton, 'Sums for the 70s: Rigamarole Versus Reason', *Teachers World*, 15 January 1971, p. 14; *Teachers World*, Letters page, J. C. Gagg, 15 January 1971, p. 20.
80 J. C. Gagg, 'A free approach – is it possible?', *Teachers World*, 5 January 1949, p. 5; *Teachers World*, Letters page, J. C. Gagg, 15 January 1971, p. 20.
81 H. Peach, 'The noise of passing bandwagons', *Teacher*, 7 July 1967, p. 13.
82 WEP A001, 1/5/98, pp. 11–12; A003, 27/7/98, p. 10; C021, 17/9/01, p. 19.
83 History in Education, Eric Houlder interviewed by Nicola Sheldon, p. 6.
84 Oxfordshire Pilot, Ox.006, questionnaire, p. 3.
85 Gordon Pemberton, 'Integrated learning', *Teachers World*, 5 January 1973, p. 15; Brenda Thompson, book review, *Teachers World*, 24 January 1975, p. 26.
86 Oxfordshire Pilot, Ox.006, interview.
87 MacLure, *The Inspectors' Calling*, p. 50.

88 DES, *Children and their Primary Schools*, p. 417.
89 *Ibid.*
90 *Teachers World*, 4 February 1966, p. 3.
91 Letters page, *Teachers World*, 1 April 1960, p. 21.
92 Peach, *Curious Tales of Old North Yorkshire*, p. 198.
93 Galton *et al.*, *Inside the Primary Classroom*, p. 159.

4

A half-reformed education? Teaching practice and local change

Until the 1980s, the control of the curriculum and of teaching methods in England and Wales theoretically lay in the hands of teachers themselves, a principle that many believed had been firmly established by the 1944 Education Act, despite increasingly frequent challenges from the late 1960s onwards.[1] This was mediated significantly by the influence of headteachers and inspectors, and by the particular climate of the local education authority within which teachers worked. Nevertheless, because of the decentralisation of education in the period under consideration, to understand what pedagogical practice actually looked like, it is necessary to turn to local case studies. The lack of central direction might lead us to expect wide variations in teaching practice between LEAs, and my three English case studies – Oxfordshire, Cambridgeshire and Sheffield – were chosen with this consideration in mind.

Oxfordshire and the West Riding of Yorkshire, where Sheffield was administered until 1974, when it became part of South Yorkshire, were both believed to be centres of non-utopian progressive practice.[2] The *Guardian* wrote in 1975 that, under chief education officer Michael Harrison, Sheffield was 'regarded as the national model of a cohesive working-class city, with the most progressive modern education'.[3] Sheffield provides a case study of a northern industrial city, specialising in steel, engineering and cutlery manufacture, and by the 1950s it was also more racially diverse than my other case study areas, with groups of Asians from the Indian subcontinent, West Indians from Jamaica, Somalis and Yemenis arriving after the Second World War, and Ugandan and Kenyan Asian, Chinese and Chilean immigrants settling in the 1970s.[4] Cambridgeshire was initially selected as a 'control' LEA; both the secondary literature and teachers' memories indicated that it was not particularly progressive, despite its experiments with village colleges, until Nuffield curriculum reform in maths and science took off from the late 1960s.[5] However, logbook evidence and HMI reports indicated that schools in the City of Cambridge and in rural Cambridgeshire, including the Isle of Ely, were much more child-centred than I had expected.[6] Practice within local authorities – including my Welsh LEA, Monmouthshire – was remarkably consistent, considering the differences in topography, school provision and training and staffing, and the lack of centralised control.

Why did schools share so many similarities in this period, and why was teachers' practice seemingly so co-ordinated – especially when many attempted to resist novel ideas? The role of HMIs in spreading non-utopian progressive ideas in this period was paramount. Inspectors not only exerted their own influence on individual schools but liaised with the local authority in appointing appropriate candidates to headships, although their degree of success was inevitably greater with certain schools than with others. The headteacher exercised a significant amount of control over teaching practice in his or her school, allowing change to happen relatively rapidly if he or she was promoting it. The Plowden Report of 1967 indicated that only a third of English primary schools had become truly 'progressive' by the 1960s, a finding which was reiterated by a number of educational research surveys in the 1970s.[7] However, these surveys were distorted by rapidly changing definitions of what it meant to be 'progressive' or 'child-centred', as well as by a perceived need to respond to the popular backlash against 'trendy' teaching.

Instead, the most obvious way to characterise the majority of primary and secondary modern schools in this period is as 'half-reformed'; non-utopian progressive methods were widely influential, but partially and incoherently implemented.[8] However, precisely because teaching practice neither became fully reformed nor remained predominantly unreformed, these shifts profoundly affected both teachers' professional identities and their concepts of childhood, as new ideas about the role of the teacher and the child's capabilities were adapted to suit the realities of the classroom. Practical barriers further constrained teachers' ability to teach according to child-centred shibboleths, even if they were willing to take these new ideas on board.

A progressive education?

Central funding for education substantially increased in the post-war period. However, as Glen O'Hara has argued, the 'paradox' of these large-scale development schemes was that they led to a 'constant sense of educational crisis'. Central government, despite the increased funds, often made ambitious promises that it could not fulfil, such as the 1964 and 1966 Labour manifestos which set new targets for smaller class sizes.[9]

As O'Hara's argument implies, the increased spending on education also meant that it was subject to increased public scrutiny, which contributed to the atmosphere of anxiety among the teaching profession in the 1950s and 1960s. Funding was also unevenly distributed, with more spent on grammar schools than on secondary moderns, and on the secondary than primary sector. By the 1970s, economic crisis had led to calls for schools to become more accountable to the public, and limited further educational reform. For example, the raising of the school leaving age (ROSLA) to sixteen was postponed to 1972.[10] While the 'progressive revolution' in education has often been dated to the 1960s or even the 1970s, my findings suggest that non-utopian progressive change was a much longer process, beginning in the late 1940s and early 1950s. Progressivism has often been conflated with permissiveness, especially by its right-wing critics, but rather than seeing progressive reform as part of the 'permissive shift' that has itself been challenged by recent historiography, I suggest that it was intertwined with fears about preserving the post-war settlement, and hence motivated by a desire to control children and adolescents, rather than to give them liberty.

The national inspectorate

The role of the national inspectorate in spreading non-utopian progressive practice, particularly in flagship counties such as Oxfordshire, Herefordshire and the West Riding of Yorkshire, is well-established in the existing historiography, with the movement personified by influential HMIs such as Robin Tanner, Christian Schiller and Alec Clegg.[11] Ken Jones argues that inspectors formed a key arm of the partnership that promoted progressive education in the inter-war period, alongside training colleges and local authority administrators, taking advantage of the decentralised system to press for change.[12] This continued, and intensified, post-war. Allan Hill, who became an HMI in 1965, recalled critically that:

> I quickly realised that some colleagues were promoting "fashionable teaching methods" such as . . . project-directed studies, discovery learning and mixed ability teaching whilst decrying and dismissing formal methods . . . It was obvious that the new and progressive methods were being marketed and taught very effectively by the colleges of education and with considerable encouragement from some HMI.[13]

HMIs were usually recruited from teaching posts through personal contact and public advertisements when they were in their mid-thirties to mid-forties, as previous experience in schools was valued. They then underwent a two-year probation period, reduced to one year after 1970, which largely constituted informal on-the-job training, encouraging the use of a common script.[14] Logbook evidence suggests that HMIs often worked in groups, with the most senior inspector formally signing off on an inspection report where the inspection had been conducted by a more junior inspector.[15] Heavy recruitment after the Second World War meant inspectors were often thrown in at the deep end. Don Porter, who became an HMI in 1946, recalled 'After a short introduction one was given a group of schools, then a small area of responsibility.'[16] HMIs themselves were recruited at the national level but worked alongside a local inspectorate, and, in the post-war period, 'advisory teachers' appointed by the LEA, although the majority of LEAs made little use of this option.[17]

Traditionally, HMIs were drawn from the social elite. As David Cannadine, Nicola Sheldon and Jenny Keating note, inter-war HMIs were, on the whole, men who had been educated at public schools, although increasing numbers of women were recruited from 1918, following changes in the civil service as a whole. The number of inspectors grew swiftly over the immediate post-war period, rising from 364 to 567 between 1945 and 1949, and these newer recruits came from a broader range of backgrounds.[18] Women were also integrated fully into the structure of the inspectorate after 1945.[19] However, the *Schoolmaster* complained in 1950 that of the 330 HMIs who inspected primary and secondary modern schools, only 187 had previous experience of teaching in those schools, and only 130 of those had taught for more than five years.[20] Jack Featherstone, who was recruited to the inspectorate in 1968, having been the head of two secondary modern schools, recalled 'I was loaned out a great deal . . . in most Divisions HMI visiting secondary schools were unable to help in that field – they had not worked in it as teachers.'[21] This indicated that despite the increasing social diversity of the inspectorate, the criterion that mattered most to teachers – previous teaching experience in a similar type of school – was still not being met. Although inspectors' attitudes had become less punitive, this still positioned them, like teacher trainers, as outsiders to the bulk of the teaching profession.

Despite the emphasis placed on the role of the national inspectorate by historians of education, little use has been made of inspectors' reports as a source, with the exception of the work of Cannadine, Sheldon and Keating on the history of history teaching.[22] Given the decentralised nature of the English and Welsh education system in the period under consideration, inspectors' reports provide a valuable guide to what HMIs considered to be important in education, and how far schools lived up to their expectations. In the 1950s, HMIs committed themselves to the inspection of every school by the end of the decade, and so evidence is especially rich for those years.[23] These reports can help us assess how broadly and consistently child-centred education was practised in schools, and how it affected teachers' concepts of childhood. They also allow us, in conjunction with logbook evidence, to examine precisely how non-utopian progressive practice was promoted. HMIs were consistently progressive; in only a very few reports did the inspector suggest that a school had become 'too' child-centred, and this was generally because the organisation was viewed to be poor and haphazard, suggesting that the criticism was of the way in which the method had been implemented, rather than of the method itself.[24] Inspectors tended to advocate an integrated local curriculum, a focus on creativity in written English, art, drama and music, and extensive provision for practical activities, especially in senior classes or schools.

A report from Ecclesfield secondary modern girls' school in Sheffield in 1950 represented a common assessment of a school that was 'moving towards progressivism' but, in the inspectors' opinion, not yet fully child-centred. Local geography and history were emphasised, weather observations and records were made and used for mathematics and gardening, and current affairs were considered once a week, which prompted discussion, debates, visits, lectures and newspapers. The improvements suggested in the report were all related to making education more practical and 'relevant'. Mathematics was praised for focusing on concepts 'to enable them to face successfully the normal problems of living' while art was to focus more on the design of objects in common use. It was believed that housecraft should be planned in a series of stages, beginning with the girls' own particular needs and extending outwards to those of the community. Linked to these recommendations were key child-centred educational suggestions such as integrating the curriculum, working in groups or as individuals, rather than whole-class teaching, and project work.[25] These recommendations were representative of inspectors' priorities in Cambridgeshire and Oxfordshire as well.[26] In Monmouthshire, similar advice was put forward, but a familiar language of behaviour, standards and discipline persisted alongside these child-centred recommendations.[27]

Teachers' relationships with inspectors also framed their response to child-centred education. The inspector was often positioned as the figure who pressurised teachers to adopt methods they did not understand or like. HMI reports from my four case study areas tended to make very similar recommendations and often used the same words and phrases, indicating that they were drawing from a common national script rather than being governed by local conditions, although the Monmouthshire inspectors, who were employed separately from their English counterparts, used a slightly more conservative tone.[28] John Blackie, an influential Cambridgeshire inspector who became chief inspector for Primary Education from 1963 to 1966 and a lecturer at Homerton thereafter, emphasised the national links of HMIs in 1970, stating that it was usual practice for the HMI to move between localities every ten years.[29] By 1965, only 50 out of 164 LEAs appointed their own local inspectors, with the remaining 114 being inspected by the national inspectorate.[30]

However, inspectors did not confine themselves to suggesting changes in reports, but worked closely with at least some schools to introduce progressivism by suggesting new ideas and arranging visits to other schools so that staff could see child-centred methods in action. This became particularly common from the 1940s onwards. At Prickwillow, an all-age rural school in Cambridgeshire, for example, HMI Fuller persuaded the head to attend an NUT two-day refresher course at Chatteris in 1949. When Miss Rhys, another HMI, visited the school in 1954, the head noted three days later that 'Following the visit of

Miss Rhys . . . The geography syllabus for Classes I and II has been altered, "The Royal Tour" being substituted'.[31] In 1954, the Queen was touring Australia and New Zealand, so this was a clear attempt to link geography lessons to current-day events that might 'naturally interest' the children. At Hook Norton in Oxfordshire in 1953, one teacher, Mr Dowling, was seen to be underperforming. The HMI, Miss Moorhouse, found that he 'was not possessed of the techniques of teaching owing to his lack of Teachers' College training' and recommended 'Dramatising and Miming . . . and visits to other schools.' In this case, this led to the teacher's resignation two weeks later.[32]

Inspectors also helped with equipment, furniture and decoration, supporting headteachers in their applications for funds to the local education authority or simply supplying the necessary items themselves. At Albury and Tiddington junior–infants in Oxfordshire in 1943, Mr Toombes suggested that the head should 'apply for decoration of building [sic] substituting a cheerful colour for the brown.'[33] At Launton juniors in the same county in 1959, Miss Bews 'called this afternoon and brought a large roll of kitchen paper and some tins of powder paint'. This equipment was associated with the child-centred New Art teaching, indicating that the inspector was both helping with the acquisition of materials and promoting a certain set of methods.[34] Schools could also employ the national inspectors as leverage against the local authority. At St Mary's Silver Street mixed secondary modern in Ely, a 1962 HMI report stated that the premises were still very poor, the school lacked technical equipment related to child-centred goals, such as a projector, wall maps and science apparatus, and there were few library books.[35] At the 'presentation of HMIs [sic] report' to the governors, the head noted in the logbook that 'This was my opportunity to have a "go" about our conditions and the mean attitude in the supply of money for the new school.'[36]

While HMIs were employed at a national level and remained in contact with national trends, they developed a strong relationship with the schools they inspected over that ten-year period as well, and this affected teachers' relationships with, and impressions of, the inspectorate. In Oxfordshire and Cambridgeshire, schools did not encounter a multitude of different and unfamiliar figures, but tended to develop long-term relationships with the local inspector. For example, at Ascot-under-Wychwood school in Oxfordshire, Mrs C. G. Garside regularly inspected the school throughout the 1930s. During wartime, Miss Courtney was the regular inspector, and during the 1950s and 1960s, Robin Tanner took her place, alongside Edith Moorhouse, the senior adviser for primary education in the county.[37] Sheffield schools, in contrast, were more likely to experience a large number of different inspectors, especially during wartime; bombings meant that this period was inevitably more chaotic for Sheffield than for the two rural counties. Greenhill County School was visited by Mr Whitworth, Mr Young, Mr Thurston, Mr Large and Miss Hall as HMIs, from 1931 to 1936 alone. The situation did not change post-war; Miss Crooks, Mr Keys, Mr Baker and several other unnamed HMIs called from the late 1940s to late 1950s.[38]

A close relationship with one inspector may have influenced headteachers' attitudes towards inspections in Oxfordshire and Cambridgeshire, judging from logbook records, which record a generally positive attitude towards both formal inspections and informal advice in these two counties. Although logbooks might be read by inspectors or other officials, making it wise for the head not to be too outspoken, headteachers had no obligation to write positive things about the HMI, but only to record their visit. In this light, the numerous appreciative remarks may largely be taken at face value. For example, the newly appointed head of Great Haseley in Oxfordshire recorded this informal and friendly conversation in 1943: 'A visit today from Mr Toombes HMI that we might become acquainted. Mr Toombes interested in my proposals & made constructive suggestions concerning the Time Table. Remarked that it would probably take two years for me to get things re-organised as I wished. I agreed heartily!'[39]

In contrast, Sheffield schools, which tended to experience numerous different inspectors, were often less receptive to advice. There were virtually no overtly positive remarks about inspectors in the Sheffield logbooks I surveyed, and a number of negative comments. For example, the head of St George's school complained in 1958 that Miss K. Payne, HMI, visited 'to see the J1 [first-year junior] class which is extremely backward. She could offer no help, or advice, in dealing with the difficult problem of teaching reading to this class.'[40] While teachers noted HMIs' suggestions in the logbooks, often there was little evidence that they actually followed up these suggestions. They also pointed out the impracticality of some ideas. The head of Carbrook Mixed Church

School made sure to note in the logbook that HMI Mr P. B. Brewerton discovered for himself the difficulties that teachers might face when organising out-of-school activities when he took forty-five children and only one teacher to Wiston Park Museum in 1944. The head commented, 'When he returned Mr Brewerton suggested that 25 children should be the maximum taken on an educational visit.'[41]

HMIs also played a role in introducing teachers to refresher courses and running these courses themselves. Mary Bews, who was an adviser for rural primary schools in Oxfordshire under Edith Moorhouse from 1949 to 1981 and helped to organise such courses, was interviewed by Philip Best in 1996. Philip had been an enthusiastic young teacher in Oxfordshire in the 1950s himself, so interviewer and interviewee tended to remember similar things and confirm each other's judgements, moulding the shape of Mary's recollections. They were also linked by a shared nostalgia for those 'better' times in education. The interview concluded with a joint musing on the negative impact of the National Curriculum and a sharing of concerns about how much had been forgotten about the positive work that had been done in the post-war period:

> Mary: I feel that some of these aspects that we've talked about . . . are rather fading away . . . and only the impression of failure seems to be left. And I'm sure that it's only an impression, but it does darken the lives of teachers and children sometimes.
> Philip: Yes, it's a shame that the media have got hold of the idea that all is negative, when really, there was so much good.
> Mary: And of course, they always emphasise the negative.

Philip rarely asked Mary direct questions in the interview, but made statements of his own that prompted her to say more on a certain topic. A common interjection was 'I remember', confirming the validity of her reminiscences in the way an interviewer who had not been there would not have been able to. He stated that he could 'well remember' on a number of occasions and that he could 'remember very vividly' Mary's work with probationary teachers, of whom he had been one. Conversely, Mary occasionally turned the tables and posed closed questions to her interviewer, stating at one point, 'With parents, we were a pioneer authority with regard to parental involvement, would you agree with that, Philip?' This 'reciprocal' interview presented a united front on how valuable and significant refresher courses in

Oxfordshire had been. Mary thought the residential weekends 'were very special, and they're still talked about' while Philip recalled 'you had a tremendous influence on we teachers'.[42] The advisory service in Oxfordshire did provide valuable help for many teachers, as logbook evidence confirmed. For example, the head of Albury and Tiddington went to a weekend course on primary education in 1964 and thought that it was 'a stimulating and very interesting weekend'.[43] However, Mary and Philip's confirmation of each other's memories and their commitment to emphasising the positive 'side' of post-war education perhaps presented an overly optimistic view of the attitudes of Oxfordshire teachers to refresher courses.

Not all teachers in the county responded positively to the inspectors' attempts to promote child-centred methods through such courses. Mel Summers, who entered teaching as an emergency trained teacher after the Second World War, and taught at St Clement's and West Oxford mixed all-age schools in the 1950s and 1960s, remembered in a private interview in 1997 that

> we went on many courses . . . Miss Biggs, HMI Biggs [known for promoting practical mathematics], she was very keen on the 'discovery method' of things, we used to laugh a bit about that.[44] She told us once about a school where she went to and she wanted the kiddies to find [calculate] pi, and she brought in these wheels, and she said they were there for about three days, and I wondered what their parents were going to say about that, but she thought it was fantastic, that they were finding pi with the discovery method [laughs]. If somebody had just told them, they could have been practising on it in a couple of minutes . . . quite funny.

This long anecdote was not directly prompted by the interviewer, who had simply asked 'How did teaching methods change during your time there? [in West Oxford school]. I mean, was it still quite formal when you arrived?'[45] The Plowden Report indicated that attendance on refresher courses among primary teachers in England and Wales by the 1960s was good, stating 'We were glad to find from the National Survey that two-thirds of all primary teachers had followed a refresher course between September 1961 and June 1964, and that on average these teachers had spent 13 days on courses.'[46] Logbook evidence from all case study areas also frequently mentions attendance on a wide variety of refresher courses.[47] However, as Mel's testimony indicates, attendance did not necessarily indicate that teachers agreed with or understood the ideas they were introduced to, especially as they may have been determined to resist new suggestions such as the discovery method which, in their eyes, lacked a practical track record in the classroom.

On a national level, teachers' relationships with inspectors improved rapidly throughout the inter-war period and the Second World War, but took a downturn in the 1950s and 1960s. In the 1920s, suspicion of the inspectorate was still widespread, as teachers possessed a strong collective memory of the detested 'payment by results' system, in place between 1862 and the late 1890s, which had been implemented by inspectors.[48] *Teachers World* ran a series of regular columns written by inspectors in this decade, from 'The inspector overheard' (1925) to 'As the inspector sees it' (1928) that challenged these assumptions, but the framing of other broadly positive articles on the inspectorate, which began with statements such as 'Why should the school inspector be a bane?' and 'The duty of the inspector . . . is to be a constructive, not a destructive critic' indicated underlying attitudes.[49] However, by the 1930s, relationships were improving; a new model for relations between teachers and inspectors was evolving, based on trust, advice and suggestions rather than commands and sanctions. *Teachers World*'s call for 'inspector stories' in 1931 indicated friendly relations between teachers and inspectors, and when teachers were invited to write in on 'detestable things in a teacher's life' in 1935, the periodical noted that 'unsympathetic inspectors are only rarely mentioned, which is a sign of the times'.[50] The *Schoolmaster* took a similar tack.[51] Interestingly, the *TES* rarely mentioned HMIs, indicating that an inspection was a much greater concern for elementary school teachers than those who taught in grammar and independent schools.

In contrast, the dominant discourse in the 1950s and 1960s indicated rising concern about inspectors, although their positive functions were still stressed. This was largely because inspectors were associated with the rise of 'modern methods'. As we have seen, they had been key architects of non-utopian progressive educational practice. The Ministry of Education's 1949 Report thought that 'During recent years criticism of Inspectors' methods . . . has tended to increase. This is due in some measure to a misunderstanding, if not an ignorance, of the work and function of Inspectors.' The *Schoolmaster*'s article on this report carried a hidden warning: 'It is no part of an inspector's function to tell any teacher what to do or how to do it, but most teachers welcome new ideas and gladly consider suggestions that might be useful.'[52] Letters from the *Schoolmaster*'s readers reflected these anxieties, drawing on familiar discourses of professional identity and craft knowledge. In the same year as the Ministry of Education report, 'Also Disturbed', an older male teacher, wrote to the periodical on

> teachers who are being subjected to every kind of pressure by HMIs and the legions of Organisers to adopt the new methods . . . Who has decided that failure has crowned the efforts of our predecessors and ourselves? . . . I cannot subscribe to the freak methods that are being foisted upon us . . . HMIs are using every means in their power to *make* us adopt these changes.[53]

This resistance to inspectors initially seems to contradict the positive attitudes towards inspections we observed in the Cambridgeshire and Oxfordshire case studies. But it must be remembered that these logbook accounts were written by headteachers, not class teachers, many of whom would have been promoted, in the 1950s and 1960s at least, by virtue of their sympathy with child-centred methods. Indeed, class teachers often found that the headteacher and inspector allied to put pressure on them to change their teaching style.

However, retrospective self-narrative accounts from teachers who started their teaching careers in the post-war period tended to remember the national inspectorate more fondly, recalling a lack of judgement and an ongoing commitment to helping teachers improve their practice. My Oxfordshire respondents, who all began teaching in the 1970s, universally praised HMIs. John taught in two different Oxfordshire schools in the 1970s and 1980s: 'What I found with the HMIs was that they come back and talk to you afterwards, and how helpful they were. These were experienced people in education. They weren't there to find out what you weren't doing, what you were doing wrongly, but if you needed help, they'd offer it, and offer advice.'[54] However, while not discounting their significance, these memories were coloured by the inevitable comparison with the regime of Office for Standards in Education (Ofsted) inspections, which began with the Education (Schools) Act of 1992 and which all these respondents remembered very negatively. Most respondents explicitly contrasted the experience of Ofsted with earlier HMI inspections. John recalled walking out of a conversation with an Ofsted inspector, as he felt 'this isn't helping me as a teacher – at all.

You're looking for faults'. He remembered the tense atmosphere created by the arrival of Ofsted: 'This is what they were doing . . . It was awful in the staffroom . . . Every teacher in that school was a good teacher.' HMIs, he thought, were 'completely different to Ofsted'.[55] Brian also contrasted his earlier experience of HMI inspections with Ofsted: 'Oh yes. Very different. I mean, I felt with them [HMIs], you could sit down and talk about things, and they would sit down with you and talk about things. Whereas now, they come in and they go out.'[56]

The Cannadine set of interviews indicate that this attitude was not confined to Oxfordshire, but was shared by teachers nationwide. Chris Culpin, who started teaching in the 1960s, recalled that

> I had once thought of being an HMI but they had become, you know, the enforcers of the judgements that I wasn't very keen on making. They were once a really respected, interesting, innovative body and I think they lost that, you know, the work of [Chris] Woodhead [head of Ofsted from 1994] turned that body into a group of people who don't have the confidence of teachers any more.[57]

While this does not mean that these respondents' memories of HMIs were false, they were inevitably rose-tinted by this dominant narrative about Ofsted. Also, this particular cohort, who had started teaching at the very end of the period under consideration, were more likely to have been receptive to the input of HMIs than older teachers, as they would have recently encountered current progressive orthodoxies during their training. In contrast, teachers who had trained earlier and gained more practical experience in the classroom were more likely to feel threatened by new ideas.

HMIs themselves emphasised the importance of establishing good relationships with teaching staff, and suggested that this had been a significant part of their training throughout the post-war period. Stuart MacLure's history of the inspectorate, which draws on more than two hundred narrative accounts by HMIs, highlights this theme. Respectful relations were recommended by the new edition of *Instructions for Inspectors* issued by Martin Roseveare, who reorganised the inspectorate after becoming senior chief inspector (SCI) in 1944. This stated: 'HM Inspector does not give directions, nor does he see that these directions are carried out . . . if he is liked and trusted by his schools . . . it is only on very rare occasions that he needs to speak with unusual emphasis.'[58]

This philosophy was absorbed by inspectors over the following decades. Roy Wake was recruited as an HMI in 1960: 'Induction: the greatest stress was on courtesy to everyone; never making notes in public if possible; never discussing a class or the teaching in front of that class or the teacher; never saying anything to the head not already said to the teacher . . . looking at teaching not the teachers.' Gordon Hamflett, who started work in 1962, concurred: 'Great emphasis was on the art of inspection . . . development of empathy in schools . . . remember that an ordinary day for HMI was an extraordinary day for the school.'[59] However, the focus of the inspectorate was to shift under Sheila Browne, SCI from 1974 to 1983, whose philosophy was 'face the centre'. In effect, the inspectorate's orientation was reversed, so HMI spent more time supplying information on the schools to the central government, and less time working with schools themselves, which led to complaints that HMI were overloaded. Fewer inspections took place in the early 1970s, and the end of the decade saw the beginning of the publication of HMI's 'Matters for discussion' (1977–82), 'Red Books' (1977–83) and HMI Surveys (1978–85), an unprecedented formal intervention by the inspectorate in curriculum and school organisation.[60]

Child-centred education in four local authorities

By considering 'progressive' in its broader sense, we can see that despite resistance from practising teachers, the adoption of non-utopian progressive practice, driven by the national inspectorate, became evident across England, and to a lesser extent, in Wales from the 1950s onwards. Looking at HMI reports and logbook records from my three major case study areas, we can identify a significant shift towards progressive practice in Oxfordshire, Cambridgeshire and Sheffield during the period under consideration, and a less significant, but still observable, shift in Monmouthshire. The common cultural script used by inspectors resulted in a series of common terms used in their reports to denote child-centred educational practice in a school. 'Practical', 'real', 'vocational' or 'activity' indicated that academic subjects, especially mathematics, were deliberately taught using concrete methods; that art and craft were integrated into the wider curriculum rather than taught as stand-alones; that the children learnt through experience; and that the curriculum related to future occupation or current activities. A 'local' education denoted that subjects, especially geography and history, were closely connected to the immediate environment of the school.

An 'individual' education, also signalled by terms such as 'project work', 'capacity' and 'ability', focused on the assessment and recording of children's ability, with children pursuing their own projects or working in groups. Finally, an 'enjoyable' or 'natural' education, with other terms used including 'creative', 'imaginative', 'interest', 'happy', 'lively' and 'enthusiasm', indicated that teaching was supposedly centred on the children's 'interests', that it promoted good social behaviour and encouraged the children to be confident and outgoing. Typical reports could be virtually identical; at Heeley Bank in Sheffield in 1945, 'the children are happy and responsive', Crowmarsh in Oxfordshire in 1950 was 'a happy place; the children are alert and friendly and they are responsive to the right demands', while Arrington in Cambridge in 1954 was 'a very happy school where the children are friendly, responsive and keen'.[61]

Data from Welsh schools somewhat modify this picture. This is not because Welsh education was subject to a significantly different set of influences from English education. Despite the establishment of a Central Welsh Board in 1896 and a Welsh Department within the Board of Education in 1907, which included a separate Welsh inspectorate, Welsh education remained under the remit of the central government in England throughout the period under consideration.[62] Gareth Elwyn Jones has argued that 'education policy was determined in London rather than Cardiff', even after 1964, when a Welsh Office and a Welsh Secretary of State for Education were established. Despite increasing attention being paid post-war by the Ministry of Education to what a distinctively 'Welsh' education might look like, these theories were not translated into practice.[63] By the 1970s, Welsh HMIs were promoting the teaching of the Welsh language, which had been a key aim of the 1967 Gittins Report. The work to date was summarised in *HMI Today and Tomorrow* (1970), which noted the establishment of the National Language Centre in Glamorgan.[64] However, this linguistic progress was not necessarily related to other areas of the curriculum, and change did not proceed rapidly. For example, the *Teacher* reported in 1974 that Glamorgan had dropped compulsory Welsh in schools due to a shortage of Welsh-speaking staff.[65]

A half-reformed education?

Instead, case study data from Monmouthshire indicate that it was subject to the same pressures as my English LEAs, but was responding rather more slowly to the new orthodoxies. Two surveys were carried out in the LEA in 1968 and 1969 that emphasised the standards that progressive inspectors expected and how far the schools still fell short. In the first report, which covered nine primary schools in the Rhymney Valley, it was noted that the schools were still too 'teacher-dominated' even though seven of them were trying to promote active learning through an Environmental Studies project, and methods were old-fashioned; children copied notes from the board and crafts were still basic and traditional. The schools needed more expression, individuality, group work and an integrated curriculum, and needed to adopt specific modern curriculums such as Nuffield Science.[66]

The 1969 survey covered a wider range of thirty-nine schools in Monmouthshire, and concluded that the children worked to a formal timetable and subjects were rarely integrated or related to the children's surroundings. Mathematics teaching showed 'little reflection of current thought or practice' and 'there is need for more up-to-date approaches in most subjects'.[67] Logbook records indicate that some schools in the area were ahead of the game. Cwncarn County, a secondary modern school, was praised in 1951 for original pattern work and vigorous painting. However, this appears to have been an atypical centre of progressivism.[68] A logbook record from Llanwenarth-ultra School in Govilon from 1962 notes that the headteacher attended a 'coloured rods' [Cuisenaire rods] course at Cwncarn, and the headteacher at Raglan School wrote that he attended the same course, indicating that Cwncarn was pioneering the use of this new maths apparatus among schools in the area.[69] An article by John Roberts, undated but probably from the late 1960s, noted that Cwncarn was the only school in Monmouthshire to try a new, experimental way of teaching the humanities through debate.[70] Therefore, it was probably not representative of the county in its willingness to try new methods, and Monmouthshire as a whole lagged behind our three English case studies.

Local factors alone did not determine whether or not a school would start to adopt child-centred methods. The attitude of the head was cited by many teachers, educational writers and lecturers as the most significant influence on the methods of a school, and headteachers retained this dominant influence throughout the period under consideration.

It could be the introduction of a new head into a school, rather than any efforts on the part of the HMIs, that turned the school in a child-centred direction, especially if the previous head had had a long period of service. Such heads could often be very aware of the need to win round the rest of the staff to their point of view. At Soham in Cambridgeshire, an all-age boys' school which was reorganised as a mixed juniors in 1958, a new head, Peter Lerway, revolutionised the teaching after his appointment in September 1963.[71] Lerway was in correspondence with the influential progressive inspector Christian Schiller about 'the middle school' in the early 1970s, indicating that he may have been exceptionally committed to progressive practice.[72]

The HMI report from 1957 indicated that the school was moving towards progressivism, having established group work, class libraries and integrated social studies and handiwork, but was restricted by some poor teaching and 'old and inconvenient' buildings.[73] When Lerway arrived, he had some initial difficulty with introducing more advanced progressive methods, and so had to think carefully about how to convince the staff. On 15 October 1963, he wrote in the logbook that he had arranged visits to Bristol and Oxfordshire for the staff, and that these had been a success:

> The whole staff . . . spent an enlightening two days meeting people who had for some years been using the approach I had been suggesting in this school. They saw, above all, that the methods I had demonstrated and advocated had been practised with success by other teachers. This . . . encouraged them to extend their already growing efforts to stimulate learning by providing first-hand experience for the children.[74]

At the end of term, he reflected that while 'From the first week of term much talk has taken place about how the school should function and all teachers appeared willing to consider new ways of approach' by December these methods were actually in practice.[75] In 1965, Lerway showed the same caution in approaching new appointees, explaining that he had to begin from the beginning in introducing 'realistic maths' to these teachers.[76]

Over the next three years, the school started using new maths apparatus, created its own 'museum', introduced family grouping, had a substantial extension to the school building approved and began keeping a range of small animals.[77] Lerway went on to become a lecturer in Lancashire.[78] His practical demonstrations of why his methods worked may have appealed to the teachers' professional ideal, as they linked the methods with practice, rather than theory. Lerway's ability to gain funds from the local authority to improve the school building, which had been recognised as a problem since the 1950s, further indicates that a headteacher's negotiating skills could be crucial to secure much-needed refurbishments.[79]

'Condemned as unfit': class sizes, school buildings and progressive reform

Teachers' full adoption of non-utopian progressivism was often constrained by practical considerations, even when they were enthusiastically committed to child-centred methods. Large class sizes were frequently cited. As Roy Lowe argues, *School and Life* (1947), the first report of the Central Advisory Council for Education (CACE) which had been established in 1944, confirmed that this continued to be an issue post-war, with large class sizes seen as one of the central problems facing primary teachers.[80] In 1959, Asher Tropp argued that a reduction in class size was the key reform desired by all teachers, both primary and secondary, claiming that over half the children in maintained and assisted schools were being taught in overcrowded classes in 1952, although he did not give figures. Peter Cunningham suggests that the average primary class ranged from forty to fifty pupils in the 1950s.[81] By 1960, the average class size was thirty-three, but 23,000 classes still contained over forty pupils.[82] Although much of the contemporary concern about large classes was centred on primary teachers, secondary teachers had to deal with large classes as well. Primary classes were seen to be of greater concern because of the younger age of the children and the more advanced implementation of non-utopian progressive methods in primary schools. Progressive shibboleths such as group and individual teaching, independent projects and class trips all became much more difficult, if not impossible, with such a large number of children.

John Brucker's experience of post-war primary education indicates the range of problems teachers faced. John's recollections were formulated in the context of another 'reciprocal' interview; in this case, he was nominally the interviewer, asking his old friend and colleague Ted Harvey about his experience of teaching, but the interview developed into a conversation between the two men, who clearly knew each other very well and had shared similar experiences.[83] John and Ted reaffirmed each other's recollections of the difficulties of post-war teaching. John started teaching in 1950 in Abingdon in Oxfordshire with a class of fifty-four children: 'Outings were rare weren't they', he commented, addressing Ted, 'you couldn't manage 54 kids'. He also began to remember the unsuitability of the school building and the equipment after Ted recalled that 'The building had been condemned as unfit . . . since 1929.' After some discussion about the characters of the children they had taught, John chipped in to add 'I do remember also the building itself being very inadequate . . . My room was heated from a pipe that went up the back of the classroom and so in the winter I tended to teach from that position hugging the pipe.' After this description, John became the more voluble of the two men. Ted had had more teaching experience than John when they met, and John's memories may have been especially vivid because they concerned his first year as a teacher.

Highlighting the challenges he faced, John stated that there was 'a lack of materials in the school' and 'no books'. Although the classroom, which consisted of three brick walls leading to a high pointed ceiling, was not the ideal educational arena, John did his best: 'I got all the kids' paintings and went even higher up towards the ceiling and it made quite a reasonable display space. Also I had a table there where I kept interesting objects.'[84] On the whole, however, he taught through 'chalk and talk' rather than more child-centred methods, which is unsurprising given that he had fifty-four children to manage. Indeed, he explicitly resisted what he had learnt about child psychology on at least one occasion:

> I do remember one lesson I gave. When we were at College it was drummed into us very clearly that when you are teaching primary school children don't talk to them for more than 10 minutes, their attention span is never longer than 10 minutes . . . One day I went off the track and started talking about stars and the night sky . . . I went on talking without stopping for three quarters of an hour and their attention was completely held because of the subject.[85]

John's knowledge of his class, on this occasion, trumped the theoretical findings of the psychologist. Ted had a similar anecdote to relate about the foolishness of a progressive inspector who caused chaos among his formerly well-behaved class by asking them to whistle.[86] Both John and Ted, therefore, like many post-war teachers, positioned themselves on a spectrum between 'traditional' and 'progressive' teaching, and emphasised the practical difficulties of progressivism.

John and Ted's post-war experiences in Oxfordshire, while not completely representative, were not atypical. As we have seen, John's class of fifty-four pupils outstripped the average class size for the 1950s, but was hardly an anomaly, especially not in a small rural school. And despite new architectural ideas and increased funds for school infrastructure, school buildings remained a significant problem into the 1960s, with the factors John cites – space, heating, plumbing and furniture – remaining continual obstacles. Progressive educationalists were aware of the crucial role that school design and classroom space played in the successful implementation of their ideas, as Tom Hulme, Andrew Saint, Catherine Burke and Peter Cunningham have shown.[87] Saint notes that there was a wave of school building from 1936–39, but these schools were built along largely conventional lines, unlike the village college movement in Cambridge, which had begun at Sawston in the late 1920s; these colleges combined schools with community centres, re-envisaging the role of the school, and hence of the teacher, in the community.[88] Post-war innovations were led by John Newsom in Herefordshire, who was the chief education officer for the county, from 1947–50. A wider advance was led by the Consortium of Local Authorities Special Programme (CLASP) from the late 1950s onwards. Unlike earlier school building programmes, post-war school architecture was notable for consulting teachers. Newsom told the Architectural Association in 1946 that 'No architect should design a school until he has sat in a school for at least a week and seen what happens,' and the primary schools built in Hertfordshire emphasised light and colour.[89] As Mathew Thomson has argued, radical educationalists in the 1970s suggested that traditional school building should be abandoned in order to allow children to engage more directly with both rural and urban environments, suggesting that the use of space remained fundamental to progressives.[90]

What ought a child-centred classroom to look like? The answer to this question changed radically throughout the period under consideration. Mary Bews conjured an image of the nineteenth-century classrooms that still persisted in post-war Oxfordshire:

> Reading autobiographies of those born at the beginning of the century who describe their schools, many of the features they mention were still evident when I started work in the rural schools in 1949. The high windows, so the

pupils couldn't see out, the tortoise stoves, that roasted the front rows while those at the back froze. The drab-coloured walls, the iron-framed double desks. One or two schools even had galleries still. Hardly any had modern sanitation. Earth closets were the norm.

In contrast, she strove to promote a much more flexible classroom design for primary schools, comprising a quiet reading area with a carpet, a working area with tables and chairs, and practical areas for arts and crafts. Finmere, the 'first purpose-built rural school' was her model, as it was 'the ideal flexible building' due to its light sliding partitions.[91] As Saint notes, the architects of this school had worked with Edith Moorhouse and observed children in existing schools to achieve its user-friendly design, and it became a model for later Oxfordshire schools such as Roxton and Freeland.[92] Mary argued that teachers could use progressive methods even in an unsuitable building: 'teachers thought up strategies to solve the problem. They moved out lockers and cupboards . . . put up trellises at curtains, they brought carpets from home, used cloakroom space for practical work.'[93] Given many teachers' lack of understanding of, and lack of confidence in, progressive methods, however, this solution may not have led to fully reformed schools, even if spatially they conformed more closely to progressive standards. Also, large class sizes were a significant barrier to group and individual teaching, even if the classroom space was reformed, as John Brucker's experience showed, and this problem persisted into the 1970s. During her primary school training in 1972–73, Carol taught in a small rural Oxfordshire school where 'there were far too many children to fit into the room – the teacher had had to take the doors off the cupboards 'cause you couldn't actually open the cupboard doors because of the press of desks and chairs.'[94]

The two images that Mary painted in her interview, however, were hardly the only options for schools, and neither was the norm during the period under consideration. Logbook evidence suggests that classroom space, like teaching methods, was largely 'half-reformed' in the 1950s and 1960s, although some schools were rebuilt, or newly built, more radically. Inter-war schools were often reminiscent of the nineteenth century, and did not simply vanish after the Second World War. Bill Johnson, who taught at Evenwood school in Yorkshire from 1942 to 1966, remembered that at the beginning of his tenure, 'the place was an old wreck' and he circled the temperature with a blue ring in the logbook each time he opened the school below freezing; he often had to thaw frozen inkwells.[95] The key post-war changes that took place at Evenwood did not involve flexible furniture and remodelled classrooms but the addition of central heating, electric lights and a resurfaced playground so the children were in less danger of slipping.[96] Ted Harvey and John Brucker's experiences of teaching in a school that had been declared unfit for purpose some thirty years before were hardly unique. As Roy Lowe notes, by 1950 almost a quarter of school buildings blacklisted in 1925 were still in use.[97]

Even when school buildings were not explicitly blacklisted, they were often old and unsuitable. The Plowden Report calculated that, in 1962, of a total of 21,055 English primary schools, almost a third had been built before 1875, and more than a quarter built before 1902.[98] This was counterbalanced by the 2,483 new primaries built between 1919 and 1944, and the 3,424 primaries built after 1945, which made up almost a third of the total, but around two-thirds of primaries still occupied pre-1919 buildings.[99] Plowden reflected that 'school building programmes since the war have favoured the secondary schools'. Of 5,472 secondaries in use in 1962, 1,869 had been built since 1945, or 34 per cent of the total; 1,619, or 30 per cent, had been built since 1919, meaning that only 36 per cent of secondaries occupied pre-1919 buildings by 1962. However, this meant that a third of pupils remained in older buildings that were unlikely to be able to cater for the needs of a modern secondary school, which required numerous specialised spaces, such as science labs.[100] The situation was even worse in Wales. The Gittins Report showed that, in 1962, only 28 per cent of Welsh primaries had been built since 1919 and, while only 22.3 per cent of English primary schools had no piped hot water and 23.8 per cent had no central heating, the figures were 65.1 per cent and 37.3 per cent in Wales.[101]

Logbook evidence confirms that the majority of primary schools, even in Oxfordshire, had not moved to the type of flexible working space that Mary describes by the 1950s and 1960s. Instead, they tended to purge themselves of nineteenth-century remnants, improve facilities, but maintain a classroom space that was a mix of familiar and novel child-centred elements. At Coveney, a small rural mixed primary in Cambridgeshire, dual stacking tables and single locker desks were introduced in 1951 to replace the old dual locker desks. This made the furniture slightly less inflexible and uncomfortable, but retained the same classroom model of a row of desks facing the teacher. Conditions also improved in 1953 when gas lighting, new stoves, new handbasins and drains were installed, although these innovations could hardly be called modern. New heating, a wireless, a record player, a projector and a coal bin were added in 1956.[102] Coveney's developments were typical of the majority of schools in our three case study areas, although schools in Oxford and Cambridge City tended to fare better than rural schools or Sheffield's more deprived urban schools.[103] However, these modernisations did not create the completely flexible environments that Mary had envisaged, and they largely took place within existing buildings.

As with child-centred methods, child-centred shibboleths about the school building and equipment also changed too quickly for schools to keep up. A separate hall for games, dancing and other activities was central to inter-war reforms, for example. However, by the 1960s, when most larger schools finally had one – Gittins noted that only 17.4 per cent of English schools and 18.9 per cent of Welsh schools with more than 100 pupils lacked a hall in 1962 – it was deemed more desirable to have a more 'open-plan' school, integrating the hall with the classrooms.[104] The Department of Education and Science (DES) report *Primary Education in England* (1978) believed that one-fifth of primary school buildings were still not 'reasonably adequate', to the extent that 'they imposed limitations on what could be undertaken'.[105] Only a tenth of classes were housed in 'open or semi-open working spaces'.[106] Nevertheless, much of the original post-war child-centred wish list had been achieved; most schools, with the exception of small rural schools, now had a hall, 'libraries and book collections were available almost universally' and two-thirds of all the classes had a 'nature' or 'interest' table.[107]

Secondary modern and comprehensive schools, while more likely to be housed in a completely new building, still struggled with similar issues. At Greenhill in Sheffield, the newly built secondary modern school was still overcrowded in 1958.[108] Norman Bridge remembered the old building in Liverpool he taught at after the war; it had old furniture, a dingy interior and dirty windows.[109] William Taylor argued that this trend was experienced more widely, and was partly due to the limited amount spent on facilities, staffing and equipment in comparison with grammars. He cited the Hertfordshire Education Committee report of 1955, which reported spending of £1 15s 4d for a child at a secondary modern school compared with £2 18s 4d for a child of similar age at a grammar.[110] As Deborah Thom notes, most secondary modern buildings before 1950 were in makeshift Hutting Operation for the Raising of the School-leaving Age (HORSA) huts, unlike grammar schools, which retained their existing buildings.[111] And even after the wave of school-building from 1951, many children of secondary age remained in unsuitable buildings or in all-age elementary schools.[112] Katherine Watson argues that a further expansion in school buildings was delayed by the postponement of ROSLA, and Glennerster and Low note that spending halved after this date in the context of wider Conservative cuts to education.[113] Thus, the infrastructure required for child-centred education remained partially reformed.

Local case studies indicate the degree to which the majority of primary and secondary schools in England and Wales were 'half-reformed' by the beginning of the 1970s. The efforts of the national inspectorate and many headteachers succeeded in getting schools to adopt a number of child-centred practices, such as relating material to the pupils' 'interests', utilising small group teaching rather than lecturing from the front of the classroom, using apparatus and teaching aids more frequently, and highlighting creative subjects. This was sometimes reflected in the physical reorganisation of the school or classroom, with the promotion of school libraries and school halls, an emphasis on moveable, flexible furniture and the display of pictures on the classroom walls. However, a lack of funding for significant innovations in many schools restricted these concrete changes. For some teachers, the priority was getting running water, or decent lighting or heating, in their school rather than fashionable furniture. Therefore, the restrictions imposed by the built environment, alongside teachers' resistance to new, untested ideas, made full progressive reform impossible in the majority of primary and secondary modern schools, even by 1979. Nevertheless, it was precisely because reluctant teachers were pressed to use half-understood child-centred methods in crowded, ill-equipped classrooms that concepts of childhood, rather than opening out space for the self-expression of the individual child as progressive educationalists had intended, became so limiting, prescriptive and potentially damaging.

Notes

1. Dean, 'Conservative governments', p. 264.
2. Cunningham, *Curriculum Change in the Primary School*, pp. 2, 49 and Jones, *Education in Britain*, p. 55.
3. 'Textbook city fails to make happiness,' the *Guardian* (1975), cited in Ward, *The Child in the City*, p. 16.
4. Mackillop, *Ethnic Minorities in Sheffield*; Carter, *Home, School and Work*, p. 18.
5. For example, WEP C081, interviewed 9/8/01, p. 18; C021, interviewed 17/9/01, p. 19; D020, interviewed 6/6/01, p. 23.
6. The Isle of Ely was originally a separate LEA but was merged into Cambridgeshire in the post-war period.
7. DES: *Children and Their Primary Schools*, pp. 101–2.
8. The terminology recalls William Fuller's famous comment that Elizabeth I's church was 'but halfly reformed'.
9. O'Hara, *Governing Post-War Britain*, pp. 153–4.
10. Woodin et al., *Secondary Education and the Raising of the School-Leaving Age*, pp. 115–19. Peter Mandler discusses the discourse of 'accountability' in 'Educating the Nation I'.
11. Cunningham, *Curriculum Change in the Primary School*, p. 49; Lowe, 'Primary education since the Second World War', p. 9.
12. Jones, *Education in Britain*, p. 54.
13. MacLure, *The Inspectors' Calling*, p. 49.
14. *Ibid.*, p. 110.
15. For example, we can trace the career of HMI C. C. Parmee in Cambridgeshire from 1932–36. Cambridgeshire Archives, C/ES 5A3: Ashley School: Logbooks, 1 June 1932 and 20 June 1932, notes that Parmee inspected but HMI A. F. Norman Butler produced the report; C/ES 51A/3-4: Logbook: Coveney School, 7 June 1934, notes that Parmee inspected but HMI H. J. B. Fox produced the report; R103/033: Logbook: Park Street Junior Middle & Infants, 12 and 13 April 1934 notes that again, Parmee visited and Fox produced the report. Parmee wrote a report jointly with Fox the following year; see St Luke's, Cambridge, Boys: Logbook, Uncatalogued, 27/28 May 1935. By 1936 he was writing the reports from other inspectors' inspections; C/ES146/A1: Stow-Cum-Quy School, Logbook, HMI Report, 9 January and 2 April 1936 noted that Miss Brown inspected, but the report was written by Parmee.
16. MacLure, *The Inspectors' Calling*, p. 128.
17. DES, *Children and their Primary Schools*, pp. 335–6.
18. Cannadine et al., *The Right Kind of History*, pp. 85, 126.
19. MacLure, *The Inspectors' Calling*, p. xxix.
20. *Schoolmaster*, 6 April 1950, p. 538.
21. MacLure, *The Inspectors' Calling*, p. 50.
22. Cannadine et al., *The Right Kind of History*, p. 5.

23 MacLure, *The Inspectors' Calling*, p. 112.
24 For example, Sheffield Archives, CA 729/S1/4-5: Sheffield Bole Hill Mixed School, Logbook, HMI Report, 7 and 8 March 1956; CA 35/934-5: Beighton, Hackenthorpe School, Logbooks, HMI Report, 17 June 1948.
25 Sheffield Archives, CA35/484, HMI Report, Ecclesfield Town County Secondary School, Yorkshire (West Riding), 11-14 July 1950, pp. 4-7.
26 For example: National Archives, ED 156/54, HMI Reports: Primary: Oxfordshire 1946-51; ED 156/4: Cambridgeshire 1946-51.
27 For example: National Archives, ED 156/90: Monmouthshire 1946-51, HMI Report, St Michael's RC Primary, Abergavenny, 25/26 June 1951, HMI Report, Llanhilleth County Primary, Abertillery, 27 November 1951; National Archives, ED 156/196: Monmouthshire 1952-55, HMI Report, Newbridge County Primary School, Abercarn, 25 November 1952, 16 January 1953.
28 For example: National Archives, ED 156/90: Monmouthshire 1946-51.
29 Blackie, *Inspecting and the Inspectorate*, p. 29. On Blackie himself, see Cunningham, *Curriculum Change in the Primary School*, pp. 49, 62.
30 Blackie, *Inspecting and the Inspectorate*, p. 20.
31 Cambridgeshire Archives, C/ES66P/9: Prickwillow School, Logbooks, 13 October 1949, 11 January 1954.
32 Oxfordshire Archives, S137/1/A1/4: Logbook, Hook Norton School, 27 January 1953.
33 Oxfordshire Archives, S4/1/A2/3: Logbook, Albury and Tiddington Junior and Infant School, 9 November 1943.
34 Oxfordshire Archives, S159/1/A1/4: Logbook, Launton Church of England Juniors, 17 April 1959. 'Miss Bews' is probably Mary Bews.
35 Cambridgeshire Archives, C/ES66A/3-4: Ely (St Mary's) Silver Street Junior Middle, Girls: Logbook, HMI Report 3-8 March 1962. This school was reorganised as a secondary school in 1949 and became mixed in 1959.
36 Cambridgeshire Archives, C/ES66A/3-4: Ely (St Mary's) Silver Street Junior Middle, Girls: Logbook, 19 October 1962.
37 Also see Oxfordshire Archives, S112/1/A1/3: Garsington Church of England School Logbook and Oxfordshire Archives, S159/1/A1/4: Logbook, Launton Church of England Juniors.
38 Sheffield Archives, Acc. 2001/26: Logbook: Greenhill County School 1 and Acc. 2001/26: Logbook: Greenhill County School 2.
39 Oxfordshire Archives, S125/2/A1/1: Logbook of Great Haseley Church of England Primary School, 17 February 1943.
40 Sheffield Archives, CA/35/5-6: St George's Church of England School, Logbook, 24 October 1958.
41 Sheffield Archives, CA/35/96, 97, 100: Logbooks: Carbrook Mixed Church School, 15 June 1944.
42 Oxfordshire Archives, OXOHA:OT 213 – Mary Bews – An adviser to Oxfordshire Primary Schools. Interviewed by Philip Best (1996).

43 Oxfordshire Archives, S4/1/A2/3: Logbook, Albury and Tiddington Junior and Infant School, 10 to 12 July 1964.
44 J. B. Biggs had a national reputation. P. G. Pile referred to 'the eager beaver types who have previously "done a Miss Biggs' weekend" on modern mathematics' in 'Trading Post', *Teachers World*, 2 January 1970, p. 11. Biggs also published a book on the subject: Biggs, *Mathematics and the Conditions of Learning*.
45 Oxfordshire Archives, OXOHA:OT 257 – Mel Summers interviewed by Malcolm Graham (1997).
46 DES, *Children and their Primary Schools*, p. 360.
47 For example: Cambridgeshire Archives, C/ES 51A/3-4: Logbook: Coveney School, 14 July 1950; C/ES.142B/1: Soham Fen Board School: Logbook, 5 April 1934; R109/056, R106/045: Milton Road Council School, Chesterton, Cambridge: Log Book, HMI Report, 17 April 1939. Oxfordshire Archives, S9/1/A1/4: Ascot-under-Wychwood Church of England School, Logbook, 2 November 1949; S76/6/A1/2: Cowley St John Girls' School Logbook, 6 May 1939. Sheffield Archives, CA 35/803-4, St Silas Church of England School Logbooks, 21 November 1960; CA/35/800-1: St Barnabas Church of England School, Alderson Rd, Logbooks, 13 and 14 October 1964; CA/35/115: Hillfoot Council School Logbook, 1944–69, 23 May 1962; Gwent Archives, CE.C60.1: Abercarn, Gwyddon Council School Logbook, 22 October 1946; CE. C60.2: Gwyddon Secondary Modern School, Abercarn, Logbook, 8–9 July 1954.
48 Ronald Gould speculated about this. Gould, *Chalk Up the Memory*, p. 45.
49 'The inspector overheard', *Teachers World*, 14 January 1925, p. 791; 'As the inspector sees it: weekly notes on teaching method', *Teachers World*, 25 January 1928, p. 895; 'A Country Headmaster', 'The blessing of inspectors', *Teachers World*, 18 January 1928, p. 828; 'Teachers and inspectors', *Teachers World*, 25 January 1928, p. 866.
50 *Teachers World*, 18 November 1931, p. 246; 'Detestable things in a teacher's life', *Teachers World*, 13 February 1935, p. 695.
51 For example, *Schoolmaster*, 7 July 1932, p. 9, where an old *Schoolmaster* article on the dreaded inspector from 1872 was reprinted as a contrast with present-day attitudes.
52 Cited in *Schoolmaster*, 6 July 1950. *Teachers World* was even more negative about inspectors in the 1950s and 1960s. See 'Onlooker', *Teachers World*, 5 February 1960, p. 3.
53 'Also Disturbed', letters page, *Schoolmaster*, 22 September 1949, p. 322.
54 Oxfordshire Pilot, Ox.005, interview.
55 *Ibid*.
56 Oxfordshire Pilot, Ox. 001, interview.
57 History in Education, Chris Culpin interviewed by Nicola Sheldon (2009), 18.
58 MacLure, *The Inspectors' Calling*, p. xxi.

59 MacLure, *The Inspectors' Calling*, pp. 128-9.
60 MacLure, *The Inspectors' Calling*, pp. ix, 113, 156, 168.
61 Sheffield Archives, CA 35/816, Heeley Bank Mixed School, HMI Report, 9-12, 15-19 and 23 January 1945; National Archives, ED 156/54, HMI Reports: Primary: Oxfordshire 1946-51; National Archives, ED 156/98, HMI Reports: Cambridgeshire.
62 Evans, 'The evolution of Welsh educational structure and administration', pp. 59-60.
63 Jones, 'Which nation's curriculum?', pp. 6-7.
64 MacLure, *The Inspectors' Calling*, pp. x, 36, 38; DES, *HMI Today and Tomorrow*, p. 32.
65 'Don't blame staff over Welsh problem', *Teacher*, 18 January 1974, p. 7.
66 National Archives, ED 156/1108: Monmouthshire 1965-69, Survey of Primary Education in the Rhymney Valley, October 1968.
67 National Archives, ED 156/1108: Monmouthshire 1965-69, A Survey of Rural Primary Schools, Monmouthshire, May-July 1969.
68 National Archives, ED 156/90: Monmouthshire 1946-51, HMI Report, Cwncarn County, 2 and 3 October 1951.
69 Gwent Archives, CE.B.21.5, Llanwenarth-ultra School Logbook, 5 and 6 April 1962; CE.B.36.1-2: Raglan School Logbook, 5 and 6 April 1962.
70 John Roberts, 'Thanks to humanities they see both sides' insert, Gwent Archives, CE. C60.2: Gwyddon Secondary Modern School, Abercarn, Logbook, p. 1.
71 Cambridgeshire Archives, C/ES/42F/5-6: Logbook, Soham Boys' Council School/ Soham Townsend Boys'/Soham Shade School, 1 September 1963.
72 Lerway, 'The middle school'.
73 Cambridgeshire Archives, C/ES/42F/5-6: Logbook, Soham Boys' Council School/ Soham Townsend Boys'/Soham Shade School, HMI Report, 28 and 29 February and 1 March 1957.
74 Cambridgeshire Archives, C/ES/42F/5-6: Logbook, Soham Boys' Council School/ Soham Townsend Boys'/Soham Shade School, 15 October 1963.
75 Cambridgeshire Archives, C/ES/42F/5-6: Logbook, Soham Boys' Council School/ Soham Townsend Boys'/Soham Shade School, undated entry, c. December, 1963.
76 Cambridgeshire Archives, C/ES/42F/5-6: Logbook, Soham Boys' Council School/ Soham Townsend Boys'/Soham Shade School, 'Autumn Term, 1965'. In the child-centred context, the 'realistic maths' Lerway mentioned probably involved the use of apparatus and practical methods.
77 Cambridgeshire Archives, C/ES/42F/5-6: Logbook, Soham Boys' Council School/ Soham Townsend Boys'/Soham Shade School, Spring Term, 1964, Summer Term, 1964, Spring Term, 1965, Autumn Term, 1966.
78 Cambridgeshire Archives, C/ES/42F/5-6: Logbook, Soham Boys' Council School/ Soham Townsend Boys'/Soham Shade School, Summer Term, 1967.

79 Cambridgeshire Archives, C/ES/42F/5-6: Logbook, Soham Boys' Council School/ Soham Townsend Boys'/Soham Shade School, Autumn Term, 1964.
80 Lowe, *Education in the Post-War Years*, pp. 31–2.
81 Tropp, *The School Teachers*, p. 255; Cunningham, 'Primary education', p. 12.
82 Lowe, *Education in the Post-War Years*, p. 103.
83 Oxfordshire Archives, OXOHA:OT 554 – Edward (Ted) Harvey interviewed by John Brucker (2000).
84 It is unclear from John's interview whether the classroom actually had only three walls or whether it had one temporary wall and three made of brick.
85 John's memory of his training college course's dictates on children's attention span is echoed by set texts written at the time he was training. For example, Alex Kennedy wrote in the second edition of *The Teacher in the Making*, p. 43, that children's attention spans were short. Some later child-centred educationalists, however, would have agreed with John that attention spans could be extended *if* the lesson was interesting. See Moorhouse, 'Philosophy', p. 1.
86 Oxfordshire Archives, OXOHA:OT 554 – Edward (Ted) Harvey interviewed by John Brucker (2000).
87 Saint, *Towards a Social Architecture*; Cunningham et al., *The Decorated School*; Hulme, 'A nation depends on its children'.
88 Saint, *Towards a Social Architecture*, pp. 36–41. For a more detailed exploration of the Village College movement and its architect, Henry Morris, see Rée, *Educator Extraordinary*.
89 Saint, *Towards a Social Architecture*, pp. 58–60, 157, 189; Cunningham, *Curriculum Change in the Primary School*, pp. 130–9; Lowe, *Education in the Post-War Years*, p. 26.
90 Thomson, *Lost Freedom*, p. 195.
91 Oxfordshire Archives, OXOHA:OT 213 – Mary Bews – An adviser to Oxfordshire Primary Schools, interviewed by Philip Best (1996).
92 Saint, *Towards a Social Architecture*, pp. 189–90.
93 Oxfordshire Archives, OXOHA:OT 213 – Mary Bews – An adviser to Oxfordshire Primary Schools, interviewed by Philip Best (1996).
94 Oxfordshire Pilot, Ox.006, interview.
95 Laurie, *A Lifetime in Schools*, p. 26.
96 Laurie, *A Lifetime in Schools*, p. 32. Unsurfaced playgrounds represented a significant hazard to pupils. Cambridgeshire Archives, St Luke's, Cambridge, Boys: Logbook, Uncatalogued, 1 May 1935, notes that 'After an accident resurfacing of the playground was requested.'
97 Lowe, *Education in the Post-War Years*, p. 27. The exact figure is 22.5%.
98 The precise figures are 6,580 and 5,986 respectively.
99 DES, *Children and Their Primary Schools*, p. 389. The precise figures are 11.3% and 16.3% respectively.
100 *Ibid.*
101 DES, *Primary Education in Wales*, pp. 458–9.

102 Cambridgeshire Archives, C/ES 51A/3-4: Logbook: Coveney School, 30 January 1951, 12 October 1951, 23 October 1951, 14 April 1953, 23 January 1956.
103 For example: Cambridgeshire Archives, R103/033: Logbook: Park Street Junior Middle and Infants; Oxfordshire Archives, S216/1/A1/4: Oxford St Philip & St James Church of England Boys Logbook 1949–65.
104 DES, *Primary Education in Wales*, p. 459. Vernon, *Hunger*, pp. 169, 171, notes that a hall was seen as desirable for all schools in the 1940s. Burke and Grosvenor, *School*, p. 103, note the new focus on open-plan buildings in the 1960s.
105 DES, *Primary Education in England*, p. 9.
106 *Ibid.*
107 *Ibid.*, pp. 51, 59, 110.
108 Sheffield Archives, Acc. 2001/26: Logbook: Greenhill County School 2, HMI Report, December 1958.
109 Bridge, *My Liverpool Schools*, p. 55.
110 Taylor, *The Secondary Modern School*, pp. 45–6.
111 Thom, 'The 1944 Education Act', p. 122. These temporary huts persisted in some schools for much longer, however.
112 Jones, *Education in Britain*, p. 27; Lowe, *Education in the Post-War Years*, p. 92.
113 Watson, 'Education and opportunity', p. 362; Glennerster and Low, 'Education and the welfare state', p. 54.

5

Primary school teachers, gender and concepts of childhood

Non-utopian progressive education, as it was implemented in English and Welsh schools, shaped new expectations for primary-aged children. The inter-war ideal of a quiet, well-behaved individual altered in response to both psychological prescriptions and social trends to shape a new image of the 'normal child' that emphasised extroversion and sociability. Schools were expected to measure development across a wider range of axes, promoting social and emotional maturity as well as physical and intellectual, which meant that 'normality' became an even more difficult ideal for the child to achieve. The introduction of the school record card after 1944 formalised this kind of assessment, introducing a range of specific milestones that children should have achieved by certain ages. Child-centred pedagogy also narrowed the expected capabilities of the junior-age child dramatically. Most obviously, the misuse of the term 'egotistic', and its imprecise application to children aged as old as eleven, encouraged parents and teachers to see children as innately selfish, unable to appreciate anything that lay outside their own 'sphere of interest'. This fundamentally altered teaching methods, as curriculums were rewritten to be concrete and practical, and linked to the child's own immediate surroundings. Nevertheless, it was still persistently asserted that children naturally belonged in rural areas, so urban children were viewed as innately deprived – even as rural pupils were stereotyped as backward and slow.

Teachers' responses to child-centred education were not created equal. Due to the strong associations between women and children, the imagining of the female teacher as a 'mother' to her pupils, and the development of non-utopian progressive practice in the primary school after the Second World War, child-centred pedagogy itself became gendered feminine in teachers' professional literature, feeding into the significant resistance exhibited by some male teachers. As we have seen, female teachers by no means capitulated to new child-centred ideas, especially when these ideas challenged their own authority and expertise, as in the case of G. L. Haynes. Nevertheless, expectations placed upon primary school teachers by progressive inspectors were perhaps greater than the similar pressures in secondary moderns, and child-centred practice could be stigmatised by its associations with a lack of discipline, firmness and 'high standards', qualities that male teachers were assumed to possess.

Non-utopian progressive education also reshaped old gendered stereotypes in new psychological language, which affected the education of girls in both primary and secondary schools. The education of primary-aged pupils was not theoretically gendered, but the norms governing seven to eleven-year-old girls' behaviour meant that they often failed to live up to child-centred expectations. For adolescent girls, the familiar child-centred maxim that the curriculum must be designed around the pupils' immediate interests encouraged teachers to provide 'realistic', often vocationally orientated, activities for teenagers, which allowed persistent gender stereotypes to remain in play. Girls' activities were orientated around the household and/or female-dominated occupations, such as typing and clerical work, whereas boys were steered towards industry and craft. While single-sex secondary schools were in decline across this period, this did not necessarily lead to a more egalitarian experience of education, and might even have served to further entrench gender differences.

The seven to eleven-year-old

In 1931, Cyril Burt wrote in *The Primary School* that '[m]uch attention has been devoted to the systematic study of children at the infant stage and also at the adolescent period, but the intermediate stage between the ages of seven and eleven, up to the present, has been comparatively neglected.'[1] Burt's assertion reflects the historiography of twentieth-century childhood. Twentieth-century British youth, especially older teenagers and young adults, have been linked to radicalism, social upheaval and modernity, and so have attracted sustained interest from historians; children under eleven, in contrast, have tended to appear in the context of the family, or been considered only in relation to histories of abuse and neglect within the home, workplace or institutional care.[2] Such histories have foregrounded the institutional status of childhood, and hence constructed a chronology asserting that the physical and legal condition of children broadly improved up to the 1970s, when a backlash against the 'rights of the child' led to a more punitive approach to juvenile justice and renewed disciplinarian attitudes in the school and the home.[3] In contrast, Mathew Thomson traces the origins of this 1970s 'backlash' back to the post-war settlement, arguing that anxieties engendered by the experience of the Second World War led to increasing restrictions on children's movements, and despite brief radical campaigns for the rights of the child, these liberal assertions were torn apart both by their own internal contradictions and by a simultaneous conservative reaction against the 'permissive society' and free discipline.[4] Similarly, I assert that it was the 1950s, not the 1970s, that was the crucial turning point for concepts of childhood in England and Wales.

The inter-war ideal for a primary-aged child was summed up in this phrase from a Cambridgeshire inspector's report from Grantchester, an all-age rural elementary, in 1933: 'The discipline is good: the children are diligent, quiet in manner and courteous.'[5] This is immediately evident across inspection records. In Oxfordshire which, as we have seen, was a more progressive county in the inter-war period, the enthusiasm and liveliness of the pupils was mentioned in 36 per cent of the surviving reports, but the importance of industry and standards was emphasised in 27 per cent and 25 per cent of the reports respectively, and discipline appears in 14 per cent. In contrast, in the forty-six reports from the 1950s, although standards are mentioned in 17 per cent, the happiness and friendliness of the pupils appears in 30 per cent, and the idea of freedom in 22 per cent.[6] It is clear that, for progressive inspectors at least, the definition of a 'good pupil' had changed over this period.

Assessments of teachers-in-training also reflect changing norms. In Sheffield, a lesson plan notebook from Southey Green Juniors kept by the head shows how new teachers at the school were advised throughout the inter-war and post-war periods. In 1937, a lesson on 'A Dutch farm' was criticised for being too noisy at times, as the children were 'too enthusiastic' when answering questions, but by 1961, a lesson on a 'journey from London to Dover' was praised because the children responded well to the questions they were asked.[7] Similar findings are evident in J. H. Frisby's consideration of examinations for the teaching certificate. The 1931 Yorkshire Board asked teachers to describe how they would deal with six different 'types' of child: 'habitually disobedient', 'nervous', 'day-dreamer', 'untidy in dress', 'mischievous' and 'spoilt'. By the 1950s, teachers were asked instead to imagine that they were dealing with an 'unsociable child', 'child who tells lies', 'highly gifted child' and a 'bullying child'.[8] The shift of emphasis from behaviour to psychology, and from the ideal of obedience to the ideal of appropriate sociability, is obvious.

Inter-war teachers' accounts reflect the expectations they had of their pupils. Delia Skelley began teaching in 1920, and recalled her experience as a student teacher in Croydon with reference to standards of behaviour: '[The children] were very polite and very nice. I enjoyed it very much indeed. No discipline problems'. Gerard Phillips became a student teacher in 1926, and remembered that discipline was 'very strictly controlled', which he felt made his life easier.[9] Some teachers were more critical of prevailing norms, such as Kathleen Young, who recalled in her retrospective memoir, written in the 1980s, that when she was teaching in the inter-war period in a London primary, 'most of one's effort was expended on keeping order', which she felt was unnecessary. The headmistress would check that no conversation could be heard from the classrooms, so Kathleen found it difficult to give individual attention to the children who needed it 'while keeping the other children absolutely quiet'.[10] Younger teachers noted generational shifts after the war. 'Miss Read' was the pseudonym of a female teacher who started teaching in Middlesex in the 1950s. In her very popular, semi-fictionalised memoir, *Village School* (1955), she recalled 'Miss Clare', a fellow teacher: 'she is now over sixty, and her teaching methods have of late been looked upon by some visiting inspectors with a slightly pitying eye. They are, they say, too formal; the children should have more activity, and the classroom is unnaturally quiet for children of that age.'[11]

The revised image of junior-aged children promulgated from the 1950s onwards both emphasised how children *should* be and stated what they *could not* be. The former shift emphasised the gregariousness, sociability, activity and practicality of the seven to eleven-year-old.

In Circular 151, issued by the Ministry of Education in 1947 and entitled 'Explanatory notes for the completion of the school record card', 'sociability' was defined as strong if the child was 'very sociable and companionable; very happy and easy in company' and weak if he or she 'keeps aloof from others; self-centred and solitary; unfriendly'. It was also asked 'Does he work better or seem happier alone or with others?' Good qualities also included being 'adventurous and independent' and bad qualities were being 'over-submissive, timid or anxious'.[12] Although the new image of the extroverted and energetic normal child that was emphasised by record cards theoretically applied to all children, it was especially relevant for this age group due to the characteristics assigned to them by developmental psychologists. The Underwood Report (1955), *Maladjusted Children*, suggested that maladjustment in this age group had been previously neglected and should be subject to intensified attention: 'It used to be held that the years between the ages of seven and twelve constituted a kind of golden age, when a child gave little trouble and lived happily and thoughtlessly, reaching an almost mature state of stability and reasonableness towards the end of the period.' Noting that 'the eighth and ninth years constitute one of the peak periods for references to child guidance clinics', Underwood suggested that this earlier characterisation was wholly false; junior-age children were neither well-adjusted nor reached a mature state by twelve.[13]

This shift tied into a wider psychological assumption that the primary school stage was the 'age of the gang', in contrast to the more socially isolated infant stage, and so solitary children in this age group were especially unusual – and possibly psychologically unhealthy. As Mary Atkinson stated in *Junior School Community* (1949), 'We realise the importance of the "gang" and of being a member of a gang.'[14] David Armstrong argued in his examination of the development of the category of the 'normal' child from the 1930s onwards, 'The solitary child . . . suffered from not being a child' and hence was construed as problematic.[15] Nevertheless, these claims were age-specific; infants were not expected to play co-operatively, while adolescents were assumed to require some space and solitude to deal with puberty, although both groups were expected to spend some time in social situations. Physically, adolescents were also expected to be withdrawn and awkward during puberty while infants were still trying to control their limbs, in contrast with the physical image of seven to eleven-year-olds in a steady state of growth.[16] Concerns about only children tied into this image of the junior age group. Donald Winnicott argued in one of his *Difficult Children* radio talks, broadcast from 1945, that only children could become 'precocious'. This was positioned as problematic because the child was not living his or her present stage of development to the full, and so became 'stunted in play'.[17]

In contrast, inter-war journals and teaching guides had very little to say about 'gangs'. When social co-operation between children was described in the 1920s and 1930s, it tended to be pictured as something that came naturally to children rather than something that had to be observed and instilled by adults. *Teachers World* reported in 1932 that the influential educational writer, Philip Ballard, had praised the Dalton Plan – which provided for individual work, rather than group work – in a speech to the Dalton Association, because children helping each other with their own projects 'often . . . proved that the child was a better teacher of the child than the adult.'[18] Ernest Campagnac, Chair of Education at the University of Liverpool, wrote in the journal in the same year that 'Children like to talk to us, but they are probably more at home with their brothers and sisters then older people.'[19] However, sociability was not necessarily seen as particularly important. The *Schoolmaster* noted in a 1931 review of the US psychologist Lewis Terman's *The Problems of the Gifted Child* that while 'gifted' children often had difficulty with social interactions within their age group, this was not a problem.[20] In the same year, the journal published 'A plea for solitude', expressing concern that 'Compulsory games . . . do not suit every child . . . All children are not moulded in the same pattern'.[21]

The post-war image of the primary-aged child was further skewed by popular misunderstandings of child psychology. One key confusion centred around the idea of 'the egocentric child'. This issue was identified by Piaget himself in his *Psychology Today* interview in 1970. When asked by the interviewer, Elizabeth Hall, 'When you say that the young child is egocentric, just what do you mean?', Piaget replied, 'That term has had the worst interpretations of any term I have used.' Indicating that this was a widely recognised issue, Hall replied, 'That's why I asked the question.' Piaget went on to clarify his use of this terminology: 'When I refer to the child, I use the term egocentric in an epistemological sense, not in an affective or moral one. This is why it has been misinterpreted. The egocentric child ... is incapable of putting himself in someone else's place, because he is unaware that the other person has a point of view.'[22] Piaget first identified this 'egocentric stage' in *The Language and Thought of the Child* (1923, trans. 1926), arguing that it began to diminish around the age of seven.[23] He expanded upon the idea in *The Child's Conception of the World* (1926, trans. 1929), where he stated that the child's 'intellectual egocentricity' means 'that the child neither spontaneously seeks nor is able to communicate the whole of his thought.'[24] For Piaget, egocentricity was not a moral failing, but a key characteristic of what he was later to term the sensori-motor and pre-operational stages of development.

In popular teaching guides, however, the idea of an 'egotistic' or 'narcissistic' child was often left open for misinterpretation, as Piaget's comments in 1970 suggested. It was often linked with the assumption that such a child was selfish or antisocial, especially as the term was often used in conjunction with such assertions. The terms were also often used to refer to older children and teenagers, despite Piaget's limitation of the full extent of the term to children under seven. These terms were misused in both the inter-war and post-war periods, but the increasing influence of non-utopian progressivism in the post-war period meant that the idea became more dominant. The psychologist Agatha Bowley argued in *Everyday Problems of the School Child* (1948) that 'children are essentially egotistic, impatient, inept, unappreciative and at the same time remarkably bombastic and over-bearing'.[25] In *Learning and Teaching* (1937, 1946 and 1959 editions) Hughes and Hughes asserted that 'It is well known that young children are, as a general rule, determined little egotists,' while *Primary Education* (1959) stated that 'During childhood there is a gradual transition from the baby's egocentric life of play towards the adult's occasional hours of freedom.'[26] Even in the 1960s and 1970s, when more reliable Piagetian textbooks emerged, the term could be used confusingly. Beard correctly wrote in her *An Outline of Piaget's Developmental Psychology for Students and Teachers* (1969) that Piaget believed young children's thought was distorted around his or her own point of view, but she phrased this in terms that could have been interpreted as condemnatory: the child is 'egocentric ... seeing everything in relation to himself.'[27]

These guides, therefore, usually associated egocentricity with undesirable characteristics, rather than using the term in the value-neutral sense that Piaget had intended. As G. A. N. Lowndes, assistant education officer to the LCC, wrote in the second edition of his history of progressive education, published in 1969: 'Piaget . . . concluded that up to 7 the average child . . . is egocentric . . . spoilt or self-centred.'[28] This erroneously linked the essential nature of the junior-aged child to self-centredness, implying that – quite apart from their need for practical, concrete experience – children are simply unable to become interested in things outside themselves or their immediate surroundings, because they are too selfish. This sat uncomfortably with the idea that seven to eleven-year-olds were essentially sociable, but this could be rationalised as a shallow kind of sociability, unlike the deeper connections forged by adolescents. The psychologist C. W. Valentine, professor of education and head of department at Birmingham, wrote in his popular textbook *Psychology and its Bearing on Education* (1950) of the 'more intense emotional bond' of early adolescent friendships, compared with the groups formed by younger children, which also do not possess true team spirit.[29]

The characteristics assigned to the primary-aged child explained many of the key tenets of the post-war child-centred programme. Group work in the classroom, for example, was a progressive shibboleth, and if it was assumed that all children naturally ought to be sociable and gregarious, it is easy to see why it was promoted, as this would ensure that education was enjoyable. The emphasis placed on group work also invoked an idealised sense of community, in response to the sense of social fragmentation felt in post-war Britain.[30] *Teachers World* columnist 'Jason' wrote in 1952 'Let's teach children to work with each other', stating that it was selfish for children to work by themselves and, contradicting the idea that they have to be 'taught' to co-operate, that 'children love coming together' to produce a piece of work.[31] As we have seen, inspectors and schools themselves placed greater emphasis on group work from the Second World War onwards, and the use of 'grouping' became one piece of evidence that a school was progressive. If children were presumed to be egotistic in the 'selfish' sense, group work may also have been encouraged to try to counteract these tendencies, as Jason's statements implied, and also linked to education for citizenship via the importance placed on 'the school community'. Ian Grosvenor and Martin Lawn explore how the post-war Ministry of Education envisaged this community as a microcosm of the wider world. The CACE (Central Advisory Council for Education) report, *School and Life*, of 1947, suggested schools ought to create 'a social structure satisfying to the pupil – a structure which he [sic] can understand and from which he may learn the discussion of practical difficulties and problems with objectivity and tolerance'.[32] However, this was necessarily an idealised image of tolerance and co-operation, not an accurate reflection of British society.

In contrast, innovative pedagogical solutions in inter-war manuals and articles tended to oppose undesirable 'class teaching' to desirable 'individual work', with little discussion of 'group work'.[33] This was particularly evident in discussions of the Dalton Plan and the Project Method, both developed in the United States, which allowed children to pursue projects by themselves, although the Project Method offered more free choice than the Dalton Plan, which retained a greater role for the teacher by envisaging the division of a set syllabus into individual assignments.[34] The psychologist C. M. Fleming encapsulated this trend in *Individual Work in Primary Schools* (1934), criticising 'the class method' and 'ability grouping' and promoting the Project Method above the Dalton Plan because it allowed for true individuality.[35] Numerous other inter-war texts highlighted these new teaching methods, such as John Adams's *Educational Movements and Methods* (1924), and *The Triumph of the Dalton Plan* (1932) by London school inspector Charles W. Kimmins and Belle Rennie, founder of Gypsy Hill training college and secretary of the British Dalton Plan association.

In the same way that shibboleths about group work were seen as desirable in the context of a post-war welfare state, the emphasis on individuality in the 1920s and early 1930s reflected broader national norms. In the 1920s and early 1930s, *Teachers World* emphasised that children became more individual as they got older, and that this development was desirable.[36] By the end of the 1930s, however, the stress upon individuality was already being tempered by concerns about sociability as the Second World War loomed. In a 1939 article on 'Free discipline and common sense', which reported a series of discussions between psychologists, it was noted that 'The world to-day offers a terrifying object lesson in the unlimited evil which can be wrought by badly adjusted individuals', citing Alfred Adler's 'insistence on social co-operation as the true measure of maturity'.[37] Similarly, a 1942 article in the *Schoolmaster* on 'Problem children' warned that 'sheer individuality' was 'dangerous' as it produced 'a misfit' when children needed to learn to live in a community.[38]

Child-centred education was also supposed to be centred around the child's interests. However, having determined the expected characteristics of primary-aged children, advice manuals and journal articles often defined the interests of this age group precisely as well, moving away from the focus on the individual and creating a less flexible curriculum. As Cyril Burt put it baldly in a radio talk in 1930: 'the same child shows very different interests at different stages of his life; whereas different children show similar interests at similar stages.'[39] This linked the language of 'interests' to developmental psychology, suggesting that there was a coherent scientific explanation for the unity of children's interests and, again, marking out children who did not conform as abnormal. As we have seen, the 1931 Hadow Report emphasised that primary children's interests were essentially practical and constructive, and from the age of nine they were increasingly interested in exploring their surroundings. However, in the inter-war period, the idea that you could generalise about the interests of an entire age group was not especially prominent, due to the focus on individual treatment. For example, in 1936 *Teachers World* promoted an 'optional period', when children would each pursue their own interests: 'In this "free" period, it was argued, the teacher would find out a good deal about the "hidden" side of the child's character – much about the likes and dislikes of individuals.'[40]

In the post-war period, the definitions of primary children's interests became much more specific. Although the idea that children of this age shared the same interests was frequently qualified in theory, it did not tend to be as nuanced in practice. Nancy Catty included a long description of the child's interests in her introduction to *Learning and Teaching in the Junior School* (1941). For example, she claimed that all children under ten were interested in living creatures, that none of them were interested in the past as opposed to 'the here and now', and that all of them would hence prefer to pursue social and environmental studies rather than history, which was more suitable for adolescents who were naturally 'interested in motives and springs of action.'[41] She qualified these statements a few pages later by noting that her description was 'generalised'; however, she went on to say, 'most people who know children as individuals and not as "classes" will agree that it is substantially true'.[42] This classic progressive move saw her rejecting a view of children that saw them as primarily situated in groups, then claiming that extensive observation of individual children had allowed her to offer a more accurate description of the group. Rather than arguing that we should not view children in a group but as individuals, she suggested that we could treat a class as a group, as long as our understanding of children was psychologically accurate, noting that there was a 'growing knowledge' of junior children's interests.[43]

In some logbooks we can glimpse how the move to child-centred teaching affected attitudes towards seven to eleven-year-old pupils at the school. Alice Freeman was headteacher at Grantchester juniors in Cambridgeshire from 1950, a tiny rural school. Although making reference to the need to enlarge these rural children's horizons and improve their speech, she maintained a positive relationship with the small number of pupils on roll (thirty-eight in 1949), writing in July 1960 as the older children left: 'Again how it hurt to lose these children – but they must go on and grow up – I realise that – but . . . !'[44] A 1957 HMI report stated that the school was 'fortunate in having a Head Mistress who identifies herself so whole-heartedly with the welfare of her pupils'.[45] Freeman praised the children's maturity when the only other teacher in the school, Miss Kendall, collapsed in assembly in 1960: 'The Juniors were quite self-contained – calmly took the Infants into their room'.[46] These terms, however, indicate that she had an older ideal of good, orderly behaviour, rather than adopting the new child-centred image of the active and extroverted child. She did engage with child-centred practices such as handicrafts and school trips to places of local interest, and got on well with the HMI, Mr Simmonds, but did not seem to be particularly knowledgeable about psychology. In 1960, she wrote 'It meant a great deal to be able to discuss with parents, their children's work, failures, hopes and psychological troubles,' but had to cross out and rewrite the term 'psychological' after misspelling it, indicating that this was not a particularly familiar word.[47] When she left the school in 1963, she stated: 'I have attempted to set the Christian ideal of friendship and help to one another', demonstrating her essentially traditional values.[48]

Grantchester's new head, Elizabeth Taylor, was a self-defined progressive; a 1972 profile of her written by a well-known progressive,

Raymond O'Malley, who had begun his career at the experimental school, Dartington Hall, and who became a lecturer in English, noted that she had been influenced by a number of progressive writers, 'but the two she spoke of with most warmth are Anna Freud and Vicars Bell'.[49] Vicars Bell was a rural schoolteacher whose memoir demonstrated child-centred education in practice.[50] O'Malley felt that she had implemented a truly progressive system: 'In this school there is a continual flow, a continual rhythm of altercation between small group and large group and individual work.'[51] However, in contrast to the warmth with which Alice Freeman had written about her pupils, Taylor's progressive and psychoanalytical stance led her to re-evaluate their quiet behaviour in negative terms. Numbers remained small during her headship, with forty on roll in 1965, but she found the children unsatisfactory according to child-centred definitions of a 'normal' junior. In 1964 she wrote after a visit to a dance festival that

> The Grantchester children were frightened and ill at ease, but did join in a few dances. The other schools danced with delighted skill. The children made almost no comment, but it was a triumph that they managed to go . . . The more experiences they can have, the more that life outside comes into the school, the more I feel they may be liberated from the apathy, the aggression, that characterises most of their behaviour.[52]

She mentioned later that year that the children were 'less aggressive', but never gave a concrete example of what constituted aggression. In October 1964, commencing a term's work based on their own interests, she felt that 'for the first time, the children have shown some curiosity'.[53] The diffident children at Grantchester were beginning to live up to child-centred norms by becoming more enquiring. Interestingly, this school had a very mixed intake – the HMI report of 1965 noted that 'The children belong to families ranging from those internationally famous for scholarship [probably the children of University of Cambridge fellows] to modest agricultural workers' – and so Taylor's judgements were not based solely, or even largely, on class-related judgements about her working-class pupils.[54] They formed as she realised that these children did not fit her ideal of what seven to eleven-year-olds should be.

The Marxist sociologists Rachel Sharp and Anthony Green offered an explanatory framework for this kind of peculiar, psychodynamic account of children's behaviour in *Education and Social Control* (1975), a study of the social environment of Mapledene Lane junior-infant school in Birmingham, a new build completed in the late 1960s on a large new local authority housing estate. Two of the three female teachers that Sharp and Green observed were deeply concerned about the 'abnormality' of most of the children in their classes, but found it difficult to describe what this meant. 'Jean and Mary, well, they're not what I would call normal little girls, by any stretch of the imagination, but there's nothing I could put my finger on to say they're abnormal.'[55] The same teacher thought that another child, Michael, was 'really odd'. He showed little interest in the activities she expected him to enjoy and although he sometimes joined groups, 'he doesn't *need* to – I can't make up my mind why he is so peculiar.'[56]

Sharp and Green suggested that it was the emphasis placed by these radically child-centred teachers on 'interest' and 'enthusiasm', and the belief that these characteristics were natural to children and would lead them to effectively self-direct their learning, that led to these pathological interpretations of their pupils' behaviour. 'Motivation and interest in the activities which the teacher approves of are necessary conditions of becoming defined as a successful pupil', Sharp and Green argued, indicating that the idea of individual choice was simply a veneer.[57] 'The key feature associated with the abnormal children was that the teacher's approach manifestly did not work for them.'[58] Like the 'apathy' exhibited by the Grantchester pupils, boredom in the classroom, in psychological terms, indicated a problem with the child. It was assumed by teachers who practised such methods that the child *must* be abnormal, odd or peculiar because 'normal' children were defined by their 'natural' curiosity.

Another central idea put forward by non-utopian progressives for the junior school curriculum was the suggestion that child-centred methods allowed children to achieve better results, especially in creative subjects, than earlier approaches to teaching. However, these methods often involved forcing children to conform to a certain idea of how their work ought to be at a given developmental stage, rather than allowing full freedom in the classroom. H. C. Dent, a prominent commentator on education and a former headteacher, editor of *TES* and Director of the Institute of Education at Sheffield, stated in 1970 that progressive education would allow, and had allowed, children to accomplish things that had been believed to be far beyond them by unlocking their creative potential.[59] This assertion, again, was one that was most often made in relation to under-elevens, rather than adolescents, and indeed, it was often held that the unique 'creative potential' of children in subjects such as art dissipated around puberty. Therefore, the positive statements made about seven to eleven-year-olds could be limiting, locking the schoolchild into a certain set of expected interests and abilities, as well as fatalistic when set in contrast to teenagers. The image of the child as an unspoilt primitive that emerged in art teaching sat in tension with the move towards social realism in creative writing, but both developments drew from similar ideas about childhood, suggesting that children were unable to comprehend anything beyond their own direct experience.

The 'New Art' movement, inspired by the work of Franz Cižek in Vienna, first emerged in the inter-war period. *Teachers World* followed the development of Cižek's ideas closely in the 1930s.[60] Cižek believed that pre-adolescent children's art should naturally resemble primitive artwork, and teaching children how to use correct perspective, for example, would constrain their natural creativity and produce inferior art.[61] Part of the movement involved supplying children with restricted materials, which Cižek thought would promote 'creative problem-solving'.[62] These ideas were strictly confined to the junior stage; Cižek argued that 'the creative instinct ceases in children around the age of eleven.'[63] The 'New Art' articles in *Teachers World* followed a consistent theme, showcasing examples of the children's work alongside quotations from viewers who did not believe they were the work of children, and sometimes including more traditional children's drawings to demonstrate how 'inferior' they were.[64]

The New Art was influential in schools in our three case-study areas, with inspectors' recommendations for art teaching continuously consistent, detailed and specific, such as the preference for bold colours, large pages and a more 'childlike' approach. These ideas were present from the 1930s onwards. The head of High Green junior-infant school wrote in 1935 that there had been a 'Staff meeting . . . to discuss some points of interest in the Sheffield Schools' Art Exhibition. Emphasised that we should allow more freedom to the child to work out his own ideas in pattern making & picture constructions. Suggested that work should be done more often with coloured film papers & that . . . potato printing should be tried.'[65] This exhibition was possibly orchestrated by Marion Richardson, a London inspector who became a key English exponent of the New Art; she had spoken to Sheffield schools on the request of the National Union of Teachers.[66] Post-war Oxfordshire reports expressed similar ideas, drawing directly on Richardson's views; a 1954 report from North Aston noted that the art is restricted 'to pattern printing and rather small pictures drawn in pencil and sometimes coloured . . . the work would have more educational value if large papers, big brushes and powder colours were available'.[67]

The New Art movement played a central role in the life histories of key child-centred reformers such as Robin Tanner and Sybil Marshall, who often asserted that it was children's art that led them to 'see the light' about child-centred education.[68] Art teaching clearly led teachers to relate to child-centred assertions more closely, perhaps because it fed into images of children as creative and unspoilt, in opposition to modernising forces in the inter-war and post-war periods. In the 1980s, when Tanner wrote his autobiography, he put this viewpoint explicitly: 'The fifties were a decade of startling change . . . We were constantly reminded that we were now living in a "Technological Age".' He conceptualised the 'modern' focus on industrial advance as greedy and materialistic, and asserted that these values increasingly dominated education, stating that 'My own views were totally opposed to our educational system.'[69] In this context, childhood became linked with a certain image of the nation that emphasised the small-scale rural community over the more impersonal urban or suburban experience, and asserted the importance of social interdependence in the context of fears about growing individualism and privatism.[70]

In the face of agricultural depression and rural depopulation from the 1870s onwards, only a fifth of Britons lived in rural areas in 1956, although, outside south-east Wales, more Welsh people were engaged in agricultural occupations than English people in the 1950s and 1960s.[71] Raymond Williams's famous statement that 'there is almost an inverse proportion, in the twentieth century, between the relative importance of the working rural economy and the cultural importance of rural ideas' has been expanded on by a number of historians.[72] The discourse on rural schools suggested that these children represented the preservation of a traditional way of life that ought to be retained at all costs, even if it meant the sacrifice of broader educational opportunities. The teacher T. H. Etherington recalled two former pupils in an advice guide of 1950; both sons of farmers, they had reached the school leaving age, but while one was keen to become a farmer, one avowed that he wanted any job but farming. For Etherington, this was not a choice that made sense: 'we knew that this difference was not so much a result of natural aptitudes as that one boy had been made to feel all along that he was a useful and essential part of the life of the farm ... The other had experienced the toil without having had set alight in him that spark of vital interest.'[73] Etherington simply assumed that these farmers' sons must have a 'natural aptitude' for farming, and so the dissenter must have been put off by other factors.

Children in child-centred rural schools were encouraged to participate in traditional country crafts and display their work, but there was little thought given to how educational these pursuits really were. At Garsington in Oxfordshire, the pupils demonstrated 'the processes of spinning, carding, weaving and dying at the County Show' in May 1954, and a BBC film was made in 1961 showing the children engaged in gathering wool, teasing, carding, spinning, washing, mordanting, dying, weaving and finally sewing their own clothes. The film praised the school's attention to 'rural studies', but such a focus imprisoned the children in a kind of time warp rather than allowing them access to 'modern' education, despite the rhetoric of modernity that surrounded these practices.[74] An earlier film focusing on three Oxfordshire rural schools, *Village School* (1954), had similar priorities; this film was so popular it was still being shown on refresher courses in the late 1970s.[75] This was despite the continuing decline of employment in rural areas, especially in traditional craft industries; as early as 1934, the *Schoolmaster* itself noted that only 6 to 8 per cent of the population were employed on the land.[76]

The New Art movement highlighted the tension in non-utopian pedagogy between the image of the child as modern and forward-looking, and childhood as a special period of primitive timelessness, as Tanner's writings make clear. David Matless and Peter Mandler have challenged the idea that rural imagery was predominantly associated with 'rural nostalgia', arguing that inter-war rurality and popular interest in the countryside might be better characterised as modernist.[77] The active construction of a rural ideal, therefore, despite its traditionalist appeal for some influential child-centred educationalists, was also tied into both inter-war and post-war projects for creating good citizens of the modern state. Child-centred educationalists focused on getting the urban child out of the city, rather than exploring the potential that the city had to offer. Mary Bews recalled the use of study centres in Oxfordshire to enable urban children to experience a rural environment, while the historian of the school journey movement, W. E. Marsden, suggests that this was one of the key motivations of the pioneers of school journeys.[78] Issues of race were also prominent after 1945; a rural childhood was implicitly white, whereas multicultural urban centres were seen as dogged by the underachievement, delinquency and violence that were stereotypically associated with children of colour.

The focus on rurality allowed this image of the nation to be adapted for both English and Welsh schools, neglecting Welsh calls for an educational system controlled by Wales itself. Apart from the concern that children should learn Welsh, much of the discussion about providing a 'Welsh' curriculum centred on the promotion of traditional Welsh rural activities.[79] As the headteacher of the first Welsh-speaking school, founded in Aberystwyth in 1939, put it in 1943: 'When I think of the term "Welsh Education", I mean something infinitely more fundamental than using Welsh as a medium of instruction. The education must draw on the native material and penetrate deeper than the matter of language . . . The education provided should be kindred to its soil.'[80] As in England, inspectors consistently recommended the pursuit of traditional arts and crafts, but ignored the experience of children who lived in urban areas such as Cardiff, Swansea and Newport.[81] The Gittins Report (1967) recognised that the traditional view of education as a ladder to social mobility in Wales ironically meant emigration from the most traditionally 'Welsh' rural areas: 'Although education should help the child to identify with his own immediate background it must, in some instances, release him from it . . . Many Welsh children will eventually leave the communities in which they were brought up, to live and work in very different circumstances . . . they enter a future which cannot be foreseen.'[82] This limited the theoretical impact of an authentically Welsh child-centred education.

Educationalists stereotyped the rural child as easier to teach than the urban delinquent, but inevitably slow-witted. The Wood Report of 1929 framed expectations for future generations of teachers by concluding that the incidence of mental defect in rural areas was almost twice that of urban areas, blaming this, in eugenic terms, partly on the persistence of 'inferior stock' in these communities after the 'better stock' had migrated from the countryside.[83] John and Ted summed up these prejudices in their reciprocal interview, recalling their experience of teaching in rural Abingdon. John stated, 'The children I feel were a really nice crowd. They were a bit country. I don't mean that in a disparaging way, but they were not the slickest bunch of characters, not the city slickers by any means, but they had a nice slow take on life and I think a good understanding of each other.' Ted added, 'Except . . . several of these youngsters [evacuees] had persuaded their parents to settle in the area so we had a rather tough little minority in there.'[84] It was rural childhood, rather than the rural child, that was idealised in the inter-war and post-war periods, and linked to broader assertions about what was 'natural' for seven to eleven-year-olds.

The teaching of creative writing, which, as Carolyn Steedman has shown, became much more dominant in primary schools after the Second World War, drew on similar ideas about children's natural abilities. However, this 'revolution in English teaching' focused on life-writing; it was seen as essential that children drew from their own daily experience, and work on imaginative subjects was discouraged.[85] *Primary Education in England* (1978) was explicit on this point: 'Where [creative writing] fell into the category described in the Bullock Report [*A Language for Life*, 1975] as "colourful or fanciful language, not 'ordinary', using 'vivid imagery'. . . very often divorced from real feeling". . . then its absence can only be applauded. At its best personal writing enabled children to recreate experiences faithfully and sincerely and arose from the context of daily life in the classroom or outside.'[86]

The stories written by adults for junior-aged children published in *Teachers World* also underwent a shift by the late 1960s; in the inter-war and immediate post-war period these had spanned a range of genres but now were confined to social realism. 'Operation Columbus' (1970), which dealt with kids in gangs on a council estate and assumed the villain's delinquency was the result of his poor upbringing, was a typical example.[87] A reader wrote in later that month to praise the new short stories: 'Some of them are a far cry from the old "once upon a time there was a little elf called Snoopy" nonsense . . . writers for children today come to grips with the real environment.'[88] This stood in opposition to inter-war attitudes to creative writing, which had stressed the appeal of fantastical stories. Joan Luxton wrote in *Teachers World* in

1931 that 'Fairy stories always excite a child; a true representation of life in an ordinary school might bore him.'[89] Geoffrey Cross, a regular contributor, made similar recommendations for pupils' own creative work in 1935: 'I never allow the child to write about himself... Children are so honest. *If you force their thoughts inwards upon themselves you limit them to actual facts, and stifle imagination which is the basis of all good writing.'*[90]

The Bullock Report (1975), a major and influential report on the teaching of English in primary and secondary schools, thought, in contrast to *Primary Education in England*, that both realistic and fantastical stories had a place in children's literature. However, Bullock was concerned that teachers had placed too great an emphasis on realism, especially in the secondary school, where it might be used 'almost exclusively [as] a source of material for personal response to social issues' which led to pupils falling back on 'the ready-made cliché reaction' gleaned from television and the press.[91] As Lucy Pearson has shown, teachers' turn towards more 'realistic' creative writing in the 1960s and 1970s reflected a wider movement within children's literature at the time, which had moved from an immediate post-war revival of fantasy stories aimed at stimulating the imagination to 'social issue' novels.[92] This was bound up with the response to Basil Bernstein's work on linguistic codes that disadvantaged working-class children at school, but ultimately highlighted a separate argument, the idea that children, due to their innate psychological limitations, could only deal effectively with material that was close to their own lives.[93] The children envisaged by advocates of realistic creative writing were a different kind of 'primitive' from those imagined by the New Art movement, but primitives they remained.

Female teachers, primary schools and the gendering of child-centred education

In both the inter-war and post-war periods, primary schools were female-dominated environments. W. A. L. Blyth noted that, in 1938, there were 14,845 male and 88,968 female primary school teachers, so women made up 86 per cent of the workforce. In contrast, by 1965, there were 32,875 male and 107,087 female teachers, so women made up only 77 per cent.[94] Despite the marriage bar in most local authorities, women predominated even more strongly in the inter-war than in the post-war period. When the figures for all elementary (primary and secondary modern) schools are considered, women lost further ground; Asher Tropp notes that the proportion of women in elementary education fell from 74 per cent in 1900 to 65 per cent in 1954.[95] This reflects the larger number of male teachers in secondary modern schools as well as the overall fall in the percentage of female teachers across the profession. Dolly Smith Wilson suggests that lobbying from militant male unions such as the National Association of Schoolmasters (NAS) also contributed to the fall in female teachers.[96] The NAS line was that women were capable of teaching young children and older girls, but were not equipped to teach older boys. For example, the NAS president, G. H. Snow, asserted in 1946 at their national conference that male teachers should teach boys as 'He has trodden the same path, partaken of the same nature, and shared the same hopes.'[97]

Women were also persistently under-represented in positions of responsibility, despite their numerical dominance. Penny Summerfield notes that while more women than men held primary headships before 1961, the situation was reversed thereafter, especially following equal pay in 1970; 80 per cent were held by men by 1987.[98] This may also reflect the decline in single-sex education, as women tended to head girls' schools. A similar situation persisted in mixed-sex unions such as the NUT.[99] Women's relative lack of promotion opportunities might have been linked to career breaks. As H. C. Dent argued, the earlier average age of marriage and the increased percentage of women marrying meant that women spent fewer years teaching after they qualified, although they might return to the profession later.[100] Additionally, the majority of emergency trained teachers, who made up a sixth of teachers in maintained schools by 1951, were male.[101]

Women teachers tended to hail from better-off backgrounds than men, but conversely, were often less qualified. Floud and Scott's 1955 figures indicate that 46 per cent of male primary teachers had been born to manual worker families, compared with 48 per cent from 'intermediate' backgrounds (these included teaching, farming, 'lesser professions', clerical and personal service – the 'lesser professions' and clerical categories dominated, with only 5 per cent from teachers' families) and 6 per cent professional and administrative. The figures were similar for male secondary modern teachers, at 47 per cent manual, 46 per cent intermediate and 8 per cent professional. Women primary teachers, on the other hand, were predominantly from 'intermediate' families; 39 per cent came from manual families compared with 52 per cent intermediate and 9 per cent professional. Their backgrounds differed even further from those of their male counterparts at secondary modern level, where only a quarter were manual while 55 per cent were intermediate and 11 per cent professional.[102]

However, female teachers were less likely to have been educated to degree level than male teachers in both the inter-war and post-war period. In 1935, 14.4 per cent of all male teachers and 4.3 per cent of all female teachers were graduates.[103] By 1963, the numbers of graduate teachers had risen but gender disparities remained; 2.5 per cent of female primary school teachers were graduates, compared with 7.4 per cent of male primary school teachers, and 13.0 per cent of female secondary modern school teachers were graduates, compared with 20.2 per cent of male secondary modern school teachers.[104] In the inter-war period, they were less likely than male teachers to have undertaken any form of teaching qualification but, as we have seen, these 'unqualified' teachers largely disappeared after the Second World War. In 1900, 40 per cent of teachers were unqualified. This had fallen to 2 per cent by 1954. Asher Tropp described this shift in the following terms in 1959 in his history of teacher training: 'The profession has shed its mass of cheap untrained female labour and has begun to move slowly towards its goal of a trained graduate profession.'[105] This assumed that female teachers' lack of formal teaching qualifications made them less 'professional', and hence less valuable, than their male counterparts.

As we have seen, 'married women returners' were being deliberately targeted by the Department of Education by the 1960s. It was recognised that it was usual for women to take a career break after having children, and these teachers were seen as a partial solution to problems of teacher supply in this decade, as the 'baby boom' generation moved from infant schools into primary and secondary schools and the raising of the school leaving age loomed.[106] In 1960, there were around 894 thousand more ten to fourteen-year-olds in the British population than there had been in 1950.[107] However, by the 1970s, demographic patterns had resulted in falling demand for these experienced teachers; the

Teacher reported in 1974 that there were 'no posts for a fifth of women who want to teach again'.[108] The number of married women returners had increased as pupil numbers fell; in 1970, there were around 158 thousand fewer ten to fourteen-year-olds in Britain than there had been in 1960.[109] This meant that women were less able to return to teaching, even if they wanted to.

Teaching discourse in the post-war period, especially in primary schools, often deliberately positioned teachers as mothers, as Carolyn Steedman argues, citing Donald Winnicott's statement that the young teacher needs to learn about mothering through 'conversation with and observation of the mothers of children in her care'.[110] As Christine Wall has shown, teaching manuals and journals often used images that associated the figures of the teacher and the mother. For example, the *Schoolmaster/Teacher*, when it pictured teachers at all, usually used images of female teachers interacting closely with the children. In a rare example, from 1954, a male teacher is shown relaxing away from his pupils, with the caption 'Pursuit of the cup that cheers . . . a familiar scene in the staffroom, where the morning break offers a few moments' respite (if you're lucky) from marking, supervision and the guerrilla warfare of the classroom.'[111] This positioned teaching as a 'natural' occupation for women but something that was less natural (and naturally enjoyable) for men, although it may be rewarding. Alison Oram suggests that the idea of the teacher as mother pre-dated the post-war period, and argues that unmarried inter-war female teachers deliberately used this image to counteract stereotypes that they were 'unnatural women' because they had not fulfilled their instinctive urges towards marriage and motherhood. For example, the NUWT attacked a doctor who had made such insinuations in 1935, stating 'he should know that in the vast majority of cases a woman teacher's work is a complete outlet for her maternal instincts.'[112] Although teachers were imagined as mothers in the nineteenth century as well, this indicates how the growth of psychological knowledge reframed a teacher's position in relation to her pupils.[113]

Child-centred education and parenting was sometimes linked to effeminacy and delinquency by professional discourse, especially as progressive practice was often seen as characteristic of the female-dominated primary school rather than the more male-dominated grammar schools. In 1960, an editorial in *Teachers World* entitled 'Poor old dad' viewed the loss of paternal authority as one of the symptoms of a more permissive society, arguing that

> many are victims of 'You mustn't lay a finger on the little darling' school of thought... This is the fault of Mums – who have read all about how to bring up children in the women's magazines. For years their heads have been stuffed with half-baked and dangerous psychology. We, in schools, have fostered the same kinds of thought.[114]

This perhaps suggests why older men were less likely to engage with this 'female' vision for education. Furthermore, child-centred education was associated with the declining authority of adults over children as a whole, as both teachers' complaints and articles such as the 'Poor old dad' piece in *Teachers World* indicate. As fatherhood became both more emotionally significant and yet more contested and uncertain than had been the case in previous generations, male teachers may have perceived a double onslaught upon both their identities as fathers and as professional providers.[115] Similarly, female teachers may have felt under pressure to employ child-centred methods both in the workplace and as mothers, which, as we have seen, could lead to uncertainty, anxiety and, in some cases, resistance.

Female teachers often recalled struggling at the beginning of their careers because children's image of the ideal teacher was 'a young married man with children', as Musgrove and Taylor observed in 1969.[116] Rosemary Deem reported the findings of a 1976 guide that showed that many probationary female teachers had difficulty controlling the boys in their classes, with one respondent, who taught in a comprehensive school, stating: 'if only they were scared of me... I can't do it the way the kids are used to because I'm not a big aggressive male, you see.'[117] This made female teachers' claims to professional identity even more contested than those of male teachers, with the assumption that 'traditional' teaching involved exercising control and discipline, whereas 'trendy' progressive education led to chaos. Neville Bennett's 1976 study, which considered the teaching styles of all third and fourth-year junior school teachers [teachers who taught nine to eleven-year-olds] in Lancashire and Cumbria, actually suggested that female teachers, especially those aged over forty, were slightly more likely to use formal teaching styles than men, being keen to retain class control with these older primary-aged children. However, this did not challenge the automatic assumptions that women were more 'child-centred', due to the mistaken association of 'progressive' education with 'permissive' child-rearing, and the belief that women were more naturally interested in both.[118]

Mathew Thomson argues that there was a distinct gender difference in teachers' responses to psychology, which linked to their engagement with child-centred education, but he suggests this was related to the type of school in which teachers worked; men were more likely to work in secondary schools and be concerned with examinations and with subject-specific teaching, while women more often worked with infants and juniors.[119] Because of the gendering of child-centred pedagogy, men were often more concerned with professional status based on subject knowledge, while women were more likely to combine the role of mother and teacher, which progressivism encouraged. Martin Lawn notes in his study of a Mass Observation diary kept by a teacher that the diarist, May, observed a gender split in responses to new trends in wartime. She recorded in 1942 'Talk to two men teachers. They advocate much more Reading, Writing and Arithmetic in schools as opposed to Art, P.E., etc.' The male teachers' interest in 'traditional' subjects as opposed to those that encouraged 'self-expression' indicated their commitment to an academic curriculum. While May herself was interested in 'activity' learning, she felt that male teachers were less involved in the new pedagogy in general.[120] Ashton *et al.*'s 1975 survey made a similar observation, noting, in contrast to Bennett, that female teachers were more progressive than male. However, unlike Bennett's study, Ashton considered teachers who taught all age groups throughout the primary school, not just the older age groups, which may help to explain the discrepancy.[121] Therefore, gender, as well as age, conditioned teachers' responses to non-utopian progressivism throughout the post-war period.

Female pupils in primary and secondary schools

Girls were not specifically envisaged as a 'problem group' in national discourse during this period. Indeed, at least at primary school age, they could be considered easier to teach than boys.[122] However, child-centred norms implicitly defined them as abnormal, even if teachers were less likely to complain about them. Childhood and adolescence were gendered very differently in child-centred writing. Manuals, texts and reports that discussed adolescents foregrounded gender by asserting that boys' and girls' interests were fundamentally different.[123] In contrast, the most popular teaching manuals for primary school teachers usually mentioned the differences between boys and girls only briefly; the term 'child' is consistently used for younger children, with gendered pronouns appearing only when the subjects approached adolescence. For example, M. V. Daniel's standard textbook *Activity in the Primary School* (1947) contrasted the 'child of seven' with 'the boy or girl of eleven', while the Plowden Report used the term 'girl' 126 times and 'boy' 119 times, compared with its 1,000+ matches for 'child'.[124] As this suggests, gender assumed greater significance at the older end of the age group, because common characteristics were seen as less usual. Daniel, who was an HMI in Manchester, thought that after the age of ten, 'the divergence between the interests of boys and girls becomes more apparent'.[125] HMIs were often concerned that children should have teachers of the same sex, but only once they reached a certain age; reports did not otherwise mention the gender of primary-aged pupils.[126] *Teachers World* and the *Schoolmaster* also had little to say on gender for this age group; Joseph Edmundson's comment in 1956 that 'the average primary school child, boy or girl, is a very healthy young animal with an almost insatiable craving for physical activity', was typical.[127]

To argue that the child-centred image of this age group remained ungendered is not to suggest that teachers did not display gendered attitudes towards their pupils in practice. As the HMI Survey Report *Curricular Differences for Boys and Girls* (1975) noted 'there is virtually no distinction made between boys and girls in the timetabling of nursery and infant schools and classes. Nevertheless, boys and girls do behave differently in these classes, and are expected to behave differently.' The report thought that this tendency only increased once children entered the junior school.[128] Girls consistently outperformed their male peers throughout primary school and on the 11-plus, and teachers were aware of this fact.[129] However, it is still significant that the theoretical image of primary-aged children was one that highlighted shared practical interests and gregarious energy, rather than gender, distinguishing them further from adolescents and adults. Becoming a fully gendered being indicated that the child was getting closer to maturity.

Furthermore, it was precisely because the image of the primary-aged child remained ungendered that girls in this age group were often seen by teachers as unsatisfactory; there was no positive ideal that they could live up to.[130] Primary-aged girls were framed as less creative and enthusiastic, incapable of independent thinking because they were too well-behaved; ironically, this may have resulted from the conflict between the set of norms that defined a 'good child' and the set that defined a 'good girl'. As Valerie Walkerdine has argued, 'girls are often defined within education as displaying characteristics of passivity, rule-following and good behaviour, which makes their status as natural children quite problematic' if 'natural children' are defined as active and defiant.[131] These norms were well-established by the inter-war period – a 1919 article in *Teachers World* defined girls as 'passive, sympathetic, faithful, patient and conservative', while boys were 'active, adventurous, variable, original and progressive' – but these characteristics took on a new meaning as the 'ideal pupil' was redefined by child-centred educationalists and developmental psychology.[132] If child-centred children were inherently 'progressive', where did that leave the 'conservative' girl?

Experiences of adolescence were much more explicitly gendered. Gender expectations had been reflected in formal working-class education since at least the early nineteenth century, whether it was provided by the state or by voluntary organisations, but became increasingly so from the 1870s onwards, as cookery and housewifery were added to the girls' curriculum, alongside needlework.[133] Gendered assumptions also governed teachers' responses to their pupils. The prevailing model was that a group of boys was more trouble, but a single girl could be a loose cannon, especially for a male teacher. A range of accounts from male secondary modern school teachers tasked with mixed classes in the 1950s and 1960s portrayed this stereotype, which persisted throughout the early and mid-twentieth century. Writing on secondary modern school discipline in 1960, Richard Farley argued, 'As a rule, girls are more docile than boys, they tend to be a little more civilised ... Their range of behaviour is narrower than that of a boys' class; one has less idiots and hooligans and less original thought.' However, 'a really difficult girl' 'can cause more trouble than half a dozen boys'.[134] Walter James, the editor of the *Times Educational Supplement*, noted in 1962 that 'Girls are usually much quieter [than boys], though occasionally you will find an uncontrollable terror in a rough class.'[135]

In his retrospective autobiography, Edward Blishen recalled the horrific experience of standing in at the local girls' school when there was a shortage of teachers there. The head had commented, 'if you've never taken girls, it might be . . . a useful experience.' He described entering the school: 'a blurred fantasy, in my vision, of tall creatures, all tee-heeing, and all unbelievably long of leg' and then a classroom of girls 'fixing me with shameless eyes'.[136] These assumptions linked to the persistent belief in the juvenile justice context that delinquent girls were rarer, but more troublesome than delinquent boys, especially because their actions tended to be linked to sexual misconduct. Pamela Cox examines the functioning of this idea in practice in inter-war England and Wales.[137] Blishen's description of his pupils, for example, recalls this link between bad behaviour and 'uncontrolled' sexuality in working-class girls. The expectation that female adolescents were 'quieter' and 'more docile' than male adolescents also confined 'normal' behaviour for girls within a narrower range. As with concepts of middle childhood, the assumption that girls were well-behaved but unoriginal affected how they were taught by child-centred teachers.

The non-utopian progressive contention that the 'natural interests' of adolescent boys and girls predisposed them towards gendered activities allowed these older stereotypes to persist. Unlike the more radical changes wrought by post-war progressivism, this assumption was already in action in the 1930s. It was possibly because this offered a way of engaging with 'modern methods' without deviating too far from the original curriculum, and also because it offered a solution to the problem of engaging the interest of older adolescents, who were often impatient to leave school and enter the workplace. In 1931, *Teachers World* suggested a course called 'The home as a project' for the 'B class' girl, where the pupil would imagine she has her own house and is furnishing it. It was argued that debates on household topics should work well as the girls would be 'pleased' to 'contribute' as 'they study goods in shop windows, catalogues and magazines with considerable interest'.[138] 'A practical course for backward boys' in the same year focused on '(a) The man's side of home maintenance and the domestic budget (b) Topical events from a newspaper.' The writer thought that 'The material dealt with has a direct appeal to the boy who was discouraged and dismayed [by academic work] . . . Here he is working with boys of his own age at a task he really wants to be able to do.'[139]

These courses were both aimed at less academic adolescents, indicating that these schemes were seen as most relevant for the low-achieving working-class pupil. Despite the progressive veneer, deviations from these gendered interests were not countenanced by *Teachers World*. When a reader wrote in 1935 to ask: 'It is proposed to let the senior girls of 13-14 attend this woodwork centre for a course of woodwork in their last year at school. Could you give me some idea of what they should be expected to do . . . ?' the editor rejected the idea, using the girls' own 'interests' to justify his suggestion:

> I suggest that you think seriously about taking *Upholstery and Furniture Repairs*... The work they do will be of real use to them in after life, the work to be done is probably waiting in their homes... The woodwork involved is such that girls can be expected to do it fairly well in their stride, and will not demand hours of, to them, dull preparatory tool manipulation.[140]

Gendered curriculums persisted into the post-war period, playing into the wider assumption that girls had less aptitude for mathematics and science than boys. In T. H. Etherington's 1950 manual, based on his own teaching practice, he sketches out examples of projects that the teacher might set in school; the boys are to do a project on the gasworks and the girls on the clothing factory. His descriptions of these projects indicate that the content is not equal in difficulty. While the boys are to do basic science, studying how coal gas is made and the uses of its by-products, the history of gas-making and street lighting, calculations of the profits of coal, meter readings and the volume of cylinders, the girls are to do less maths and science, focusing on where wool comes from and how it is made into cloth, the reasons for locating the factory where it is, the history of clothmaking and calculations of the weekly earnings of workshops.[141]

The logbooks of Sheffield schools also indicate that vocational provision was often gendered. The new focus on youth employment after 1945 meant that schools took a greater role in directing pupils explicitly towards appropriate lines of work, a task that risked utilising both gender and class stereotypes.[142] To take some examples from Sheffield logbooks, at Beighton secondary modern in 1953, the senior girls were sent to visit the Children's General Hospital and boys the Sheffield Transport Maintenance Depot. The 1954 report noted that housecraft now had more emphasis on cooking food in relation to meals, and budgeting would be introduced, emphasising the practical element of this female-only subject.[143] At Southey Green secondary modern in 1955, girls made visits to a bakery, a laundry and a sweet factory, whereas at

Bole Hill all-age school in 1951, the senior boys visited the Iron & Steel Federation exhibition.[144] More broadly, girls were often tasked with studying biology and 'hygiene', while boys tackled a broader course of basic science that included some chemistry and physics, although it was still a watered-down version of the academic curriculum.[145]

Despite the child-centred contention that these courses suited the girls' 'natural interests' and hence would be innately enjoyable, girls often disliked such lessons. Stephanie Spencer's oral history interviewees had all attended secondary modern schools in the 1950s, and recalled how much they had hated domestic science classes. Paula commented, 'we made really weird things in cookery, we never made anything I wanted to eat. I remember making soup – we never ate soup in our house. It's awful isn't it, such a waste of money.'[146] While these girls' experience was clearly affected by the intertwining of class and gender, Mary Evans and her peers had similar feelings about domestic science teaching at their girls' grammar school in the same decade.[147] Interestingly, by the 1970s, some girls in comprehensive schools had started to demand such an approach; the HMI Survey on *Girls and Science* (1980) noted that its respondents expressed views such as 'I would try to relate it [science] more to everyday things that would probably interest girls more, such as how equipment in the home works.'[148] However, as ever, it is difficult to disentangle what these pupils 'really thought' from their awareness of the dual sets of expectations they should be conforming to as female adolescents; it is also unclear how far this survey cherry-picked evidence from its respondents to fit established views about child-centred education.

Single-sex secondary education was in relative decline by the 1970s, with less than a third of state secondary schools remaining single-sex – and this proportion was dominated by single-sex grammars, meaning that an even greater percentage of working-class adolescents were in mixed-sex schools.[149] This was hailed by contemporaries as a sign that education was becoming more equal for adolescent girls. R. R. Dale's 1974 multi-volume study of mixed and single-sex education, which came down emphatically on the side of mixed schools, argued that mixed schools were more 'natural' for both girls and boys as they replicated conditions within the family and in adult life.[150] However, Dale's findings were challenged by the social scientist Rosemary Deem, who published *Women and Schooling* in 1980. Deem argued that Dale's study had actually shown that girls performed slightly less well academically in mixed-sex schools and were less likely to take maths and science subjects than if they attended single-sex schools.[151] Dale, she suggested, had emphasised the social benefits of mixed-sex schooling in his analysis, but this should be challenged 'since one of the things it may involve is breaking down girls' resistance to the imposition of various stereotypes of femininity to a greater extent than is found in single-sex schools'.[152] As we have seen, the way in which gendered progressive norms functioned in secondary modern and comprehensive schools supported Deem's view; girls were sanctioned for stepping outside gendered norms, and might have been seen as socially immature for doing so.

While the argument that schools should reproduce a 'natural' mixed-sex environment appeared compelling to left-wing educationalists in the 1970s – A. S. Neill had made similar claims for mixed-sex Summerhill in the 1930s – the feminist rejoinder might be that there is nothing 'natural' about education under patriarchy, especially if one expects schools to resist prevailing gendered norms.[153] It was well-established in the 1970s that fewer girls than boys took maths and science subjects to a high level, and that this was more common in mixed than single-sex schools.[154] For example, the HMI Survey Report *Curricular Differences Between Boys and Girls* (1975) was clear that 'in matters of subject choice, mixed schooling tends to underline rather than to blur the distinction between the sexes.'[155] This could have been due to formal curricular arrangements; certain subjects were often 'blocked' together by the timetable, discouraging girls from mixing arts and sciences.[156] Benn and Simon's study of the comprehensive school (*Halfway There*, 1970) found that 50 per cent of the schools they surveyed limited some subjects to boys only and 49 per cent to girls only.[157] However, both teachers and fellow pupils could informally discourage girls from taking maths and science. The HMI Survey *Girls and Science* (1980) recorded some of these attitudes. Girls internalised negative feedback; they frequently expressed 'the view that physical sciences were really for the boys' even when the subject was compulsory, and felt more comfortable with biology, seen as a 'female' science, than with chemistry and physics.

Boys dominated class discussion, as one girl recounted: 'I would try to have more all-girls classes than mixed because you tend to feel overshadowed in a class, especially by boys who tend to have a better flair for the subject. This makes you feel embarrassed or stupid about asking for something to be explained or saying that you don't understand.' This girl had already assumed that boys had a 'better flair' for science and that girls needed to be taught separately to make up for girls' supposed inadequacies.[158] Both male and female teachers confirmed these attitudes; one girl, who had taken science subjects, said that 'The senior mistress thinks girls should take ladylike subjects such as needlework, so I decided to show her that girls are just as good at science as boys are.'[159] As the writers Anna Coote and Beatrix Campbell argued in the second edition of their popular second-wave feminist text *Sweet Freedom* (1982), schools could not escape the patriarchal society in which they existed, and the conscious or unconscious bias of teachers. It was not enough simply to appeal to the idea that 'mixed-sex' education mirrored the 'real world'.[160]

Arguments about the 'naturalness' of mixed-sex education, instead, should be understood in the context of concern for the social and sexual development of adolescent boys, rather than the intellectual achievement of adolescent girls. This was evident in the examples that Dale chose to cite in his study. He pointed out that a majority of boys preferred mixed-sex education, making statements such as 'women's and girls' influence calms down excess'. Even one male respondent who preferred single-sex education pointed out that it could be bad for social life: 'there is a tendency for shyness to arise.'[161] The push for mixed-sex education could also be seen not as an attempt to address educational equality but as a panacea for the intensified fears about male homosexuality that emerged from the 1950s onwards.[162] As Chris Waters has argued, single-sex institutions were seen in the post-war period to produce homosexual encounters and 'corrupt' young men.[163] A. S. Neill stated in 1945 that single-sex schools were 'unnatural and dangerous'.[164] Rebecca Jennings has shown that, while public discourse focused on homosexual acts between boys at schools, fear of lesbianism came into play as well after the 1950s, with schoolgirl 'crushes' diminishing in fictional representations, moving away from the 'kissing' and 'bed-sharing' depicted in school fictions of the 1920s.[165] Contact with the opposite sex at a young age, thereafter, was believed to steer both girls and boys on an appropriately heterosexual path. Girls' academic interests were sacrificed in the name of securing social norms.

As the majority of schools began 'moving towards progressivism', teachers' concepts of childhood were reforged by a half-implemented form of child-centred education. Maturational stages and the separation of childhood and adulthood became explicit in popular post-war teaching guides and implicit in the organisation of training, schools and classes. Child-centred education was associated with femininity, and encountered resistance from teachers who felt that it threatened their existing craft and subject knowledge, and who did not have faith in its methods. However, as teachers adopted methods they did not necessarily understand, a more rigid and limited concept of the seven to eleven-year-old emerged, based on a set of rules and methods rather than on a thorough understanding of the psychology behind the recommendations. As this image was linked to the assertion that children were essentially incapable of understanding concepts outside their own experience, interests and wants, it reconfigured this age group as self-centred, in need of 'social training' to become fit for co-operation and collaboration in the adult world. Gender also conditioned teachers' responses to both primary and secondary school pupils, as norms of girlhood came into conflict with norms of childhood and adolescence. Female teachers, meanwhile, were expected to be more progressive than men but were castigated and professionally penalised for being so.

Individuality, so prominent in inter-war educational texts, became subordinate to sociability and co-operation in the post-war period, to fit the child for membership of a community.[166] The move towards a social vision for education in the post-war period was formed in the context of a social democratic consensus and the increased theoretical emphasis on collectivism. Whereas individuality had been positively associated with the liberal British polity in the inter-war period, defined against the military uniformity imposed by the Nazi state, it became less theoretically desirable after the experience of the Second World War.[167] The decreased emphasis on the individuality of the child in the educational setting also occurred alongside the post-war growth in sociology. As both Thomson and Burchell have argued, there was a transition from the psychological to the sociological approach in understanding child development by the 1960s, which emphasised the relation of the child to his or her environment and family, rather than the analysis of the child in individual isolation.[168] This did not represent a replacement of psychological with sociological concerns, but rather the emergence of what has been termed the 'psycho-social', which maintained that the individual personality was developed through collective experience.[169] Children's individual talents and interests were no longer foregrounded; it became more important to ensure that primary-aged children were following the correct developmental paths towards adulthood, despite the assertion that the primary stage should be treated as valuable in its own right.

Notes

1. Board of Education, *The Primary School*, p. 33.
2. Histories of child welfare, crime and health that feature children, but do not engage with concepts of childhood, include Behlmer, *Friends of the Family*; Cooter (ed.), *In the Name of the Child*; Horn, *Young Offenders*; Humphries, *Hooligans or Rebels?*
3. For example, Hendrick, *Child Welfare: England*, p. 1; Hendrick, *Children, Childhood and English Society*, p. 9; Cunningham, *Children and Childhood in Western Society*, pp. 18, 177, 190; Heywood, *The History of Childhood*, pp. 27–30.
4. Thomson, *Lost Freedom*, pp. 1–2, 20.
5. Cambridgeshire Archives, C/ES79/A2, Grantchester School, Logbook, 27 February 1933.
6. Compiled from Oxfordshire Archives.
7. Sheffield Archives, CA 35/680: Southey Green Juniors: Headteacher's Notes on Criticism Lessons, 15 June 1937 and 19 January 1961.
8. Frisby, 'The History of Educational Psychology Teaching', p. 141.
9. Cunningham and Gardner, *Becoming Teachers*, pp. 173–4, 189.
10. Young, *The Green Velvet Dress*, pp. 37–8.
11. Read, *Village School*, pp. 16–17.
12. Sheffield Archives, Acc.2001/26, 9.
13. DES, *Report of the Committee on Maladjusted Children*, p. 17.
14. Atkinson, *Junior School Community*, p. 26.
15. Armstrong, *Political Anatomy of the Body*, p. 27.
16. Board of Education, *The Primary School*, pp. 24–5.
17. Winnicott, 'Only child', pp. 14–15. See the broader discussion of the 'problematic' nature of only children in Violett, 'Only Children Growing Up in Britain'.
18. '500 speeches on education', *Teachers World*, 13 January 1932, p. 510.
19. E. T. Campagnac, 'The teaching of literature', *Teachers World*, 29 June 1932, p. 490.
20. *Schoolmaster*, 2 April 1931, p. 628.
21. 'A plea for solitude', *Schoolmaster*, 1 October 1931, p. 481.
22. Hall, 'A conversation with Jean Piaget', p. 28.
23. Piaget, *The Language and Thought of the Child*, pp. 41, 46.

24 Piaget, *The Child's Conception of the World*, p. 6.
25 Bowley, *Everyday Problems of the School Child*, p. 3.
26 Hughes and Hughes, *Learning and Teaching*, 2nd edn, p. 29; Ministry of Education, *Primary Education*, p. 24.
27 Beard, *An Outline of Piaget's Developmental Psychology*, p. 9. Also see Ridgway and Lawton, *Family Grouping in the Primary School*, p. 52.
28 Lowndes, *The Silent Social Revolution*, p. 115.
29 Valentine, *Psychology and its Bearing on Education*, pp. 569–70.
30 For example, Daniel stated that children must both express individuality and conform to the demands of the community through small group work in *Activity in the Primary School*, p. 57.
31 'Jason', *Teachers World*, 2 January 1952, p. 1.
32 Grosvenor and Lawn, 'Days out of school', p. 381.
33 For example: Kennedy-Fraser, *Education of the Backward Child*; Fleming, *Individual Work in Primary Schools*; Raymont, *Modern Education*; Potter (ed.), *The Practical Junior Teacher*.
34 For more on this, see Adams (ed.), *Educational Movements and Methods*.
35 Fleming, *Individual Work in Primary Schools*, p. 9.
36 'J. St. CH', 'Liberty or license', *Teachers World*, 14 January 1920, p. 563; 'The final year at an elementary school: individual work, private study and sectional teaching', *Teachers World*, 5 January 1921, p. 606; F. Roscoe, 'The junior school: a critical survey of the new Hadow report on the primary school', *Teachers World*, 18 February 1931, p. 809.
37 'Free discipline and common sense: practical advice on handling the "difficult" child', *Teachers World*, 16 August 1939, p. 10.
38 W. Sternwhite, 'Problem children and children's problems', *Schoolmaster*, 7 May 1942, p. 309.
39 Burt, 'Mental development', p. 901.
40 'The optional period', *Teachers World*, 26 August 1936, p. 987.
41 Catty, *Learning and Teaching in the Junior School*, pp. 7, 105.
42 *Ibid.*, p. 10.
43 *Ibid.*, p. 32.
44 Cambridgeshire Archives, C/ES79/A2: Logbook: Grantchester School, HMI Report, 27 June 1949; 29 July 1960.
45 Cambridgeshire Archives, P179/25/13: Grantchester Church of England HMI Report, 28 June 1957.
46 Cambridgeshire Archives, C/ES79/A2: Logbook: Grantchester School, 12 October 1960.
47 Cambridgeshire Archives, C/ES79/A2: Logbook: Grantchester School, 12 December 1951; 28 July 1960. Cambridgeshire Archives, P179/25/13: Grantchester Church of England HMI Report, 28 June 1957.
48 Cambridgeshire Archives, C/ES79/A2: Logbook: Grantchester School, 30 October 1963.

49 Cambridgeshire Archives, C/ES79/A2: Logbook: Grantchester School, insert, Profile: 'Grantchester School' by Raymond O'Malley (May–June 1972), Vol. 22, 4, 1973, New Zealand Department of Education.
50 Bell, *Dodo*.
51 Cambridgeshire Archives, C/ES79/A21: Logbook: Grantchester School, insert, Profile: 'Grantchester School' by Raymond O'Malley (May–June 1972), Vol. 22, 4, 1973, New Zealand Department of Education.
52 Cambridgeshire Archives, C/ES79/A2: Logbook, Grantchester School, 1 May 1964; HMI Report, 28 June 1965.
53 Cambridgeshire Archives, C/ES79/A2: Logbook: Grantchester School, 11 June 1964 and 23 October 1964.
54 Cambridgeshire Archives, C/ES79/A2: Logbook: Grantchester School, HMI Report, 28 June 1965.
55 Sharp *et al.*, *Education and Social Control*, p. 72.
56 *Ibid.*, p. 136-8.
57 *Ibid.*, p. 157.
58 *Ibid.*, p. 118.
59 Dent, *Century of Growth*, p. 101.
60 For example: R. Eccott, 'A Cižek class in London', *Teachers World*, 8 August 1934, p. 677.
61 *Ibid.*
62 'The art of the paper-cut', *Teachers World*, 27 June 1934, p. 511.
63 R. and A. Eccott, 'What about the new art in the senior school?', *Teachers World*, 10 October 1934, p. 50.
64 A. Sanderson, 'An art course for senior schools', *Teachers World*, 21 January 1931, p. 659. Also see Tanner, *Double Harness*, p. 100.
65 Sheffield Archives, CA.35/667-9: High Green Junior and Infant School Logbooks, 17 October 1935.
66 Tanner, *Double Harness*, p. 100.
67 Oxfordshire Archives, S11/1/A1/1: North Aston C of E Junior School Logbook, 26 January 1954.
68 Tanner, *Double Harness*, pp. 25, 74, 148–50; Marshall, *An Experiment in Education*, pp. 9, 20.
69 Tanner, *Double Harness*, pp. 148–50.
70 On ideas of growing individualism, especially among the working class, and challenges to this idea, see Thomson, *Lost Freedom*, p. 80; Donnelly, *Sixties Britain*, p. 11; Todd and Young, 'Baby-boomers' to 'beanstalkers', p. 452; Devine, *Affluent Workers Revisited*.
71 Laing, 'Images', p. 144; Sandbrook, *Never Had it So Good*, p. 32; Howkins, 'The discovery of rural England', pp. 62–88. DES, *Primary Education in Wales*, p. 13.
72 Short, *The English Rural Community*, p. 1; Rose, *Which People's War*, pp. 200-3.
73 Etherington, *In and Out of School*, p. 8.

74 Oxfordshire Archives, S112/1/A1/3: Garsington Church of England School Logbook, 4 March 1954, 27 January 1961, 7 March 1961.
75 Cunningham, *Curriculum Change in the Primary School*, pp. 121, 155.
76 'Meeting of rural school teachers', *Schoolmaster*, 6 April 1934, p. 597.
77 This is discussed in Barron, 'Little prisoners of city streets', pp. 166–81.
78 Oxfordshire Archives, OXOHA:OT 213 – Mary Bews – An adviser to Oxfordshire Primary Schools, interviewed by Philip Best (1996); Marsden, 'The school journey movement to 1940', p. 79. Barron, 'Little prisoners of city streets'.
79 Jones, 'Which nation's curriculum?', p. 7.
80 Cited in Elfed-Owens, 'The implementation of the National Curriculum', p. 17.
81 Tisdall, 'Kindred to its soil'.
82 DES, *Primary Education in Wales*, p. 207.
83 Board of Education, *Report of the Mental Deficiency Committee*, pp. 80–1.
84 Oxfordshire Archives, OXOHA:OT 554 – Edward (Ted) Harvey, interviewed by John Brucker (2000).
85 Steedman, 'State-sponsored autobiography', p. 44.
86 DES, *Primary Education*, p. 49.
87 'Operation Columbus: a short story for juniors', *Teachers World*, 2 January 1970, p. 15.
88 H. Miles, Letters page, *Teachers World*, 16 January 1970, p. 9.
89 J. Luxton, 'What the children's theatre has taught me', *Teachers World*, 23 September 1931, *Teachers World*, p. 949.
90 G. Cross, 'Children and the pen', 26 June 1935, *Teachers World*, p. 473.
91 DES, *A Language for Life*, pp. 7, 131.
92 Pearson, *The Making of Modern Children's Literature*.
93 Bernstein, *Class, Codes and Control*.
94 Blyth, *English Primary Education*, p. 154.
95 Tropp, *The School Teachers*, p. 262.
96 Wilson, 'Fighting the "damnable" triumph of feminism', pp. 670–2.
97 *Teachers World*, 24 April 1946, p. 2.
98 Summerfield, 'Women in Britain since 1945', p. 66.
99 Martin, 'Thinking education histories differently', p. 527.
100 Dent, *Century of Growth*, p. 133.
101 Dent, *The Training of Teachers*, p. 125.
102 Floud and Scott, 'Recruitment to teaching', p. 540.
103 Tropp, *The School Teachers*, p. 246.
104 Blyth, *English Primary Education*, pp. 156, 158.
105 Tropp, *The School Teachers*, p. 262.
106 Dent, *Century of Growth*, p. 133.
107 'UK Population Estimates 1838–2015', Office for National Statistics, www.ons.gov.uk/aboutus/transparencyandgovernance/freedomofinformationfoi/populationbyagegenderandethnicity.

108 'Waste: no posts for a fifth of women who want to teach again', *Teacher*, 11 January 1974, p. 16.
109 UK Population Estimates.
110 Steedman, 'The mother made conscious', p. 156.
111 Wall, 'Picturing an occupational identity', p. 332.
112 Oram, 'To cook dinners with love in them', p. 106.
113 Steedman, 'The mother made conscious', p. 149, dates the idea back to Froëbel.
114 'Poor Old Dad', *Teachers World*, 3 June 1960, p. 3.
115 King, *Family Men*.
116 Cited in Deem, *Women and Schooling*, p. 122.
117 Deem, *Women and Schooling*, p. 121.
118 Bennett, *Teaching Style and Pupil Progress*, p. 63.
119 Thomson, *Psychological Subjects*, p. 192.
120 Lawn, 'What is the teacher's job?' p. 62.
121 Ashton et al., *The Aims of Primary Education*, p. 52.
122 J. W. Marriott, 'Junior expression', *Teachers World*, 7 February 1940, p. 23; K. Ollerenshaw, 'Girls and their education', *Teachers World*, 26 November 1965, p. 11.
123 Tisdall, 'Inside the blackboard jungle', pp. 501–2.
124 Daniel, *Activity in the Primary School*, p. 42. Other examples include Hughes and Hughes, *Learning and Teaching*; Atkinson, *Junior School Community*; Marshall, *An Experiment in Education*.
125 Daniel, '*Activity in the Primary School*', p. 34.
126 National Archives, ED 156/54: HMI Reports: Primary: Oxfordshire 1946–55.
127 J. Edmundson, 'What kind of apparatus?', *Teachers World*, 9 May 1956, p. 9.
128 DES, *Curricular Differences for Boys and Girls*, pp. 2–3.
129 Walkerdine, 'It's only natural', pp. 84–5.
130 Thom, 'Better a teacher than a hairdresser?', p. 130.
131 Walkerdine, 'Developmental psychology', p. 120.
132 'Mr Casson', 'How to teach girls', *Teachers World*, 1 January 1919, p. 369.
133 Oram, 'Inequalities', p. 116.
134 Farley, *Secondary Modern School Discipline*, p. 65.
135 James, *The Teacher and His World*, p. 91.
136 Blishen, *A Nest of Teachers*, p. 157; also see Braithwaite, *To Sir, With Love*.
137 Cox, *Gender, Justice and Welfare*.
138 A. L. Nixon, 'The home as a project', *Teachers World*, 4 February 1931, p. 716
139 F. Hughes, 'A practical course for backward boys', *Teachers World*, 21 January 1931, p. 636.
140 Letters page, *Teachers World*, 18 December 1935, p. 549.
141 Etherington, *In and Out of School*, pp. 81–5. H. C. Dent sketches out a similar programme for girls in a secondary modern school, suggesting that they do a project on 'Ourselves and Our Homes'. See Dent, *Secondary Modern Schools*, p. 108.

142 On the rise of 'vocational guidance', see Watts, *The Teacher's Guide to Intelligence*, pp. 7, 24; Wooldridge, *Measuring the Mind*, p. 142.
143 Sheffield Archives, CA/35/21-27: Beighton Boys Dept School Logbooks, 7 October 1953, HMI Report, 6-8 July 1954. This school was in Derbyshire LEA until 1967 when the parish of Beighton became part of Sheffield.
144 Sheffield Archives, CA/35/72-4: Southey Green Senior School Logbooks, headteacher's report to the school governors, 1955; CA 729/S1/4-5: Sheffield Bole Hill Mixed School, Logbook, 19 March 1951.
145 For example, Sheffield Archives, CA/35/72-4: Southey Green Senior School Logbooks, HMI Report, 25-28 June 1951; National Archives, ED 109/9239, Owler Lane East County Secondary School, Sheffield, 19, 20 and 21 October 1953; National Archives, ED 109/9044, HMI Report, Hook Norton County Secondary School, Oxfordshire, 22-24 June 1954.
146 Spencer, 'Reflections on the "site of struggle"', p. 446.
147 Evans, *A Good School*, p. 12.
148 DES, *Girls and Science*, p. 21.
149 Deem, *Women and Schooling*.
150 Dale, *Mixed or Single Sex School?*, p. 231. A similar point was implied by DES, *Working papers*, pp. 9-10.
151 Deem, *Women and Schooling*, p. 43.
152 Deem, 'State policy and ideology', p. 38.
153 Neill, *Summerhill*, p. 99.
154 DES, *Girls and Science*, pp. 8-11.
155 DES, *Curricular Differences for Boys and Girls*, p. 22.
156 Deem, *Women and Schooling*, p. 43.
157 *Ibid.*, p. 63.
158 DES, *Girls and Science*, p. 18.
159 *Ibid.*, p. 10.
160 Coote and Campbell, *Sweet Freedom*, pp. 177-85.
161 Dale, *Mixed or Single Sex School?*, p. 235.
162 Houlbrook, *Queer London*; Buckle, *The Way Out*.
163 Waters, 'The homosexual as a social being', p. 197.
164 Jennings, *Tomboys and Bachelor Girls*, p. 29.
165 *Ibid.*, pp. 21-3.
166 Grosvenor and Lawn, 'Days out of school'.
167 Selleck, *English Primary Education and the Progressives*, pp. 87-8.
168 Thomson, *Lost Freedom*, p. 133; Burchell, 'The Adolescent School Pupil', p. x.
169 Hayward, 'The invention of the psychosocial'; Burchell, 'The Adolescent School Pupil'.

6

Secondary school teachers, class and status

Adolescence, like childhood, became a more restrictive and limiting category after the Second World War. Developmental psychology emphasised the minimal capabilities of the under-sixteens in fields such as logical thinking and theoretical reasoning. Moreover, the development of a non-utopian progressive curriculum in secondary modern and comprehensive schools, far from opening up educational opportunities, reasserted old assumptions about class and gender in psychological language. As we have seen, it was assumed that working-class girls would be 'naturally interested' in appropriate manual occupations that were already dominated by women, as well as in marriage and motherhood. Following on from this, although developmental psychologists asserted that adolescents should be attaining the more advanced maturational stages by the end of compulsory education, in practice educationalists often assumed that their working-class pupils would never reach this point, arguing that they could only engage with topics that were concrete, rather than abstract. This shaped pedagogical practice in both secondary modern and comprehensive schools.

The fates of grammar school pupils, and the experience of the grammar school itself, have attracted a huge amount of attention from historians of mid-twentieth-century Britain concerned with class and social mobility. Yet the institution within which the majority of adolescent pupils were educated – the secondary modern – has been remarkably neglected by the historiography, partly because of the difficulty of finding former secondary modern school pupils who will discuss what is still seen as a shameful experience.[1] This chapter demonstrates that understanding what happened inside secondary modern and comprehensive schools is crucial not only for our understandings of age, but also for constructions of class and of gender. Child-centred education, unable to gain a significant foothold in grammar schools, provided secondary modern schools with their guiding philosophy.[2] By claiming to provide a profound reassessment of the needs of the non-academic adolescent, progressivism offered these new institutions a positive rationale for their existence, a rationale that was sorely required in the face of mounting criticism from parents, reports from government advisory committees and certain local education authorities.[3]

The 1950s witnessed a media panic over post-war juvenile delinquency, which asserted that pampered teenagers had forsaken their parents' values for instant gratification and violent crime.[4] In the 1960s, race as well as age was foregrounded, following the 1958–59 race riots in Notting Hill, as 'social problem films' switched their focus to immigrant youth.[5] The media creation of generational conflict had real consequences for adolescents, but historians such as Selina Todd, Hilary Young and Gillian Mitchell have challenged the idea that this 'generation gap' was a lived reality in the 1950s.[6] This novel historiographical shift chimes with an older tradition of sociological research dating back to the 1960s that challenged stereotypes of threatening youth.[7] More recent sociological work concurs with this basic point; the majority of young people in the 1950s and 1960s were not juvenile delinquents or counter-cultural rebels 'resisting through rituals', but unremarkable individuals who generally agreed with their parents' values.[8] If the 'generation gap' was not a reality, then 1950s fears might fit Geoffrey Pearson's model in *Hooligan*, where he notes that concerns about the younger generation reoccur throughout history.[9]

This narrative is certainly one convincing explanation of attitudes towards youth in post-war England. However, while it seems evident that the 'generation gap' has been exaggerated, this chapter will argue that teachers' attitudes towards youth were more complex than this model suggests, and cannot be fully accounted for either by Pearson's model of recurring generational conflict or the more recent suggestion of a media-created generation gap that masked a harmonious reality. In the inter-war period, utopian progressive educationalists focused on youth as the hope for the future, presenting a remarkably positive concept of the rising generation, and this was largely reflected in teachers' attitudes as well. However, as non-utopian progressive education became increasingly implemented in schools after the Second

World War, teachers' concepts of youth became more qualified, pessimistic and ambivalent. The changing class profile of the profession after the war resulted in a different relationship with pupils, but this cannot be reduced to the simplistic sociological model that suggested middle-class teachers were unable to understand their working-class pupils.[10] Even in secondary modern schools, which drew more middle-class recruits, the majority of teachers were not from professional or elite families in the 1950s.[11]

The distance observed by sociologists between teachers and their working-class pupils may have arisen less from a sense of difference than of similarity. Teachers who were keen to safeguard their professional image did not want to identify themselves with pupils who hailed from manual workers' families. This concern was deepened by the relative fall in teachers' pay throughout the post-war period, meaning that some skilled manual workers could command higher wages than trained 'professional' teachers.[12] Male teachers, in particular, felt the need to assert a 'masculine' professional identity in response to two perceived threats: child-centred methods, gendered feminine, and emergency-trained teachers, usually men, who threatened their craft knowledge and authority through less professional and more practical forms of masculinity. When working-class pupils overturned their teachers' expectations by achieving academically, they could be stigmatised as abnormal and maladjusted, especially if they were female and/or from an ethnic minority.

Adolescence

Since the introduction of the concept of adolescence in the late nineteenth century, the precise age range covered by this stage, as well as the characteristics of the stage itself, have frequently shifted.[13] As Sally Shuttleworth has argued, adolescence could be defined as extending into the mid-twenties or even to thirty, and this idea of a 'long adolescence' persisted intermittently throughout the twentieth century.[14] For obvious reasons, however, writers on education tended to confine their definitions of adolescence to a tighter time frame, given that pupils were only in school for a certain proportion of their teenage years. Between the inter-war and post-war periods, however, the age range covered by 'adolescence' shifted, and its characteristics were redefined.

This was obviously affected by the raising of the school leaving age from fourteen to fifteen in 1947, and to sixteen in 1972, but other factors were also in play.

The beginning of adolescence was defined by the Hadow Report of 1926 as eleven, but most inter-war writers, in line with G. Stanley Hall, argued that it truly began at thirteen or fourteen.[15] This break fit with the school leaving age, which was thirteen until 1921 and fourteen thereafter, and also with employment provision, as the 1933 Children and Young Persons Act prohibited the employment of children under thirteen during school hours, although allowing pupils to be exempted from the final school year if they were in employment. This left the period from eleven to thirteen as an awkward transitional stage. When these definitions are scrutinised more closely, however, it seems that this transitional stage was more akin to what post-war writers would term 'adolescence' than their 'adolescent' stage was. Adolescence proper was portrayed as mature and stable by inter-war writers on education. A. H. Allsopp's guide for the student teacher argued in 1936 that the role of emotional instability in adolescence had been overplayed, and it was a period when 'true self-control' could emerge.[16] Constance Bloor, whose text was cited by R. J. W Selleck as one of the 'best-known and most widely read' in training colleges in his history of progressivism, thought that adolescents had mastered self-discipline and could understand abstract principles.[17]

When inter-war psychologists and educationalists did define adolescence as commencing at eleven, they tended to place more emphasis on its turbulence, rather than its rationality.[18] Early adolescence was frequently compared to a 'new birth' by inter-war writers, who argued that it was analogous to the upheaval of infancy rather than the stability of childhood. J. S. Ross's popular set text for student teachers, *Groundwork of Educational Psychology* (1931), stated that 'The adolescent no longer exhibits the stability that marked his later childhood, but loses his bearings and finds himself in a strange world ... he is badly adjusted physically and mentally, being clumsy and awkward in bearing, moody and intractable in manner ... In a word, like the infant, he has to begin again the work of adapting himself to his environment. Many of his characteristics are those of infancy repeated on a higher level.'[19] The psychologist Ernest Jones, writing in *The British Journal of Psychology* in 1922, explicitly compared unstable adolescence to stable childhood: 'In many respects youth is more closely parallel to infancy than to the intervening period of childhood, which is relatively stable and has some of the characteristics of maturity.'[20]

This reflected current research in developmental psychology, which tended to emphasise an early adolescence that resolved into stable maturity around the age of fourteen or fifteen, or even earlier. Jean Piaget's early work had little to say about adolescents, but gestured towards the idea that adult reasoning power emerged after the age of eleven or twelve. In *The Child's Conception of the World* (trans. 1929), he wrote: 'But by then [twelve years old] the child is no longer a child and his mental structure is becoming that of the adult.'[21] Piaget's early work contrasted with his post-war approach to the adolescent. In *The Growth of Logical Thinking from Childhood to Adolescence* (1958), co-authored with Bärbel Inhelder, Piaget used the more complex sequence of maturational stages he had developed to lengthen adolescence. Piaget and Inhelder argued that a 'new set of operational structures' emerged from twelve to fifteen during the formal operational stage; it was only when this stage was complete that adult cognitive capacity was attained.[22] During this period, they suggested, recalling the older discourse about adolescence as a 'new birth', the adolescent returned to a form of 'cognitive egocentricism', which Piaget had previously associated with the under-sevens.[23] Piaget and Inhelder argued that adolescence began when the individual started to take up adult roles and ended when he/she had fully assumed them.[24] This decoupled adolescence from a strictly defined age range and related it more closely to environmental circumstances. However, these qualifications in Piaget and Inhelder's work did not tend to be taken up by British child-centred educationalists, who continued to conceptualise adolescence as maturational.

Progressive educational texts from the late 1940s onwards tended to assume a lengthened adolescence while neglecting the role of the environment in its formulation. Adolescence was extended at both ends of the spectrum; better nutrition meant that biological puberty commenced earlier for both boys and girls, indicating that eleven or twelve was a sensible theoretical age for adolescence to begin, whereas developmental psychologists increasingly asserted that it extended well past fifteen.[25] Arnold Gesell's work on youth in the 1950s observed a trend towards more abstract thinking up to the age of fifteen, and perhaps well beyond it, as his book stopped at sixteen.[26] A series of research papers on moral autonomy in the 1960s by an educational psychologist implied that adolescents of sixteen had not yet attained moral autonomy, and so were still developing towards adulthood.[27] This lengthened adolescence was not without precedent; 'youth' could be considered to extend into the mid-twenties from at least the early modern period onwards in Britain.[28] However, the new terminology of 'adolescence' assigned a tighter definition to this life-stage, linking it more closely to an undeveloped set of cognitive capacities that were present not solely through lack of life experience, but through an, as yet, incomplete maturational sequence. The idea of a stable and rational state was postponed well beyond the official school leaving age.

Inter-war writers, while acknowledging that adolescence could be a turbulent period, tended to consider that this age-stage possessed its own uniquely positive qualities as well, in keeping with the greater influence of utopian progressive ideas in the 1920s and 1930s. Teaching journals emphasised that youth both needed and deserved better treatment, with the *Schoolmaster* concerned for the fate of the young worker in 1931 who was 'denied the warmth and colour that youth has the right to ask of his surroundings'.[29] These tendencies became especially obvious in discussions of juvenile delinquency, with S. F. Hatton writing in *London's Bad Boys* (1931) that 'riots' were 'nothing more serious than the symptoms of healthy, vigorous, adventurous adolescence', drawing on the wider inter-war trend to sympathise with 'natural' youthful misbehaviour. Adolescents, he believed, naturally sought out wonder and beauty: 'At no period of our life is our mind so open to impression as during adolescence . . . athirst for all that is fine and lovely.'[30] This linked to the inter-war assumption that adolescents tended to be overly introspective, or 'daydreaming', but this was not viewed as a wholly negative quality, unless it became excessive.[31] Indeed, older nineteenth-century psychological thinking had valued introspection as a useful process for finding out more about oneself, and so this quality could be seen as a sign of adulthood.[32] The 'new psychology', due to its emphasis on the unconscious mind, could also conceptualise daydreaming as a useful process, as *Teachers World* noted in 1931.[33]

These qualities were still attached to concepts of adolescence in the post-war period, but had been reformulated as immature and undesirable traits because they separated the adolescent from his or her peer group. Most obviously, adolescents were stigmatised as essentially self-centred, with rising concerns about juvenile delinquency linking their selfish natures to their offences. Avner Offer has considered how 'self-control' became a more valuable trait in affluent societies such as Britain and the US after the Second World War; adolescents were increasingly castigated for lacking this quality, and for being driven by consumerism and impulsivity.[34] Healthy daydreaming had become unhealthy 'brooding', as a 1947 article in the *Schoolmaster*, aimed at emergency trained teachers, summarised: '[Adolescents] tend to brood and think a great deal about themselves.' This linked to wider critiques of youth culture from both the right and the left; adolescents in the 1950s and 1960s were seen as existing in a 'fantasy' or 'dream' world by socialists, who criticised their supposedly materialistic culture, recalling the 'candy-floss world' criticised by Richard Hoggart.[35] Right-wing commentators, meanwhile, blamed television and the cinema for promoting an 'unreal' view of life, encouraging pointless daydreaming.[36]

Working-class adolescents could also be castigated as 'unrealistic' when they expressed ambitions that reached beyond manual labour and low-paid white collar employment, such as clerking or secretarial work. In the 1950s and 1960s, this was often linked to the 11-plus, and an assumption that these teenagers had already proved themselves to be 'non-academic' and therefore needed to prepare for practical occupations. Mary, a secondary modern school pupil in London in the late 1950s, remembered that

> I just felt quite strongly that we were written off at the eleven plus. Some people did have the opportunity of taking the exam again at 13 but a lot were so demoralized anyway so there was this big divide . . . that if you went to secondary [modern] school you weren't academic and therefore you were more or less just brought up to be wives and mothers and that was all you could expect from that.'[37]

Hundreds of children's essays submitted to the Camberwell Libraries' annual essay competition in 1951–52 on 'What I want to be when I leave school' indicated that these messages were internalised at an early age. Respondents, who were aged between seven and thirteen, depicted their career plans as characterised above all by realism, with many children explicitly stating that they wanted to do the same job as one of their relatives. Girls were especially practical in their ambitions. Joan, who was nearly thirteen when she wrote her essay, recalled that she had wanted to be an actress 'from the day I started school . . . but

I don't suppose that ambition will ever be fullfilled [sic]. When I was eight I had many whims and fancy's [sic]'. She anticipated leaving her secondary modern school at fifteen.[38] This contrasted with the more exciting and dream-like futures, the 'overwhelming sense of possibility', imagined by inter-war child writers, despite the grimmer economic backdrop of the 1930s.[39]

While the spread of comprehensive schools in the 1970s removed the stigma of the 11-plus for most pupils, aspirations continued to be policed. This was especially true for immigrant adolescents, who were badged as having 'unrealistic aspirations' by a number of sociological studies during the decade. Y. P. Gupta reported in the *British Journal of Sociology* in 1977 that more British South Asian school-leavers wanted to remain in school beyond leaving age, compared with their white counterparts, and frequently aspired to enter professional occupations; this reflected the findings of David Beetham's earlier study in Birmingham.[40] Beetham and Gupta believed that these achievements would be impossible for this largely working-class immigrant group. However, J. H. Taylor's follow-up study of South Asian young men in Newcastle upon Tyne in 1976 demonstrated that a large percentage of those who had expressed such desires had achieved their ambitions; twenty-one of his sample were still in school at the time of interview in 1968, and of this group, fourteen were at a university or polytechnic by 1971, outperforming the white sample that Taylor had selected as a control group. One young man, Mahmoud, had got into university on the second try to read electrical engineering. Taylor recounted that 'His headmaster admitted to me that none of the staff thought he would get even one advanced level.'[41]

While South Asians struggled, black immigrant pupils, who tended to have emigrated from the West Indies, were subject to even more systemic discrimination, as Sally Tomlinson has shown. Black pupils were more likely than other immigrant groups to be seen as innately incapable, rather than disadvantaged by environmental circumstance.[42] Black students were explicitly aware that teachers thought they had 'unrealistic ambitions'. A black child attending a secondary modern school said to the social researchers Derek Humphrey and Gus John, who published *Because They're Black* in 1971, 'When the time comes for us to think of choosing jobs [the teachers] always say we aim too high. They know they deliberately didn't teach us a damn thing and they even tell some of us we're going to end up on the factory floor or on the buses. They got a hope!'[43] Dipak Nandy wrote in *Race Today* in 1969, considering immigrant communities in Birmingham, that high aspirations 'may also reflect an understanding by coloured immigrants and their children that in an alien *and* white world they must aim higher and be better to get as far as their white counterparts.'[44]

These studies tended to focus on black boys, but Mary Fuller considered the position of black girls at a secondary modern school in the 1970s, arguing that they gave the outward impression of being uncommitted to education but were in fact ambitious and determined, performing well in school subjects. When asked what their future aspirations were, they were notably more aspirational than their white female counterparts in the early 1950s. Michelle stated that 'I want a proper job [before getting married] and some kind of skill . . . The picture of myself is an active one, always doing something, I don't know what. Maybe I'll be a housewife or something like that, but I always picture myself working.'[45] One fifteen-year-old Jamaican girl interviewed by Humphrey and John was planning to leave her secondary modern school to take a typing course after her CSEs. 'I did well in everything else except history and so I failed. I tried learning up everything in history as quickly as I could before the exam, but I got all muddled up.' Given that she had taken her 11-plus only three months after arriving in Britain, she felt that she had deserved a place at a grammar school.[46] These young people were certainly not living in a 'candy-floss world'.

The adolescent in the secondary modern and comprehensive school

Secondary modern schools emerged after the 1944 Education Act as the third arm of the tripartite system of grammar, secondary modern and technical schools in England and Wales that, in practice, usually operated as a bipartite system.[47] It has often been asserted that secondary moderns had no distinctive educational rationale, and it is certainly true that any justification for their existence was worked out fully after the fact.[48] Ivor Goodson has argued that the secondary modern schools, unlike junior or grammar schools, had an unusual freedom to experiment with progressive methods, as they were – at least temporarily – free from the demands of examinations.[49] While increasing numbers of secondary modern school pupils took O Levels in the early 1960s, entrants still represented a small fraction of the total population, and Certificates of Secondary Education (CSEs) were not sat until 1965.[50] Junior schools, especially in the higher classes, became increasingly focused on the 11-plus, while grammars had to concentrate on General Certificates of Education (GCEs), comprising O and A Levels. Apart from Goodson's essay and Cannadine et al.'s examination of history teaching, however, there has been very little consideration of secondary modern curriculums.[51] My findings suggest that the secondary modern school defined its pupils as working-class not simply in a *negative* sense – not middle-class, not academic – but *positively* via child-centred methods that designed the curriculum around their perceived vocational needs. This offered secondary modern schools a reason for their existence at a time when they were often criticised by advisory reports such as those issued by CACE in 1954 and 1956, and by the Robbins Report of 1963, as well as by parents, and those education authorities who were early supporters of comprehensives.[52] However, it also frequently committed them to familiar ideas about gender and class, which were augmented by the age of the pupils under their authority.

The ineffectiveness of the 11-plus in identifying high-achieving pupils and in promoting social mobility has been conclusively shown.[53] This affected some groups more frequently than others. As is well known, numerous girls were denied grammar school places, despite performing better than boys in the 11-plus, because of the perceived need to ensure that a certain number of places were reserved for boys. This practice was defended using developmental assertions that girls accelerated earlier than boys, both physically and mentally, but tailed off more quickly.[54] Adolescents were also subject to an arbitrary regional lottery; the proportion selected for grammars varied from 64 per cent in Merioneth, reflecting the relatively more generous provision of grammar schools across much of Wales before their abolition in that country, to 8 per cent in Gateshead.[55] However, despite their regional advantage, bilingual Welsh-speaking pupils faced more difficulties with the 11-plus than their monoglot English-speaking counterparts in Wales; few tests were available in Welsh, cultural differences affected performance, and children from rural areas and Ysgolion Cymraeg ('Welsh Schools', bilingual schools for Welsh-speaking children set up in Anglicised districts) might especially struggle. Even if a bilingual child passed the test, instruction in Welsh secondary schools was almost always solely in English, which disadvantaged them further.[56]

The idea of the comprehensive school circulated as early as the 1930s with discussions of 'multilateral' education entering pedagogical discourse, especially within the Labour Party.[57] However, it was only after the 1944 Education Act, which established the principle of separate secondary education, that comprehensives in their modern form, as part of a wider system of schools that focused on the education of the adolescent, could emerge. The development of comprehensives in the 1950s was relatively slow, confined to especially progressive LEAs such as Leicestershire, which produced the Leicestershire Plan for comprehensivisation as early as 1957, and to rural LEAs that made use of them out of necessity, such as Caernarvon and Cardigan in Wales.[58] Sheffield, alongside other northern cities, produced a comprehensive reorganisation scheme in 1962–63, and Labour's 1965 Circular 10/65 required LEAs who had not already developed such plans to do so.[59]

In 1961, more than 70 per cent of adolescent pupils were in secondary modern schools and 20 per cent in grammar schools, meaning that comprehensive schools educated less than 10 per cent of the population.[60] In contrast, by the end of the 1960s, a third of pupils were in comprehensives.[61] The newly elected Conservative government replaced Circular 10/65 with Circular 10/70 in 1970, allowing LEAs to decide whether or not to proceed with plans for comprehensivisation, although Circular 10/65 was reinstated in its turn by Circular 4/74 in 1974. Similarly, Labour's 1976 Education Act, requiring all schools to be non-selective, was abolished by the Conservatives in 1979. Despite this political back and forth, about 80 per cent of English state-educated adolescents were educated in comprehensive schools by 1980 and 85 per cent by 1986.[62] In Wales, the shift was earlier and more complete, with 85 per cent of state-educated adolescents in comprehensive schools by 1975 and 99 per cent by 1986.[63]

Despite the emphasis placed by developmental psychologists on the development of abstract reasoning abilities throughout adolescence, secondary modern and comprehensive school curriculums were often influenced more by progressive junior school practice than by a consideration of the needs of the adolescent. Despite the assumption that adolescent development was maturational and hence universal, working-class and middle-class adolescents were treated very differently in practice. A Piagetian account of developmental stages influenced a report of the Cheshire Education Committee on the secondary modern school in 1958; however, the committee were not referring to Piaget and Inhelder's later corpus of work. Instead, they erroneously extended his conclusions about the junior-aged child to the secondary modern school pupil, justifying this move by asserting that those of below-average intelligence 'will rarely reach that stage of maturity when they act rightly from inner conviction'.[64]

H. C. Dent's consideration of the secondary modern school in the same year reached similar conclusions, asserting that 'at some point in the intelligence scale the capacity for systematic and progressive learning becomes so slight as to be almost negligible, leaving accumulative learning as the main means to knowledge'.[65] The Newsom Report of 1963, dealing with 'half our future', thought that 'the abstract thinking of mathematics, and the concepts behind the scientific method will be beyond their reach'.[66] All these reports assumed, therefore, that maturational development halted for the less academic pupil, and so he or she would never reach the higher stages of thought characteristic of mental adolescence. It was hence appropriate to treat secondary modern school pupils like junior school children, as long as appropriate consideration was given to their vocational needs. Dent wrote that such pupils' 'interest in learning can only be evoked and retained when they see before them immediately obvious, readily attainable, and personally relevant goals', recalling the progressive assertions about junior school children's need for practical, concrete experience.[67] Not only would adolescence not be completed before leaving school, it was now asserted that some young people would never become capable of abstract thought.

The vocational demands placed on the secondary modern and comprehensive school meant that, unlike the junior school, it could not completely commit itself to the progressive ideal of education enabling the young person to live his or her present developmental stage to the full, but needed to engage with the needs of prospective employers.[68] In response to these pressures, child-centred currents in the secondary modern suggested that adolescents, unlike children, were naturally interested in the world of work, and so it was appropriate that their education should be shaped in response to the next stage in their lives.[69] This kind of education was mocked retrospectively by educationalist Dennis Lawton in 1981, who pointed out how it implicitly narrowed 'non-academic' pupils' horizons: 'it would not be satisfactory for some to be studying physics and chemistry whilst others would be having a walk around the gasworks.'[70] The 'interests' of adolescents tended to be defined to fit familiar scripts of gender, class and locality, in contrast to the 'interests' of junior children which, while rigid, were relatively non-gendered and non-stratified, and centred on an idealised conception of rural childhood rather than linking tightly to the locality where the child actually lived. However, in other respects, adolescent education was more conservative than primary school progressivism, often cleaving more closely to older curriculums. The child-centred contribution to these curriculums was to justify them in a new psychological language that linked them with modernity and progress, rather than continuity.

Non-utopian progressive assumptions about the limitations of adolescents' thought processes were utilised most heavily when the 'class gap' between 'middle-class teachers' and their 'working-class pupils' was considered, as it was suggested that developmental psychology could help the teachers understand how these children learnt. Unlike junior school children, whose limitations were defined with no reference to class, this was of more concern for secondary modern pupils and of little concern for more academic adolescents in grammar schools. In the 1962 report on Shiregreen County Secondary in Sheffield, the inspectors noted that the pupils came mostly from working-class housing estates. The report argues, 'For most of the pupils, life out of school does not appear to contribute widely in terms of language or experience, and thus poses problems throughout the curriculum' and suggests that the teachers need specialist, perhaps psychological, knowledge about how such children learn, in order to teach effectively. It was argued that in the teaching of mathematics, some teachers 'are aware of the stages through which the pupils must pass in the development of their thinking and cultivate the formation of ideas' but 'elsewhere there is a more precipitate approach to forms of calculation'.[71] This implicitly referenced Piaget's ideas on cognitive stages of development.

Other HMI reports from Sheffield also made reference to the presumed limitations of the pupils' lives outside school in poor, urban localities and hence the special role of the school in making good these perceived deficiencies. A 1955 report on Carbrook Mixed Church School, which was surrounded by factories and workers' houses, and hence smoke and noise, similarly argued that the school rightly placed emphasis on 'the social side of its work' but criticised the fact that only one group of girls took housecraft: 'In an area where experience of the kind is so much needed this can only be deplored.'[72] At Huntsmans' Gardens, which was situated in a poor area, the inspector wrote in 1957 that imaginative and descriptive composition was strong among the older pupils although there was little opportunity for direct observation of the natural world.[73] This suggests why fewer of these comments appear in Cambridgeshire and Oxfordshire logbooks and reports, despite widespread rural poverty throughout this period. These adolescents were conceptualised as especially deprived because they lived in an urban setting. Urban, working-class pupils were hence divided from middle-class adults, because of both their background and age.

These attitudes were reflected in the provision of 'ROSLA curriculums' in comprehensives to address the extra year of schooling provided to all adolescents after 1972. HMI Jack Dale, who started work as an inspector in 1970, said

> I recall vividly the programmes specially prepared for the ROSLA students, often boys ... The theory of many of these courses, flawed from the beginning, was that such pupils were essentially of a different kind from their fellows. Accordingly they had to be catered for not only by a different time-table but by a quite separate syllabus from other students ... Naturally, the kids saw through it from the start.[74]

Many teachers had opposed ROSLA on the basis that working-class children were already bored with school and wanted to enter the 'real' work of work, and so these courses were often vocationally orientated.[75] The *Teacher* thought that Michael Holt's maths workbooks, published in 1974, were especially appropriate for ROSLA pupils as they related to the pupils' 'interests, background and experience' – the reviewer noted that they discussed drugs, contraception and abortion.[76]

HMI surveys of particular local education authorities often revealed that little provision had been made for ROSLA as pupils were seen to be 'marking time before they could go to work.'[77] This was despite the fact that the adult 'world of work' – as the Newsom Report had put it in 1963 – that pupils were being prepared to enter was fundamentally altered in the following decade with the economic downturn after the 'oil shock' of 1973.[78] HMI's first 'Red Book' on the school curriculum, published in 1977, pointed out that vocational provision 'assumes that on the whole there is a "world of work" for pupils to go into . . . many pupils are leaving school to become unemployed . . . An unquantifiable number of pupils at 16 faces, for the next few years at any rate, an uncertain future, of periods of work of various kinds interleaved with periods out-of-work.'[79] School leavers in the 1970s would encounter different challenges from school leavers in the 1950s, but curriculums failed to alter in response.

The development of CSEs, introduced in 1962 and first sat in 1965, had been intended to give some direction to secondary modern and comprehensive school curriculums. Local control over the development of CSE Mode 3 syllabuses, which were teacher-designed, could be valuable, as the Rampton Report (1981) noted. Some CSE boards in areas of high immigration had taken the opportunity to incorporate West Indian culture and history into the examinations, with one board including West Indian authors in its set book list for English and another Mode 3 syllabus dealing with the 'social and economic history of the West Indies'.[80] However, these initiatives were not representative of wider practice, and CSEs as a whole were resisted by many teachers, who thought they, like the extra year, were a waste of time for non-academic adolescents.[81] As ROSLA approached in the early 1970s, it was still assumed by headteachers that between a quarter and a half of comprehensive school pupils would take no examinations at all.[82]

This state of affairs was the result of deliberate policy choices as well as neglect and indifference. The Crowther Report was emphatic about the purpose of the 'modern school' when discussing whether or not it should offer external examinations to its pupils:

> None of the advocates of external examinations for modern schools, so far as we know, contemplates their going more than one-third, or one-half at the furthest, down the scale of intellectual ability. We should enter a vigorous protest if they did. The majority ought not to be subjected to an external examination, and their interest must be protected. They are, after all, the main concern of the modern schools.[83]

However, even the 'main concern of the modern schools', the pupils who were placed in lower academic streams, felt let down intellectually by their schools. One Sheffield boy surveyed in the early 1960s said that 'in the lower classes you do easier things – easier than you need to'. Another said that 'when you had finished [your work], instead of going on to teach something more advanced, they just told you to get out a book and read'.[84] Bill Francis, who started as an HMI in 1968, confirmed these impressions in his description of inspecting science lessons: 'the conventional wisdom in science was that work had to spring from practical applications, but some lesson notes sent in seemed to assume that this was the sole requirement . . . I thought the idea of "too academic for them" coloured many perceptions'.[85]

Therefore, once they had failed to pass the 11-plus, both 'backward' and 'bright' working-class adolescents were liable to be framed as problematic pupils, because they challenged assumptions about the way intelligence worked in the 'normal' secondary modern school child. Mathew Thomson has noted that the idea of 'mental deficiency', current during the first half of the twentieth century, included a vast range of different conditions, and often included children with physical disabilities such as deafness and poor eyesight.[86] Children with Down's syndrome, autism, dyslexia and attention deficit hyperactivity disorder (ADHD), to take a cluster of very different examples, may have been lumped together as 'mentally deficient'. A. D. B. Clarke and Ann M. Clarke note that the presence of the extra chromosome that allowed accurate diagnosis of Down's was not discovered until 1959, and at least until then, it was retained under the umbrella of 'deficiency' or 'subnormality'. Bonnie Evans has shown that autism did not become a significant classificatory category in Britain until the late 1960s; meanwhile, Philip Kirby argues that DES's resistance to the concept of dyslexia led to the term being excluded from the Warnock Report on *Special Educational Needs* (1978), so official recognition would have to wait until the late 1980s.[87] While ADHD, as Matthew Smith has shown, did not become a dominant diagnosis in Britain until the 1990s, 'hyperactivity' was still occasionally mentioned as a disorder from the 1970s onwards. Paul H. Wender's American book, *The Hyperactive Child*, was reviewed in *Teachers World* in 1974 and highlighted as an 'important book' because it showed that 'two per cent of all children are hyperactive'.[88]

'Mental deficiency' was often associated with other defects of character in the inter-war period, but because these were not framed in the psychologised language that would become the norm in post-war

England and Wales, it was implicitly suggested that they were less pathological and more mutable. Form 306 M, 'Report on Child Examined for Mental Deficiency', requested a list of 'Personal and Social Qualities' such as 'appearance, general bearing, habits . . . will power, co-operation with others' and 'Temperamental Conditions' such as 'temper, fear . . . docility, curiosity . . . solitariness'. This form was introduced in 1925 and was in use until well after the Second World War.[89] The Mental Health Act of 1959 removed the legal term 'mentally deficient', and, as Evans argues, this led to a significant increase in the numbers of children defined as both 'maladjusted' and 'educationally subnormal' attending special schools; there was an increase from 1,742 to 6,293 in the case of 'maladjusted' children, and 32,815 to 51,768 in the case of 'educationally subnormal' children. The numbers continued to increase after the Education (Handicapped Children) Act 1970 and the closure of all remaining schools for 'subnormal' children.[90] Wales had the lowest proportion of all areas in the 1960s of handicapped children and children treated in child guidance clinics, which the Gittins Report (1967) thought indicated inadequate detection of such children in Wales. When Welsh children were designated as having 'special needs', they could be further isolated by being sent to English special schools.[91]

'Maladjusted' children were defined by the Handicapped Pupils and School Health Service Regulations of 1945 as 'pupils who show evidence of emotional instability or psychological disturbance', and the Underwood Report of 1955 elaborated on this definition, arguing that 'It is characteristic of maladjusted children that they are insecure and unhappy, and that they fail in their personal relationships.' The report was at pains to stress that this definition was 'so worded as to include the withdrawn, introverted child, who may on the surface be quiet and well-behaved'.[92] Once again, children who did not fit specific behavioural criteria might be at risk of being labelled as 'maladjusted'. However, this was less likely if the child was viewed as intellectually 'normal'. In Launton school in Oxfordshire in 1961, one pupil was reported for bullying another boy '& was insolent when approached about it . . . the boy's general behaviour is not very satisfactory'. When the matter was discussed with the boy's parents, the head reflected that 'For the present I prefer not to treat this as a "special case" as I feel the root of the problem may be that the boy feels to some extent "different" from others & I am concerned with helping him to feel as normal as possible; intelligence is probably average & any disturbance is probably emotional.'[93] This suggests that pupils who were labelled both 'mentally deficient' and 'maladjusted' may have been more likely to be recommended for treatment. Little was expected of this group of children. In 1977, Mary Wilson, who was the director of a Schools Council project on the education of 'disturbed' pupils, found that 42 per cent were 'severely underachieving' and suggested in the *Teacher* that 'If you can get a group of severely disturbed children in a school, get them happy, to concentrate and not hit one another over the head you have achieved a lot.'[94]

Diagnoses of learning difficulties, behavioural maladjustment and other special educational needs were also racialised. In 1969, it was noted by E. J. B. Rose in a report commissioned by the Institute of Race Relations that migrant children, especially West Indian boys, were three to four times more likely to be declared educationally subnormal (ESN) than white British children.[95] Concern about the achievement of immigrant children, who made up 1.8 per cent of the school population in 1966, coalesced after a series of studies in the 1960s that focused on West Indian pupils.[96] Institutional bias in schools was highlighted by Nicholas Hawkes's 1966 book, *Immigrant Children in British Schools*, which noted that 'West Indian streams' were still too common. 'One borough education officer had admitted in print that there was at one time a tendency to assume that immigrant pupils were automatically C-stream material.'[97] This prefigured later discussions of 'unrealistic aspirations'.

The West Indian community strongly resisted the racist inference that the relatively poor school performance of West Indian children was in any way related to innate intelligence, and by the late 1970s their arguments had begun to gain some hearing. A report on 'Ethnic Minorities in Sheffield' in 1981 noted that 'Repeatedly they [the Rastafarian community in Sheffield] stress that schools, by ignoring the culture and heritage of their black pupils, stultify their development and undervalue them so that often they opt out either by not trying or by being disruptive.' The use of Creole was a particular point of contention: 'In the past, teachers have seen Creole as a symptom of linguistic inadequacy, but West Indian community leaders feel increasingly that in adolescence, many West Indian children opt for patois as a defence against teacher's belief that they are inadequate and will underachieve.'[98] Despite the sympathetic tone of this section of the report, an implicit comparison was made with Sheffield's ethnically Indian migrant communities – who had originated not only from India but Tanzania, Kenya and Uganda – when it was stated that 'Most Indian children were born here. They fit into Sheffield schools without difficulty.'[99] Ethnically Chinese immigrants, mostly from Guangdong and Hong Kong, were even more highly praised: 'They take an interest and pride in their children's education and their facility with English and our education system means they can play a much more active part.'[100]

The 1981 Rampton Report supported the claims of West Indian communities to some extent. It stated that 'we are convinced from the evidence that we have obtained that racism, both intentional and unintentional, has a direct and important bearing on the performance of West Indian children in our schools.'[101] Attitudes of teachers were directly implicated: 'Many teachers feel that West Indians are unlikely to achieve in academic terms but may have high expectations of their potential in areas such as sport, dance, drama and art.'[102] The report also highlighted the important role of language, and the fact that many teachers mistakenly believed that the language of West Indian children was 'inadequate for learning, deficient or restricted', or that the use of dialect would interfere with their learning of standard English.[103] Nevertheless, the report still approvingly quoted an earlier NFER review that had suggested that West Indian parents 'lack understanding of the developmental importance of play, toys, communication and parent-child interaction in the early years', summarising the findings in its own words: 'West Indian parents ... may not fully appreciate the need to spend time talking and listening to their children to develop their linguistic skills.'[104] This simply shifted the blame for the supposed inadequacies of West Indian children from the child to the parent, and from a psychological explanation to a sociological one. Even by the late 1970s, it was suspected that West Indian children were still not only more likely to be declared 'educationally subnormal', but to be excluded from school or sent to a 'disruptive unit'.[105] Implicitly, they were not 'normal' children because they were not white and often not British-born.

Although black parents faced the biggest challenges, white parents could also find themselves in conflict with the school and LEA over whether their 'mentally deficient' or 'ESN' child should remain in mainstream education or be sent to a special school, which might mean boarding away from home. The local authority could make a school attendance order compelling a child to attend a particular school, and while the Underwood Report stressed that these 'powers of enforcement' had never been used, 'presumably because the co-operation both of the parents and the child is ordinarily regarded as an essential prerequisite of success in treatment', this could have been perceived as a threat by both children and their parents.[106] The Mental Health Act of 1959 allowed parents extra time to appeal 'against a local education authority's decision that their child was incapable of being educated in school', which the Warnock Report of 1978 saw as a direct response to 'unhappiness, particularly amongst parents, about the labelling of some children as not being entitled to education' while noting that this did not necessarily silence criticism of the system.[107]

Contested cases crop up regularly in Cambridgeshire, Oxfordshire and Sheffield school logbooks, especially in the period immediately following the Mental Health Act.[108] Such protests usually led to different kinds of compromises being made with parents. In 1960, the headteacher of Chippenham End in Cambridgeshire noted that a junior school pupil had 'previously been tested and recommended for a place at the ESN residential school, but his parents are unwilling to let him go'. The local HMI agreed to investigate an ESN day class.[109] At Prickwillow in the same year, the assistant school medical officer 'gave [a pupil] . . . an Intelligence Test with a view to him being admitted to Wilburton Manor ESN School. The child's mother said that whatever was the outcome of the test, she would not allow him to attend'. When the results of the test were returned two months later, the head recorded that 'He is found to be ESN, but it is recommended that he remain at this school and be re-examined in 1962.'[110] However, parents who felt unable to wage these kinds of battles with the school or LEA may have silently acquiesced to the removal of their child from mainstream schooling.

While children with special educational needs or learning disabilities suffered, on the other hand, working-class adolescents who displayed exceptional academic ability were also frequently disparaged by postwar non-utopian progressive educationalists, with their 'brightness' or 'giftedness' linked with undesirable behaviour and poor emotional and social adaptation. This, initially, appears puzzling; with the widespread deployment of intelligence testing from the 1920s onwards, high intelligence was seemingly valorised by educational institutions.[111] In the inter-war period, indeed, there was considerable official interest in how to identify and educate these kinds of children, a discourse which went hand in hand with the assumption that they would constitute a natural minority in the elementary school. The Hadow Report on *Psychological Tests of Educable Capacity* (1924), argued that 'dull children, however much they tried, would never develop beyond a certain point'. Recognising that children with higher 'intelligence quotients' would not necessarily distinguish themselves in their schoolwork, the report warned that 'the school should be criticised not so much for failing to adapt itself to such exceptional personalities as for failing to discover them'.[112]

Even in the 1920s and 1930s, it was frequently argued that exceptional intelligence was innately linked to psychological problems. The 1924 Hadow Report went on to state that 'brilliant children frequently had grave faults of character which, if not corrected, limited effectively their educable capacity'.[113] There were concerns about how these talented individuals could be encouraged to contribute to society. In a 1923 *Teachers World* article on 'The gifted pupil', F. B. Kirkman, who had worked for the Board of Education from 1917 to 1921, noted the prominence of the topic in German and US literature, and stressed the need for 'gifted' children to develop a strong sense of social obligation.[114] Nevertheless, the emphasis still tended to be directed towards how teachers should deal with bright children, rather than coding the children themselves as the problem.

In contrast, in post-war England and Wales, working-class children who fell outside the range of their expected intellectual norms were explicitly penalised. Clever children were stereotyped as 'cocky', and developmental claims that their accelerated academic development was abnormal were used to undermine their success. This was reflected both in official reports and in the teaching press. 'Jason' stated in *Teachers World* in 1952 that he disapproved of marking because 'it contributes to the smugness of bright children', while in 1954, 'Essem' [for S.M. or sec. mod.], one of the more conservative editors, remembered a teacher who wanted to have a C class as 'the A people are inclined to be a bit cocky; and I can't stand cocky people.'[115] In 1962, Christopher Sly, the resident psychologist, argued that 'an attitude towards gifted children which is akin to resentment' is not uncommon among teachers. One Warwickshire teacher was quoted as saying: 'I have a lot of faith in steady plodders and honest triers . . . many of the flash-in-the-pan bright boys . . . often turn out to be undependable and inconsistent.'[116] This indicated teachers' practical struggles to deal with a large class with a wide range of ability as well as a resentment directed towards children who failed to fit this working-class stereotype of a 'steady plodder'. Underwood recognised teachers' concerns while extending a degree of sympathy to what it termed the 'exceptionally bright child': 'He may suffer from boredom and frustration; and because of his intellectual superiority, he may give his teachers the impression that he is deliberately pert and provocative. Particularly as he gets into his teens, he may become intolerant of the inevitable discipline and restrictions of school.'[117]

Crucially, these discussions focused on the 'A stream' pupils in secondary modern schools or comprehensives, rather than grammar school pupils, for whom giftedness was regarded as a desirable norm. The difference in tone was indicated by the prioritisation of the social and emotional needs of gifted children in non-selective education, often alongside the unspoken assumption that these children would be socially incompetent. Plowden strongly suggested that children be kept with their chronological age group wherever possible: 'The presumption should be that children are better with their friends in their own age group, unless there is clear evidence to the contrary.'[118] This assumed, as was usual by the 1960s, that chronological age matched developmental age, and so children would always be able to get along best with peers of their own chronological age. Similarly, Alice Yardley's article on 'The intellectually different child' (*Teachers World*, 1974) assumed such a child would have few friends: 'The child who always wins, who appears to be a knowall or "talk like a book", who devises rules which others find difficult to follow, isn't popular with his peers.' The article concluded that 'Gifts not shared with others deteriorate and ways must be found of helping the gifted child to offer what he has for the benefit of others.' This positioned the gifted child as a misfit who must learn to contribute to society, rather than considering the individual needs of the gifted child in his or her own right.[119]

This position was summarised by the report of the proceedings of the first world conference of the National Association for Gifted Children in 1975, which stated that the aims of the organisation included 'To focus world attention on gifted children and their valuable potential contribution to the benefit of mankind' and 'To explore the nature of their talents *and resultant problems* in childhood and adolescence' [my italics].[120] Gifted children were an important 'global asset', but they were also seen as inherently difficult. American psychiatrist Pamela Mason's contribution to the conference had barely a positive word to say about the character of the intellectually gifted child: 'They become more withdrawn, more anxious, more difficult, more deviant, more self-willed than the average child . . . They tend to have unusual bizarre ideas, minority attitudes . . . At school some of these children are described as a sore trial . . . and others show severe aggression and antisocial behaviour.'[121] Gifted children were simultaneously important for the future progress of society, and innately disturbing because they violated developmental expectations for childhood and adolescence, hence the profound ambivalence displayed even by an organisation that was supposed to represent their interests.

Reports on 'retarded' or 'slow' children in post-war England and Wales often justified their remit by claiming that too much attention had been paid in the past to the education of the exceptional child. For example, the Crowther Report, *15-18* (1959), argued that 'there is a tendency of long historical standing in English educational thought . . . to concentrate too much on the interests of the abler pupils in any group that is being considered and to forget about the rest.'[122] This was an argument that was reversed in the following decades by advocates for the 'gifted' child; the National Association for Gifted Children argued that significant money and resources had been devoted to the study of the mentally disabled, and that there should be a similar amount of attention paid to the exceptionally able.[123] Ben Evan Owen wrote in *Teachers World* in 1970 that in the eleven issues of *Educational Research*, the NFER's journal, to date, there had only been one two-part article on highly intelligent children compared with nine articles on the 'backward'.[124] Both these sets of claims indicate something important, despite their obvious contradictions. In secondary modern and comprehensive schools, pupils who fell outside intellectual norms for their age group were penalised. Once pupils had taken the 11-plus, it was assumed that their intellectual development ought to remain within certain boundaries, and secondary modern schools failed to cater for their brighter pupils. At the same time, work on the mentally disabled or 'backward' child did not necessarily translate to any improvement in conditions either. Both these outlying groups were marginalised by a school system focused on the education of the 'normal' working-class child.

Sociology, teachers and professional status

In the 1950s, secondary modern schools became prominent in public discourse as 'blackboard jungles' – a phrase taken from the title of the American film *The Blackboard Jungle* (1955) – indisciplined, violent places where teachers struggled to keep control. A series of British novels written by former teachers repeated this theme, including Edward Blishen's *Roaring Boys* (1955) and E. R. Braithwaite's *To Sir, With Love* (1959), which was filmed in 1967.[125] The teaching press reacted negatively to some of these novels, pointing out the writers' relative lack of teaching experience and objecting to their portrayal of the teaching profession. The *Schoolmaster* argued that the school in Michael Croft's *Spare the Rod* (1954) was more typical of schools forty years earlier, stating, 'Secondary modern school teachers have every right to be justly indignant at this alleged "sympathetic and faithful" portrait of their work.'[126] This cultural narrative was so dominant in teachers' minds that the journal was still complaining about it in 1966, when David Jordan castigated 'professional failures writing about blackboard jungles to excuse their own inadequacy'.[127] Nevertheless, most of the texts were received positively by teachers, who believed that they emphasised how difficult their jobs actually were, and hence how worthy they were of respect.[128] As late as the 1970s, the comprehensive school was described as 'the concrete jungle' by one of the *Teacher*'s correspondents, who used this language to argue that teachers working in urban areas should be paid more; 'hard work is required to stimulate children ... whose only window on the world may lie some ten storeys above a city street.'[129] The reception of this narrative linked to a wider sense that the status of teachers was declining in society, coupled with increasingly permissive attitudes towards children and adolescents – the kinds of attitudes that were depicted in 'blackboard jungle' fiction.

While the blackboard jungle narrative was frequently presented in 1950s media, an academic backlash took place in the early 1960s, when sociologists began to argue that adolescents were not, on the whole, a social concern. This work chimes with Jon Lawrence's recent summary of the history of sociology in Britain from 1930 to 1962, where he argues that, broadly speaking, post-war sociologists moved away from the 'social problem' remit of the inter-war period to an interest in 'social engineering' that extended beyond the poorest, presenting detailed ethnographic studies that emphasised the heterogeneity of the group under consideration.[130] For example, John Barron Mays' survey of deprived Liverpool schools stated that 'There was no evidence whatsoever which gave credence to any idea of a "Blackboard Jungle" existing in the Inner City areas,' arguing that a fall in delinquency from 1951 to 1958 had led to better discipline and staff–pupil relationships.[131] Peter Laurie's 1965 *The Teenage Revolution* centred around the idea that the 'sexuality and violence' of teenagers was often 'the fitful fantasy of adults'. He argued that this hysteria in the media was especially characteristic of the late 1950s, due to a surge in juvenile crime from 1955 to 1958 that saw teenage convictions rising from 10 per 1,000 in 1945 to 21 per 1,000 in 1958. 'It is as if the collective adult mind had become neurotically imprinted with the idea of the menacing teenager,' Laurie argued, suggesting that this attitude had persisted despite a subsequent drop in adolescent crime.[132] The 1963 Newsom Report supported these sociologists' conclusions, noting that the majority of headteachers 'who supplied evidence about the attitudes of pupils in their secondary modern and comprehensive schools agreed that the great majority of their pupils were co-operative, and that the picture sometimes presented of "the blackboard jungle" is overdrawn and inaccurate.'[133]

However, while these contemporary sociological studies effectively challenged the idea that post-war working-class adolescents were inherently delinquent, the 'culture gap' they identified between the middle-class teacher and working-class pupil was too broad a generalisation. It is certainly true that teachers in secondary modern schools in the 1950s were very unlikely to have attended a secondary modern school themselves. However, the majority of them hailed from working-class backgrounds, as we have seen, and had not experienced higher education outside teacher training. In 1956, only a fifth of teachers in secondary modern schools were university graduates; the remaining four-fifths had either trained in two-year training colleges (three-fifths) or were emergency-trained teachers (one-fifth).[134] The significant proportion of emergency-trained teachers, who would have had a broader range of experiences than the average recruit, is also of interest. Dent asserted, citing the Ministry of Education report on the emergency training scheme, *Challenge and Response* (1950), that these students were even less receptive to psychology, and by extension, progressivism, than the average training-college student; they arrived 'in college in the state of mind as of one hurrying for a train, and anything which appeared to stay or deflect their progress towards becoming efficient practical teachers in the shortest possible time was regarded with something more than impatience.'[135] Two-thirds of these recruits were male, and three-quarters of these trained to teach secondary school pupils, explaining the large proportion that entered the secondary moderns.[136]

The varied backgrounds of these recruits, coupled with the large number of teachers from working-class families that trained via more traditional pathways, meant that the problem in the secondary modern schools was not as simple as a clash between middle-class and working-class 'cultures'. Instead, socially mobile teachers became increasingly anxious about their standing in society, and felt the need to distinguish themselves as professionals by asserting their superior social status and distance from their working-class pupils. Later recruits would also have been likely to acquire marks of middle-class culture through a period in grammar school.[137] This reflects Savage's and Hinton's analyses of middle-class self-ascriptions in the post-war period; both observe that middle-class subjects characteristically defined themselves as 'above' class by virtue of cultural superiority, something which teachers could lay claim to.[138] Farley appealed to such cultural pretensions in his 1960 advice guide, writing, 'In cities especially, the teacher is often a lone figure at a bus stop, waiting to be whisked away to some schoolboy's dream land of cultured and gracious living,' and went on to add that 'It is a paradox of our social system that the more sensitive and educated citizens may have to seek their livelihoods in the teaching of the insensitive and mentally dull.'[139] This linked the child-centred discourse about the inherent limitations of the working-class pupil to the 'culture gap' that some teachers were determined to widen.

Post-war teachers, like other middle-class professionals, felt threatened by reductions in both pay and status. Ronald Gould, the General Secretary of the NUT, stated in his address to the Annual Conference in 1955 that 'Wages have declined in value until each one of us can look and see unskilled and socially unimportant jobs being better paid; the actual classroom work of teaching has steadily become more exacting and more exhausting.'[140] Asher Tropp's 1959 history of the teaching profession made a similar argument, noting that the Burnham salary scales were an asset to the profession during the inter-war depression, but post-war inflation meant that the purchasing power of teachers had declined rapidly in comparison with manual wage labourers.[141] Figures on wage levels during the 1950s indicate that teachers' complaints had real substance. Guy Routh's data indicate that male teachers were paid on average less than some groups of skilled manual workers, such as engineering fitters, coalface workers and railway engine drivers in 1955, and while they outstripped all these groups except coalface workers by 1960, they were still paid less than foremen.[142] In relation to male teachers, female teachers fared even worse across the decade, with equal pay not introduced until 1961. However, their pay compared favourably with groups of skilled female manual workers, with the best-paid group in Routh's data, upholsterers, earning substantially less throughout the 1950s.[143] Routh also notes that from 1913 to 1924 teachers increased their pay lead over the national average salary, but experienced a substantial relative reduction from 1936 to 1955, so may have experienced a decline in relation to other groups of middle-class professionals as well.[144]

Reductions in pay, however, mattered to teachers for more than financial reasons; many teachers increasingly felt that they did not receive the respect they had before the war, and linked this development to progressive methods. John Blackie was a well-known progressive inspector, but at the West Riding Vacation Course in Bingley in 1957 he argued, 'Now the pupils are beginning to have ideas of their own, and their parents too . . . It is a paradox that just when the teacher's claim to be a professional person is beginning to have real substance his professional authority is being increasingly challenged.'[145] John Gabriel's 1957 survey catalogues such complaints from a sample of British teachers. Common responses included 'The way children disregard commands nowadays makes life impossible in a large community' and 'The cheek and impudence of children is colossal. They are the "British Untouchables" and encouraged in this by the regulations.' Teachers frequently mentioned the problem of the 'growing tendency towards free discipline', suggesting that they perceived the issues to be broader than their troubles with a particular class.[146]

As we have seen, child-centred methods were resisted by men because they were gendered feminine. The large cohort of emergency-trained teachers in secondary modern schools may have made male teachers even more anxious about their claims to masculine authority. Teaching was a reserved occupation during the war, so these teachers would have been confronted with a group of men who had served in the forces and hence contributed to the war effort more 'directly' than they had been able to. Furthermore, many teachers, both male and female, associated the emergency training scheme with a dilution of their professional identity – their claim to cultural superiority – because it implied that the craft of teaching could be learnt in a single year, softening the entry requirements. Ronald Gould expressed concern over the scheme in 1950, reflecting that doctors and lawyers had not relaxed their standards. This drew on a wider definition of 'a profession' that highlighted the need for a significant period of training.[147] As we have seen, concerns that teachers' professional authority was decreasing were not new in the post-war period, and would be repeated a generation later. However, the particular narrative that coalesced in the 1950s and 1960s about why this was happening was significant.

Advice manuals for teachers created their own version of this narrative by using the language of warfare to describe staff–pupil relationships in the secondary modern school, influencing the image of teaching adopted by new recruits. Gilbert Highet, the author of a popular guide of 1951 that had been reprinted five times by 1963, commented in his introduction that 'I have met school-teachers who were literally terrified of their pupils, and sighed with relief when the bell rang and they were released from intimidation.'[148] The opening chapter of Richard Farley's guide to *Secondary Modern School Discipline* was called 'Into Battle' and the chapter 'On being one of the boys' included sub-headings such as 'schoolboy guerrilla tactics', commenting that 'Senior boys ... show a streak of viciousness unparalleled in former school times.'[149] In *Teaching Without Tears* of 1961, R. I. Bowley thought that 'The teacher who ignores the pellet whizzing across the room might just as well give the signal to open fire' and that 'surprise is as effective in the classroom as on the battlefield'.[150]

The experience of the 'first day as a teacher', especially in the secondary modern school, became an anxiety-laden cultural script in this period. This trend may have been linked to the decline of pupil-teachers, which meant that young teachers had to face a class for the first time after leaving college. Previously, they might have started teaching in the same school that they had attended, which might have been less frightening, and also meant that the transition from pupil to teacher would have been experienced more gradually. This kind of concern was less evident in the inter-war period. Dora Saint ('Miss Read') remembered that she 'loved' her teaching practice, and that her first post in a school 'wasn't nerve-racking because we had a marvellous headmistress' although 'I was faced with fifty-six eight-year-olds in my first post.'[151] *Teachers World* and *Schoolmaster* correspondents in the inter-war period were similarly non-committal about their first day on the job, indicating that these oral history interviewees had not simply forgotten having a terrible experience because so many years had passed. Maurice Kidd recounted his experiences after one year's teaching to *Teachers World* readers in 1934, warning them that 'You must expect to be stared at a good deal at the first morning', but made no suggestion of anything else that would be particularly troublesome about the first day.[152] This may indicate the absence of cultural scripts via which inter-war teachers could explore their unhappy experiences, rather than a relatively easier first day on the job but, even so, the absence of such scripts is interesting in itself.

A popular discourse of 'baptism by fire' had certainly become more available by the late 1940s. Patricia Dawson, who started teaching in the 1950s, gave an account of her teaching practice that tallies more closely with the representations in advice guides and memoirs: 'I think I felt quite depressed – it was hard, you either kept classroom control and taught very little, or you had mayhem round you and tried to do some teaching. It was not easy, and particularly the split site. It was dreadful . . .'[153] The emphasis on the gulf between adults and adolescents positioned teaching as a much more daunting endeavour than it had been previously. By the 1970s, this kind of narrative had become standard. I asked my Oxfordshire respondents what their 'first day' teaching had been like, and they all had negative recollections. When I asked Kevin, for example, who started teaching at a secondary modern school, 'What was it like being in front of a class for the first time by yourself?', he answered, 'Pretty scary . . . it's about confidence, isn't it?'

Teachers felt that respect from both pupils and parents was decreasing near the end of their careers regardless of when they had started teaching. However, in the case of teachers who started their careers from the 1940s onwards, parents were genuinely becoming more involved in schools, which some staff might have perceived as threatening. In all four of my case study LEAs, open days and exhibitions of work became more common in the 1930s and 1940s, and parents' associations were often formed in the 1950s and 1960s, with parents holding fundraisers, commenting on school policy and attending talks. This tendency was much more marked in England than in Wales; the Gittins Report of 1967 noted that while 25 per cent of schools in England had PTAs [parent-teacher associations] by this date, this was the case with only 5 per cent of Welsh schools. While 81 per cent of English schools had open days, it was only 31 per cent in Wales.[154] Therefore, teachers who taught in England were much more likely to come into contact with their pupils' parents. Logbook evidence demonstrates how schools and teachers tried to convince parents of the value of child-centred teaching methods. At Morley School's Open Evening in Cambridge in 1950, the local paper reported that 'The hall was packed to overflowing with parents' who were told that 'throughout the infant and junior schools the child is studied as an individual and encouraged to learn at the rate that suits its own emotional and intellectual development.' The school's logbook recorded that more than 400 parents were in attendance.[155]

Schools often complained that parents were reluctant to become closely involved in school life, but tended to resent their 'interference' when they did show up. Immigrant parents, in particular, were frequently castigated by schools for not showing enough interest in their children's education while simultaneously stigmatised as inadequate. West Indian parents were singled out as an especially problematic group, despite running vigorous community programmes supporting the out-of-school education of their children, felt to be necessary because of the institutional racism of the school system.[156] Meanwhile, South Asian parents tended to be closely interested; Kamlesh, interviewed by J. H. Taylor in Newcastle upon Tyne in 1968, said 'They [my parents] are pretty keen, they always attend the lectures, you know, the lectures at school and see my teachers regularly.'[157] This compared favourably with the involvement of white parents in the same city.[158]

Parents and schools clashed most frequently over children's results in the 11-plus. As Peter Mandler has shown, far from being indifferent to educational outcome, working-class parents passionately wanted their children to be admitted to grammar schools.[159] Schools were unsympathetic to these concerns, and tended to interpret them as due to a lack of knowledge about the present system, with headteachers arguing, in line with the spirit of the 1944 Education Act, that grammar and secondary modern schools were of equal merit – they simply catered for a different 'type' of child. The headteacher of Bole Hill juniors in Sheffield took pre-emptive action in 1954 by writing a letter to parents which stated that 'no child ever <u>fails</u> this examination' as it is only intended to find out which kind of school the child is best suited to. 'Obviously it would be sheer folly to inflict on your child the rigours of an intensely academic course . . . if your child's abilities and aptitudes are non-academic and more practical in character. A child with this type of mind would profit most from a less exacting and more practical course.' However, the letter revealed the intense contradictions inherent in this policy when it noted that only a quarter of children would receive grammar school places in Sheffield – regardless of their 'natural aptitudes' – and asked parents to give 'confidence and sympathetic understanding . . . to those children who will be transferred to the Secondary Modern Department at Bole Hill'.[160] This is unlikely to have allayed parental fears. For authorities that did not adopt a comprehensive system early on, these disputes continued into the 1960s.[161]

Some teachers had positive recollections of parental involvement in schools. Connie Norman, who taught in the relatively deprived area of Rose Hill in the City of Oxford post-war, felt that 'the more parents got involved with the school, the better it would be' and remembered that some lonely young mothers used the school as a meeting-point.[162] However, Oxfordshire parents remembered this period rather differently. Doreen Essex was an exceptionally involved parent, having served on her children's school's PTA for three to four years, even though it was not well attended by other parents. She 'respected' the teachers, but even she felt that:

> There was that division between – though they were very nice, the teachers – there was that division between teachers and parents . . . to a certain extent, you saw the teachers as the expertise in teaching your children. You didn't feel that you'd got the expertise . . . They teach in a different way . . . the way I was taught was far far removed from the way my two were taught.[163]

Doreen's testimony reveals that parents could feel marginalised when they didn't understand the rationale behind what schools were doing and felt that they had to treat the teachers as 'the experts'; any objections were framed as conservative and backward.[164] While this development was not solely tied to child-centred methods, some parents found these innovations particularly confusing, as they were so divorced from their own educational experience. In Wales in 1961, 79 per cent of parents surveyed by the Parental Attitudes Survey which formed part of the Gittins Report disliked schools which 'gave a lot of freedom' and one-third wanted schools to be more strict, but they were unlikely to have expressed their views; 83 per cent had had no discussion with their child's teacher about teaching methods, a figure which was only slightly lower, at 75 per cent, for English parents.[165] Sharp and Green's 1975 study of Maplethorpe primary school revealed how this issue intensified in the 1970s, as a larger number of schools adopted the integrated day and family grouping, two organisational methods centred on increased freedom in the classroom. When working-class parents complained that their children were bored, teachers blamed the parents, with one teacher saying 'it's now widely recognised that working-class mothers do not prepare their children well enough for school'. Parents were discouraged from helping their child with academic activities as they can 'do the children a lot of harm'.[166]

Sharp and Green recorded the impact this had on parents, who made statements such as 'We don't think we can help them very much because the teacher said that they have their own methods and it would . . . only muddle them.'[167] This was further reflected in the psychologists John and Elizabeth Newsom's study of parents of seven-year-olds in Nottingham in 1977. A policeman's wife said 'I'm always up in arms about reading in school, because I don't think they do enough . . . he was on one reading book, and he'd been on it for months . . . I said that he was bored . . . she [the teacher] explained to me how different they teach . . . this is the modern method'.[168] Parents' concerns about their children's boredom and lack of progress were written off as a lack of understanding of progressive practice, an argument that parents themselves partly accepted.

In a period of post-war affluence, teachers' anxieties about their pupils and their own professional status increased rather than decreased.

This reflects a wider phenomenon described by both Peter Stearns and Barry Glassner, who asserted that in modern societies where risks are greatly reduced, perceived risks, ironically, become more threatening.[169] However, this response may become more understandable if we reflect on the difference between fear and anxiety. Risks that we can combat and address induce fear, but not anxiety. In contrast, anxiety is more corrosive and persistent because it centres on the risks we cannot directly engage with, risks that are more characteristic of modernity. Teachers' anxieties came to coalesce around the assertion that it was progressive education that had undermined both authority and discipline. However, this 'backlash' against progressivism cannot fully explain the increase in pessimism. Progressivism itself moulded new, anxiety-laden concepts of adolescents, by emphasising their limited maturational capacities and their separation from adults. This necessitated greater protection for vulnerable youth, but also positioned them as a greater threat because of their inability to navigate the adult world. Moreover, child-centred methods both emphasised the gulf between adolescence and adulthood, and emphasised the need for gender- and class-based provision for adolescents' 'natural' interests, reinforcing the stereotype of selfish working-class youth, unable to appreciate anything beyond their own narrow frame of reference. Pupils with special educational needs and pupils of colour were especially othered and marginalised.

Historians of education have tended to locate a commitment to a progressive, egalitarian education within the comprehensive school. Secondary moderns, in contrast, are seen as outdated before they were even instituted, subject to extensive criticism from the public as well as from official commissions and local education authorities. This chapter has demonstrated that, despite their undeniably pernicious effect on social mobility, secondary modern schools were, in many ways, at the forefront of educational change in the post-war period. Unlike the grammar school, where, as Mary Evans observed, a certain type of achievement was valorised with no reference to the needs of the child in the real world, secondary moderns engaged directly with the call to make education more natural, practical and enjoyable, although this meant sacrificing the individuality of their pupils.[170] In short, they remade old stereotypes in novel ways, and passed this legacy on to comprehensives.

Notes

1. SESC, 'Secondary moderns'. Existing historical work on secondary modern schools includes McCulloch, *Failing the Ordinary Child?*, Spencer, 'Reflections on the "site of struggle"'; Tisdall, 'Inside the blackboard jungle'; Carter, '"Experimental" secondary modern education in Britain'.
2. For example: Evans, *A Good School*.
3. Jones, *Education in Britain*, p. 47.
4. Early examples include Abrams, *The Teenage Consumer*; Fyvel, *The Insecure Offenders*, as well as numerous articles in popular newspapers such as the *Daily Mail*. See Laurie, *Teenage Revolution*, p. 18. More recent historiographical discussions of this phenomenon include Osgerby, *Youth in Britain since 1945*, and Jackson and Barrie, *Policing Youth*.
5. Sandbrook, *Never Had it So Good*, p. 342.
6. Todd and Young, 'Baby-boomers' to 'beanstalkers'; Mitchell, 'Reassessing "the generation gap"'.
7. Musgrove, *Youth and the Social Order*; Eppel and Eppel, *Adolescents and Morality*.
8. Davis, *Youth and the Condition of Britain*; Mills, 'Using the personal to critique the popular'.
9. Pearson, *Hooligan*.
10. For example, Mays, *Education and the Urban Child*, p. 85. Mays' approach is discussed (and taken as read) in Jones, *Education in Britain*, p. 41, who notes that the Newsom Report (1963) identified similar class divisions.
11. Floud and Scott, 'Recruitment to teaching', p. 540.
12. Routh, *Occupation and Pay in Great Britain*, pp. 186, 194.
13. Tinkler, 'Youth', p. 215.
14. Shuttleworth, *The Mind of the Child*, p. 10.
15. Board of Education, *The Education of the Adolescent*, 1926, p. 132; Hall, *Adolescence*, pp. ix, xix.
16. Allsopp, *The Essentials of Psychology*, pp. 97, 108.
17. Bloor, *The Process of Learning*, p. 189. Selleck, *English Primary Education and the Progressives*, p. 121.
18. Raymont, *Modern Education*, p. 9.
19. Ross, *Groundwork of Educational Psychology*, pp. 146–7.
20. Cited in Wheeler, *The Adventure of Youth*, p. 24.
21. Piaget, *The Child's Conception of the World*, p. 32. Also see Piaget, *The Language and Thought of the Child*, p. 46.
22. Piaget and Inhelder, *The Growth of Logical Thinking*, p. xxii.
23. Ibid., pp. 343, 346.
24. Ibid., pp. 335–7.
25. It was also recognised that girls entered puberty earlier than boys. Tanner, *Growth at Adolescence*, pp. 1–3.

26 Gesell *et al., Youth*, p. 468.
27 Edwards, 'Some studies of the moral development of children', pp. 200–11.
28 For example, see Griffiths, *Youth and Authority*.
29 'Fourteen to eighteen', *Schoolmaster*, 1 October 1931, p. 481.
30 Hatton, *London's Bad Boys*, pp. 14, 17, 34.
31 Wheeler, *Creative*, p. 147.
32 Tansley, *The New Psychology*, p. 10.
33 *Teachers World*, 19 August 1931, p. 767.
34 Offer, *The Challenge of Affluence*.
35 Black, *The Political Culture of the Left in Britain*, p. 74; Mandler, 'Two cultures', p. 139.
36 Thomson, *Lost Freedom*, p. 109.
37 Spencer, 'Reflections on the "site of struggle"', p. 448.
38 Oxford, Bodleian Libraries: Opie 35, Folder 1, Folios 1–220.
39 Langhamer and Barron, 'Children, class, and the search for security'.
40 Abbas, *The Education of British South Asians*, p. 30; Taylor, *The Half-Way Generation*, p. 67.
41 Taylor, *The Half-Way Generation*, pp. 151–2.
42 Tomlinson, *Race and Education*, p. 35.
43 *Ibid*.
44 Taylor, *The Half-Way Generation*, p. 167.
45 Fuller, 'Black girls in a London comprehensive school', p. 57.
46 Humphrey and John, *Because They're Black*, p. 25.
47 Sanderson, *The Missing Stratum*.
48 Mandler, 'Educating the Nation I', p. 11.
49 Grosvenor and Lawn, 'Days out of school', p. 382.
50 Lowe, *Education in the Post-War Years*, p. 117. Watson, 'Education and opportunity', p. 362.
51 Goodson, *School Subjects and Curriculum Change*; Cannadine *et al., The Right Kind of History*, pp. 113–25. Gary McCulloch and Liz Sobell make this point in 'Towards a social history of the secondary modern schools', pp. 275–86.
52 Watson, 'Education and opportunity', p. 361. Parents frequently complained to schools about the 11-plus and were not won over by teachers' arguments about the secondary modern being the 'right' type of school for their child. See Cambridgeshire Archives, C/ES66P/9: Prickwillow School Logbook, 14 May 1953; Oxfordshire Archives, OXOHA:OT338, Interview with Maurice Brown, 8 September 1995; Sheffield Archives, CA 729/S1/4-5: Sheffield Bole Hill Mixed School, Logbook, letter to parents, 28 June 1954.
53 Marsden and Jackson, *Education and the Working Class*.
54 Watts, 'Pupils and teachers', p. 145.
55 MacLure, *The Inspectors' Calling*, p. 57.
56 DES, *Primary Education in Wales*, p. 157.
57 SESC, 'Comprehensive schools'.

58 *Ibid.*
59 O'Hara, *Governing Post-War Britain*, p. 163.
60 Cannadine et al., *The Right Kind of History*, p. 109.
61 McCulloch, 'Secondary education', p. 44.
62 Watson, 'Education and opportunity', p. 363. Glennerster and Low, 'Education and the welfare state', p. 60.
63 'Delays as sprawling Dyfed moves towards reorganisation', *Teacher*, 1975, p. 3. Glennerster and Low, 'Education and the welfare state', p. 60.
64 Cheshire Education Committee, *The Secondary Modern School*, p. 18.
65 Dent, *Secondary Modern Schools*, p. 197.
66 DES, *Half Our Future*, p. 113.
67 Dent, *Secondary Modern Schools*, p. 171. Also see Jeffreys, *Revolution in Teacher-Training*, p. 53.
68 Taylor, *The Secondary Modern School*, p. 16, argued that the concerns of the Hadow Report of 1926 had been answered by the acceptance of the fact that it was the job of the secondary modern schools to prepare working-class pupils for working-class occupations.
69 For example, Dent, *Secondary Modern Schools*, pp. 41, 171; Newsom, *The Education of Girls*, p. 210; Loukes, *Secondary Modern*, p. 63; Reeves, 'Education after the war', pp. 137–40. Adolescents might also participate in part-time work when still at school; see Mayall and Morrow, *You Can Help Your Country*, p. 3.
70 Lawton, 'The curriculum and curriculum change', p. 119.
71 Sheffield Archives, CA35/484: Shiregreen County Secondary School, HMI Report, 6–8 February 1962, pp. 4–6.
72 Sheffield Archives, CA/35/96, 97, 100: Logbooks: Carbrook Mixed Church School, HMI Report 28 and 29 November 1955. A 1951 report on Southey Green Senior School, which was also in an industrial district, made a similar comment about the lack of housecraft for girls. See Sheffield Archives, CA/35/72-4: Southey Green Senior School Logbooks, HMI Report, 25–28 June 1951.
73 Sheffield Archives, CA/35/761: Huntsmans' Gardens Mixed School Logbook, HMI Report, 22 and 23 October 1957.
74 MacLure, *The Inspectors' Calling*, p. 171. As this indicates, concerns about ROSLA often centred on boys; see Burchell, 'The Adolescent School Pupil', p. 181.
75 Woodin et al., *Secondary Education and the Raising of the School-Leaving Age*, p. 86.
76 'To reach the ROSLA pupils', *Teacher*, 1974, p. 13.
77 Woodin et al., *Secondary Education and the Raising of the School-Leaving Age*, p. 219.
78 DES, *Half Our Future*, p. xvii.
79 DES, *Working papers*, p. 18.
80 DES, *West Indian Children in our Schools*, p. 38.
81 Hargreaves, *Social Relations in a Secondary School*, p. 4.

82 Woodin et al., *Secondary Education and the Raising of the School-Leaving Age*, p. 136.
83 Ministry of Education, *15–18*, p. 87.
84 Carter, *Home, School and Work*, pp. 69–70.
85 MacLure, *The Inspectors' Calling*, p. 169.
86 Thomson, *The Problem of Mental Deficiency*, pp. 7–8.
87 Clarke and Clarke, 'The historical context', pp. 12, 17; Evans, 'How autism became autism'; Kirby, 'A brief history of dyslexia'.
88 *Teachers World*, 11 January 1974, p. 27.
89 Sutherland, *Ability, Merit and Measurement*, pp. 77–9.
90 Evans, 'The foundations of autism', p. 281.
91 DES, *Primary Education in Wales*, pp. 437–8.
92 DES, *Report of the Committee on Maladjusted Children*, p. 22.
93 Oxfordshire Archives: S159/1/A1/4: Logbook, Launton C of E Juniors, 5 October and 6 October 1961.
94 M. Wilson, 'No good waiting for children to overcome emotional problems', *Teacher*, 21 January 1977, p. 11.
95 Wilson, 'Gender, race and the ideal labour force', p. 96.
96 DES, *West Indian Children in our Schools*, p. 6.
97 Hawkes, *Immigrant Children in British Schools*, p. 50.
98 Mackillop, *Ethnic Minorities in Sheffield*, pp. 38–9.
99 *Ibid.*, p. 55.
100 *Ibid.*, p. 58.
101 DES, *West Indian Children in our Schools*, p. 12.
102 *Ibid.*, p. 13.
103 *Ibid.*, p. 23–5.
104 *Ibid.*, p. 43.
105 *Ibid.*, p. 50.
106 DES, *Report of the Committee on Maladjusted Children*, p. 36.
107 DES, *Special Educational Needs*, p. 28.
108 Cambridgeshire Archives: R109/056, R106/045: Milton Road Council School, Chesterton, Cambridge: Log Book, 22 November 1967; C/ES44 A 1-5: Chippenham End School, Logbook, 19 February 1960; C/ES66P/9: Prickwillow School, Logbooks, 4 March 1960, 17 May 1960; Sheffield Archives: CA 35/320, 323: Carbrook Council Junior School Logbooks, 29 July 1957.
109 Chippenham End, Logbook, 19 February 1960.
110 Prickwillow, Logbook, 4 March 1960. I have omitted the pupil's name to preserve confidentiality.
111 Sutherland, *Ability, Merit and Measurement*, p. 189.
112 Board of Education, *Psychological Tests of Educable Capacity*, p. 67.
113 *Ibid.*, p. 93.
114 F. B. Kirkman, 'The gifted pupil', *Teachers World*, 10 January 1923, p. 746.

115 'Jason', 'Gather round my desk', *Teachers World*, 2 April 1952, p. 5; Essem, *Teachers World*, 6 October 1954, p. 1.
116 Christopher Sly, *Teachers World*, 7 September 1962, p. 23.
117 DES, *Report of the Committee on Maladjusted Children*, p. 32.
118 DES, *Children and Their Primary Schools*, p. 284.
119 A. Yardley, 'The intellectually different child', 18 January 1974, *Teachers World*, p. 19.
120 Gibson and Chennells (eds), *Gifted Children*, opp. p. 1.
121 Mason, 'Disturbances', pp. 214–15.
122 Ministry of Education, *15–18*, p. 87.
123 Gibson and Chennells (eds), *Gifted Children*.
124 'Teachers' bookshelf', *Teachers World*, 16 January 1970, p. 30.
125 The novels in question are: Croft, *Spare the Rod*; Blishen, *Roaring Boys*; Hughes, *Down the Corridors*; Townsend, *The Young Devils*; Braithwaite, *To Sir, With Love*.
126 *Schoolmaster*, 6 August 1954, p. 192.
127 D. Jordan, 'The quaint, rude, undisciplined British', *Teacher*, 1 July 1966, p. 16.
128 For example: Taylor, *The Secondary Modern School*, p. 37; *Teachers World*, 2 September 1956, p. 2.
129 S. C. Traves, 'Justice in the concrete jungle', *Teacher*, 11 January 1974, p. 6.
130 Lawrence, 'Class, "Affluence" and the study of everyday life in Britain', pp. 274–80.
131 Mays, *Education and the Urban Child*, pp. 70, 73, 85.
132 Laurie, *Teenage Revolution*, pp. 8, 18–19, 123.
133 Cited in Evans, *Attitudes and Interests in Education*, p. 56.
134 Loukes, *Secondary Modern*, p. 89.
135 Dent, *The Training of Teachers*, p. 125; also see Lowe, *Education in the Post-War Years*, p. 29.
136 Gosden, *The Evolution of a Profession*, p. 289.
137 Tropp, *The School Teachers*, p. 228.
138 Savage, 'Changing class identities'; Hinton, 'The "class" complex'.
139 Farley, *Secondary Modern School Discipline*, pp. 91, 123.
140 Cited in Gosden, *The Evolution of a Profession*, pp. 77–8.
141 Tropp, *The School Teachers*, p. 227.
142 Routh, *Occupation and Pay in Great Britain*, pp. 70, 95, 101.
143 *Ibid.*, pp. 70, 104.
144 *Ibid.*, p. 194.
145 Blackie, 'Authority', p. 128.
146 Gabriel, *Analysis of the Emotional Problems of the Teacher*, pp. 17–19, 41.
147 Cited in Cunningham, 'Teachers' professional image and the press', p. 40.
148 Highet, *The Art of Teaching*, p. 10.
149 Farley, *Secondary Modern School Discipline*, p. 72.
150 Bowley, *Teaching Without Tears*, pp. 24, 27.

151 Oxfordshire Archives, LT 799: Miss Read.
152 M. Kidd, 'What my first year's service has taught me', *Teachers World*, 22 August 1934, p. 729.
153 P. Dawson: www.history.ac.uk/history-in-education/browse/interviews/interview-patricia-dawson-12-april-2010, interviewed by Nicola Sheldon, p. 5.
154 DES, *Primary Education in Wales*, p. 422.
155 Cambridgeshire Archives: R10069 (C/ES): Logbook, Morley Memorial School, 1931–67, 29 November 1950.
156 DES, *West Indian Children in our Schools*, p. 42; Hawkes, *Immigrant Children in British Schools*, p. 13; Mackillop, *Ethnic Minorities in Sheffield*, p. 68.
157 Taylor, *The Half-Way Generation*, p. 162.
158 Hackett, *Foreigners, Minorities and Integration*, p. 168.
159 Mandler, 'Educating the Nation I', pp. 13–14.
160 Sheffield Archives: CA 729/S1/4-5: Sheffield Bole Hill Mixed School, Logbook, Letter to parents, 28 June 1954.
161 Oxfordshire Archives: S159/1/A1/4: Logbook, Launton C of E Juniors, 20 February 1963; Cambridgeshire Archives, C/ES44 A 1-5: Chippenham End School, Logbook, 25 June 1964.
162 Oxfordshire Archives, OXOHA:LT 276 – No. 79 Connie Norman, '*My Choice*', BBC Radio Oxford, undated.
163 Oxfordshire Archives, OXOHA:OT 304 – Doreen Essex interviewed by Mike Beal and Anne Burrell (1994).
164 Walkerdine, 'It's only natural', p. 83.
165 DES, *Primary Education in Wales*, p. 410.
166 Sharp *et al.*, *Education and Social Control*, p. 58.
167 *Ibid.*, p. 206.
168 Newson *et al.*, *Perspectives on School*, p. 31.
169 Stearns, *American Fear*; Glassner, *The Culture of Fear*.
170 Evans, *A Good School*, p. 19.

7

The 'backlash' against progressivism

In 1969, Basil Bernstein, a professor of the sociology of education at the Institute of Education in London who would become best known for his work on the ways in which linguistic codes disadvantaged working-class children at school, wrote in a collection of critical essays on the Plowden Report that 'waiting for Plowden' had already given way to 'baiting Plowden'.[1] Bernstein's opinion was not mainstream in 1969; the media and expert response to Plowden was overwhelmingly positive.[2] Nevertheless, Bernstein's critique, in collaboration with his colleagues at the Institute, prefigured the controversies surrounding the report that unfolded in the 1970s, which extended to encompass what Plowden symbolised – child-centred educational practice itself. Bernstein's major concern was the 'narrowly psychologistic' view of the child that Plowden promoted and what he saw as its sloppy sociological methodology.[3] His colleague, co-contributor and editor of the volume, Richard Peters, professor of the philosophy of education at the Institute, was more concerned with what he saw as the inherent contradictions in Plowden's philosophy. He noted that there was a tension between two central claims relating to the purpose of the primary school in the Report: fitting children for society and creating a community where they would live first and foremost as children, not future adults. He suggested that it was impossible to measure indices of development without imposing value-judgements, and questioned the artificial split between, for example, intellectual and moral development. In conclusion, he wrote, targeting the child-centred idea that children possessed all the resources for growth within themselves, 'it is not enough, therefore, to say that children should learn to be themselves at school; we must give them the equipment to find out properly what sort of selves they want to be.'[4]

A progressive education?

Far from being a conservative outpost, the London Institute of Education had occupied a central place in the progressive revolution. It had been the base for such famous in-service courses as Susan Isaacs' Child Development Diploma in the inter-war period, continued by Dorothy Gardner post-war, and it had also hosted the pioneering inspector Christian Schiller's one-year training course from 1956–63, which went on to produce a number of significant alumni.[5] Its participation in 'Plowden-baiting' hence stemmed from a recognition of the inherent tensions in contemporary child-centred practice, not a reactionary backlash against progressivism as a whole. This text demonstrates, as Peter Cunningham has argued, that there was both continuity and change in the anti-progressive 'backlash' that began to gather speed from the 1970s onwards.[6] The traditional story told by some historians of education and childhood focuses on the mobilisation of dissent by the series of infamous *Black Papers* from 1968 onwards and its consolidation by a series of key events in the 1970s. These ranged from the closure of the flagship progressive William Tyndale junior-infant school in London in 1976 after parent protests, and the publication of Neville Bennett's *Teaching Styles and Pupil Progress* in the same year, which suggested that formal teaching in primary schools led to better results.[7] Teachers were blamed for what was perceived as a breakdown of discipline in schools caused by progressive education, which had led to falling standards, a hypothesis that was linked, somewhat inaccurately, to the psychiatrist Michael Rutter's *Fifteen Thousand Hours* (1979).[8] This traditional narrative implies that the successful implementation of progressive methods, in the context of growing criticism of 'the permissive society', led to a reaction against the teaching profession. Control of the curriculum was wrested from teachers by central government, acting under the belief that educational experimentation had gone too far in both primary and secondary schools.[9]

However, although there is truth in this narrative, it tells a one-sided story. Like Bernstein and his colleagues, many of the key contributors to the 1970s debate over progressivism were not enemies of child-centred education. Neville Bennett, a professor of educational research, opposed poorly implemented child-centred practice and the muddled formulations of Plowden rather than 'activity' methods properly defined.[10] His early research indicated that, properly practised, a degree of child-centred education in classes led by experienced teachers gave better results than a solely formal approach, although this was not the conclusion he chose to emphasise in the text.[11] Indeed, he published a second report on his research a few years later, suggesting that his earlier findings had been misleading.[12] Michael Rutter, leading a research team composed of a social worker, an educational psychologist and a developmental psychologist, did not imply that progressive education played a role in encouraging poor behaviour, and indeed argued that a large amount of praise combined with 'few and firm' disciplinary measures encouraged good behaviour in the classroom, tying into progressive assertions.[13] Finally, even the *Black Papers*, though more obviously reactionary, pulled in contributors, such as Cyril Burt, who had been associated with progressivism in its early days, contributing to the sense that something had *gone* wrong rather than *been* wrong from the start.[14]

The part of the story that is missing from traditional historical narratives, therefore, is the problems within non-utopian progressivism itself that fuelled challenges from both its supporters and its opponents. Teachers have been presented as the victims of a top-down 'attack', but as we have seen, a significant proportion of the profession resisted child-centred education from within.[15] Moreover, their resistance contributed to the partial implementation of child-centred methods that distorted and weakened their application in the classroom. Critics such as Bennett attacked schools that misunderstood the meaning of terms such as 'activity methods' and reduced the role of the teacher to that of an observer.[16] Peters concurred, challenging the dogmatic acceptance of child-centred ideas that prevented genuine innovations, such as the teaching of French in the primary school, resisted because it would necessitate whole-class teaching and hence move away from the individualistic emphasis of progressivism.[17] Both Cunningham and Thomson have gestured towards the complex nature of the 1970s 'backlash' against both progressive education and movements for 'the rights of the child'. We have already considered Thomson's statements about the incompatibility of the developmental model of childhood and the children's rights movements.[18] I would suggest that his argument both extends to educational practice and encapsulates a wider shift in concepts of childhood that took place from the 1950s onwards. Teachers' concepts of childhood did not change suddenly in the 1970s in response to a conservative backlash against permissivism. They shifted from the late 1940s and early 1950s as child-centred education and parenting reformulated the nature of the child in response to developmental psychology and child psychiatry. Even teachers who had once self-defined as progressive could find themselves being criticised as obstructively conservative if they disagreed with the latest innovations. It was the existing tensions within child-centredness that drove the later 'backlash' as much as conservative fears about delinquency and the decline of traditional values.

Redefining progressivism

W. A. L. Blyth wrote in 1984 that progressivism, as a term, 'would appear to have in-built obsolescence.'[19] What had been progressive in the 1930s or the 1950s was no longer progressive by the 1970s. Traditional historiographical accounts depict the 1970s as an unfinished, and brief, progressive revolution. This ignores the much longer history of both utopian and non-utopian progressive education, the enormous changes that were brought about in schools, and teachers' persistent impressions that educational ideals were constantly in flux. Indeed, contemporaries often remembered the 1950s or the 1960s as the 'peak' of progressivism, implying that a more balanced approach was developing in the 1970s. Dennis Lawton suggested in 1981 that progressivism was the product of the 1950s and was now settling down into a more reasonable version of itself, mentioning the 'exaggerated child-centred views which were very common in the optimistic days of the fifties and sixties and reached a climax in the Plowden Report'.[20] Shirley Williams, who at the time was Secretary of State for Education, told the North of England Education Conference in 1977 that 'modern methods' were too difficult for most teachers to use. The *Teacher*'s indignant response to this both criticised the vagueness of her language and implied that things had changed for the better in this decade: 'to lump together any innovatory ideas and condemn them with the label "modern" is absurd . . . Modern methods are not the answer to all educational problems, as some HMIs appeared to think in the 1960s, nor are they the curse that the DES now appears to be suggesting.'[21] Interestingly, HMIs, rather than teachers, were here carefully blamed for any potential excesses.

In the 1960s and 1970s, studies of non-utopian progressive practice in primary schools – similar studies did not tend to be carried out in secondary moderns or comprehensives – often concluded that progressivism was not dominant even in the supposedly more progressive primary sector. Certainly, reactionary critics such as the authors of the *Black Papers* (1968–1977), who claimed that schools now completely lacked discipline due to teachers' commitment to the gospel of free education, were obviously exaggerating.[22] Studies such as Patricia Ashton et al.'s *The Aims of Primary Education* (1975), Neville Bennett's *Teaching Styles and Pupil Progress* (1976), Michael Bassey's *Nine Hundred Primary School Teachers* (1978) and Maurice Galton et al.'s *Inside the Primary Classroom* (1980) deliberately engaged with the *Black Papers* by refuting their claims that child-centred education had led to chaotic classrooms and falling standards. Bennett argued that while the 'strident' *Black Papers* saw progressive education as 'the root of all evil', only 18 per cent of teachers in his study actually taught 'in the manner prescribed by Plowden' and so it seemed unlikely that progressivism had had much impact on the education system as a whole.[23] Bassey commented that 'there does not seem to be any danger of the schools in Nottinghamshire moving into the so-called "progressive methods" in which "children do as they please".'[24] Maurice Galton, Brian Simon and Paul Croll went the furthest, declaring that 'anarchy and confusion' did not prevail in primary classrooms and that progressive teaching, as defined by Plowden, 'hardly exists in practice'.[25]

The challenge posed by the *Black Papers* prefigured a shift in the wider public mood in the 1970s after high-profile scandals such as that of William Tyndale in London, a junior–infant school which was taken over in the 1970s by a handful of radical progressives and was forcibly inspected in 1975 by the ILEA following parent protests, with seven teachers being dismissed after a parliamentary enquiry.[26] In this context, studies by educational professionals clearly felt they had to respond to these accusations of indiscipline. Bassey's study was conducted for NFER, Ashton's for the Schools Council's 'Aims of Primary Education' project. Galton's book was part of the Observational and Classroom Learning Evaluation (ORACLE) project, with which he was involved from the mid-1970s, while Simon was a Marxist historian of education who had been a leading advocate for comprehensives.[27] In short, all had a stake in the current system of education. However, their assertions that reform had been minimal actually expose the shifting meanings of the terms 'progressive' or 'child-centred' education both before and after the Second World War.

Bennett divided teachers into twelve 'types' depending on their teaching styles, and declared that only 'Type 1', which corresponded to only 9 per cent of the teachers he observed, fit with a 'Plowden' definition of progressivism. This type was characterised by integration of the curriculum, no assessment, and pupil choice of work and seating.[28] However, it is arguable whether this corresponded either to Plowden's definition of progressivism or to contemporary ideas of what was considered to be progressive. Bennett noted himself that the majority of the teachers he observed used 'mixed styles', drawing from both supposedly 'traditional' and 'progressive' pedagogies, which highlighted the rigidity of his methodology.[29] Furthermore, we can question Bennett's definitions of traditional and progressive. Bennett thought that in a progressive classroom pupils 'learn primarily by discovery techniques', teaching is 'not confined to classroom base' and 'pupils participate in curriculum planning', but this kind of free, open-plan classroom was, as we have seen, a relatively recent progressive ideal.[30] Similarly, while Bassey claimed to have found 'a lack of "gimmicky" progressive methods' in the classrooms he observed, only 19 per cent of teachers used whole class work for more than 10.25 hours a week, spending the rest of their time on individual or group work, as child-centred educators recommended. Children were not usually allowed to choose their own assignments, but again, this kind of self-directed work was a relatively recent progressive tenet – and even then, only 37 per cent of teachers did not use self-directed work at all.[31] In terms of the integrated curriculum that Bennett had seen as central to progressivism, Bassey used 'thematic studies' rather than history and geography as one of his basic subject categories, indicating that this approach was often employed in schools.[32]

Galton *et al.* drew heavily upon the recent HMI survey *Primary Education in England* (1978), arguing that it showed limited change in primary schools. Like the other studies, the survey was on the defensive, taking pains to stress that 'a quiet working atmosphere was established in nine out of ten of the classes whenever it was needed', that 'there is little support for any view' suggesting that 'the basic practices of reading and writing ... are neglected in primary schools', and that 'the findings of this survey do not support the view which is sometimes expressed that primary schools neglect the practice of the basic skills in arithmetic.'[33] The survey cited NFER tests, conducted in 1975, which showed that reading standards among eleven-year-olds had continually improved since previous sets of external tests in 1955, 1960 and 1970; there were no equivalent tests with which to compare performance in mathematics.[34] Evidently, HMIs felt they had to defend the current system of primary education in a hostile public climate.

The uncomfortable relationship between the terms 'child-centred' and 'progressive', so frequently used as synonyms by their advocates, might help to explain why these surveys assumed that so little change had taken place. Earlier child-centred methods, by becoming orthodox, had by definition ceased to be progressive. *Primary Education in England* argued that three-quarters of teachers employed a 'mainly didactic' approach, implying that traditional teaching was still dominant in schools, but their definition of 'mainly exploratory' was stringent; 'mainly exploratory' teachers had to allow children to find their own solutions to problems, with no explanations given, and allow them to choose how to tackle the work.[35] The report thought that one in twenty, or 5 per cent of teachers, used this approach all the time, which actually seems strikingly high.[36] Meanwhile, 'mainly didactic' teachers were characterised as such simply because the teacher 'directed the children's work in accordance with relatively specific and predetermined intentions . . . explanations usually, though not always, preceded the action taken by the children'.[37]

This approach could be congruent with an otherwise 'progressive' style of teaching, as the report showed; nine out of ten teachers used group work, 'in almost all the classes children had the opportunity to talk informally among themselves at some time in the course of the working day', and three-quarters of classes for eleven-year-olds incorporated structured debate.[38] 'In just over half of the classes children did some writing on subjects of their own choice not connected directly with other current school work', half the classes incorporated outdoor activities, and 90 per cent of nine and eleven-year-olds did integrated humanities work, often in the form of topics such as '"homes", or "life on the farm" or "children of other lands"'.[39] And yet most of these teachers were classified by HMI as 'mainly didactic'. This only makes sense if one assumes that the report was using a very strict definition of 'progressive' and 'child-centred', assuming that 'child-centred' meant 'entirely self-directed by the child' and that 'child-centred' also equalled 'progressive'. However, this was not the way the terms had been, or were, used by the majority of schools and teachers, even in the late 1970s.

Non-utopian progressivism had always functioned by framing other kinds of practices, equipment and attitudes as 'traditional'. Now it became caught in its own logic, having to retrospectively redefine innovations that had been seen as cutting-edge in earlier decades as traditionalist and old-fashioned. This played out in concrete terms in a report in the *Teacher* in 1974, which declared that CLASP schools, part of a flagship programme of school-building in the late 1950s, were now seen as fire risks due to their undivided cavity roofs, which allowed fires to rapidly spread. The article pointed out that the 1971 school-building regulations would render such schools illegal were they to be built today.[40] The journal also utilised the idea that things had come 'full circle', and so it was difficult to apply 'traditionalist' labels to the past, in an article on a 110-year-old teacher, Sarah Ellen Morgan, who had started teaching in the late nineteenth century. 'As she describes teaching the huge classes of her day, sometimes 60 strong, it becomes clear that there was much less rote learning than is popularly imagined. She says the only way to teach anything in such situations was to divide children into groups and find good leaders.'[41] In seeking to portray non-utopian progressive pedagogy as radical and innovative, educationalists often found they had to deny the changes that had taken place in earlier decades.

Teachers themselves refused to take this view of the situation. In the 1970s, teachers often rejected new ideas by using the mantra that there had already been 'too much change' or 'change was moving too fast'. *Teachers World* criticised the 'frantic pace' of change in 1971, pointing out the massive amount of educational research that was currently under way:

> Primary school teachers in particular are still reeling under the successive blows to their traditional values and practices which have fallen upon them since the early 1960s . . . There are currently 98 curriculum development projects under the aegis of the Schools Council. The National Foundation for Educational Research, too, has a full agenda of investigations in hand . . . the Select Committee on teacher education . . . the 22 Area Training Organisations are conducting individual inquiries into teacher training, and Lord James . . . is about to start work [on the James Report on teacher training].[42]

Teachers often explicitly resisted the findings of educational researchers, which they characterised as outside interference with their craft knowledge.[43] This could lead to the lumping of all novel suggestions

The 'backlash' against progressivism

into the 'modern methods' category, regardless of whether they had much to do with how teachers actually taught or not. The *Teacher*, arguing that there had been 'too much change too soon', in 1974, mentioned community schools, ROSLA, permissiveness, school reorganisation, pupil participation inside schools, new curriculums and teaching methods.[44] The Rampton Report of 1981, discussing how to interweave the culture, experiences and heritage of West Indian children into school curriculums, noted that some teachers 'see this approach as the latest in a long line of politically influenced forms of "progressive" education', quoting one teacher: '"We have had mixed ability; we've gone Community and now it's bloody multi-cultural"'.[45] Therefore, if there was reflexive resistance against non-utopian progressive education in this decade, it was coming as much from within the teaching profession as from outside it, even though the latest generations of recruits had been trained under the progressive regime.

The non-utopian progressive tradition was also outflanked in this decade by a new wave of radical utopian educational thought with the emergence of the 'deschooling' movement, which drew from key US works such as Paul Goodman's *Compulsory Miseducation* (1962), John Holt's *How Children Fail* (1969) and Ivan Illich's *Deschooling Society* (1971).[46] These texts were in many ways very different, but put forward certain key arguments: children learn little in school as it is presently constituted, and so it is a waste of time and money; schools simply exist to socialise children into appropriate social and economic roles; many resources for learning are found outside the classroom; schools underline and enshrine class inequality. The solutions the writers put forward were equally varied, but, as Ian Lister's *Deschooling: A Reader* (1975) summarised, they focused on 'disestablishing schools', bringing education into the community, facilitating apprenticeships, reconstructing the outside world inside the school and giving pupils more power to run schools.[47]

However, these texts focused on American schools, which were much less progressive than English and Welsh schools in this period, and tended to attack an image of the 'traditional' school rather than particular pedagogical practices. Illich wrote about 'programmed instruction' as opposed to 'learning skills', and although he recognised the existence of more 'liberal' forms of education, he had very little to say about them, as he believed the teacher–pupil relationship was fundamentally oppressive.[48] He specifically complained about methods that mainstream progressive educationalists would have also rejected, such as passive 'instruction', the artificial division of the curriculum into set subjects, and textbooks.[49] Hence, child-centred educationalists in England and Wales could easily reject his views by arguing that his image of 'a school' was very different to the schools that actually existed. Ironically enough, *Deschooling Society* and *How Children Fail* were familiar set texts on teacher training courses by the late 1970s.[50] As Thomson has argued, projects idealised by the 'deschoolers', such as the adventure playground movement, which became influential in London in the late 1940s under the direction of Margery Allan, could become simply extensions of traditional playgrounds rather than a uniquely creative space.[51] Work on early progressive playgrounds in the United States has highlighted their gendered nature, and these tensions played out in Britain as well.[52] The child-centred emphasis on practical construction in these 'junk playgrounds' reflected the assumption that the child was always male, and may have turned off some potential participants; 80 per cent of British playground users in the post-war period were boys.[53]

Nevertheless, the 'deschoolers', while having little institutional impact, challenged non-utopian progressive claims to know best about what children needed and wanted.[54] Drawing on Philippe Ariés's *Centuries of Childhood* (1962), Illich argued that childhood itself was a modern concept institutionalised by compulsory education divided up into age-stages, and that it was 'a burden' that would be removed by deschooling, allowing society to become 'liveable for the young'.[55] John Holt similarly thought that 'Children are subject peoples. School for them is a kind of jail.' In contrast to the child-centred version of the school as a nurturing environment for creativity, he suggested that they might 'escape . . . by withdrawing the most intelligent and creative parts of their minds from the scene'.[56] Colin Ward's photographs of children creatively exploring cityscapes were influenced by Illich, and he quoted the anthropologist Margaret Mead, who had explored the different meanings of childhood and adolescence in non-western cultures, in his influential *The Child and the City* (1975): 'It's a good thing to think about the child as long as you remember that the child doesn't exist. Only children exist. Every time we lump them together we lose something.'[57] Like inter-war utopians such as Lane, Neill and

Russell, deschoolers were diametrically opposed to non-utopian progressive pedagogy, because they were committed to a different concept of childhood. They did not emerge from child-centred educational traditions, but reacted against them by denying the validity of their claims.

Politics and the teacher: becoming 'accountable'

Changes in the position of the teaching profession in the 1970s and early 1980s intensified the concerns about pay and status that many teachers had experienced in the 1950s and 1960s. During wartime, and in the immediate post-war period, teachers had been in such demand due to the rising birth rate and the raising of the school leaving age that the profession had been forced to alter its entry standards by admitting emergency-trained teachers. While this had contributed to increased anxiety among certain groups of teachers, and fed into concerns about the falling status of the profession, teachers were at least assured of employment once they had finished their training college course. From the mid-1970s, as the birth rate fell for the first time since the war, this would no longer be the case.[58] By the early 1980s, the colleges were producing more teachers than there were teaching posts available, and teachers faced unemployment and increased competition for both jobs and promotion opportunities.[59] The profession was also becoming subject to increased external controls on two interlinked fronts: via central government and via the inspectorate. The Plowden Report, as Mike Savage notes, embedded the importance of research in informing educational practice by calling for a new survey every ten years.[60] A major HMI survey of 1964 drawn upon by Plowden revealed the origins of a more homogenised inspectorate when it mapped out a new way of classifying schools on a numerical scale of one to nine. The descriptors ranged from 'In most respects a school of outstanding quality', echoing the later language of Ofsted, to 'A bad school where children suffer from laziness, indifference, gross incompetence or unkindness on the part of the staff'.[61]

As Peter Cunningham has argued, the function of the HMI began to change as early as the House of Commons Select Committee of 1967/8, which suggested that, as well as constructing national surveys, they should produce curricular guidelines.[62] A major document along these lines was produced in 1977 with the publication of *Curriculum 11–16*, alongside a series of *Surveys* and *Matters of Discussion* in the same period, and the publication of inspection reports from the early 1980s.[63] And although the National Curriculum was not introduced by central government until 1988, the 1981 Education Act introduced the parents' right to choose the school and required schools to publish their examination results.[64] These moves undermined the system in which non-utopian progressive education had been introduced, threatening congenial relations between both inspectors and schools and different schools in the same area. They further affected the declining professional autonomy of the teacher by beginning to impose central control on teaching methods via an increasingly formalised process that would culminate in the National Curriculum.

The HMI Surveys produced in the 1970s indicate that the inspectorate itself was beginning to turn away from the kind of child-centred education that had been promoted by Plowden, perhaps in response to both educational researchers and the concerns of teachers. *HMI Today and Tomorrow* (1970) started to adopt the language of 'accountability' that a number of historians have seen as characteristic of educational discourse in this decade.[65] 'Education today claims a larger share of national resources, in money, materials and manpower, than it has ever done ... Public interest in educational issues and in the nature and quality of the education provided is becoming keener and more sophisticated', the report stated.[66] This was in line with wider international shifts in the relationship between schools and the state by the late 1970s and early 1980s. For example, in the US, Ronald Reagan's National Commission of Excellence in Education's report *A Nation at Risk* (1983) picked up on similar arguments about falling standards in schools and the need for centralised action.

HMIs responded to this climate by framing the HMI's role as an 'observer' for the DES rather than solely 'advisor' for schools, which marked a significant shift in the inspectorate's remit.[67] 'Policy decisions depend for their validity on knowledge of material circumstances ...', *HMI Today and Tomorrow* argued. 'It follows that a Department which has a field force of its own observers enjoys a considerable advantage'.[68] Not all HMIs were happy about this shift; as MacLure pointed out. A number complained that they spent increasing amounts of time on policy-related tasks and less time at schools from the mid-1970s onwards.[69] Joe Wiles felt that the HMI had become institutionalised: 'The Inspectorate that I joined in 1964 was a very different organisation from that I left in 1984 . . . it [had] allowed full scope for the conscientious and inspiring maverick.'[70] After the appointment of Sheila Browne as SCI in 1974 and the shift in the HMI's relationship to the central government, Trevor Fletcher, who had become an HMI in 1963, thought that 'This new view of HMI ran counter to much that I had been taught as a new entrant.'[71]

By the late 1970s, the shift within the inspectorate was not solely confined to responsibilities and duties but had started to influence their educational ideals as well. *A View of the Curriculum* (1980) was commissioned by the DES as part of 'the process of reaching a national consensus on a desirable framework for the curriculum'.[72] This not only formalised the informal influence that HMI had wielded over teaching methods for decades, but revealed that the inspectorate's priorities had shifted. The report opened by making a point that had become familiar during the 1970s, returning to the central tension within child-centred education that had remained unrecognised by Plowden:

> 'The curriculum' has to satisfy two seemingly contrary requirements. On the one hand it has to reflect the broad aims of education which hold good for all children, whatever their capacities and whatever schools they attend. On the other hand it has to allow for differences in the abilities and other characteristics of children, even of the same age . . . This necessary tension between common and individual needs exists however the school system is organised.[73]

The report made use of the relatively novel language of 'skills' to claim that while local curriculums might differ, their underlying aims remained the same, and it was this that HMI were attempting to codify – there was no suggestion that they were attempting to introduce a scheme on the lines of the National Curriculum. The report explicitly noted concerns about the implication of certain child-centred forms of curriculum, such as integrated study: 'Where traditional subjects have been replaced by grouped interdisciplinary or 'integrated' studies, it is even more important that the learning objectives be clearly established, since familiar landmarks may be less visible.'[74] It also criticised the idea, expressed by both Hadow and Plowden, that children of a certain age shared the same interests: 'As children make progress their interests diversify and what is a stimulus to one may be a barrier to another.'[75]

A progressive education?

Nevertheless, the more utilitarian tone of the report did not signal a 'backlash' against child-centred education. In many ways, the assumptions made by HMI were rooted in the logic of non-utopian progressive educationalists. Shared skills were more important than specific content; teachers were responsible for pupils' emotional and social development, as well as their intellectual and physical needs; streaming was often 'too crude' a tactic to provide for individual needs; 'geographical circumstances' conditioned children's development and should be taken into account in their teaching; 'painting, modelling, music-making, dancing and storytelling' were important in primary schools, as was practical work, especially in science.[76] Education should still be local, practical and enjoyable, but the balance between 'individual' and 'natural' had shifted; *A View of the Curriculum* suggested that too much weight had been placed on the latter at the expense of the former. Unsurprisingly, then, it had little to say about the 'child' and much more about the 'school'.

The idea of 'accountability' promoted by HMI, the DES and, to an extent, by the teaching press was intended to frame the increasingly militant teachers' strikes of this decade as selfish and individualistic. The *Teacher*, as the NUT's journal, was naturally more sympathetic to strike action, reporting extensively on teachers' demands. When the Houghton Report (1974) delivered teachers a substantial pay rise, most of the January 1975 issues of the journal were dedicated to discussing it, and the staffroom reaction was summarised as 'Good – but not enough'.[77] *Teachers World* deliberately adopted a 'neutral' stance on strikes; a 1970 article on 'Strikes – common sense and conscience', following the first ever national teachers' strike from 1969–70, argued that militancy had led to 'a new sense of unity in the profession' but refused to support teachers who fully withdrew their labour, arguing that strikers should simply not participate in out-of-school extracurricular activities.[78] The journal barely mentioned the Houghton Report, despite its obvious relevance to its readership.[79] This stance may not have proved popular with readers, given the journal's termination in 1975 due to low sales. Union action had been an issue that had divided teachers since at least the inter-war period, as it was felt that strike action challenged teachers' professional status, but the debate fundamentally shifted in the 1970s.[80]

The increase in teacher militancy associated the profession publicly with the organised left, especially after the later wave of strikes in the mid-1980s, which may have contributed to the right-wing myth that teachers in the 1970s were all 'loony lefties' forcing 'trendy' progressive methods upon unwilling children. But although the language of the political left and right became increasingly used by teachers from the 1970s onwards, this model is not especially helpful for understanding either teachers' own views or the nature of the progressive educational movement. We have already seen that teachers were not usually enthusiastic converts to child-centred education. Non-utopian progressivism, with its much longer history, was not innately left-leaning or radical. As we have seen, it was deeply implicated in developments that commanded cross-party support, such as the 1944 Education Act, implemented by Labour but steered through Parliament by the Conservative politician R. A. Butler and passed under the wartime coalition government. Dennis Dean has argued that post-war Conservatives 'laid claim' to this act, publishing the White Paper *Secondary Education for All: A New Drive* in 1958 under Macmillan to try and 'capture a slogan created by the Left'.[81]

This White Paper did not push for the expansion of a 'traditional' kind of secondary education, but praised modern developments: 'There are few more encouraging aspects of British life to-day than the sight of a primary class getting on with their work in bright and airy surroundings; or of older children learning for the first time how to make the best use of a library'.[82] The report noted that there had been no decline in 'basic standards' but also reported favourably on the 'artistic pursuits' of pupils.[83] It criticised large classes and all-age schools, concurring with the progressive commitment to an individualised, separate secondary education.[84] While it supported the retention of selection, it must be remembered that this could have been seen as a child-centred commitment in the 1950s. Labour did not fully commit itself to the adoption of comprehensives until 1955 for similar reasons to those stated by the White Paper: 'there must remain a substantial element of selection . . . if we are to do justice to the different needs of individual children. For children do differ considerably in their mental powers, in their special gifts, in vigour, in industry, and in their ability to concentrate.'[85] The paper retained the 1944 commitment to a decentralised education system controlled by local authorities, and did not rule out experiments with comprehensives when suitable for the needs of a locality.[86] In short, on the eve of the 1960s, Conservative rhetoric on education sounded thoroughly progressive; this was not a language confined to the Labour Party or to other 'left-wing' organisations.

The idea that progressivism was inherently left-wing was also due to the false equation of non-utopian progressive educational practice with the 'permissive shift' that was believed to be sweeping the country in the 1950s and 1960s. This was spelt out by the writers of the Black Papers.[87] Cyril Burt wrote that 'parents and members of the public at large are beginning to wonder whether the free discipline, or lack of discipline, in the new permissive school may not largely be responsible for much of the subsequent delinquency, violence and general unrest that characterise our permissive society.'[88] As Francis Musgrove has argued, these concerns were only loosely linked to actual practice in schools: 'The real occasion for Black Paper One [published in 1968] was not the state of primary schools but university expansion and student unrest.'[89] Contributors bought into a simplistic narrative that linked 'permissive' child-rearing – personified by Dr Spock – and education to radical activism among students and other occupational groups.[90] Although historians have challenged the idea of a 'permissive shift' in this period, there has still been some tendency to assume that child-rearing and education had become more 'permissive' in both Britain and the US.[91] However, as we have seen, non-utopian progressive or child-centred pedagogies did not necessarily allow children any more freedom than their 'traditional' counterparts, and so cannot be accurately characterised as permissive from the child's point of view. Deschooling advocates, indeed, criticised child-centred education from a left-wing perspective, suggesting that it merely modified the conditions of children's institutionalisation rather than attacking them at the root. Children's agency was still limited, and children's voices were not listened to.

'The new conservatism': children, childhood and 'child-centred' education

If there was an intellectual backlash against child-centred education in the 1970s, it focused upon the model's inherent contradictions and shortcomings. All children and adolescents were, to various degrees, defined as abnormal by non-utopian progressive pedagogy, because it was unlikely that any individual would be able to perfectly conform to the theoretical image of their age group. Furthermore, they could never really be seen as normal while they were envisaged as incomplete adults. As Lorna Ridgway and Irene Lawton argued in *Family Grouping in the Primary School* (1968), 'although some children have exceptional problems and difficulties, *all* children have some of these problems some of the time' due to 'their feelings of inadequacy in an adult world'.[92] As childhood itself functioned as an axis of oppression, when these identities intersected with gender, class, race and disability, children and adolescents shouldered triple or quadruple burdens.[93]

The white, able-bodied male child was the invisible norm for child-centred educationalists.[94] Familiar gender expectations ascribed to primary-aged girls in the inter-war period were modified but not challenged by child-centred post-war primary schools. Immigrant children, who were often children of colour, were framed as pedagogical problems because of their 'underachievement', yet when they expressed ambition and drive, they were seen as being 'unrealistically ambitious'. Children with learning difficulties were often removed from mainstream schooling altogether, while 'gifted' children were ignored. Although child-centred education theoretically celebrated individual 'difference', these children were viewed as too 'different' to be accommodated by the system. Finally, working-class children were often seen as stupid, apathetic and disengaged, terms that took on a new significance in the child-centred primary school where 'interest' was valued so highly. As Sharp and Green put it in 1975, far from being a radical, left-wing ideology, child-centred pedagogy, when practised in a certain way, could be seen as 'a modern form of conservatism'.[95]

Developmental psychology, as understood by child-centred educationalists in the 1960s, came under attack from within the movement in the 1970s. The most significant shift was the internalisation of the idea that growth was not chronological and uniform, and that individual children would develop at their own rate. This came in the context of 'growing public hostility' to intelligence testing after the discrediting of Cyril Burt from the mid-1970s onwards among claims that he had falsified much of his original data.[96] This started to become evident in child-centred texts by the late 1970s. Margaret Donaldson's *Children's Minds* (1978) insisted that 'the evidence now compels us to reject certain features of Jean Piaget's theory of intellectual development', arguing that children's abilities have been underestimated and it should not be assumed that 'most children are not capable of real intellectual achievement', reflecting the inter-war work of Susan Isaacs, although Donaldson did not cite her.[97] Donaldson, a developmental psychologist, called for 'a more effective psychology' rather than criticising the knowledge system itself, but her criticisms are still notable given the dominance of Piagetian thought in child-centred educational discourse throughout the post-war period.[98]

Meanwhile, the version of developmental thought that had been presented to teachers by teacher training colleges, refresher courses, popular teaching guides and the teaching press continued to mediate the experiences of children in schools. The HMI Survey *Girls and Science* (1980) unwittingly revealed that many of the aspects of science teaching that female students found difficult were child-centred. After decades of work on the importance of practical education, science now centred on experimental work, but this could be challenging for girls who had 'little previous experience of practical electricity', unlike boys, who were 'likely to have had such experiences at home', and so girls tended 'to lack confidence in the laboratory'.[99] One inspector observed first-hand how girls were discouraged in mixed-sex classrooms because of the emphasis on practical skill, rather than note-taking, which girls were 'good at':

> A group of girls who had little previous experience of practical physical science, especially of electricity, experienced difficulties when first asked to connect batteries, bulbs, switches and meters together. Some boys began to mock the girls and to interfere with their experiment, thinking it funny that girls should encounter difficulty with what seemed to them to be an elementary piece of work.[100]

The child-centred emphasis on class discussion and participation could also turn girls off science lessons, as they found it difficult to speak in front of boys who were much more confident, regardless of ability. Encouraging pupils to 'find things out' or 'discover answers for themselves' rather than being instructed by the teacher could make this situation worse. 'One teacher, when asked by an able girl if he could explain a point, asked her to work it out for herself. This was the method regularly adopted by this teacher simply because he was trying to encourage self-reliance, but the girl found this approach to her difficulties rather worrying.'[101] This kind of 'discovery learning' presupposed that the pupil had a natural confidence in the subject.

It is important to note that gendered assumptions and attitudes did not persist in schools *despite* child-centred education, but were central to the way that it functioned. Both boys and girls who did not fulfil gendered norms could be subject to sanction by progressive teachers. Katherine Clarricoates, who undertook eighteen months of observation in four British primary schools in the late 1970s, recounted the experiences of seven-year-old Michael, who was stigmatised by teachers for engaging in 'cross sex-role behaviour' by playing with dolls, baking with his mother and making doll dresses. Teachers claimed that they had to discourage Michael from these activities so he could form successful relationships with his peer group – seen as central to healthy development.[102] Nevertheless, on the whole, boys were seen as more 'successful children' because they were better at fulfilling the child-centred dictate that children should be sociable, extroverted, active and independent.

In Clarricoates' study, teachers admitted that girls got the best results in their classes, but only because of their conformist nature. One teacher said 'The girls ask the right questions simply because it's expected of them'; another said 'I think it's more to do with wanting to please rather than being intelligent.'[103] When compared with their male counterparts, girls came off worst, and this was framed in terms of interest: 'Boys are interested in everything, and are prepared to take things seriously'. Boys were seen as more 'capable of learning', which was unsurprising when learning was defined as active pursuit.[104] This finding was reflected in my Oxfordshire oral history interviews as well. Ruth, who taught mathematics at an Oxford comprehensive school in the 1970s, when asked if 'the children responded differently' to progressive methods such as group work and discovery learning, said 'The boys did more . . . Boys are very different in the way they learn . . . They tell me I'm being sexist when I tell the kids this at school. The girls tend to be more precise, they do what you tell them to do, they write down every step. The boys think it more . . . they like the investigation type stuff more.'[105] On the other hand, when girls displayed aggressive, independent behaviour, this was policed much more strictly than when boys committed similar transgressions, as Clarricoates' study showed. Craig was allowed to get away with 'harassing his classmates' while Sarah's 'outbursts of temper' marked her as 'a problem child': 'Little girls do not do that.'[106] Girls' social and emotional development was hence more harshly judged, while their superior intellectual development was excused or denied – leaving them as failed children.

Official policy stated that disabled pupils should be more fully integrated into the mainstream from the late 1960s onwards, with films such as *'So we're different but . . .'* (1977), which dealt with physically disabled children, being produced by the DES, but this was not necessarily the case in practice. Sheffield saw a large drop in admissions to ESN schools in the early 1970s, which the *Teacher* thought was due to an expansion in the area's psychological services, which meant that pupils were staying in mainstream schools that were not equipped to teach them. Dennis Spooner, a teacher representative on Sheffield's Education Committee, argued that 'If Sheffield is going to adopt a policy of total integration then it must provide the facilities in the ordinary schools.'[107] Teachers who were put in sole charge of ESN classes were often too badly overworked to provide their pupils with the appropriate amount of attention. One explained 'My average day is ten hours, and often runs nearer 15, so I am just too tired and too overworked to give any depth of thought.'[108] Disabled pupils faced both physical barriers and prejudiced attitudes when they were 'mainstreamed', as Lynn, who was special needs co-ordinator in her Oxfordshire school, recalled. She had resisted the practice of pulling ESN pupils out of 'ordinary' classrooms for one-on-one treatment, because she felt this made them feel like 'the thick group'.[109] Jan was also in charge of an Oxfordshire special needs department in the late 1970s, which she reorganised entirely when she took over. As she recalled, 'it was run by an ex-military chap . . . the youngsters used to come in and take their file off, sit down, open it, not speak.'[110] She told the headmaster, 'if you want the special needs department run as it is now . . . I'm not interested . . . I would want a daily newspaper, a three-piece suite, a cooker, cups, cutlery, china . . . they're not coping in this school, we need to offer them something different . . . He said you can have all that.'[111]

The overwhelming importance of appropriate interaction with one's peer group was used by non-utopian progressive educationalists to justify the exclusion and isolation of physically and mentally disabled children. Elizabeth Anderson's consideration of physically disabled children in both mainstream and special schools, published in 1973, revealed these assumptions. 'Teasing' was a common problem when children were 'integrated' into the mainstream, but Anderson presented this as something that disabled children simply had to get used to: 'it is necessary for personality development that children learn to assert themselves.'[112] She suggested that it was the disabled child's fault when he or she was bullied, as the child contributes 'to the unhealthy situation by his negative self-evaluation and . . . his hostility towards others, by his unskilled and unrealistic behaviour which may include either assertive aggressiveness or withdrawing non-contribution and by his insensitive and defensive reception of feedback from others.'[113] However, Anderson still suggested that mainstreaming disabled children was desirable, as it was good for them to understand from an early age how the world saw them: 'parents must not enter into too great a "conspiracy of cheerfulness", otherwise the child may have the devastating experience of being brought face to face with his shortcomings in a hostile rejecting environment . . . the child has to face the responsibility for his own adjustment to the new school world . . . he has to ward off possible attacks (verbal or otherwise) of classmates, and to make himself acceptable to them.' [114] Disabled children were positioned as responsible if they were verbally and physically assaulted, as their lack of integration with their peer group was not seen as due to prejudice or discrimination but their own social shortcomings. This was the natural outcome of a child-centred education that valorised 'peer relationships' as the measure of a child's social and emotional development.

Immigrant and ethnic minority children suffered from the same set of normative assumptions about childhood and adolescence. Researchers and campaigners who wanted to discuss problems of racism in schools often ran up against the argument that children 'don't see race' and so discussing race with them would have undesirable consequences. Taysir Kawwa, who went on to become an educational psychologist at a London child guidance centre, vividly described his encounters with staff when researching ethnic prejudice among white adolescents in a North London comprehensive school in 1962:

> once when I was talking to three members of the staff . . . one of them accused me in bitter tones of being destructive: "You come and destroy what has taken us ages to build up", and of course she meant I was destroying the tolerant spirit she had been inculcating into the children. Another member of staff offered to give me what I wanted without going to the trouble of

asking the children, he said he could tell me exactly what the children felt and thought about all coloured people. This and other forms of objection to my work grew more and more bitter on the grounds that by asking the children about their opinions I was exciting or fanning racial hatred.[115]

Kawwa's findings on ethnic prejudice among white adolescents aged eleven to seventeen spoke for themselves. Typical statements in answer to his questionnaire on views of black people and Greek Cypriots included:

> [Are black people and Cypriots good for the country? In what way?] 'Yes, for keeping the Kit-Kat factories going.' (Boy, 15)

> Myself I think they get jobs as easy as a finger snap, as for us we are thousands out of work, they should give all white people first chance. (Girl, 16)

> They rape innocent white girls. Give them an inch and they take a yard. (Girl, 14)

> I would like them to be chucked out of all the schools and chucked out of the country (Boy, 13)

> I like a few of them but the majority I don't like they [are] dirty, bullying, bigheaded (Boy, 13)

> They got [sic] to get money for food and clothes to live or they will die and they will take up all of our cemetery of English peoples [sic] graves (Girl, 13)[116]

Although the school in question is not named in Kawwa's thesis, correspondence between its headmaster and County Hall reveals that this study was carried out at one of the most famous 'progressive' schools of this period, Risinghill.[117] While the headmaster, Michael Duane, supported Kawwa's study and wrote in his report that '[t]here has certainly been no evidence at all that relations between the children have deteriorated', it is clear that many of his staff were of a different frame of mind; the study was terminated abruptly after one staff member threatened to resign.[118]

Kawwa's experiences were not unique. The idea that children were naturally free of ethnic prejudice continually reoccurred in work on race relations in schools in the 1960s and 1970s.[119] Interestingly, the opposing argument, that young children were incapable of exercising empathy, returning to Piagetian ideas about moral development, was also put forward in relation to both racial prejudice and prejudice against those with disabilities.[120] Anderson wrote that 'it is unrealistic to expect very young children to show compassion' even though she was discussing children of all ages.[121] Therefore, romanticised and stereotypical expectations of children created a hostile climate for both ethnic minority and disabled pupils, especially for those who were members of both groups.

Sharp and Green showed how working-class children were vulnerable to value judgements in their study of Maplethorpe primary in the early 1970s. They concluded that 'the well-intentioned "radical practices" of the progressive educator produced effects very similar to the hierarchical differentiation of pupils characteristic of formal methods.'[122] Maplethorpe practised self-directed education, and teachers had little time for children who wanted more formal instruction: 'Children learn by doing . . . and children who don't seem to have enough confidence to get cracking and do something – these are the kids who worry me . . . the extraverted ones . . . the children who are confident, reasonably relaxed kids . . . these are the kids we can help.' Certain teachers deliberately used class judgements to stigmatise their pupils, such as Mrs Carpenter, who thought that most of her pupils 'are thick and those who aren't thick are disturbed'. Mrs Buchanan, who came from a working-class background herself, resisted the other teachers' assumptions about working-class families: 'I think most of the rest of the staff tend to teach families rather than individuals. If they've had one problem child from a family then the rest of that family that come to school are immediately labelled as problems.' However, she still had little time for children who were not showing what she considered to be appropriate social development, such as seven-year-old Glenn, who was bullied by the other children: 'He cries a lot, he whinges and whines. He moans a lot – I think this is what annoys the other children . . . He's got no friends . . . He doesn't talk much to me. I don't think he likes me very much.'

While female, ethnic minority, working-class and disabled pupils suffered most, all children were liable to fail to live up to the child-centred standards of what constituted a healthy child. Well-behaved children, whatever their class background, were less likely to run up against child-centred assumptions about inappropriate or abnormal development. Mary was exceptionally good at reading for her age but, as Sharp and Green observed, 'The fact that she is "no trouble" will mean that the teacher will indulge her requests to read without this being taken to be symptomatic of having pressurizing parents who are unprepared to wait for readiness to emerge.' In contrast, Daniel, who was rebellious, but not backward in his academic work, was seen as 'abnormal' as 'he was not sufficiently deferent to the teacher's authority . . . He would not take her word, but wanted reasons.' The Nottingham parents of seven-year-olds interviewed by the Newsons in 1977 looked at these issues from the other side. One middle-class child, the son of a company director, was struggling at school and, according to his mother:

> He's frightened to death of school. I think this is because he can't apply his mind to the subjects, and he goes to a state school where there's no individualistic teaching either – which is all to the good, I'm not against it, I'm very *for* it, because I think he must learn to mix with others; but he's frightened, you see, that they can do it and he can't.[123]

Child-centred teaching enforced a different set of orthodoxies on school pupils, and children would struggle as profoundly to live up to these expectations as they had when they were taught traditionally.

The Integrated Day (1970) by Mary Brown and Norman Precious included a series of case studies of children as they moved through the primary school where these value judgements could be seen in practice. David was seen as a consistently problematic child because he was 'friendless' and preferred doing things by himself, despite his active participation in other aspects of school life; at ten, he wrote a play for another group of children to perform, joined an orchestra and contributed to the school newspaper. In contrast, Pat, who was confident and outgoing, was praised as 'mature' for her age.[124] Nine-year-old Charles also ran into trouble for not fitting adult expectations of childhood: 'Charles needs a lot of understanding. His presumptuous, bumptious manner could easily be misunderstood. He takes liberties and presumes an acceptance of his mature standards which are unusual for a child of his age.' At ten, Charles, working on a piece for the school magazine, 'Interviewed new teachers for their impression of the school!'; the exclamation mark indicates that his teacher thought this was transgressive, tying into a discourse of unhealthy precocity and the assumption of an unequal relationship between children and adults.[125]

Child-centred education united modern developmental models of childhood with an older, more romantic image of the child as unspoilt and innocent, unable to discriminate against others or demonstrate deliberate malice. Children were 'free of prejudice' at the same time as they were 'unable to show compassion'. They naturally united with each other in co-operative play while excluding those peers – and *only* those peers – who did not live up to appropriate developmental standards.[126] In other words, children lived in both a natural paradise and a Darwinian jungle, maturationally unable to demonstrate real empathy for each other, and yet somehow protected from the challenges of the 'real adult' world.[127] This concept of childhood, and also of a childlike adolescence, was to prove inadequate for any radical project that wanted to give more freedom to the pupil in the classroom. As Ian Lister argued in 1975: 'Both the progressives and the traditionalists assert that they want to protect children – from each other. They have become ... complementary parts of the same protection racket ... the younger [children] are, the more marginal they become ... It is the political weakness of the young that has made them so vulnerable to educational researchers and to utopian experiments.'[128]

Utopian progressive ideas about childhood made a partial comeback in the deschooling movements of the 1970s, although even these radical discourses strayed occasionally into more prescriptive notions of childhood, as was seen in the 'playwork' ideas that surrounded adventure playgrounds. However, 'deschooling', like utopian progressivism, was fundamentally divorced from non-utopian or child-centred pedagogy, which rested on the 'schooling' of the child to fit normative, developmental conceptions of childhood. These new movements pointed out that non-utopian progressive pedagogy did not extend true freedom to the child in the classroom, arguing that schools, as institutions, had failed in their purpose. The inherent contradiction between what was natural for children and what was specific to each child started to unravel, with official reports moving away from discussion of the characteristics of childhood and focusing instead on the functions of the school, a shift that progressive educators might have decried as 'traditionalist' but which was still rooted in other child-centred values. Finally, deschoolers noted that the existing education system, despite its theoretical claims, did not really value the child in his or her own right, but tended to think about pupils in terms of the adult roles they would later inhabit.

As the contradictions within child-centred education were brought to light by educational researchers in the 1970s, teachers, far from leading a left-wing charge to allow children freedom in schools, remained as uncertain about its claims as they had been in the preceding decades. Despite the high profile of conservative attacks such as the Black Papers, child-centred education was assailed from within as well as from without during this decade, with its most novel ideas starting to lose the support of its key institutional allies – the national inspectorate. The language of 'backlash' does not fully capture this process, which had been in train since the mainstreaming of non-utopian progressive education in the 1950s. However, fears about indiscipline and unrest in schools did provide the DES, now under Thatcher's government, with an excuse to extend its control over education into the 1980s. Furthermore, as James Avis has argued, child-centred pedagogy was vulnerable to appropriation by the New Right as, unlike utopian progressivism, it lacked a coherent radical political programme.[129] The concepts of childhood and adolescence that non-utopian progressive educationalists had promoted did not disappear as their influence waned, but persisted, now separated from their origins, as a basic form of common sense about what children were really like.

Notes

1 Bernstein and Davies, 'Plowden', p. 55.
2 O'Hara, *Governing Post-War Britain*, p. 177.
3 Bernstein and Davies, 'Plowden', p. 60.
4 Peters, 'Philosophy', pp. 2, 5, 12.
5 Wooldridge, *Measuring the Mind*, p. 12; Smith, *To Understand and to Help*, p. 131; Griffin-Beale (ed.), *Christian Schiller*, p. xii; Cunningham, *Curriculum Change in the Primary School*, p. 58.
6 Cunningham, *Curriculum Change in the Primary School*, p. 213.
7 For example, Ball and Goodson, 'Understanding teachers', pp. 3–5; Bennett, *Teaching Styles and Pupil Progress*; Wooldridge, *Measuring the Mind*, pp. 385–93. Despite his massive contribution to the early history of educational psychology and progressive practice, Wooldridge's book is less innovatory on the 1960s and 1970s.
8 Rutter *et al.*, *Fifteen Thousand Hours*.
9 Though not necessarily subscribing to the 'traditional narrative' I outline here, Philip Gardner has charted teachers' declining professional autonomy from the 1970s onwards. Gardner, 'Classroom teachers and educational change'.
10 Bennett, 'Changing perspectives on teaching'.
11 Bennett, *Teaching Styles and Pupil Progress*, pp. 157, 160.

12 MacLure, *The Inspectors' Calling*, p. 189.
13 Rutter et al., *Fifteen Thousand Hours*, pp. 123, 185–6.
14 Burt, 'Mental differences', p. 16.
15 Hilliard (ed.), *Teaching the Teachers*, p. 12, argued that the *Black Papers* represented the feelings of a large number of teachers.
16 Bennett, 'Changing perspectives on teaching'.
17 Peters, 'Philosophy', pp. 16–18.
18 Thomson, *Lost Freedom*, p. 185.
19 Cited in Cunningham, *Curriculum Change in the Primary School*, p. 4.
20 Lawton, 'The curriculum and curriculum change', p. 121.
21 'Labels of convenience', *Teacher*, 14 January 1977, p. 2.
22 Cox and Dyson (eds), *Black Paper 1*.
23 Bennett, *Teaching Styles and Pupil Progress*, pp. 5, 149.
24 Bassey, *Nine Hundred Primary School Teachers*, p. 7.
25 Galton et al., *Inside the Primary Classroom*, p. 156.
26 Auld, *William Tyndale Junior and Infants Schools Public Inquiry*.
27 Bassey, *Nine Hundred Primary School Teachers*; Ashton et al., *The Aims of Primary Education*; Cunningham, *Curriculum Change in the Primary School*, p. 2; McCulloch, 'A people's history of education'.
28 Bennett, *Teaching Styles and Pupil Progress*, p. 54.
29 *Ibid.*, p. 149.
30 *Ibid.*, p. 38.
31 Bassey, *Nine Hundred Primary School Teachers*, pp. 7, 28.
32 *Ibid.*, pp. 22, 39–41.
33 DES, *Primary Education in England*, pp. 26, 51–3.
34 *Ibid.*, p. 83.
35 *Ibid.*, pp. 26–7.
36 *Ibid.*, p. 27.
37 *Ibid.*, p. 26.
38 *Ibid.*, pp. 42, 46.
39 *Ibid.*, pp. 47, 59, 74.
40 H. Brook, 'Closing the fire roof gap . . . CLASP schools are safe, but who will pay to make them even safer?', *Teacher*, 18 January 1974, p. 3.
41 M. Denett, 'Independent of any man . . . but *The Schoolmaster* played Cupid', *Teacher*, 28 January 1977, p. 3.
42 'Talking the new year in', *Teachers World*, 1 January 1971, p. 3.
43 G. Wratten, 'Classroom researcher destroys own data', *Teacher*, 17 January 1975, p. 4.
44 'Too much change too soon', *Teacher*, 4 January 1974, p. 1.
45 DES, *West Indian Children in our Schools*, p. 29.
46 Thomson, *Lost Freedom*, pp. 194–206.
47 Lister (ed.), *Deschooling*, p. 10.
48 Illich, *Deschooling Society*, pp. 12–13, 31.

49 *Ibid.*, pp. 39-40, 80.
50 Oxfordshire Pilot, Ox.009, questionnaire, p. 1; Oxfordshire Pilot, Ox.008, interview.
51 Thomson, *Lost Freedom*, p. 206.
52 Hines, 'They do not know how to play'; Gagen, 'Too good to be true'.
53 Newstead, 'Shadows and mystery'.
54 Thomson, *Lost Freedom*, pp. 127, 195-206.
55 Illich, *Deschooling Society*, pp. 26-8.
56 Holt, *How Children Fail*, p. 156.
57 Ward, *The Child in the City*, p. vi.
58 Cunningham, *Curriculum Change in the Primary School*, p. 213.
59 Ball and Goodson, 'Understanding teachers', p. 3.
60 Savage, *Identities and Social Change*, p. 206.
61 DES, *Children and Their Primary Schools*.
62 Cunningham, *Curriculum Change in the Primary School*, p. 221.
63 *Ibid.*; Ball and Goodson, 'Understanding teachers', p. 5.
64 Ball and Goodson, 'Understanding teachers', p. 5.
65 P. Mandler, 'Educating the Nation I', pp. 20, 25; Cunningham, *Curriculum Change in the Primary School*, p. 221; MacLure, *The Inspectors' Calling*, p. ix.
66 DES, *HMI Today and Tomorrow*, p. 23.
67 *Ibid.*
68 *Ibid.*
69 MacLure, *The Inspectors' Calling*, p. 113.
70 *Ibid.*, p. 129.
71 *Ibid.*, p. 164.
72 DES, *Girls and Science*, p. 1.
73 *Ibid.*
74 *Ibid.*, p. 16.
75 *Ibid.*, p. 8.
76 *Ibid.*, pp. 2, 10-11.
77 'Good – but not enough', *Teacher*, 3 January 1975, p. 3.
78 'Strikes – common sense and conscience', *Teachers World*, 16 January 1970, p. 3.
79 *Teachers World*, 3 January 1975, p. 3.
80 'The NUT as a trade union', *Teachers World*, 20 January 1926, p. 800; Grace, 'Teachers and the state in Britain'.
81 Dean, 'Conservative governments', pp. 247, 253.
82 Ministry of Education, 'Secondary education for all', pp. 207-8.
83 *Ibid.*, p. 208.
84 *Ibid.*
85 Francis, 'A socialist policy for education?', p. 332; Ministry of Education, 'Secondary education for all', p. 209.
86 Ministry of Education, 'Secondary education for all', p. 210.

87 Cox and Dyson (eds), *Black Paper 1*.
88 Quoted in Wooldridge, *Measuring the Mind*, p. 388.
89 Musgrove, 'The Black Paper movement', p. 107.
90 Wooldridge, *Measuring the Mind*, p. 385.
91 Thomas, 'Will the real 1950s please stand up?'; Stearns, *Anxious Parents*.
92 Ridgway and Lawton, *Family Grouping in the Primary School*, p. 50.
93 James and Prout, *Constructing and Reconstructing Childhood*.
94 Burman, *Deconstructing Developmental Psychology*, p. 70.
95 Sharp et al., *Education and Social Control*, p. viii.
96 Wooldridge, *Measuring the Mind*, pp. 286–9.
97 Donaldson, *Children's Minds*, pp. 121, 126, 140.
98 Walkerdine, 'Child-centred pedagogy', p. 153.
99 DES, *Girls and Science*, p. 15.
100 *Ibid.*, pp. 17-18.
101 *Ibid.*, p. 18.
102 Clarricoates, 'The importance of being Ernest', pp. 35–6.
103 Clarricoates, 'The importance of being Ernest', p. 29.
104 *Ibid.*, p. 33.
105 Oxfordshire Pilot, Ox.007, interview.
106 Clarricoates, 'The importance of being Ernest', p. 31.
107 'The missing ESN children', *Teacher*, 24 January 1975, p. 7.
108 'Some very special classes', *Teacher*, 17 January 1975, pp. 6–7.
109 Oxfordshire Pilot, Ox.006, interview.
110 Oxfordshire Pilot, Ox.012, interview.
111 *Ibid.*
112 Anderson, *The Disabled Schoolchild*, p. 118.
113 *Ibid.*, p. 122.
114 *Ibid.*, p. 131.
115 Kawwa, 'Ethnic Prejudice and Choice of Friends', p. 6.
116 *Ibid.*, pp. 143–5, 238–9, 249, 252.
117 Institute of Education, Michael Duane Archive, MD/5/5/39, letter from Michael Duane to 'Dr Hay', 13 July 1962. On Risinghill, see Berg, *Risinghill*.
118 Institute of Education, Michael Duane Archive, MD 5/5/39, 'Sociological Research – Risinghill', p. 2; Kawwa, 'Ethnic Prejudice and Choice of Friends', p. 7.
119 Bhatnagar, *Immigrants at School*, p. 60.
120 Blyth, *Development, Experience and Curriculum in Primary Education*, p. 90
121 Anderson, *The Disabled Schoolchild*, p. 123.
122 Sharp et al., *Education and Social Control*, p. vii.
123 Newson et al., *Perspectives on School*, p. 25.
124 Brown and Precious, *The Integrated Day in the Primary School*, pp. 94–6.

125 *Ibid.*, p. 113.
126 Burman, *Deconstructing Developmental Psychology*, p. 265.
127 *Ibid.*, pp. 268-9.
128 Lister, *Deschooling*, p. 6.
129 Avis, 'The strange fate of progressive education', p. 138.

Conclusion: the reinvention of childhood?

In 1960, Philippe Ariès published his landmark *Centuries of Childhood*, introducing the idea of treating childhood as a constructed and historically contingent category rather than as a natural state. Ariès divided his text into three major sections, of which the second and most substantial, taking up at least half of the book, focused upon 'Scholastic life'. In this, he argued that an increased interest in education in early modern France in the sixteenth and seventeenth centuries led to the 'discovery of childhood'. As girls were initially excluded from schools, elite boys became 'the first specialised children'.[1] In addition, Ariès related the structure of mass schooling in the late nineteenth century to constructions of childhood, stating that age-grouped classes resulted in 'a striking differentiation between age groups which are really quite close together . . . In the past, the span of life and childhood was not cut up into such thin slices. The school class has thus become a determining factor in the process of differentiating the ages of childhood and early adolescence.'[2]

While Ariès's argument that childhood was an elite early modern creation has been rightly refuted by historians, there has been relatively little attention paid to his claim that the organisation of public schooling was necessarily bound up with the construction of childhood, beyond the statement that the institution of compulsory schooling and the raising of the school leaving age formalised and extended childhood and adolescence in Western Europe and the United States in the nineteenth and twentieth centuries.[3] Nevertheless, the closer attention paid to chronological age in England and Wales from the inter-war period onwards, starting with 'Hadow reorganisation' in the 1930s, was the beginning of a fundamental shift in concepts of childhood within educational institutions, segmenting it into developmental stages and widening the gulf between childhood and adulthood. Understanding the 'nature' of the child meant defining children as a monolithic group, creating a set of expectations that children of all ages struggled to live up to. By the 1970s, Ariès's assertion that childhood was not fixed and inevitable was providing inspiration for a new set of radical reformers, who, like their utopian progressive predecessors, were less interested in what children *were* than what they *could be*.[4]

The popular narrative that situated children and adolescents as a permanently problematic group, selfish, indisciplined and uneducated, may have peaked in the 1970s, but it had its roots in the post-war settlement. Contemporary commentators, indeed, explicitly argued that the undesirable political attitudes of university students were directly related to the child-centred parenting they had received in the 1950s.[5] Therefore, any suggestion that there was a 'sharp downturn' in public attitudes towards childhood and youth from the 1970s onwards, emerging as a backlash to the 'permissive shift' of the 1960s, ignores this longer pessimistic history.[6] For the children who formed part of this generation, the recognition of their own significance might have bolstered their sense of self, but might also have left them with a sense of promises left unfulfilled, as was reflected by the accounts collected by Liz Herron in *Truth, Dare or Promise: girls growing up in the fifties* (1984). These retrospective self-narratives tapped into the contemporary sense that something had gone wrong since the optimistic days when British people, and especially British children, had 'never had it so good'. Carolyn Steedman's assertion that 'I think I would be a very different person now if orange juice and milk and dinners at school hadn't told me, in a covert way, that I had a right to exist, was worth something' is the line most frequently quoted by historians, and this was a statement echoed by other female contributors.[7] As Stef Fixner, born in 1945, wrote: 'We're the Post-War Generation, and we're tall for our age, and healthy, and will grow bigger than the grown-ups.'[8]

Nevertheless, others perceived the hidden cost of these post-war prizes: Harriett Gilbert, born in 1948, believed that the popular explanation 'for why we thought and behaved as we did was that we had simply failed to grow up. Pumped full of National Health orange juice, further education, our parents' relative prosperity, we were seen as a

Conclusion

Peter Pan generation.'[9] Child-centred parenting and teaching demanded sacrifice from parents and teachers; the children who were the object of these efforts were expected to be both passive and grateful. As John and Elizabeth Newson discovered in their work in Nottingham in the early 1960s, both middle-class and working-class mothers had already adopted child-centred parenting methods – and were already expressing unease about how their children had turned out, once given more freedom at home. The Newsons thought that 'parents are finding that they have got something more than they bargained for . . . it is not always so easy to accept the more spirited, disrespectful child which is the result'. As one bricklayer's wife put it: 'they're not so well behaved today as they were when we was young. They don't think so much of other people, of their parents, these days.'[10]

One of the contributors to Herron's collection was Valerie Walkerdine, born into a working-class family in 1947. Walkerdine's writing reflected her own academic work as a critical psychologist in the early 1980s. Unlike some of the other contributors, and in tension with Herron's relatively optimistic introduction to the collection, she emphasised promises that had been broken rather than kept: 'In the fifties, when I felt set up, set up to want, to want to be different, special, when I was chosen to be one of the children of the post-war boom . . . They set me up to want, fashioned my desires, and then held out the promise that if I were a good girl, by dint of my own efforts, it could all come true.'[11] Although Walkerdine's career might be read by outsiders as the product of a triumphant vision of social mobility, the direction her own research was taking at the time positioned her as intensely critical of the idea of a 'good girl' who got her reward for hard work. In 1983 and 1984, she published two essays arguing that one of the key planks of this post-war settlement – a child-centred education based on developmental psychology – was inherently oppressive.[12] When she summarised the basic impetus behind this work decades later, it was clear that her key convictions had not changed:

> [C]hildhood is always produced as an object in relation to power . . . developmental psychology understands children's thinking as becoming more and more like that of adults. It figures therefore that children's thinking is assumed to be different from adult thinking and that this difference is understood as a deficiency, a natural deficiency that will be put right as the child grows up.[13]

A progressive education?

By the 1970s, teachers, parents and the wider public had started to be afraid that children were not growing up as it had been anticipated that they would – that this 'Peter Pan generation' had, in fact, failed to become the socially responsible and emotionally mature citizens that the welfare state demanded. This was unsurprising. The logic of child-centred education and child-centred parenting was that children were fundamentally separate from adults, distinguished by their developmental immaturity. Working-class, immigrant, ethnic minority, female and disabled children could find it especially difficult to 'prove' that they were healthy children who would become healthy adults. As non-utopian progressive educators had positioned 'growing up' as a process that was much more fraught with difficulty than it had been in the past, it was natural that it attracted greater concern. As greater resources were put into childhood and education, society expected to see significant and measurable results – and appropriate gratitude.

The use of 'adulthood' as the yardstick against which the failings of childhood were measured in post-war Britain indicates the need for greater historical work on adulthood as a constructed category in its own right; the few existing texts tend to be sweeping and ahistorical.[14] Literary scholars have started to consider this question in greater depth for earlier periods. Claudia Nelson, Sari Edelstein and Teresa Michals have all engaged with adulthood and its relationship to childhood in key literary texts to analyse how these categories altered in both British and American literature over the eighteenth and nineteenth centuries. Michals, in particular, has produced a fascinating analysis of how the nature of readership altered over this period, and how the idea of 'adults' books' and 'children's books' emerged from changing ideas of adulthood rather than childhood.[15] Nevertheless, we need to continue to consider childhood as a relational category, shaped with reference to what it meant to be 'mature' in a given place or at a given time, and to see adulthood itself as a state that is in constant flux, with no fixed meanings over time. Developmental psychology advanced new sets of expectations for adults as well as for children and adolescents in post-war Britain, Western Europe and the United States.

The move within child-centred education from considering the child as an individual to children as a group reflects wider themes in mid-twentieth-century British history that have traced the rise of the democratic subject and the increasing importance of the social sciences in the

Conclusion

post-war period.[16] These shifts also related to theoretical developments in child psychology and psychoanalysis throughout this period, with the individualistic approach of Cyril Burt and Susan Isaacs gradually supplanted by Jean Piaget's increasingly elaborated concept of maturational developmental stages and the environmentalist psychoanalytical approach of the neo-Kleinians John Bowlby and Donald Winnicott. By considering the Second World War as a catalyst rather than a turning point, this book joins a growing body of historiography that has reassessed the importance of the 1950s in altering ideas of romantic love, identity and selfhood.[17] Drawing on recent work by both Thomson and Shapira, it has been argued that the figure of the baby and young child was key to the constitution of ideas of democratic selfhood during the war, and the figure of the older child and adolescent in the post-war period, reflecting the slightly later shift in concepts of school-age childhood and youth in comparison with those focused on the under-fives.[18]

Teachers occupied a unique position in relation to children. Unlike, for example, educational psychologists, child psychiatrists or parents, they combined a theoretical knowledge of childhood with extensive experience of a range of actual children. Often from working-class backgrounds, but acquiring a form of professional authority, they were, as Andrew Burchell has put it, 'both insiders and outsiders' to the communities that surrounded them.[19] This book has suggested that the conflict between theoretical psychological knowledge and practical craft knowledge was central for teachers' identities and for child-centred education in practice during the inter-war and post-war periods, as they were increasingly enjoined to engage with educational psychology. This conflict between theory and practice, however, was significant beyond the internal struggles of the teaching profession itself. It shaped the operation of non-utopian progressivism in schools, reformulated teachers' concepts of childhood and fed into educational change. The teaching profession cannot be taken to be representative of the adult population as a whole. However, as the national significance of education grew, parental interest increased, and teachers themselves became vocal contributors to media debate, their assertions about children wielded disproportionate influence. In this context, considering children in 'the school class' as well as in the clinic, the street and the home is vital to understanding the shift in concepts of childhood and adolescence that took place in the post-war years in England and Wales.[20]

A progressive education?

Notes

1. Ariès, *Centuries of Childhood*, p. 58.
2. *Ibid.*, p. 172.
3. Zelizer, *Pricing the Priceless Child*.
4. Lister (ed.), *Deschooling*, p. 5.
5. Musgrove, 'The Black Paper movement', p. 107.
6. For example, Hendrick, *Child Welfare: England*, p. 1; Hendrick, *Children, Childhood and English Society*, p. 9; Cunningham, *Children and Childhood in Western Society*, pp. 18, 177, 190; Heywood, *The History of Childhood*, pp. 27–30.
7. Steedman, 'Landscape for a good woman', p. 119. Cited, for example, in Robinson *et al.*, 'Telling stories about post-war Britain', pp. 277–8; in Waters, 'Autobiography, nostalgia and the changing practices of working-class selfhood', p. 183; in Thomson, *Lost Freedom*, p. 80; and in Vernon, *Hunger*, p. 195.
8. Fixner, 'The oyster and the shadows', p. 80.
9. Gilbert, 'Growing pains', p. 45.
10. Newson and Newson, *Infant Care in an Urban Community*, p. 233; Newson and Newson, *Four Years Old in an Urban Community*, p. 523.
11. Walkerdine, 'Dreams from an ordinary childhood', pp. 63, 66.
12. Walkerdine, 'It's only natural'; Walkerdine, 'Child-centred pedagogy'.
13. Walkerdine, 'Developmental psychology', p. 117.
14. Mintz, *The Prime of Life*; Waters *et al.*, *Coming of Age in America*.
15. Nelson, *Precocious*; Edelstein, *Adulthood and Other Fictions*; Michals, *Books*, pp. 1–2.
16. Thomson, *Lost Freedom*; Shapira, *The War Inside*.
17. Langhamer, *The English in Love*; Rose, *Which People's War?*
18. Thomson, *Lost Freedom*; Shapira, *The War Inside*.
19. Burchell, 'The Adolescent School Pupil', p. 36.
20. Ariès, *Centuries of Childhood*, p. 172.

Bibliography

Manuscript sources

Cambridge: Faculty of Education Library, University of Cambridge, Wartime Evacuation Project Archive
Cambridge: Shire Hall, Cambridgeshire Archives
Ebbw Vale: Gwent Archives
London: Institute of Education, Michael Duane Archive
London: London County Council Archives
London: National Archives
Newcastle: Oxfordshire Pilot, in possession of author
Oxford: Bodleian Libraries, Special Collections, Archive of Iona and Peter Opie
Oxford: Oxfordshire History Centre
Sheffield: Sheffield Archives

Periodicals

Teachers World 1918–75
The Schoolmaster and Woman Teacher's Chronicle 1918–62
The Teacher 1963–79
Times Educational Supplement 1918–79

Printed sources

Abbas, T. *The Education of British South Asians: ethnicity, capital and class structure* (Hampshire, 2004).
Abrams, M. *The Teenage Consumer* (London, 1959).
Adams, J. (ed.) *Educational Movements and Methods* (London, 1924).
Adams, J. *Modern Developments in Educational Practice* (London, 2nd edn, 1928).
Allsopp, A. H. *The Essentials of Psychology for Student Teachers* (London, 1936).
Anderson, E. M. *The Disabled Schoolchild: a study of integration in primary schools* (London, 1973).

[Anon.] *The Extra Year: a report of the Joint Committee of Investigation representing the Association of Education Committees and the National Union of Teachers* (London, 1938).

Ariès, P. *Centuries of Childhood* (London, 1962).

Armstrong, D. *Political Anatomy of the Body: medical knowledge in Britain in the twentieth century* (Cambridge, 1983).

Ashton, P., Kneen, P., Davies, F. and Holley, B. J. (eds) *The Aims of Primary Education: a study of teachers' opinions* (London, 1975).

Atkinson, M. *Junior School Community* (London, 1949).

Auld, R. *William Tyndale Junior and Infants Schools Public Inquiry: a report to the ILEA* (London, 1976).

Avis, J. 'The strange fate of progressive education', in Centre for Contemporary Cultural Studies, *Education Limited: schooling and training and the New Right since 1979* (London, 1991).

Bailey, V. *Delinquency and Citizenship: reclaiming the young offender, 1914–1948* (London, 1987).

Baines, G. 'Social and environmental studies', in V. R. Rogers (ed.) *Teaching in the British Primary School* (Ontario, 1970).

Ball, S. J. and Goodson, I. F. 'Understanding teachers: concepts and contexts', in Ball and Goodson (eds) *Teachers' Lives and Careers* (East Sussex, 1985).

Ballard, P. *The Changing School* (London, 1925).

Barron, H. '"Little prisoners of city streets": London elementary schools and the School Journey Movement, 1918–1939', *History of Education*, 42, 2 (2013).

Bassey, M. *Nine Hundred Primary School Teachers* (Berks, 1978).

Beard, R. M. *An Outline of Piaget's Developmental Psychology for Students and Teachers* (London, 1969).

Beekman, D. *The Mechanical Baby: a popular history of the theory and practice of child raising* (London, 1979).

Behlmer, G. K. *Friends of the Family: the English home and its guardians* (Stanford, 1998).

Bell, V. *Dodo: the story of a village schoolmaster* (London, 1950).

Bennett, N. *Teaching Styles and Pupil Progress* (London, 1976).

Berg, L. *Risinghill: death of a comprehensive school* (London, 1968).

Berlin, I. 'Two concepts of liberty (1958)', in *Four Essays on Liberty* (Oxford, 1969).

Bernstein, B. *Class, Codes and Control: volume 1 – theoretical studies towards a sociology of language* (London, 1971).

Bernstein, B. and Davies, B. 'Some sociological comments on Plowden', in R. S. Peters (ed.) *Perspectives on Plowden* (London, 1969).

Bhatnagar, J. *Immigrants at School* (London, 1970).

Biggs, J. B. *Mathematics and the Conditions of Learning: a study of arithmetic in the primary school* (Slough, 1967).

Black, L. *The Political Culture of the Left in Britain, 1951–64: old Labour, new Britain?* (Basingstoke, 2002).

Bibliography

Blackie, J., 'Authority in education', in *Good Enough for the Children?* (London, 1963).
Blackie, J. *Good Enough for the Children?* (London, 1963).
Blackie, J. *Inspecting and the Inspectorate* (London, 1970).
Blackie, J. *Inside The Primary School* (London, 1971).
Blishen, E. *Roaring Boys* (London, 1955).
Blishen, E. 'The task of the secondary modern school', *The Listener* (21 February 1957) pp. 303–5.
Blishen, E. *A Nest of Teachers* (London, 1980).
Bloor, C. *The Process of Learning: some psychological aspects of learning and discipline in school* (London, 1930).
Blundell, D. *Education and Constructions of Childhood* (London, 2012).
Blyth, W. A. L. *English Primary Education: a sociological description* (London, 1965).
Blyth, W. A. L. *Development, Experience and Curriculum in Primary Education* (Kent, 1984).
Board of Education, *Psychological Tests of Educable Capacity and their Possible Use in the Public System of Education* (London, 1924) [Hadow].
Board of Education, *The Education of the Adolescent* (London, 1926) [Hadow].
Board of Education, *Report of the Mental Deficiency Committee* (London, 1929) [Wood].
Board of Education, *The Primary School* (London, 1931) [Hadow].
Board of Education, *Infant and Nursery Schools* (London, 1933) [Hadow].
Board of Education, *A Handbook of Suggestions for Teachers* (London, 1937).
Board of Education, *A Handbook of Suggestions for Teachers* (London, 1944).
Bowley, A. *Everyday Problems of the School Child* (London, 1948).
Bowley, R. I. *Teaching Without Tears: a guide to teaching technique* (London, 1961).
Bowley, R. I. *Teaching Without Tears: a guide to teaching technique* (London, 2nd edn, 1967).
Braithwaite, E. R. *To Sir, With Love* (London, 1959.)
Braster, S., Grosvenor, I. and Pozo Andres, M. Mar del (eds) *The Black Box of Schooling: a cultural history of the classroom* (Brussels, 2011).
Brearley, M. *Fundamentals in the First School* (Oxford, 1969).
Brehony, K. J. 'A new education for a new era: creating international fellowship through conferences 1921–1938', *Paedogogica Historica* 40, 5–6 (2004).
Bridge, N. *My Liverpool Schools* (Portinscale, 1992).
Brooke, S. 'Gender and working class identity in Britain during the 1950s', *Journal of Social History,* 34, 4 (2001).
Brown, M. and Precious, N. *The Integrated Day in the Primary School* (London, 1968).
Buckle, S. *The Way Out: a history of homosexuality in modern Britain* (London, 2015).

Burke, C. and Grosvenor, I. *School* (London, 2008).

Burman, E. *Deconstructing Developmental Psychology* (East Sussex, 2nd edn, 2008).

Burt, C. 'The development of reasoning in schoolchildren', *Journal of Experimental Pedagogy*, 5 (1919).

Burt, C. 'Mental development', *The Listener*, 3, 901 (1930).

Burt, C. *The Young Delinquent* (London, 3rd edn, 1938).

Burt, C. 'The education of the young adolescent: the psychological implications of the Norwood Report', *British Journal of Educational Psychology*, 13 (1943).

Burt, C. 'The mental differences between children', in C. B. Cox and A. E. Dyson (eds) *Black Paper 2: the crisis in education* (London, 1968).

Cannadine, D., Keating, J. and Sheldon, N. *The Right Kind of History: teaching the past in twentieth-century England* (London, 2011).

Carter, L. '"Experimental" secondary modern education in Britain, 1948–1958', *Cultural and Social History*, 13, 1 (2016).

Carter, M. P. *Home, School and Work: a study of the education and employment of young people in Britain* (London, 1962).

Catty, N. *Learning and Teaching in the Junior School* (London, 1941).

Cheshire Education Committee, *The Secondary Modern School* (London, 1958).

Clarke, A. D. B. and Clarke, A. M. 'The historical context', in B. Stratford and P. Gunn (eds) *New Approaches to Down Syndrome* (London, 1996).

Clarricoates, K. 'The importance of being Ernest … Emma … Tom … Jane … : the perception and categorisation of gender conformity and gender deviance in primary schools', in R. Deem (ed.) *Schooling for Women's Work* (London, 1980).

Cox, C. B. and Dyson, A. E. (eds) *Black Paper 1: fight for education* (London, 1968).

Coote, A. and Campbell, B. *Sweet Freedom: the struggle for women's liberation* (Oxford, 2nd edn, 1987).

Cooter, R. *In the Name of the Child: health and welfare, 1880–1940* (London, 1992).

Copelman, D. *London's Woman Teachers: gender, class and feminism, 1870–1930* (London, 1996).

Cox, C. B. and Dyson, A. E. (eds) *Black Paper 2: the crisis in education* (London, 1968).

Croft, M. *Spare the Rod* (London, 1954).

Cronin, J. E. *The Politics of State Expansion: war, state and society in twentieth-century Britain* (London, 1991).

Cunningham, H. 'The rights of the child from the mid-eighteenth to the early twentieth century', *Aspects of Education*, 50 (1994).

Cunningham, H. *Children and Childhood in Western Society since 1500* (Harlow, 1995).

Cunningham, P. 'Open plan schooling: last stand of the progressives', in R. Lowe (ed.) *The Changing Primary School* (East Sussex, 1987).

Bibliography

Cunningham, P. *Curriculum Change in the Primary School since 1945: dissemination of the progressive ideal* (London, 1988).

Cunningham, P. 'Teachers' professional image and the press 1950–1990', *History of Education*, 21, 1 (1992).

Cunningham, P. 'Narrative and text: women, teachers and oral history', *History of Education*, 29, 3 (2000).

Cunningham, P. 'Primary education', in R. Aldrich (ed.) *A Century of Education* (London, 2002).

Cunningham, P. and Gardner, P. 'Oral history and teachers' professional practice: a wartime turning point?', *Cambridge Journal of Education*, 27, 3 (1997).

Cunningham, P. and Gardner, P. 'Teacher trainers and educational change in Britain, 1876–1996: "a flawed and deficient history"?', *Journal of Education for Teaching*, 24, 3 (1998).

Cunningham, P. and Gardner, P. *Becoming Teachers: texts and testimonies 1907–1950* (London, 2004).

Cunningham, P., Gardner, P. and Hussey, S. 'Wartime experiences and the teacher's role', *Cambridge School of Education Newsletter*, 7 (2001).

Cunningham, P., Burke, C. and Howard, J. (eds) *The Decorated School: essays on the visual culture of schooling* (London, 2013).

Dale, R. R. *Mixed or Single Sex School? – Volume III: attainment, attitudes and overview* (London, 1974).

Daniel, M. V. *Activity in the Primary School* (Oxford, 1947).

Davies, W. T. and Shepherd, T. B. *Teaching: begin here* (London, 1949).

Davis, A. *Modern Motherhood: women and family in England, c. 1945–2000* (Manchester, 2012).

Davis, A. *Pre-School Childcare in England, 1935–2010* (Manchester, 2015).

Davis, J. *Youth and the Condition of Britain: images of adolescent conflict* (London, 1990).

Dean, D. 'Conservative governments, 1951–64, and their changing perspectives on the 1944 Education Act', *History of Education*, 24, 3 (1995).

Deem, R. *Women and Schooling* (London, 1978).

Deem, R. 'State policy and ideology in the education of women, 1944–80', in L. Dawtrey, J. Holland and M. Hammer (eds) *Equality and Inequality in Education Policy* (Avon, 1995).

Delap, L. '"Disgusting details which are best forgotten": disclosures of child sexual abuse in twentieth-century Britain', *Journal of British Studies*, 57, 1 (2018).

Dempster, J. J. B. *Purpose in the Modern School* (London, 1958).

Dent, H. C. *Education in Transition: a sociological study of the impact of war upon English education 1939–1943* (London, 1944).

Dent, H. C. *Secondary Modern Schools: an interim report* (London, 1958).

Dent, H. C. *Century of Growth in English Education, 1870–1970* (London, 1970).

Dent, H. C. *The Training of Teachers in England and Wales 1800–1975* (London, 1977).
DES, *Report of the Committee on Maladjusted Children* (London, 1955) [Underwood].
DES, *Primary Education* (London, 1959).
DES, *Half Our Future* (London, 1963) [Newsom].
DES, *Children and Their Primary Schools: a report of the Central Advisory Council for Education (England)*, Volume I: The Report (London, 1967) [Plowden].
DES, *Children and Their Primary Schools: a report of the Central Advisory Council for Education (England)*, Volume II: Research and Surveys (London, 1967) [Plowden].
DES, *Primary Education in Wales* (London, 1967) [Gittins].
DES, *HMI Today and Tomorrow* (London, 1970).
DES, *Teacher Education and Training* (London, 1972) [James].
DES, HMI Survey, *Curricular Differences for Boys and Girls* (London, 1975).
DES, *A Language for Life* (London, 1975) [Bullock].
DES, *Working Papers by HM Inspectorate* (London, 1977) ['Red Book 1'].
DES, *Special Educational Needs: report of the committee of enquiry into the education of handicapped children and young people* (London, 1978) [Warnock].
DES, *Primary Education in England* (London, 1978).
DES, HMI *Matters for Discussion* 8, 'Developments in the B.Ed degree course' (London, 1979).
DES, HMI Survey, *Girls and Science* (London, 1980).
DES, *West Indian Children in our Schools: interim report of the committee of inquiry into the education of children from ethnic minority groups* (London, 1981) [Rampton].
Devine, F. *Affluent Workers Revisited: privatism and the working class* (Edinburgh, 1992).
Dixon, T. *Weeping Britannia: portrait of a nation in tears* (Oxford, 2015).
Donaldson, M. *Children's Minds* (London, 1978).
Donnelly, M. *Sixties Britain: culture, society and politics* (Harlow, 2005).
Drummond, M. J. 'Susan Isaacs: pioneering work in understanding children's lives', in M. Hilton and P. Hirsch (eds) *Practical Visionaries: women, education and social progress 1790–1930* (Essex, 2000).
Edelstein, S. *Adulthood and Other Fictions: American literature and the unmaking of age* (Oxford, 2019).
Edwards, E. *Women in Teacher Training Colleges 1900–60: a culture of femininity* (London, 2001).
Edwards, J. B. 'Some studies of the moral development of children', *Educational Research* 7, 3 (1965).
Eppel, E. M. and Eppel, M. *Adolescents and Morality: a study of some moral values and dilemmas of working adolescents in the context of a changing climate of opinion* (London, 1966).

Bibliography

Etherington, T. H. *In and Out of School* (London, 1950).

Evans, B. 'How autism became autism: the radical transformation of a central concept of child development in Britain', *History of the Human Sciences*, 26, 3 (2013).

Evans, B. 'The foundations of autism: the law concerning psychotic, schizophrenic and autistic children in 1950s and 1960s Britain', *Bulletin of the History of Medicine* 88, 2 (2014).

Evans, L. W. 'The evolution of Welsh educational structure and administration 1881–1921', in *Studies in the Government and Control of Education* (London, 1970).

Evans, K. M. *Attitudes and Interests in Education* (London, 1965).

Evans, M. *A Good School: life at a girls' grammar school in the 1950s* (London, 1991).

Farley, R. *Secondary Modern School Discipline: with special reference to the 'difficult' adolescent in socially depressed industrial areas* (London, 1960).

Field, G. G. *Blood, Sweat and Toil: remaking the British working class, 1939–45* (Oxford, 2011).

Findlay, J. J. *The Children of England: a contribution to social history and education* (London, 1923).

Fixner, S. 'The oyster and the shadows', in L. Herron (ed.) *Truth, Dare or Promise: girls growing up in the fifties* (London, 1985).

Fleming, C. M. *Individual Work in Primary Schools* (London, 1934).

Fleming, C. M. *Adolescence* (London, 1948).

Floud, J. and Scott, W. 'Recruitment to teaching in England and Wales', in A. H. Halsey, J. Floud and C. A. Anderson (eds) *Education, Economy and Society: a reader in the sociology of education* (New York, 1961).

Floud, J. E., Halsey, A. H. and Martin, F. M. (eds) *Social Class and Educational Opportunity* (London, 1956).

Fowler, D. *The First Teenagers: the lifestyle of young wage-earners in inter-war Britain* (London, 1995).

Francis, M. 'A socialist policy for education? Labour and the secondary school, 1945–51', *History of Education* 24, 3 (1995).

Francis, M. 'Tears, tantrums and bared teeth: the emotional economy of three Conservative prime ministers, 1951–1964', *Journal of British Studies,* 41, 3 (2002).

Froebel, F. *Froebel's Chief Writings on Education,* trans. S. S. F. Fletcher and J. Welton (London, 1912).

Fuller, M. 'Black girls in a London comprehensive school', in R. Deem (ed.) *Schooling for Women's Work* (London, 1980).

Fyson, A. and Ward, C. *Streetwork: the exploding school* (London, 1973).

Fyvel, T. R. *The Insecure Offenders: rebellious youth in the welfare state* (London, 1961).

Gabriel, J. *An Analysis of the Emotional Problems of the Teacher in the Classroom* (London, 1957).

Gagen, E. 'Too good to be true: representing children's agency in the archives of playground reform', *Historical Geography*, 29 (2001).

Gallway, A. 'The rewards of using archived oral histories in research: the case of the Millennium Memory Bank', *Oral History*, 41, 1 (2013).

Galton, M., Simon, B. and Croll, P. *Inside the Primary Classroom* (London, 1980).

Gardner, P. 'Classroom teachers and educational change 1876–1996', *Journal of Education For Teaching*, 24, 1 (1998).

Gardner, P. 'Teachers', in R. Aldrich (ed.) *A Century of Education* (London, 2002).

Gardner, P. 'Oral history in education: teacher's memory and teachers' history', *History of Education*, 32, 2 (2003).

Gesell, A., Ilg, F. L. and Ames, L. B. *Youth: the years from ten to sixteen* (New York, 1956).

Giardiello, P. *Pioneers in Early Childhood Education: the roots and legacies of Rachel and Margaret McMillan, Maria Montessori and Susan Isaacs* (Oxon, 2014).

Gibson, J. and Chennells, P. (eds) *Gifted Children: looking to their future* (London, 1976).

Gilbert, H. 'Growing pains', in L. Herron (ed.) *Truth, Dare or Promise: girls growing up in the fifties* (London, 1985).

Glassner, B. *The Culture of Fear: why Americans are afraid of the wrong things* (New York, 1999).

Gleadle, K. *Borderline Citizens: women, gender and political culture in Britain, 1815–1867* (Oxford, 2009).

Glennerster, H. and Low, W. 'Education and the welfare state: does it add up?', in J. Hills (ed.) *The State of Welfare: the welfare state in Britain since 1974* (Oxford, 1990).

Goodson, I. *School Subjects and Curriculum Change* (Kent, 1983).

Gosden, P. H. J. H. *The Evolution of a Profession: a study of the contribution of Teachers' Associations to the development of school teaching as a professional occupation* (Oxford, 1972).

Gould, R. *Chalk Up the Memory* (Birmingham, 1976).

Grace, G. 'Teachers and the state in Britain: a changing relation', in M. Lawn and G. Grace (eds) *Teachers: the culture and politics of work* (East Sussex, 1987).

Griffin-Beale, C. (ed.) *Christian Schiller: in his own words* (London, 1979).

Griffiths, P. *Youth and Authority: formative experiences in England, 1540–1640* (Oxford, 1996).

Grosvenor, I. and Lawn, M. 'Days out of school: secondary education, citizenship and public space in 1950s England', *History of Education*, 33, 4 (2004).

Hackett, S. *Foreigners, Minorities and Integration: the Muslim immigrant experience in Britain and Germany* (Manchester, 2016).

Hall, E. 'A conversation with Jean Piaget and Barbel Inhelder', *Psychology Today*, 3 (1970).

Hall, G. S. *Adolescence: its psychology and its relations to physiology, anthropology, sociology, sex, crime, religion, and education* (New York, 2 vols, 1904).

Bibliography

Halsey, A. H. *Change in British Society* (Oxford, 4th edn, 1995).
Hamilton, E. R. *The Teacher on the Threshold* (London, 1945).
Hamley, H. R, 'Introductory survey', in Nunn, P. (ed.) *The Education of Backward Children and Juvenile Delinquency in England and Wales* (London, 1936).
Hamley, H. R., Oliver, R. A. C., Field, H. E. and Isaacs, S. (eds) *The Educational Guidance of the Schoolchild: suggestions on child study and guidance embodying a scheme of pupils' records* (London, 1937).
Hardman, C. 'Can there be an anthropology of children?', *Journal of the Anthropological Society of Oxford*, 4, 2 (1973).
Hargreaves, D. *Social Relations in a Secondary School* (London, 1967).
Hayward, R. 'The invention of the psychosocial: an introduction', *History of the Human Sciences*, 25, 2 (2012).
Heathorn, S. *For Home, Country and Race: constructing gender, class and Englishness in the elementary school, 1880–1914* (London, 2000).
Hendrick, H. *Child Welfare: England 1872–1989* (London, 1994).
Hendrick, H. *Children, Childhood and English Society 1880–1990* (Cambridge, 1997).
Hendrick, H. *Child Welfare: historical dimensions, contemporary debate* (Bristol, 2003).
Heywood, C. *The History of Childhood: children and childhood in the west from medieval to modern times* (Cambridge, 2001).
Heywood, C. '*Centuries of Childhood* : an anniversary – and an epitaph?', *Journal of the History of Childhood and Youth*, 3, 2 (2010).
Hatton, S. F. *London's Bad Boys* (London, 1931).
Hawkes, N. *Immigrant Children in British Schools* (London, 1966).
Highet, G. *The Art of Teaching* (London, 1951).
Highmore, B. 'Playgrounds and bombsites: postwar Britain's ruined landscapes', *Cultural Politics*, 9, 3 (2013).
Hill, J. C. *The Teacher in Training* (London, 1935).
Hilliard, F. H. (ed.) *Teaching the Teachers: trends in teacher education* (London, 1971).
Hines, M. 'They do not know how to play: reformers' expectations and children's realities on the first progressive playgrounds of Chicago', *Journal of the History of Childhood and Youth*, 10, 2 (2017).
Hinton, J. 'The "class" complex: Mass Observation and cultural distinction in pre-war Britain', *Past and Present*, 199, 1 (2008).
Hirsch, P. 'Apostle of freedom: Alfred Adler and his British disciples', *History of Education*, 34, 5 (2005).
Hoggart, R. *The Uses of Literacy* (London, 1957).
Hollins, T. H. B, 'Desirable changes in the structure of courses', in F. H. Hilliard (ed.) *Teaching the Teachers: trends in teacher education* (London, 1971).
Holmes, E. *What is and What Might Be* (London, 1911).
Holmes, E. *The Tragedy of Education* (London, 1913).

Holmes, E. 'The confessions and hopes of an ex-inspector of schools', in E. Holmes (ed.) *Freedom and Growth and Other Essays* (London, 1923).

Holmes, G. *The Idiot Teacher: a book about Prestolee School and its headmaster E. F. O'Neill* (London, 1952).

Holt, J. *How Children Fail* (London, 1969).

Horn, P. *Young Offenders: juvenile delinquency from 1700 to 2000* (Stroud, 2010)

Horwood, C. *Keeping Up Appearances: fashion and class between the wars* (Gloucestershire, 2005).

Houlbrook, M. *Queer London: perils and pleasures in the sexual metropolis, 1918–1957* (Chicago, 2005).

Howkins, A. 'The discovery of rural England', in R. Colls and P. Dodd (eds) *Englishness: politics and culture 1880–1920* (Kent, 1986).

Howlett, J. *Progressive Education: a critical introduction* (London, 2013).

Hoyle, E. and John, P. *Professional Knowledge and Professional Practice* (London, 1995).

Hughes, A. G. and Hughes, E. G. *Learning and Teaching: an introduction to psychology and education* (London, 1937).

Hughes, A. G. and Hughes, E. G. *Learning and Teaching: an introduction to psychology and education* (London, 2nd edn, 1947).

Hughes, A. G. and Hughes, E. G. *Learning and Teaching: an introduction to psychology and education* (London, 3rd edn, 1959).

Hughes, F. *Down the Corridors* (London, 1956).

Hulme, T. '"A nation depends on its children": school buildings and citizenship in England and Wales, 1900–1939', *Journal of British Studies*, 54, 2 (2015).

Humphries, S. *Hooligans or Rebels? An oral history of working-class childhood and youth 1889–1939* (Oxford, 1981).

Humphry, D. and John, G. *Because They're Black* (Middlesex, 1971).

Hunter, E. *The Blackboard Jungle* (London, 1955).

Hurt, J. *Elementary Schooling and the Working Classes, 1860–1918* (London, 1979).

Hussey, S. 'The school air-raid shelter: rethinking wartime pedagogies', *History of Education Quarterly*, 43, 4 (2003).

Illich, I. *Deschooling Society* (Middlesex, 1971).

Isaacs, S. *The Nursery Years: the mind of the child from birth to six years* (London, 1929).

Isaacs, S. *Intellectual Growth in Young Children* (London, 1930).

Isaacs, S. *The Children We Teach: seven to eleven years* (London, 1932).

Isaacs, S. *Social Development in Young Children* (London, 1933).

Jackson, L. A. with Barrie, A. *Policing Youth: Britain 1945–70* (Manchester, 2014).

James, A. and Prout, A. (eds) *Constructing and Reconstructing Childhood: contemporary issues in the sociological study of childhood* (London, 1997).

James, W. *The Teacher and His World: a young person's guide* (London, 1962).

Jeffreys, M. V. C. *Revolution in Teacher-Training* (London, 1961).

Bibliography

Jennings, R. *Tomboys and Bachelor Girls: a lesbian history of post-war Britain 1945–71* (Manchester, 2007).

Jones, G. E. 'Which nation's curriculum? The case of Wales', *The Curriculum Journal*, 5, 1 (1994).

Jones, G. E. 'Perspectives from the brink of extinction: the fate of history of education study in Wales', *History of Education*, 42, 3 (2013).

Jones, K. *Education in Britain: 1944 to the present* (Cambridge, 2003).

Jones, K. *Beyond Progressive Education* (London, 1983).

Kennedy, A. *The Teacher in the Making* (London, 1936).

Kennedy, A. *The Teacher in the Making* (London, 2nd edn, 1944).

Kennedy-Fraser, D. *Education of the Backward Child* (London, 1932).

King, L. *Family Men: fatherhood and masculinity in Britain, 1914–1960* (Oxford, 2015).

King, L. 'Future citizens: cultural and political conceptions of children in Britain, 1930s–1950s', *Twentieth Century British History*, 27, 3 (2016).

Krebs, P. M. *Gender, Race and the Writing of Empire: public discourse and the Boer War* (Cambridge, 1999).

Laats, A. *The Other School Reformers: conservative activism in American education* (Cambridge, MA, 2015).

Laing, S. 'Images of the rural in popular culture 1750–1990', in B. Short (ed.) *The English Rural Community: image and analysis* (Cambridge, 1992).

Lane, H. *Talks to Parents and Teachers* (London, 1928).

Langhamer, C. *Women's Leisure in England 1920–60* (Manchester, 2000).

Langhamer, C. *The English in Love: the intimate story of an emotional revolution* (Oxford, 2013).

Langhamer, C. and Barron, H. 'Children, class, and the search for security: writing the future in 1930s Britain', *Twentieth Century British History*, 28, 3 (2017).

Lawn, M. 'What is the teacher's job? Work and welfare in elementary teaching, 1940–1945', in M. Lawn and G. Grace (eds) *Teachers: the culture and politics of work* (East Sussex, 1987).

Lawrence, J. 'Class, "affluence" and the study of everyday life in Britain, c. 1930–64', *Cultural and Social History*, 10, 2 (2013).

Lawton, D. 'The curriculum and curriculum change', in B. Simon and W. Taylor (eds) *Education in the Eighties: the central issues* (London, 1981).

Laurie, B. *A Lifetime in Schools 1910–1966: in Bishop Auckland, Crook, Wolsingham, West Auckland and Evenwood: memories of my father, William Johnson* (Bishop Auckland, 1998).

Laurie, P. *Teenage Revolution* (London, 1965).

Lister, I. (ed.) *Deschooling: a reader* (Cambridge, 1974).

Lewis, J. *Women in Britain since 1945: women, family, work and the state in the post-war years* (Oxford, 1992).

Locke, J. *Some Thoughts Concerning Education* [1689] (Oxford, 1989).

Loukes, H. *Secondary Modern* (London, 1956).
Lowe, R. (ed.) *The Changing Primary School* (East Sussex, 1987).
Lowe, R. 'Primary education since the Second World War', in R. Lowe (ed.) *The Changing Primary School* (East Sussex, 1987).
Lowe, R. *Education in the Post-War Years: a social history* (London, 1988).
Lowe, R. *The Death of Progressive Education: how teachers lost control of the classroom* (London, 2007).
Lowndes, G. A. N. *The Silent Social Revolution: an account of the expansion of public education in England and Wales, 1895–1935* (London, 1937).
Mackillop, J. *Ethnic Minorities in Sheffield* (Sheffield, 1981).
MacLure, S. *The Inspectors' Calling: HMI and the shaping of educational policy 1945–1992* (London, 2000).
MacMunn, N. *The Child's Path to Freedom* (London, 1921).
Mander, J. *Classroom Teaching* (London, 1950).
Mandler, P. 'Two cultures – one – or many?', in K. Burk (ed.) *The British Isles since 1945* (Oxford, 2003).
Mandler, P. 'Educating the Nation I: Schools', *Transactions of the Royal Historical Society*, 24 (2014).
Mannin, E. *Common Sense and the Child* (London, 1931).
Marsden, B. and Jackson, D. *Education and the Working Class* (London, 1962).
Marsh, L. *Alongside the Child in the Primary School* (London, 1970).
Marshall, S. *An Experiment in Education* (Cambridge, 1963).
Marten, J. (ed.) *Children and Youth during the Gilded Age and Progressive Era* (New York: London, 2014).
Martin, J. 'Thinking education histories differently: biographical approaches to class politics and women's movements in London, 1900s to 1960s', *History of Education*, 36, 4 (2007).
Marsden, W. E. 'The school journey movement to 1940', *Journal of Educational Administration and History*, 30, 2, (1998).
Marwick, A. *The Sixties: cultural revolution in Britain, France, Italy and the United States, c.1958–c.1974* (Oxford, 1998).
Mason, P. 'Emotional disturbances in the gifted child', in J. Gibson and P. Chennells (eds) *Gifted Children: looking to their future* (London, 1976).
Matless, D. *Landscape and Englishness* (London, 1998).
Mayall, B. and Morrow, V. *You Can Help Your Country: English children's work during the Second World War* (London, 2011).
Mays, J. B. *Education and the Urban Child* (Liverpool, 1962).
McCulloch, G. and Sobell, L. 'Towards a social history of the secondary modern schools', *History of Education*, 23, 3 (1994).
McCulloch, G. *Failing the Ordinary Child? The theory and practice of working-class secondary education* (Buckingham, 1998).
McCulloch, G. 'Secondary education', in R. Aldrich (ed.) *A Century of Education* (London, 2002).

Bibliography

McCulloch, G. 'A people's history of education: Brian Simon, the British Communist Party and *Studies in the History of Education, 1780-1870*', *History of Education*, 39, 4 (2010).

McDougall, W. *An Introduction to Social Psychology* (London, 22nd edn, 1931).

Mead, M. *Coming of Age in Samoa: a psychological study of primitive youth for western civilisation* (London, 1928).

Michals, T. *Books for Children, Books for Adults: age and the novel from Defoe to James* (Cambridge, 2014).

Middleton, J. 'The experience of corporal punishment in schools, 1890-1940', *History of Education*, 37, 2 (2008).

Mill, J. S. *On Liberty and Other Writings* (Cambridge, 2008).

Mills, H. 'Using the personal to critique the popular: women's memories of 1960s youth', *Contemporary British History*, 30, 4 (2016).

Ministry of Education, *Primary Education: suggestions for the consideration of teachers and others concerned with the work of primary schools* (London, 1959)

Ministry of Education, *15-18* (London, 1959) [Crowther].

Mintz, S. *The Prime of Life: a history of modern adulthood* (Harvard, 2015).

Mitchell, G. A. M. 'Reassessing "the generation gap": Bill Haley's 1957 tour of Britain, inter-generational relations and attitudes to rock 'n' roll in the late 1950s', *Twentieth Century British History*, 24, 4 (2013).

Moorhouse, E. 'The philosophy underlying the British primary school', in V. R. Rogers (ed.) *Teaching in the British Primary School* (Ontario, 1970).

Morgan, A. E. *The Needs of Youth* (London, 1939).

Mort, F. 'Social and symbolic fathers', *Journal of British Studies*, 38, 3, (1999).

Musgrove, F. *Youth and the Social Order* (London, 1964).

Musgrove, F. 'The Black Paper movement', in R. Lowe (ed.) *The Changing Primary School* (East Sussex, 1987).

Neill, A. S. 'Introduction' in E. Mannin, *Common Sense and the Child* (London, 1931).

Neill, A. S. *That Dreadful School* (London, 1937).

Neill, A. S. *Summerhill: a radical approach to education* (London, 1962).

Nelson, C. *Precocious Children and Childish Adults: age inversion in Victorian literature* (Baltimore, 2012).

Newsom, J. *The Education of Girls* (London, 1948).

Newson, J. and Newson, E. *Infant Care in an Urban Community* (London, 1963).

Newson, J. and Newson, E. *Four Years Old in an Urban Community* (London, 1968).

Newson, J. and Newson, E. with Barnes, P. *Perspectives on School at Seven Years Old* (London, 1977).

Nunn, D. *Britannia Calls: Nottingham schools and the push for Great War victory* (Nottingham, 2010).

Nunn, P. *Education: its data and first principles* (London, 1920).

Nunn, P. *Education: its data and first principles* (London, 3rd edn, 1945).

Nunn, P. (ed.) *The Education of Backward Children and Juvenile Delinquency in England and Wales* (London, 1936).

O'Hara, G. *Governing Post-War Britain: the paradoxes of progress, 1951–1973* (Hampshire, 2012).

Offer, A. *The Challenge of Affluence: self-control and well-being in the United States and Britain since 1950* (Oxford, 2006).

Oram, A. 'Inequalities in the teaching profession: the effect on teachers and pupils, 1910–39', in F. Hunt (ed.) *Lessons for Life: the schooling of girls and women, 1850–1950* (Oxford, 1997).

Oram, A. '"To cook dinners with love in them"?: sexuality, marital status and women teachers in England and Wales, 1920–39', in K. Weiler and S. Middleton (eds) *Telling Women's Lives: narrative inquiries in the history of women's education* (Buckingham, 1999).

Osgerby, B. *Youth in Britain since 1945* (Oxford, 1998).

Overy, R. *The Morbid Age: Britain and the crisis of civilisation, 1919–39* (London, 2009).

Owen, R. 'A new view of society (1816)', in H. Silver (ed.) *Robert Owen on Education* (Cambridge, 1969).

Ozga, J. and Lawn, M. *Teachers, Professionalism and Class: a study of organized teachers* (London, 1981).

Partington, G. *Teacher Education in England and Wales* (London, 1999).

Peach, H. *Curious Tales of Old North Yorkshire* (Wilmslow, 2003).

Pearson, G. *Hooligan: a history of respectable fears* (London, 1983).

Pearson, L. *The Making of Modern Children's Literature in Britain: publishing and criticism in the 1960s and 1970s* (Farnham, 2013).

Pekin, L. B. *Progressive Schools: their principles and practice* (London, 1934).

Perkin, H. *The Rise of Professional Society: England since 1880* (London, 1989).

Pestalozzi, J. H. *How Gertrude Teaches Her Children: an attempt to help mothers to teach their own children,* trans. L. E. Holland and F. C. Turner (Syracuse, NY, 1904).

Peters, R. S., '"A recognisable philosophy of education": a constructive critique', in R. S. Peters (ed.) *Perspectives on Plowden* (London, 1969).

Piaget, J. *The Language and Thought of the Child,* trans. M. Warden (London, 1926).

Piaget, J. *The Child's Conception of the World,* trans. J. Tomlinson and A. Tomlinson (London, 1929).

Piaget, J. *The Moral Judgement of the Child,* trans. M. Gabain (London, 1932).

Piaget, J. 'Jean Piaget', in E. G. Boring, H. S. Langfield, H. Werner and R. M. Yerkes (eds) *A History of Psychology in Autobiography,* Vol IV, (Massachusetts, 1952).

Piaget, J. and Inhelder, B. *The Growth of Logical Thinking from Childhood to Adolescence,* trans. A. Parsons and S. Milgram (London, 1958).

Portelli, A. *The Battle of Valle Giulia: oral history and the art of dialogue* (Madison, 1997).

Potter, F. F. *The Practical Junior Teacher,* Vol III (London, 1931).

Purdy, B. *A. S. Neill: 'bringing happiness to some few children'* (Nottingham, 1997).

Bibliography

Ravitch, D. *Left Back: a century of battles over school reform* (New York, 2000).
Raymont, T. *Modern Education: its aims and methods* (London, 1931).
Read, Miss. *Village School,* in *The Chronicles of Fairacre* (London, 1964).
Rée, H. *Educator Extraordinary: the life and achievement of Henry Morris 1889–1961* (London, 1973).
Reese, W. J. *America's Public Schools: from the common school to 'No Child Left Behind'* (Baltimore, 2011).
Reeves, M. 'Education after the war', *New Era*, 21, 6 (1940).
Ridgway, L. and Lawton, I. *Family Grouping in the Primary School* (London, 2nd edn, 1968).
Riley, D. *War in the Nursery: theories of the child and mother* (London, 1983).
Roberts, E. *Women and Families: an oral history, 1940–1970* (Oxford, 1995).
Roberts, N. 'Character in the mind: citizenship, education and psychology in Britain, 1880–1914', *History of Education*, 33, 2 (2004).
Robinson, E. *The Language of Progressive Politics in Modern Britain* (Basingstoke, 2017).
Robinson, E., Schofield, C., Sutcliffe-Braithwaite, F. and Thomlinson, N. 'Telling stories about post-war Britain: popular individualism and the "crisis" of the 1970s', *Twentieth Century British History*, 28, 2 (2017).
Robinson, W. '"That great educational experiment": the City of London Vacation Course in Education 1922–1938: a forgotten story in the history of teacher professional development', *History of Education*, 40, 5 (2011).
Rogers, V. R. (ed.) *Teaching in the British Primary School* (Ontario, 1970).
Rose, J. *The Intellectual Life of the British Working Classes* (London, 2nd edn, 2010).
Rose, N. *The Psychological Complex: psychology, politics and society in England, 1869–1939* (London, 1985).
Rose, N. *Governing the Soul: the shaping of the private self* (London, 1990).
Rose, S. O. *Which People's War?: national identity and citizenship in Britain 1939–45* (Oxford, 2003).
Ross, J. H. *Groundwork of Educational Psychology* (London, 1931).
Routh, G. *Occupation and Pay in Great Britain 1906–79* (London, 2nd edn, 1980).
Rubenstein, D. and Simon, B. *The Evolution of the Comprehensive School, 1926–1972* (London, 1972).
Russell, B. *On Education* (Oxon, 2010, first pub. 1926).
Rutter, M., Maughan, B., Mortimore, P., Ouston, J. with Smith, A. *Fifteen Thousand Hours: secondary schools and their effects on children* (London, 1979).
Saint, A. *Towards a Social Architecture: the role of school building in post-war England* (New Haven: London, 1987).
Sandbrook, D. *Never Had it So Good: a history of Britain from Suez to the Beatles* (London, 2005).
Sanderson, M. *The Missing Stratum: technical school education in England, 1900–1990s* (London, 2nd edn, 2015).

Savage, M. 'Changing class identities in post-war Britain: perspectives from Mass Observation', *Sociological Research Online*, 12, 3, 6 (2007).

Savage, M. *Identities and Social Change in Britain since 1940: the politics of method* (Oxford, 2010).

Schmidt, S. 'The feminist origins of the midlife crisis', *Historical Journal*, 61, 2 (2018).

Scotland, A. and Mackenzie Wood, J. *The Book of Interests* (London, 1939).

Scott, J. C. *Seeing Like a State: how certain schemes to improve the human condition have failed* (New Haven, 1998).

Selleck, R. J. W. *English Primary Education and the Progressives 1914–1939* (London, 1972).

Shapira, M. *The War Inside: psychoanalysis, total war and the making of the democratic self in postwar Britain* (Cambridge, 2013).

Sharp, R. and Green, A. with Lewis, J. *Education and Social Control: a study in progressive primary education* (London, 1975).

Shelton, H. S. *Thoughts of a Schoolmaster: or common sense in education* (London, 1934).

Short, B. (ed.) *The English Rural Community: image and analysis* (Cambridge, 1992).

Shuttleworth, S. *The Mind of the Child: child development in science, literature and medicine, 1840–1900* (Oxford, 2010).

Sikes, P. J. 'The life-cycle of the teacher', in S. J. Ball and I. F. Goodson (eds) *Teachers' Lives and Careers* (East Sussex, 1985).

Silberman, C. *Crisis in the Classroom: the remaking of American education* (New York, 1970).

Silver, H. 'Knowing and not knowing in the history of education', *History of Education*, 21, 1 (1992) pp. 97–108.

Smith, F. and Harrison, A. S. *Principles of Class Teaching* (London, 1937).

Smith, L. A. H. *To Understand and to Help: the life and work of Susan Isaacs* (London, 1985).

Smith, M. 'Hyperactive around the world?: the history of ADHD in global perspective', *Social History of Medicine*, 30, 4 (2017).

Spencer, F. H. *An Inspector's Testament* (London, 1938).

Spencer, S. 'Reflections on the "site of struggle": girls' experience of secondary education in the late 1950s', *History of Education*, 33, 4 (2004).

Steedman, C. '"The mother made conscious": the historical development of a primary school pedagogy', *History Workshop Journal*, 19–20 (1985).

Steedman, C. 'Landscape for a good woman', in L. Herron (ed.) *Truth, Dare or Promise: girls growing up in the fifties* (London, 1985).

Steedman, C. 'State-sponsored autobiography', in B. Conekin, F. Mort and C. Waters (eds) *Moments of Modernity: reconstructing Britain 1945–1964* (London, 1999).

Stearns, P. N. *Anxious Parents: a history of modern childrearing in America* (New York, 2003).

Bibliography

Stearns, P. *American Fear: the causes and consequences of high anxiety* (Oxon, 2006).

Stewart, J. *Child Guidance in Britain, 1918–1955: the dangerous age of childhood* (London, 2013).

Stewart, W. A. C. *Progressives and Radicals in English Education 1750–1970* (New Jersey, 1972).

Sturt, M. and Oakden, E. C. *Modern Psychology and Education: a text-book of Psychology for students in training colleges and adult evening classes* (London, 1926).

Sturt, M. and Oakden, E. C. *Modern Psychology and Education: a text-book of Psychology for students in training colleges and adult evening classes* (London, 3rd edn, 1938).

Summerfield, P. 'Women in Britain since 1945: companionate marriage and the double burden', in J. Obelkevich and P. Catterall (eds) *Understanding Post-War British Society* (London, 1994), pp. 58–72.

Summerfield, P. *Reconstructing Women's Wartime Lives: discourse and subjectivity in oral histories of the Second World War* (Manchester, 1998).

Summerfield, P. and Peniston-Bird, C. *Contesting Home Defence: men, women and the Home Guard in the Second World War* (Manchester, 2007).

Sutherland, G. *Ability, Merit and Measurement : mental testing and English education 1880–1940* (Oxford, 1984).

Swinnerton, B. 'The 1931 Report of the Consultative Committee on the Primary School: tensions and contradictions', *History of Education*, 25, 1 (1996).

Tanner, J. M. *Growth at Adolescence* (Oxford, 1955).

Tanner, J. M. and Inhelder, B. (eds) *Discussions on Child Development: a consideration of the biological, psychological and cultural approaches to the understanding of human development and behaviour* [The Proceedings of the Meetings of the WHO Study Group on the Psychobiological Development of the Child, Geneva 1953–56] (London: Tavistock, 1971).

Tanner, R. *Double Harness* (London, 1987).

Tansley, A. G. *The New Psychology and its Relation to Life* (London, 1920).

Taylor, J. H. *The Half-Way Generation: a study of Asian youth in Newcastle upon Tyne* (Berks, 1976).

Taylor, W. *The Secondary Modern School* (London, 1963).

Thane, P. 'Girton graduates: earning and learning, 1920s–1980s', *Women's History Review*, 13, 3 (2004).

Thom, D. 'The 1944 Education Act: the "art of the possible"?', in H. L. Smith (ed.) *War and Social Change: British society in the Second World War* (Manchester, 1986).

Thom, D. 'Better a teacher than a hairdresser? "A mad passion for equality" or, keeping Molly and Betty down', in F. Hunt (ed.) *Lessons for Life: the schooling of girls and women 1850–1950* (Oxford, 1997).

Thom, D. '"Beating children is wrong": domestic life, psychological thinking and the permissive turn', in L. Delap, B. Griffin and A. Wills (eds) *The Politics of Domestic Authority in Britain since 1800* (London, 2009).

Thomas, G. *Education: a very short introduction* (Oxford, 2013).
Thomas, N. 'Will the real 1950s please stand up?: views of a contradictory decade', *Cultural and Social History*, 5, 2 (2008) pp. 227–36.
Thomson, M. *The Problem of Mental Deficiency: eugenics, democracy, and social policy in Britain, c.1870–1959* (Oxford, 1998).
Thomson, M. *Psychological Subjects: identity, culture and health in twentieth-century Britain* (Oxford, 2006).
Thomson, M. *Lost Freedom: the landscape of the child and the British post-war settlement* (Oxford, 2013).
Tinkler, P. 'Youth', in F. Carnevali and J.-M. Strange (eds) *Twentieth-Century Britain: economic, cultural and social change* (Harlow, 2nd edn, 2007).
Tisdall, L. '"That was what life in Bridgeburn had made her": reading the autobiographies of children in institutional care in England, 1918–1946', *Twentieth Century British History*, 24, 3 (2013).
Tisdall, L. 'Inside the "blackboard jungle": male teachers and male pupils at British secondary modern schools in fact and fiction, 1950–59', *Cultural and Social History*, 12, 4 (2015).
Tisdall, L. 'Education, parenting and concepts of childhood in England, c. 1945 to c. 1979', *Contemporary British History*, 31, 1 (2017).
Titmuss, R. M. *Problems of Social Policy* (London, 1950).
Todd, S. *Young Women, Work and Family in England, 1918 to 1950* (Oxford, 2009).
Todd, S. and Young, H. '"Baby-boomers" to "beanstalkers": making the modern teenager in post-war Britain', *Cultural and Social History*, 9, 3 (2012).
Todd, S. *The People: the rise and fall of the working class 1910–2010* (London, 2014).
Tomlinson, S. *Race and Education: Policy and Politics in Britain* (Maidenhead, 2008).
Tonkin, E. *Narrating Our Pasts: the social construction of oral history* (Cambridge, 1992).
Townsend, J. *The Young Devils* (London, 1958).
Tropp, A. *The School Teachers: the growth of the teaching profession in England and Wales from 1800 to the present day* (London, 1959).
Valentine, C. W. *Psychology and its Bearing on Education* (London, 1950).
Vernon, J. *Hunger: a modern history* (Harvard, 2007).
Walkerdine, V. 'It's only natural: rethinking child-centred pedagogy', in A-M. Wolpe and J. Donald (eds) *Is There Anyone Here From Education?: education after Thatcher* (London, 1983).
Walkerdine, V. 'Developmental psychology and the child-centred pedagogy: the insertion of Piaget into early education', in J. Henriques, W. Hollway, C. Urwin, C. Venn and V. Walkerdine (eds) *Changing the Subject: psychology, social regulation and subjectivity* (London, 1984).
Walkerdine, V. 'Dreams from an ordinary childhood', in L. Herron (ed.) *Truth, Dare or Promise: girls growing up in the fifties* (London, 1985).
Walkerdine, V. 'Developmental psychology and the study of childhood', in M. J. Kehily (ed.) *An Introduction to Childhood Studies* (Maidenhead, 2008).

Wall, C. 'Picturing an occupational identity: images of teachers in careers and trade union publications 1940–2000', *History of Education,* 37, 2 (2008).
Ward, C. *The Child in the City* (London, 1978).
Warr, E. B. *The New Era in the Junior School* (London, 1937).
Waters, C. '"Dark strangers" in our midst: discourses of race and nation in Britain, 1947–1963', *Journal of British Studies,* 36 (1997).
Waters, C. 'Autobiography, nostalgia and the changing practices of working-class selfhood', in G. K. Behlmer and F. M. Leventhal (eds) *Singular Continuities: tradition, nostalgia and society in modern Britain* (Stanford, California, 2000).
Waters, C. 'The homosexual as a social being in Britain, 1945–1968', in B. Lewis (ed.) *British Queer History: new approaches and perspectives* (Manchester, 2013).
Waters, M. C., Carr, P. J., Kefalas, M. J. and Holdaway, J. (eds) *Coming of Age in America: the transition to adulthood in the twenty-first century* (London, 2011).
Watson, J. B. *Psychological Care of Infant and Child* (New York, 1928).
Watson, K. 'Education and opportunity', in F. Carnevali and J.-M. Strange (eds) *Twentieth-Century Britain: economic, cultural and social change* (Harlow, 2nd edn, 2007).
Watts, A. F. *The Teacher's Guide to Intelligence and Other Psychological Testing* (London, 1954).
Watts, R. 'Pupils and teachers', in R. Aldrich (ed.) *A Century of Education* (London, 2002).
Webster, D. *Looka Yonder! The imaginary America of populist culture* (London, 1988).
Wheeler, O. A. *Creative Education and the Future* (London, 1936).
Wheeler, O. A. *The Adventure of Youth: the psychology of adolescence and its bearing on the extension and reform of adolescent education* (London, 1945).
Willcock, H. D. *Report on Juvenile Delinquency* (London, 1949).
Willmott, P. and Young, M. *Family and Kinship in East London* (London, 1957).
Willmott, P. *Adolescent Boys of East London* (London, 1966).
Wilson, D. S. 'A new look at the affluent worker: the good working mother in post-war Britain', *Twentieth Century British History,* 17, 2 (2006).
Wilson, D. S. 'Fighting the "damnable triumph" of feminism: battles between teachers' unions in interwar Britain', *Gender and Education,* 19, 6 (2007).
Wilson, D. S. 'Gender, race and the ideal labour force', in L. Ryan and W. Webster (eds) *Gendering Migration: masculinity, femininity and ethnicity in post-war Britain* (Hampshire, 2008), pp. 89–103.
Winnicott, D. 'The only child', in *Difficult Children: a series of broadcast talks* (Worcester, 1947).
Woodin, T., McCulloch, G. and Cowan, S. *Secondary Education and the Raising of the School-Leaving Age: coming of age?* (Hampshire, 2013).
Wooldridge, A. *Measuring the Mind: education and psychology in England, c.1860–c.1990* (Cambridge, 1994).

Wooldridge, A. 'The English state and educational theory', in S. J. D. Green and R. C. Whiting (eds) *The Boundaries of the State in Modern Britain* (Cambridge, 1996).
Wright, S. 'Teachers, family and community in the urban elementary school: evidence from English school log books c.1880–1918', *History of Education*, 41, 2 (2012).
Wylie, C. D. 'Teaching manuals and the blackboard: assessing historical classroom practices', *History of Education*, 41, 2 (2012).
Young, H. 'Being a man: everyday masculinities', in L. Abrams and C. G. Brown (eds) *A History of Everyday Life in Twentieth-Century Scotland* (Edinburgh, 2010).
Young, K. *The Green Velvet Dress: memories of sixty years in London and Somerset* (East Lothian, 1989).
Zelizer, V. *Pricing the Priceless Child: the changing social value of children* (Chicago, 1980).
Zweig, F. *The Worker in an Affluent Society: family life and industry* (London, 1961).

Unpublished dissertations

Burchell, A. 'The Adolescent School Pupil, Psycho-Social Theory and Practice, and the Construction of a Pedagogy of Discipline in Britain, 1911–1989' (unpub. PhD thesis, University of Warwick, 2018).
Elfed-Owens, P. 'The Implementation of the National Curriculum in Wales' (unpub. PhD thesis, UCL Institute of Education, 1996).
Frisby, J. H. 'The History of Educational Psychology Teaching in English Training Colleges During the First Half of the Twentieth Century' (unpub. M.Ed thesis, University of Nottingham, 1969).
Kawwa, T. 'Ethnic Prejudice and Choice of Friends Amongst English and Non-English Adolescents' (unpub. MA Education thesis, Institute of Education, University of London, 1963).
Pooley, S. 'Parenthood and child-rearing in England, c.1860–1910' (unpub. PhD thesis, University of Cambridge, 2010).
Robinson, P. 'Ideology in Teacher Education' (unpub. MSc Long Essay, University of London Institute of Education, 1971).
Violett, A. 'The Public Perceptions and Personal Experiences of Only Children Growing Up in Britain, c. 1850–1950,' (unpub. PhD thesis, University of Essex, 2018).

Internet sources

Bennett, N. 'Changing perspectives on teaching–learning processes in the post-war era' (1987) online at www.educationengland.org.uk/documents/plowden/plowdenore-05.html, accessed 3 October 2018.

Bibliography

Cannadine, D., Keating, J. and Sheldon, N. History In Education Project, www.history.ac.uk/history-in-education/about.html, accessed 3 October 2018.

Gillard, D. 'Education in England: the history of our schools', www.educationengland.org.uk/index.htm, accessed 3 October 2018.

'How Generation Z will change the world', http://time.com/5250542/generation-z/, 23 April 2018, accessed 3 October 2018.

HMSO, 'Secondary education for all: a new drive' (London: Her Majesty's Stationery Office, 1958), www.filestore.nationalarchives.gov.uk/pdfs/small/cab-129-95-c-58-239-39.pdf, accessed 3 October 2018.

Kirby, P. 'A brief history of dyslexia', *The Psychologist*, March 2018 www.thepsychologist.bps.org.uk/volume-31/march-2018/brief-history-dyslexia, accessed 3 October 2018.

Lerway, P. 'The middle school: teaching and learning, time and tasks – recognising some problems', in Papers of Louis Christian Schiller (1895–1976), Institute of Education, London, CS/K3, online at www.archive.ioe.ac.uk/DServe/dserve.exe?dsqIni=Dserve.ini&dsqApp=Archive&dsqDb=Catalog&dsqCmd=Show.tcl&dsqSearch=(RefNo=='CS/K/3'), accessed 3 October 2018.

Middleton, S. and May, H. *Early Childhood Herstories: an oral history project on the changing educational ideas of teachers in New Zealand*, 1996, www. files.eric.ed.gov/fulltext/ED403052.pdf, accessed 3 October 2018.

Secondary Education and Social Change project (SESC), 'Comprehensive schools', online at https://sesc.hist.cam.ac.uk/wp-content/uploads/2018/02/Briefing-paper-Comprehensives.pdf, accessed 30 May 2019.

Secondary Education and Social Change project (SESC), 'Secondary moderns', https://sesc.hist.cam.ac.uk/wp-content/uploads/2018/02/Briefing-paper-Secondary-modern-schools.pdf, accessed 30 May 2019.

Tisdall, L. '"Kindred to its soil": educating Welsh children in post-war Wales', guest blog post on the Four Nations blog, 31 October 2016 www.fournationshistory.wordpress.com/2016/10/31/kindred-to-its-soil-educating-welsh-children-in-post-war-wales/, accessed 3 October 2018.

Other

Newstead, S. '"Shadows and mystery": the importance of history in the future development of the playwork profession', paper given at the Children's History Society's Horrible Histories Conference, King's College London, 18 June 2016.

Index

1944 Education Act 6, 14–15, 51, 53, 71–3, 108, 184, 186, 206, 229

abstract reasoning 14, 53, 57–8, 176, 179–81, 186–7
activity methods *see* child-centred
Adams, John 29, 146
Adler, Alfred 146
adolescence 10, 14–15, 20, 28, 33, 53, 72–3, 161–3, 169, 176, 178–87, 198, 208, 224, 235, 239–40
  'generation gap' 1–2, 4, 10, 20–1, 30–2, 99, 160, 177, 246–8, 245, 249
  see also juvenile delinquency
adulthood 4, 10, 12, 14–15, 26–8, 53, 63–4, 66, 169–70, 181, 208, 246, 248
adventure playgrounds 224, 239
America *see* United States
'Ann' [Oxfordshire interviewee] 69
anthropology *see* social science
apparatus 6, 13, 84, 96, 114, 123–4, 131
architecture *see* school buildings
Area Training Organisations 59
Ariés, Philippe 224, 245–6
arithmetic *see* mathematics
art *see* creative subjects, 'New Art'
Ashton, Patricia 70, 92, 161, 219
ATOs *see* Area Training Organisations

babies *see* infants
Ballard, Philip 27, 30, 39, 72, 143
Bassey, Michael 219–20
Bennett, Neville 160–1, 216–17, 219–20
Bernstein, Basil 156, 215–16
Bews, Mary 114, 116–17, 127–30, 154
bipartite system *see* tripartite system
'blackboard jungle' *see* juvenile delinquency, urban pupils
Black Papers (1968) 97, 216–17, 219, 230, 240
Blishen, Edward 163–4, 199
Board of Education 12, 16–17, 26, 32, 37, 51, 57, 64, 89, 122, 196
  Handbooks of Suggestions (1937, 1944) 16, 36, 64–5
Bowlby, John 249
Bowley, Agatha 43, 144
boys *see* male pupils
brain development *see* neuroscience
'Brian' [Oxfordshire interviewee] 68, 71, 97, 120
Brize Norton 11, 44, 76
Bühler, Charlotte 10
Burt, Cyril 12, 52, 54–7, 60, 64, 71, 139, 147, 217, 230–1, 249
  Young Delinquent (1938) 55–6

CACE *see* Central Advisory Council for Education
Cambridge 73, 109, 122, 127, 130, 205

273

Cambridgeshire 13, 17–18, 54–5, 73, 108–9, 113–15, 119, 121, 124, 129, 140, 148, 189, 195
Campagnac, Ernest 30, 143
Canada 30
'Carol' [Oxfordshire interviewee] 71, 94–5, 128
Catty, Nancy 147
Central Advisory Council for Education 125, 146
character *see* citizenship
child-centred 2, 5–17, 25–31, 33–45, 50, 52–3, 62, 76–7, 83–9, 94–101, 109, 112–14, 117, 119, 121–31, 138–9, 145–56, 159–69, 177–80, 185–7, 201, 203, 205, 207–8, 215–40, 246–9
'lip service' 13, 101–3
child health *see* paediatrics
child guidance 52, 98, 142, 235
see also psychoanalysis
children of colour 15, 108, 154, 177–8, 183–4, 190, 193–4, 205, 231, 235–7, 248
children's literature 155–6, 248
Chinese 108, 194
see also children of colour, immigrant pupils
chronological age 10–12, 53, 63–4, 66–7, 72, 75–7, 197, 245
citizenship 5–6, 12, 21, 33–4, 37–8, 41, 45, 51, 145
Čižek, Franz 151
class identities 14, 63, 89–90, 176–9, 188–9, 199–202, 247–9
see also working-class pupils
classroom practice *see* curriculum
Clegg, Alec 110
cookery *see* practical subjects
comprehensive schools 13, 15, 60, 85, 87, 130, 160, 166–7, 176, 183–90, 197–200, 206, 208, 218–19, 229, 233, 235

creative subjects 112, 114, 122–3, 126, 131, 149–52, 155–6, 224, 228
creative writing 151, 155–6
see also creative subjects
Crowther Report [*15–18*, 1959] 190, 198
CSEs *see* examinations
current affairs 112, 114, 122
curriculum 2–3, 8–9, 15–17, 26–7, 31, 33, 36–8, 40–5, 71, 88, 108–9, 112–13, 116, 121–3, 139, 147, 150, 154, 161–6, 176, 185–90, 216, 220, 222, 224, 226–8

Dalton Plan 2, 30, 35, 96, 143, 146
dance *see* creative subjects
Daniel, M.V. 64–5, 162
Dawson, Patricia 62–3, 75, 98, 204
'Debbie' [Oxfordshire interviewee] 94–5
Deem, Rosemary 160, 166–7
democracy 6, 38, 169, 248–9
Dent, H.C [Harold]. 38, 150–1, 157
Department of Education and Science 130, 226–8, 234, 240
deschooling 10, 223–4, 230, 239
developmental psychology 3, 10, 12–13, 15, 26–33, 50–8, 60–78, 83, 87, 94, 103, 142–4, 147, 150–1, 163, 169–70, 176, 180–1, 185–8, 194, 196–8, 215, 217–18, 231–2, 238–9, 246–8
formal operational stage *see* abstract reasoning
social and emotional development 3, 138, 142–4, 228, 233–7
stages of development 3–4, 10, 12, 15, 33, 36, 42, 50–8, 60–78, 89, 186–8, 231–2, 246, 249
Dewey, John 2, 10, 26, 40–1
'discovery learning' *see* child-centred
disabilities 15, 98, 191, 195, 198, 231, 234–7, 248
drama *see* creative subjects
drill *see* traditional education

Index

'educationally sub-normal' pupils *see* mental deficiency
Education and Social Control (1975) 149–50, 207, 231, 237–8
egocentric *see* egotism
egotism 10, 14, 138, 143–6, 180
elementary schools 6, 8, 15, 30, 35, 37–9, 44, 118, 131, 140, 157, 196
eleven-plus *see* 11-plus
ESN pupils *see* mental deficiency
Etherington, T.H. 152–3
ethnic minorities *see* children of colour
examinations 13, 17, 71, 84, 161, 184, 190, 206, 226
    11-plus 6, 84–5, 162, 182–6, 191, 198, 205–6
    Certificate of Secondary Education 190
    for teachers 39, 59, 61–2, 88, 141
    O Levels 185
'exploding school' *see* deschooling

family grouping 53, 66, 75–7, 96, 102, 124, 207
Farley, Richard 163, 201
fatherhood 93, 159–60
female pupils 139, 150, 161–9, 184, 232–3, 237, 247–8
female teachers 14, 93–5, 138–9, 156–61, 168, 179, 202–3
First World War 3, 17, 35, 37, 39, 72
freedom in education *see* permissivism
Freud, Anna 149
Froëbel, Friedrich 36, 40, 59
future 3–5, 20, 30–1, 37, 41, 45, 177, 184, 190, 198

Galton, Maurice 84–5, 219–220
gang *see* group
gardening *see* nature, practical subjects
geography 2, 37, 41–3, 112, 114, 122, 220

Germany 2, 28, 30, 169
Gesell, Arnold 10, 54, 66
'gifted' child 141, 143, 195–8, 231
girls *see* female pupils
Gittins Report [*Primary Education in Wales,* 1967] 75, 122, 129, 130, 154, 192, 205, 207
grammar schools 6, 13, 18, 60, 63, 71, 74, 110, 118, 131, 159, 166, 176–7, 184–6, 188, 197, 201, 206, 208
Greek Cypriots 236
    see also children of colour, immigrant pupils
group 4, 33–5, 52, 64–5, 96, 103, 123–5, 128, 131, 143, 145–6, 149, 220–1, 233–5

Hadow Report 1926 [*The Education of the Adolescent*] 32–5, 40, 72, 179, 245
Hadow Report 1931 [*The Primary School*] 3, 32–6, 40–1, 44–7, 64, 72, 74, 147, 227
Hall, G. Stanley 54, 179
    see also developmental psychology
history 2, 8, 42–3, 62, 87, 97–8, 101, 112, 122, 147, 165, 184–5, 190, 220
HMIs 17, 39, 102, 110–12, 122, 162, 191, 195, 227–8
    HMI reports 109, 113–15, 124, 148–9, 188–9
    HMI surveys 77, 121, 162, 166–7, 189, 220–1, 225–6, 232
    relationship with teachers 102, 116–21
    training 111
Holmes, Edmond 1, 39
homosexuality 168
housecraft *see* practical subjects
Hughes, A.G. and Hughes, E.G. 34–5, 63–4, 144
humanities *see* geography, history, local studies, teaching methods

ILEA *see* Inner London Education Authority
Illich, Ivan 223–4
immigrant pupils 15, 177, 183–4, 193, 205, 231, 235, 248
see also children of colour
individuality 12, 27–8, 33–5, 52, 54–6, 60, 64, 96–7, 103, 122, 125, 128, 131, 143, 146–50, 170, 197, 205, 220, 227–9, 231, 248
infants 15, 94, 179
infant schools 11, 14–15, 32, 40, 54, 72, 75–6, 139, 142, 150, 158, 162, 216
Inhelder, Bärbel 58, 66, 180
Inner London Education Authority 7, 219
in-service training *see* refresher courses
inspectors *see* HMIs
Institute of Education 31, 55, 59, 62, 66, 150, 215–16
integrated day 42, 75, 96–7, 100–2, 112, 121, 123–4, 207, 220–1, 227, 238
intelligence tests 71, 187, 193–6, 231
IQ testing *see* intelligence tests
Isaacs, Susan 12, 26, 52, 54–8, 60, 62, 64–5, 216, 232, 249
Children We Teach (1932) 55
Intellectual Growth in Young Children (1930) 55, 57
Malting House School 54, 58
Social Development in Young Children (1933) 55, 58

James Report [1972] 59, 70–1, 222
'Jan' [Oxfordshire interviewee] 88–9, 234
'John' [Oxfordshire interviewee] 99, 119
'junk playgrounds' *see* adventure playgrounds
juvenile delinquency 55, 177, 181–2

Kawwa, Taysir 235–6
Klein, Melanie 54

Lane, Homer 25–7, 224
LCC *see* London County Council
LEAs *see* local education authorities
Leach, Penelope 94
Lister, Ian 11, 239
local educational authorities 16, 64, 108–25, 194–5
local studies 112, 122, 148, 227–8
Locke, John 40
logbooks 17–18, 73, 109, 111–24, 128–9, 205
logical thinking *see* abstract reasoning
London County Council 39, 55, 72, 145
'Lynn' [Oxfordshire interviewee] 63, 99, 101–2, 234

McDougall, William 60–1
see also 'new psychology'
MacMunn, Norman 2–3
'maladjusted' pupils 52, 55, 142, 178, 192–3
male pupils 161–4, 168, 224, 231–3
male teachers 14, 37, 92–3, 119, 139, 156–61, 168, 178, 201–3
manual occupations 38, 92, 157–8, 176, 178, 182, 202
Marshall, Sybil 69, 152
mathematics 42, 100, 112–13, 117, 121, 123, 165, 187–8, 221, 233
maturational *see* developmental psychology
memoirs *see* self-narratives
mental deficiency 51–2, 98, 154–5, 191
see also intelligence testing
metalwork *see* practical subjects
'Michael' [Oxfordshire interviewee] 67–8
Ministry of Education 59, 65, 93, 118–19, 122, 142, 145, 201

modernity 4–5, 34, 37, 40, 43, 45, 95–102, 152–4, 208, 218, 224, 229, 231, 238
Monmouthshire 13, 17, 109, 113, 121, 123
Montessori, Maria 10, 26–7
motherhood 93–4, 138, 159–61
music *see* creative subjects

NAS *see* National Association of Schoolmasters
National Association of Schoolmasters 157
National Foundation for Educational Research 77, 194, 219–20
National Union of Teachers 18, 28, 86, 88–9, 113, 157, 201
National Union of Women Teachers 44, 159
nature 36, 96, 130
needlework *see* practical subjects
Neill, A.S. 1–2, 4, 14, 26–7, 30, 40, 52, 167–8, 224
neuroscience 66
'New Art' 114, 151–3, 156
  see also Cižek, Franz
New Education Fellowship 26, 28
New Era 26–8
'new psychology' 25, 181
Newsom Report [*Half Our Future*, 1963] 187, 189, 200
Newson, John and Newson, Elizabeth 238, 247
NFER *see* National Foundation for Educational Research
North America *see* United States and Canada
Nunn, Percy 31–2, 34
NUT *see* National Union of Teachers
NUWT *see* National Union of Women Teachers

Office for Standards in Education 119–20

Ofsted *see* Office for Standards in Education
O'Neill, E.F. 29–30
oral history 17–20, 43, 84, 91–2, 100, 102, 166, 204, 233
Oxford 20, 71, 74, 76, 117, 130, 206, 233
Oxfordshire 11, 13, 16–17, 20, 67–8, 73–6, 84, 87–9, 91–4, 99, 108, 110, 113–22, 124, 126–9, 140, 152–4, 189, 192, 195, 204, 206, 233–4

paediatrics 50–1
parents 3, 5, 8–10, 38, 55, 83, 94, 99, 116–17, 138, 148, 155, 159, 177, 185, 192, 194–5, 202, 204–7, 218, 226, 230, 235, 238, 246–9
parent–teacher associations [PTAs] 205–7
  see also fatherhood, motherhood
'payment by results' 39, 72, 118
Peach, Howard 69, 98, 100–1
pedagogy *see* teaching methods
permissive shift *see* permissivism
permissivism 5, 7–9, 25, 110, 140, 160–1, 199, 216–17, 230, 246
Pestalozzi, Johann 36, 40
Peters, Richard 215, 217
physical growth *see* paediatrics
Piaget, Jean 3, 12, 16, 26, 52–4, 58, 61, 65–6, 94, 143–5, 180
  Child's Conception of the World (1926) 144
  critiques of 57
  Growth of Logical Thinking from Childhood to Adolescence (1955) 58, 180, 187
  Language and Thought of the Child (1923) 144
  Moral Judgment of the Child (1932) 58
  name recognition of 67–8
  see also developmental psychology, Inhelder, Bärbel
Play Way 2, 29

Plowden Report [*Children and Their Primary Schools,* 1967] 3, 7, 63, 65–6, 73, 75–7, 93, 102, 109, 117, 129, 162, 197, 215–20, 225–7
practical subjects 14, 27, 36, 38, 41–4, 84, 96–7, 101, 112–13, 117, 121, 128, 138–9, 145, 147, 153–4, 162–6, 168, 182, 187, 191, 206, 208, 224, 228, 232, 249
primary schools 3, 6–7, 9, 11, 13–16, 18–19, 32, 34, 36–7, 40–4, 56, 60, 63–6, 70–2, 75–6, 84, 95–6, 99, 101, 109–11, 113, 115–17, 123, 125–31, 138–70, 188, 207, 215–22, 228–33, 237–8
Project Method 2, 29, 96, 146
psychiatry 218
psychoanalysis 2, 15, 50–2, 60, 249
puberty 4, 142, 151, 180
see also adolescence, adolescents
pupils 13–15, 20, 27–9, 33, 35, 39, 41–2, 69, 74, 76–7, 84, 88, 90, 92–3, 97–9, 125–31, 138–41, 152–3, 156, 159–67, 176, 178–9, 183, 185–93, 197–205, 207–8, 220, 223, 228–9, 232–4, 237–9
  discipline 83, 95, 148–50, 159, 163–4, 199–200, 202–4, 207–8
pupil-teachers *see* unqualified teachers

raising of the school-leaving age 110, 131, 189–90
Rampton Report [*West Indian Children in Our Schools,* 1981] 190, 194, 223
Rastafarian *see* children of colour, immigrant pupils, West Indians
recapitulation theory 50, 54
refresher courses 59, 70–1, 78, 99, 102–3, 113, 116–17, 153, 232
Revised Code *see* 'payment by results'
ROSLA *see* raising of the school-leaving age
Rousseau, Jean-Jacques 40

rural pupils 73–6, 116, 127–30, 138, 140, 148–9, 152–5, 185, 188–9
Russell, Bertrand 2, 15, 30, 225
'Ruth' [Oxfordshire interviewee] 94–5, 233
Rutter, Michael 217

secondary modern schools 6, 9, 13–15, 18, 58, 60, 63, 71, 74, 85, 109–12, 114, 123, 130–1, 139, 157–8, 163–7, 176–208, 218
Second World War 3, 6, 9–10, 12, 14–15, 19, 29, 35, 38, 40, 51–3, 58, 62, 73, 77, 84, 103, 108, 111, 117–18, 128, 138–40, 145–6, 155, 158, 169, 176, 182, 192, 219, 249
  evacuation of children 55, 84
Schiller, Christian 62, 110, 124
schools *see* elementary schools, primary schools, secondary modern schools
  class size 9, 13, 16, 35, 77, 110, 125–8
  furniture 6, 103, 114, 127, 129–31
  organisation of 2, 41, 53, 56, 66, 71–2, 75–77, 96, 102, 112, 121, 124, 145–6, 184, 207, 231, 245
  playgrounds 129
  record cards 112, 122, 138, 142
  school buildings 4, 6, 73, 76, 114, 124–31, 222
  school subjects 2, 31, 41–3, 87, 96–7, 101, 161, 167–9, 220
  single-sex 139, 157, 166–8
  state expenditure on 6, 72, 110
school councils *see* self-government
Schools Council 193, 210, 222
Schoolmaster and Woman Teacher's Chronicle 18, 29–31, 35, 42, 64, 91, 98, 111, 118–19, 143, 147, 153, 159, 162, 181–2, 199, 204
science 2, 62, 109, 114, 123, 129–30, 165–8, 191, 228, 232
  Girls and Science (1980) 166–8, 232
self-government 2–3, 29–31

Index

selfhood 19–20, 182, 201, 246
self-narratives 19–20, 28, 35, 67, 88, 119, 141, 149, 249
Sheffield 13, 17, 61, 108, 112, 115, 121–2, 130, 140, 150–2, 165, 186, 188, 190, 193–5, 206, 234
Spock, 'Dr' [Benjamin] 9, 230
social science 63, 70, 88–9, 100, 169, 183, 199–200, 215, 248
sociology *see* social science
South Asians 183, 205
  see also children of colour, immigrant pupils
standards *see* traditional education
Steedman, Carolyn 9, 155, 159
Summers, Mel 76, 102, 117

Tanner, Robin 110, 115, 152
Teacher 18–19, 69, 95, 100, 122, 159, 189, 193, 199, 218, 222, 228, 234
teachers 1, 11, 14, 16, 26, 42, 50, 55, 70–1, 73, 76, 95–9, 109, 114, 116–17, 127–30, 138, 146–8, 159–61, 163, 165, 205, 207, 217, 221, 232–4, 237–8
  advice guides for 34–5, 58–67, 165, 179
  clothing 91–2
  emergency-trained 59, 69, 85, 117, 157, 178, 182, 200–1, 203, 225
  first day 141, 203–4
  headteachers 31, 44, 76, 91, 109, 119, 123, 148, 150, 154, 195, 206
  'left-wing' 4, 7, 228–31, 240
  lesson plans 62, 140–1, 191
  'married women returners' 92–3, 158–9
  new teachers 84, 90–1, 126
  qualifications 59–60
  pay and conditions 199–203
  professional expectations of 86–8, 102, 119–20, 225–6
  set texts 63–8, 179, 224
  status 31, 83, 86–90, 95–7, 199
  strikes 228
teacher trainers 4, 58–67, 112
teacher training colleges 17, 20, 29, 52, 58–68, 70–2, 75, 83–4, 158, 200, 222, 224, 232
trendy *see* new teachers
unqualified teachers 84, 89–90, 158, 204
Teachers World 18–19, 29–31, 35, 37, 41–2, 64, 72, 91, 98, 100, 102, 118, 143, 145–7, 151, 155, 159–60, 162–5, 181, 191, 196–8, 204, 222
teaching methods 2, 5, 7, 10, 13–17, 25–6, 29–30, 35, 42–5, 50, 61–2, 65, 71–4, 83–103, 108, 111–14, 117–19, 121, 123–31, 138, 141, 146, 150, 160, 164, 169, 178, 184–5, 202–5, 207–8, 216–29, 233, 237, 247
  cyclical 87
  'modern methods' *see* child-centred
  team-teaching 97, 101
  thematic 220
  see also local studies
technical schools 28, 71, 184
teenagers *see* adolescence, adolescents
Times Educational Supplement 18, 37–8, 42, 118, 150
traditional education 5, 9, 25–6, 28–9, 38–45, 95, 100, 123, 127, 160–1, 220–3, 227, 229–30
  drill 30, 38, 41–4, 101
  standards 7, 10, 20, 98, 113, 139–41, 203, 216, 219–21, 226, 229
traditionalism *see* traditional education
tripartite system 6, 56, 71, 184

unconscious mind *see* 'new psychology'
Underwood Report [*Mental Deficiency*, 1955] 142, 192, 195, 197
United States 7, 9–11, 20, 30, 35, 39–40, 51, 65, 143, 146, 182, 196, 223–4, 226, 230, 245, 248

urban pupils 127, 130, 138, 152, 154, 188–9, 199

vertical classification *see* family grouping
vertical grouping *see* family grouping
vocational education 28, 33, 41, 121, 165, 185, 187, 190

Wales 73, 75, 77, 109, 121–2, 129–30, 152, 154, 185–6, 192, 205, 207
Walkerdine, Valerie 27, 163, 247
Ward, Colin 14, 224
Watts, Frank 41–2
welfare state 3, 6, 12, 21, 146, 248

West Indians 108, 190, 193–4, 205, 223
see also children of colour, immigrant pupils
West Riding 11, 84, 108, 110, 202
WHO *see* World Health Organisation
William Tyndale junior-infant school 7, 216, 219
Winnicott, Donald 143, 249
woodwork *see* practical subjects
working-class pupils 14–15, 28, 35, 37–8, 43, 108, 149, 156, 163–5, 176, 178, 182–201, 206–8, 215, 231, 237, 247–9
World Health Organisation 58

youth *see* adolescence, adolescents

EU authorised representative for GPSR:
Easy Access System Europe, Mustamäe tee 50,
10621 Tallinn, Estonia
gpsr.requests@easproject.com

www.ingramcontent.com/pod-product-compliance
Lightning Source LLC
Chambersburg PA
CBHW051604230426
43668CB00013B/1972